A Tale of Boxes

The Role of Myth in Creating and Changing Our Stories

Robert T. Latham

For Introductory Prices
Go To:
www.mythinglink.com

A Tale of Boxes: The Role of Myth in Creating and Changing Our Stories

Cover illustrations by Mike Kloepfer, Arvada, Colorado.

Published by Wheatmark®
610 East Delano Street, Suite 104
Tucson, Arizona 85705 U.S.A.
www.wheatmark.com

International Standard Book Number: 978-1-60494-259-0
Library of Congress Control Number: 2009923569

Dedicated to

Cindy, Robin, Sherry, Christy, and Harry IV

To Bob

Contents

Creating Cultural Stories

Creating America's Story

Addenda

Introduction

Boxes
(Reality and Freedom)

Every myth is a box—a set of boundaries that prescribes the nature and limits of my vision.

My story is a tale of boxes—the identities they create, the relationships they nourish, the values they empower, the struggles they generate, and the life they become.

To change my story is to change my mythic box. What ensues from such change is an alteration of the meanings I make and the person I am.

Freedom is the privilege of choosing my own box.

Stories
(Jack and Jill)

Jack and Jill
Went up the hill
To fetch a pail of water.
Jack fell down
And broke his crown
And Jill came tumbling after.

—Nursery Rhyme

Jack is a story. Jill is a story. The hill is a story. Going up the hill is a story. Fetching is a story. The pail is a story. The water is a story. Jack falling is a story. Breaking his crown is a story. Jill tumbling after is a story. All of these smaller stories make up the larger story of the nursery rhyme.

Existence

Everything that exists is a story. Every atom and every human is one. And every story is a tale of encounter with other stories. My story is what I create from the meanings I give to my experiences. Your story is what I encounter as I create my story. Our story is what we create together as we weave history.

Web

The stories of everything that has existed, exists now, and will exist eventually converge into an interdependent web of existence. This web is the story of the whole. There are no isolated stories. All stories nurture and feed off of each other. Every action of my story ultimately affects the action of all other stories. I cannot enter any story without some alteration of both that story and my own.

4

Hero

We are born into stories within stories, yet we move through life enclosed within our own story. Others may pass through our story, but it never belongs to them. This is why our story is always larger than life. We are its hero and all other stories appear smaller by comparison.

Paradox

Our stories forever mingle in paradox. Even when we encounter the same moment I cannot see what your story sees. Even when we embrace profoundly I cannot know the meaning to your story. And even when we are together we are still alone in our separate stories. Yet I have no story without your story. We create the story of each other while remaining the only composer of our own story.

Death

When we die our story both ends and continues. It ends as a reflection of our personal choices in its shaping. It continues as others choose to shape its parts into their own stories.

Creation

There is nothing in creation but stories.

We clasp the hands of those that go before us,
And the hands of those who come after us.
We enter the little circle of each other's arms
And the larger circle of lovers,
Whose hands are joined in a dance,
And the larger circle of all creatures,
Passing in and out of life, who move also in a dance,
To a music so subtle and vast that no ear hears it
Except in fragments.

—Wendell Berry

Story Is Life
Life Is Story

PART I

Creating Personal Stories

A myth is a view of reality. We are born into a world of myth designed by the authorities of our existence to define who we are and will become. Somewhere along our story line we are given the opportunity, through maturity, to determine our own mythic destiny. To do so, we must understand the role myth plays in creating our personal stories and take control of this creation. Otherwise, we remain pawns of other mythic forces.

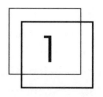

1

The Weaver
(A Metaphor of Creating)

When we next meet we'll have a tale to tell.
—Byron (*Don Juan*)

The Loom

I am born and I die. And in between, I am the weaver of a tale. This tale is the creation of my life story. It is the tapestry of my existence. The loom upon which I weave is constructed from the stuff of my birth. Its blueprint is the givens of my entry into life—the historical moment, the geographic location, the family circumstance, and the genetic boundaries. Yet the weaving itself is mine alone. The materials I use are of my choosing. And the movement of the shuttle is by my hand. With these materials and these movements, I weave my tale.

The Design

The materials I use are the relationship choices I make in my life. They become the threads, textures, and colors of my tapestry. The movements of the shuttle are the meanings I give to my experiences. They determine the style and design of my tapestry. Every moment of my life, I am feeding choices and meanings into my loom and creating the pattern of my living. There are no trivial choices or meanings in the weaving of my story. Every choice or meaning may initiate a new design.

The Character

The character of my living is shaped by these materials and movements. Sometimes the story I am weaving is full of sadness, despair, and curse. Because of this I may wish my life to end. Sometimes the story I am weaving is full of joy, hope, and blessing. Because of this I may wish to live forever. My story is interwoven with curse and blessing. Yet, whatever the character of the tapestry I create, I cannot stop weaving. Weaving is the same as being alive. Only when my loom dies does my creating cease. Until that moment, I must weave. And the weaving is of my character.

The Freedom

That which affirms my freedom to weave my own life story is my capacity to create covenants. Every covenant I make imposes boundaries on my behavior, yet each boundary is self-subscribed. Every covenant I break releases me from prior boundaries. Yet each release is self-submitted. So every covenant I make or break bears the signature of my freedom. Only death can divest me of this privilege; until then, I remain the weaver.

The Skills

The art of weaving is in my skills. Each skill I possess is a lesson learned and every story I create offers a lesson. If I do not learn the lesson of a story, I will confront it in other stories until I do. The faster I learn, the more abundant my skills. Since the skills I learn are from life itself, the state of my loom is unimportant. Whatever skills I possess are a measure of my will to learn. And the design of my weaving is a reflection.

The Sacred

My stories are made sacred through reverence. I revere my relationships by endowing them with the equality of kinship. The more profound my reverence, the greater the depth and quality of my story. When I grant reverence to my relationships, I create a covenant of sacredness with life itself. This covenant empowers me with the integrity of wholeness. This wholeness connects all my relating in a web of spiritual communion. And from this measure of wholeness I weave my larger story of sacred design.

The Story

I am the weaver of a tale and what I weave is the story of my life.

The tale runs as it pleases the teller.

> —Thomas Fuller

We sleep, but the loom of life never stops. And the pattern which was weaving when the sun went down, is weaving when it comes up tomorrow.

> —Henry Ward Beecher

2

Fine, Regular, Perk, or Drip?
(How We Create Our Stories)

It is the mind which creates the world around us, and even though we stand side by side in the same meadow, my eyes will never see what is beheld by yours, my heart will never stir to the emotions with which yours is touched.
—George Gissing

Mind is the only creative agency known to science, to philosophy, or to religion.
—Ernest Holmes

We are what we think. All that we are rises with our thought. With our thoughts we make our world.
—The Buddha

Why?

On September 11, 2001, terrorists flew commercial airplanes into the World Trade Center's twin towers and the Pentagon. The towers fell into rubble, and the Pentagon sustained serious damage. The American public was rocked onto its heels with shock. This shock went deeper than the initial impact of the loss of human life and material destruction. It descended into the very psyche of the culture and returned with this incredulous question: "Why?" What could possibly have prompted such an action that disregarded not only the lives of the innocent but also the perpetrators? This question continues to haunt the American psyche.

Using the emotional impetus of this event and its psychic shock, the Bush administration initiated a war in Iraq. The nation's response was divided. While some viewed the war as a patriotic necessity, others viewed it as an unprincipled travesty. Soldiers sent to wage the war had a similar polarity of response. How can such a radical difference in meaning from the same experience be possible?

This question of why, in respect to the disregard of destruction, is as old as the human story. It is a staple of history. Here are a few examples:

> ➤ Why would the early European Christians and Muslims of the Mediterranean area aggressively seek each others' destruction?
> ➤ Why would powerful European nations conquer, colonize, exploit, and brutalize weaker nations for centuries?
> ➤ Why would early Americans pursue a policy of Native American Indian genocide and concurrently allow the enslavement of imported Africans, doing so in the name of freedom and democracy?
> ➤ Why would America, for all practical purposes, make women into second-class citizens for most of its history?
> ➤ Why would America, once its slaves were freed, continue to subject the African Americans of generations that followed to economic and social bondage?
> ➤ Why would Nazi Germany, during the Second World War, institute the deliberate practice of Jewish genocide?
> ➤ Why would America, during the Second World War, incinerate cities full of innocent men, women, and children with firebombs?
> ➤ Why is both the political and religious world enamored of the glories of purposeful suicide?
> ➤ Why would Japan, during the Second World War, exterminate masses of people by subjecting them to hideous medical procedures and biological terrorism?
> ➤ Why would various countries around the world resort to ethnic cleansing as a rightful purpose?

These questions of why translate into larger questions characteristic of the human story, such as:

> ➤ Why do we feel superior to other people?
> ➤ Why do we conflict over social, political, and religious beliefs?
> ➤ Why do we accept some people and reject others?

> ➤ Why do we interpret the same events with opposing views?
> ➤ Why do we insist that our way of seeing is the only right one?
> ➤ Why do we kill each other because of contentions over different ways of seeing things?

The question that summarizes all such questions is this:

What causes us to see life so differently?

This is the most critical question of our existence and understanding it is the key to wisdom. I began to glimpse the answer to this question in the mid-1960s during the bourgeoning conflicts of the civil rights movement. While the terrorist attack of September 11 shocked because of its audacity and immediate density of life loss, the audaciousness and life losses associated with the subjugation of the black population over the course of American history causes this event to pale in comparison. Even in the so-called enlightened days of the 1960s, black citizens were still the brunt of dehumanizing and brutal behavior by white citizens.

In the middle of this decade I was living in Franklin County, North Carolina. It was a time of increasing tension and violence over race relations. Franklin County was tobacco farming country, where racial inequality was longstanding. Economically, this inequality was reflected in the difference in the housing of white land owners and that of black laborers. The land owners generally lived in comfortable and substantial houses; the laborers generally lived in squalid conditions and miserable shacks. While there were modest exceptions, this economic inequality was the rule. Educationally, this inequality was reflected in separate schools for blacks and whites. While the quality of education was fairly good for whites, it was less than satisfactory for blacks. The white population exerted a lot of energy justifying and maintaining these inequalities.

At that time the federal government initiated a requirement that the Franklin County School Board open itself to a token integration program called Freedom of Choice. This program permitted black pupils to take classes in white schools if their applications met certain criteria. One criterion was that the class was not being offered in black schools and another was that the applicant must justify taking the class as a necessity for educational achievement.

More than thirty applications from black pupils were received. After careful deliberation, the school board announced that none of the applicants met the criteria for acceptance. The Franklin County school system would remain segregated. The black community expressed outrage, but the school board held firm.

Later, a member of the school board confided to me why none of the applications had met the criteria. The gage regarding justification of educational achievement was developed after the applications were received and studied. It was then designed to ensure that none of the applicants would qualify.

I was scandalized by this social deviousness and approached the Federal Bureau of Investigation with the information. After a preliminary investigation, I was asked to be a key witness in a federal lawsuit against the Franklin County School Board. Along with the request came a warning that being such a witness might bring violent retaliation from the more bigoted and militant part of the white community. The specific basis of this warning was the existence of an active Ku Klux Klan organization in the area. My own personal fears and those of my family had to be weighed in my response. The ground of these fears was the same white prejudice that had created such an inhumane and bitter lifestyle for the black community. However, the possibility of our own maltreatment seemed dwarfed by comparison and an unworthy reason for failing to pursue racial justice. So I agreed to be a witness.

Immediately a campaign of intimidation was launched to encourage my withdrawal. My family was also the target of this campaign. My child was verbally and physically abused by school classmates. Day and night we received a constant flow of heavy-breathing and death-threat phone calls. For over a year we could not leave or enter our driveway without first picking up the nails that were flung there by passing motorists. Attempts were made to fire me from my job. Although these attempts failed, other methods were used to exert economic pressure as further leverage. The Ku Klux Klan visited us with their flaming cross as an additional warning message. My family lived in constant fear. But our traumas were small in comparison to those of the black community. They were experiencing far more violent attempts at intimidation. They were living their own deeper, longstanding fears.

During this drama the white community was divided. This division existed long before I arrived in Franklin County. The Freedom of Choice issue served only to give it highly visible focus. Some saw integration as a threat to their values and gave support to the intimidation campaign. Others saw integration as the fulfillment of their values and gave support to those who were the brunt of the intimidation. And some, who claimed friendship before I became a witness against the school board, became my enemies afterward.

Realization

This experience caused me to reflect on the capacity for opposing responses to life circumstance that exists in each of us humans. On the one hand, we permit our prejudices to dictate how we relate to others. We divide our world into us and them. We reject, we hate, we make violence. On the other hand, we permit our compassion to dictate how we relate. We embrace the world around us. We accept, we love, we make peace. These contrasting ways of relating were graphically expressed during my venture in Franklin County.

This contrast placed the question about why we see life so differently in bold relief for me. My own answer to this question began with a realization. It is not what we see that creates our differences. It is the way we see. Each of our minds sees through a different eye. This eye is not a gift of birth. It is created by the mind that uses it. The question is how our mind creates its own way of seeing. To answer this question is to know why we see things differently. But it is more than that. It is the prerequisite for taking control of my own life and being able to effectively influence the world around me.

Myth

The eye through which my mind sees is called a myth. The popular definition of myth is that of a falsehood or illusion. The reason for this definition is that stories that convey myths are often fictional and the content and the carrier become confused. However, I am using the word myth in its more traditional definition as a lens that gives focus to our encounter with life—as a way of seeing. Myth is the eye I use to translate experience into meaning. It is a view of reality. In this sense, everybody sees life through a myth. There are no exceptions. It is the prerequisite of being a meaning-maker.

The Questions

The puzzle is where this mythic eye comes from. The solution is that my mind creates it from the answers I give to life's most compelling questions. These compelling questions are those that all humans, irrespective of time or circumstance, are called upon to answer. They are inherent in what it means to be human. They fasten themselves to our mind at birth and confront us until the moment of our death. They will not let us rest until we answer them in some way. Answering them is the only way we have of creating meaning and the only affirmation we have that we are human.

Before the availability of writing materials and the printing press, perceptions of truth were conveyed through verbal stories. These stories were handed down by word of mouth from one generation to the next. Their purpose was to answer the questions that concerned humans about the mystery of their existence. As these stories were passed down through history, they evolved in both narrative and context as successive generations changed and the need to modernize for the sake of communication became clear. What was paramount to the tellers was not historical accuracy, rather, the power of the answer implied in the story. The truth they wished to convey was not in the accuracy of the details of the story, but in the clarity of the answer to the question being addressed.

Every culture had a set of stories that answered such questions for its people. The Greeks and Romans had stories about the actions of gods and goddesses that explained why things were the way they were. In Western culture we are more familiar with the stories in the Hebrew book of Genesis in the Bible. Genesis means "beginnings." There are stories in Genesis that seek to answer questions about such issues as:

➢ Who is responsible for everything?
➢ How did creation come into being?
➢ Where did humans come from?
➢ Why do humans suffer?
➢ How did evil enter the human drama?
➢ Why do people speak different languages?

The problem is that there is no end to the questions we have about the mystery of our existence. The answer we might give to one ques-

17

dditional questions. So over time, philosophers and
ought to reduce these questions to those most essen-
ing the meaning of human existence. The answers to
come the core of our view of reality. They are a way
owers us to give meaning to our experience. They
become the heart of our personal myth.

What are these compelling questions? What follows is a core version. Without the answers to these questions, we cannot fully create
the meanings necessary to perceive and communicate our sense of reality. Listed under each question is a set of clue words. When someone
uses one of these words, it may hint that an answer to the question is
being revealed. Under each set of clue words is an example of such usage. The examples are reflections of the diverse answers often heard in
American culture.

(1) **Who am I?** This is the question about the nature of my being. Am I good or evil, worthy or unworthy, equal or unequal,
powerful or impotent, in control or out of control? Everyone
lives an answer.

   Clue words: good, evil, ordained, being, nature, morality,
control, character, body, soul, powerful, impotent, human, divided, responsible, choice, will, worthy, unworthy, whole, broken, essence, sin.

   Example: "Humans are born sinful and powerless."

(2) **How do I know what I know?** This is the question about my
source of authority. Where does my knowing come from? Is it
within me or outside me? How do I know what I claim I know
is true? Everyone lives an answer.

   Clue words: inspiration, revelation, reason, intuition, em-
pirical, experience, observation, culture, learning, education,
conditioning, wisdom, authority, manifest, truth, knowledge.

   Example: "This is true because I experienced it."

(3) **Who or what is in charge?** This is the question about my ultimate value. What is greater than everything else? Who/what
governs the universe? What/who is the dynamic force or essence
that creates and sustains existence? Everyone lives an answer.

Clue words: goddess, god, Allah, Buddha, Creation, ultimate, universe, ruler, govern, human, maker, creator, supreme, principle, power, force, author, cosmos, value, dynamic.

Example: "Nothing is greater than the universe."

(4) **What is my purpose?** This is the question about the source of my well-being. What sustains my sense of self-worth? What fulfills my deepest longings? What gives meaning to my life? Why do I exist? How am I saved or made whole? How am I made happy? Everyone lives an answer.

Clue words: salvation, payoff, trade-off, deliverance, potential, happiness, meaning, fulfillment, purpose, claim, wholeness, redemption, evolution, growth, duty, satisfaction, meaning, contribute, cause, attain, stewardship, glorify.

Example: "Life is fulfilled by attaining wealth and power."

(5) **What does my death mean?** This is the question about the meaning of time in my existence. What happens to me when I die? How does my death relate to my birth? What meaning does death give to my life? Is my existence bound to time? Everyone lives an answer.

Clue words: afterlife, heaven, hell, purgatory, last things, reincarnation, karma, reward, punishment, annihilation, transition, transformation, nothing, vindication, time, timeless, cycle, death, destiny, future, memory, spirit, body, soul, end, justification, rule, change, energy, matter, influence, form, final, deed.

Example: "When I die I am reincarnated into a new life to learn the lessons I have not yet learned."

A Complete Myth

Max Weber once suggested that humans are animals suspended in webs of significance that we, ourselves, have spun. To use Weber's metaphor, these spun webs of significance are our answers to the compelling questions that, in their mutual support, form our mythic view of reality.

Sometimes stories or statements of mythic significance only illuminate one or two strands in this web. However, any complete view of reality will contain at least the answer strands of those five compelling questions. These strands make up the web framework to which all other significant mythic strands find a sustaining connection.

Control

From the moment of my birth, the authority figures in my life are programming answers to these compelling questions into my mind. I do not have to be aware of these answers for them to exist. Every attitude and action of my living is their reflection. The meaning they create is my mind's natural response to experience. However, I cannot be in control of my life until I consciously define these answers for myself.

Answer Examples

Generally, a person can define these answers with clarity in a few sentences per question. Following are two abbreviated example sets. The first example set is a composite of answers drawn from people in my former religious environment.

Who am I? I am born loved by God but sinful and impotent to change this condition without God's help.

How do I know what I know? The Bible is my source of authority and the voice of God gives me personal life direction.

Who/What is in charge? Nothing is greater than God, who is in control and is the creator of all that exists.

What is my purpose? God has forgiven my original sin and made me whole and worthy through my belief in Jesus's death and resurrection. My purpose is to glorify God in my living.

What does my death mean? Because God has saved me, my death will only be a doorway into Heaven where I will live with God forever.

The following second example set is a composite of some answers given by people in my present religious environment.

Who am I? I am worthy by virtue of being alive. I am co-moral with the capacity to choose between good and evil. I am responsible for the choices I make.

How do I know what I know? My personal experience, the accumulated wisdom of history, and all of creation are my sources of knowing. I am my own final authority.

Who/What is in charge? The universe is the ultimate value. It is an interdependent web of existence of which I am only a part. Everything that exists was birthed and is sustained by the universe.

What is my purpose? I am made whole by growing into my potential for nobility. Nobility is living with honor, principle, and integrity within myself; with respect, acceptance, and compassion toward others; and with gratitude, caring, and cooperation toward nature. My investment in nobility sustains my sense of self-worth.

What does my death mean? I must live deliberately and without waste because the gift of my life dies when my body dies. However, even after my body dies, my influence continues in the life of other humans and that of the planet.

The Mythic Eye

The answers I give to these questions become my mythic eye. This eye determines the way my mind sees. It is my view of reality. Following is a diagram that illustrates how these answers become the lens through which I define my relationships.

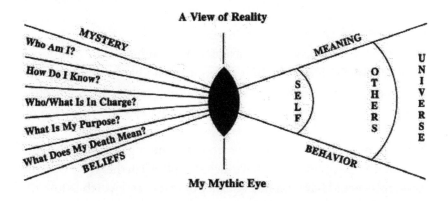

There are three primary dimensions that encompass all of my relating—my relationship to myself, my relationship to others, my relationship to the universe. As illustrated in the diagram, the meaning I give to all of my relationships and the attitudes and actions these meanings spawn are determined by my mythic eye. This eye is the answers of belief I give to the questions that reside in life's mystery, and the eye that is used is the eye that is seeing. As the Hebrew Talmud points out:

We do not see things as they are; we see things as we are.

A Historical Example

Here is an example from my experience in North Carolina of how relationships are determined by the mythic eye. Consider the question: *Who am I?* The actions and attitudes of the majority of white people in Franklin County revealed that they saw themselves as part of a superior race. The flip side of this view was that black people were a benighted race characterized by social and moral inferiority. That whites generally lived and worked in conditions of comfort while blacks generally lived and worked in conditions of misery was cited as *prima facie* evidence confirming this view as reality.

Attendant to the view that whites were superior was the notion that they were more valuable to the social enterprise than blacks. This notion absolved the white community of any guilt over using blacks as a cheap labor force. When asked to justify this utilitarian attitude toward blacks a typical response would be an incredulous: "But we love our niggers!" This response was a way of saying that low wages and shoddy housing supplied to black laborers was good enough for inferiors and, indeed, was an act of kindness.

Although such economic considerations reinforced the conditions of inequality, the issue of white superiority and black inferiority was at its heart a mythic one. This was most graphically reflected through church attendance segregation. The public worship experience of a religion is the celebration of what is most valued in its mythic view. The exclusion of the black community from worshiping in white churches was a mythic prohibition. To have included blacks in the white worship experience would have implied equality of status and worth before the white god. It would have threatened the perception of white superiority. The true "Community of God" was confirmed by pigmentation as well as salvation. Even permitting blacks to occupy such back space as a balcony partook of the implication of equality. However, for blacks to occupy such space would have been viewed as admission, on their part, of a corresponding inferiority. It was no different than sitting in the back rows of public transportation.

In contrast to this spirit of exclusion, black congregations welcomed any whites who were willing to worship in their churches. And whites could sit anyplace they wished just as did the blacks. This revealed that black people answered the question *Who am I?* in a fashion that equated them with whites. The belief that their god viewed all humans as equal transcended their quarrel with the white community over contentions of social and economic maltreatment. In brief, the true Community of God was confirmed by a salvation that disregarded skin pigmentation.

Essentially, the answer to the question of *Who am I?* by the majority of the white community was to claim a superior human worth by virtue of birth into a superior race. In contrast, the general black community's answer to this question was to claim an equal worth with all humans by virtue of creation's endowment. These two opposing answers to this crucial mythic question was the chief source of racial conflict in Franklin County. Answers to the other compelling questions were framed in compliance.

Mythic Integrity

The foregoing analysis of the differences in how the majorities of the black community and the white community answered the question of *Who am I?* was only one facet of their respective mythic eyes. As implied, their answers to the other compelling questions also played a critical role in shaping their relationships. Mythic views of reality tend to house compatible, integrated, and mutually supportive answers. The answer to one question becomes inextricably intertwined with the answers to all the other questions. Thus, to threaten the validity of one answer is normally to threaten the validity of the other answers. This is why it is so difficult to change a mythic system. Our myth is our identity, and mythic change initiates a crisis of identity.

As an example, consider this question: *What is my purpose?* Purpose is our perceived path toward life satisfaction, wholeness and, in religion, salvation. Inherent in fulfilling our purpose is our sense of sustained self-worth. Thus, our sense of purpose and our sense of self-worth are bound together in unity. If asked, the white community would have claimed some noble sense of purpose such as glorifying their god or providing sufficiently for their family. However, if purpose is reflected by attitudes and actions that prioritize living, then the basic purpose of the majority of Franklin County's white community was viewing and treating themselves as beings superior to other races. Concurrently, this meant keeping the black community in its place of inferiority. In doing so, the superior worth of the white community was affirmed (not to mention the economic benefits the white community accrued from the black community remaining in its inferior social status). Thus, to condone any action that implied the equality of the black community, such as permission to attend white schools, was not only prohibitive, it was a violation of the mythic view of reality by which white people lived. It was the prelude to a severe identity crisis and some significant measure of social chaos, not to mention serious economic loss.

On the other hand, considering the actions and attitudes of the black community as a whole, their implied purpose was to live in a circumstance of equal opportunity supported by the white community's lifestyle. It was to be viewed and treated as worthy social peers.

Contradiction

That notions of superiority of race and human worth were contradictory to the biblical authority they claimed (*How do I know what I know?*) was not an issue the majority of the white community was willing to face. So adamant was this refusal that any white person pointing out this apparent contradiction was condemned as a "nigger lover." This labeling was intended to consign that person's own worth to the level of blacks themselves. This consignment was a ploy used to not only refuse confronting the question but to avoid the potential anguish of change that would be necessitated by acknowledging the contradiction.

To have rectified this contradiction and altered their answers to be inclusive of the black community would have dictated the painful mythic transaction of recreating their social identity and relocating the source of their self-worth. It would have demanded an admission that they were responsible for creating and maintaining the conditions in which the black community lived. It would have demanded attitudes that would have changed the structure of race relationships. It would have demanded actions that would have had adverse impact on their financial status.

For most, such a price was too high to pay. It was easier to rationalize their prejudice-based answers and keep black people "in their place" through social segregation, economic suppression, psychological abuse, and intimidation through violence.

The irony of this racial conflict is that both the black and white communities claimed the same religious authority and Christian label. Yet their respective answers to the questions of *Who am I?* and *What is my purpose?* created radically different views of reality.

Conclusions

This experience in North Carolina exposed four bottom-line truths about the role of myth to me:

> ➤ Irrespective of geography or historical moment, our relationships are defined by the vision of our mythic eye.
>
> ➤ We are willing to do most anything to make reality conform to our mythic vision—howsoever irrational, absurd, reprehensible, or brutal it may be.
>
> ➤ We can change our mythic eye any time we are willing to pay the personal and social price.
>
> ➤ Normally, changing our myth requires a life-altering experience before we are willing to pay the personal and social price.

No Exceptions

Conscious awareness of being a mythic creature is not a prerequisite to being myth-driven. Scratch below the surface of any major attitude or action of living and one or more answers to the compelling questions of existence will be revealed. Every value cited as impetus toward decision-making is a symptom of our answers. The myth constituted by our answers is the wellspring of every dream and disappointment in our relationships and of all meanings given to our past-present-future. All of living is a mythic gesture.

Any Answer

However indirect or convoluted the expression of our answers, they are still answers. Consider the question *Who or what is in charge?* This is the question about the ultimate value in creation. In Western culture it has been traditionally viewed as the god question. However, there are innumerable ways to answer this question without resorting to god-labels. Even if the cosmic dimension of an answer is reduced to making humans the highest value, this is still an answer. Even if the response is a denial of being in charge from any source, this is still an answer. Even if the reply is noncommittal doubt, this is still an answer. An answer is an answer, and any answer will participate in defining our mythic view of reality.

The same is true of the answer given to any of the other compelling questions. To be a meaning-maker requires giving an answer—and any answer will fulfill this necessity. There are no exceptions to this rule. It governs all human existence.

Self-Interest and Myth

Whatever the myths in contention in Franklin County, they were all geared to the self-interest of the holder. This is true of every myth. Self-interest is my impulse to survive and be viewed as worthy. I was born with this impulse. It is innate to my humanness. It drives all the forces of my existence.

Self-interest is not synonymous with the absorbed egocentric narcissism of selfishness. It has no pre-existing moral inclinations of its own. I can as easily fulfill its urging through attitudes and actions that are caring and compassionate toward others as I can through those that are calloused and contemptuous.

It is the path I choose for its fulfillment that colors self-interest with moral quality. And this path will always be consistent with my myth. Myth instructs the satisfaction of self-interest. And my living will reflect the moral character of this instruction. The reflected living of people in both Franklin County and across the South during this period illustrates this point. Myth instructed some to satisfy their self-interest through ignoble attitudes and actions while it instructed others to find satisfaction through noble attitudes and actions. Personal, community, and cultural myth define the meaning of morality and make all moral judgments. Morality and myth are sine qua non to each other.

Conscience and Myth

The racial conflicts in Franklin County were about differences in perceived right and wrong. What some perceived to be right, others perceived to be wrong. Where did these contradicting perceptions come from? They came from conscience. Conscience is my inner voice that tells me whether attitudes and actions are right or wrong. And my conscience is created by my myth. The answers I give to life's compelling questions converge to imply a set of values. These values are the voice of my conscience. They are my standard for making moral judgments.

The racial conflicts in Franklin County rose from conflicts of myth

expressed through conflicts of conscience. Those white people holding the myth of white racial superiority had a value-conscience that
did not protest when black people were treated in demeaning ways.
Their conscience did not require respectful behavior toward inferiors.
This is why shoddy housing, second-rate schools, and low wages were
viewed as social favors rather than social travesties. In contrast, most
black people had a value-conscience that spoke of racial equality and
demanded corresponding attitudes and actions of respect. This conscience viewed shoddy housing, second-rate schools, and low wages as
expressions of social injustice. Whatever the skin color and whatever
the myth being lived, everyone in Franklin County was motivated by
conscience.

There were both black and white people in Franklin County who
claimed that those who lived the myth of white racial superiority were
without conscience and particularly those who expressed this sense
of superiority through injustice and brutalizing attitudes and behaviors. How did they come by this claim? They did so by comparing the
conscience of the myth being judged with the conscience of their own
myth. Since the values of the myth being judged were alien to their
own values, they concluded that it was without conscience. But this
was a misperception.

Myths of racial superiority, whatever they might be, are all con-
science-centered. This conscience is grounded in the values of supreme
bloodline and corresponding skin color. These values announce that
those of the superior race are of greater worth than those of other races. Historically, such a conscience condones views and behaviors that
express contempt for the racially inferior. No matter how morally perverted a myth may seem in comparison to my own, it possesses a conscience that instructs the attitudes and actions of its followers. Here is
the principle:

> *Just as meaning cannot be made without a myth, a myth cannot
> exist without a conscience.*

So the issue is never whether a conscience is present, but the nature of the conscience that is present. The human without a conscience
does not exist. That a conscience is totally alien to one's own or one's
community or one's culture only means that it is a conscience not com-

patible with or understandable by one's own mythic eye. Thus, so-called psychologies that imply lack of conscience are grounded in the mythic norms of community and culture and not in the grounding reality of human experience. Such psychologies are useful in processing cultural concerns but also skew perceptions about myths that drive human living.

Law and Myth

It appears that the Franklin County School Board, in its attempt to thwart racial integration, suppressed the civil rights of a large group of citizens. Yet, this board was composed of upstanding community members who, otherwise, believed in supporting the law. How is it possible to support law in general while violating law in particular and feeling morally justified in doing so? To broaden the question, how is it possible that an entire nation can found itself on ideals and laws of civil rights integral to its Constitution and yet, with clear conscience, deny access to these civil rights to a large segment of its citizens? The answer to these questions lies in myth.

The myth of white racial superiority has dominated and shaped American history. This myth, fueled by the spirit of manifest destiny in the nation's westward expansion, led to the near genocide of the Native American population. This myth was the impetus for the questionable actions taken toward Mexico by the American government that eventuated in the land grab of that vast territory called the Southwest and California. This myth was the moral justification for the almost century-long enslavement of African Americans and the equally long post-Civil War obstruction of their civil rights. This myth, throughout American history, has sanctioned all manner of contemptuous attitudes and inhumane behavior toward racial minorities.

Following the Civil War, the Fourteenth and Fifteenth Amendments were added to the American Constitution. These amendments guaranteed equal protection under the law and voting rights for black citizens. In addition, Congress passed two Civil Rights Acts that guaranteed equal access to public transportation. Yet so-called Jim Crow laws were instituted in both the North and South that negated these protections and rights. The United States Supreme Court gave support to these unconstitutional laws. It was not until the 1954 ruling in the Brown versus Board of Education case (Topeka, Kansas) and the impact of the following civil rights movement that the Supreme Court began upholding the constitutional and civil rights of black citizens.

Why, for almost one hundred years, did the Supreme Court allow the Constitution and congressional law to be deliberately violated by state laws? The answer is because the mythic attitudes of the majority of the courts were agreeable with these violations. Between the 1860s and the 1950s the Constitution and congressional law did not change. What changed was the court's mythic conscience. Here is the principle:

> *It is not law that governs a culture's application of its myth. It is myth that governs a culture's application of its law.*

Law can be ignored, bent, or broken to suit mythic whim. Sometimes this happens because of strong moral indignation and is called "civil disobedience." This was the impetus for violating segregation laws by civil rights advocates. Sometimes this happens to reinforce the control of mythic prejudice. This was my interpretation of the actions of the Franklin County School Board. Whatever the reason for ignoring, bending, or breaking cultural law, it is prompted by mythic viewpoints.

And whether there is negative or positive consequence depends on the mythic response of community. The laws of segregation, activities of discrimination, and civil rights violations aimed at the black citizenry in the nation's South were given positive support by a regional community whose majority affirmed the myth of white racial superiority. Only when the larger national community became outraged at the arrogance of this mythic support did it begin drawing negative consequences. The application of cultural law is always mythically selective. Whatever the branch or expression of national or local government, attitudes and actions will be determined by prevailing mythic views.

The law has always been myth's servant. Myth will create the law, force the interpretive compliance of existing law, or ignore the law's presence. In whatever way myth chooses to use the law to its own advantage, it will do so without guilt, because guilt requires the violation of conscience. The shadow of this truth falls across all of human history, irrespective of time and place. It is a shadow that retrospect reveals without effort.

Nothing has changed in the American culture in this respect since the 1950s. The Supreme Court still interprets the American Constitution and the laws of the land through the eyes of myth. One recent example is the decision of this body in respect to the 2000 presidential election and its ruling in the Florida recount controversy. This court was even so bold as to indicate in its ruling that its decision was a one-time announcement that applied only to the peculiarity of this event. In brief, it acknowledged that its decision was not one pertaining to general or constitutional law but one devoted to this specific circumstance. This acknowledgment flaunted the mythic dimension of its decision.

More often than not, the court will be divided in its mythic opinion, and the interpretation handed down will be that of the mythic majority. If this were not the case, then all of its decisions would be unanimous. That the highest court in the land is controlled by mythic view rather than by strict legal interpretation may be disconcerting, but that is the truth of history. At the beginning of the twenty-first century, one national conservative religious leader saw fit to publicly pray for his god to remove three liberal members of the Supreme Court so that a president who favored the views of this leader's constituency would be able to appoint justices with a more conservative mythic view, thus tipping the mythic balance of power of the court. This illustration again affirms that all human interaction, whatever its sphere, is myth-driven and that so-called objectivity is mythically based.

Affinity and Myth

We humans have two basic affinities in terms of mythic response to the social world around us. These affinities comprise polar possibilities. Everyone will find themselves somewhere on the continuum between these possibilities. They have to do with consort and conflict, with agreement and disagreement, with like and dislike. The depth or intensity of this affinity will determine the nature of our relationship with the other humans in our environment of living. That nature also takes on an expression that ranges from ideological to physical, from being a debate to being a war. In the choices we make about this affinity, we either create a community of bonding or we create a conflict of destruction. We either support or contend. It is in dialogue and story-telling that we determine the nature of our affinities. The upshot is a myth alignment that is as natural as breathing.

The Vehicles

To communicate our myths, the answers to the compelling questions are often embodied in story form. Rosemary R. Ruether, in her theology of feminism, reminds us:

> *It is through generating stories of our own crisis and hope and telling them to one another that we light the path.*

This observation underscores two of the essential purposes of myth: revealing perceived truth and offering perceived hope. The truth revealed is about answers to life's compelling questions. The hope offered is about a better future. The stories of Jesus, Mohammed, the Buddha, and Joseph Smith, Jr., are examples from religion. The American Revolution, "How the West Was Won," the Civil War, and World War II are examples of American national stories. The personal stories we tell about who we are and what we believe are examples from individual living.

Stories are used because they are easy to remember and to reference. Moreover, since the intention of any myth is to capture our devotion, the story form is valuable because it touches our passions with its imagination, aliveness, and drama.

The story used can be either factual or imaginary. It does not matter as long as it conveys the answers to the questions. Factual war stories are often used as vehicles for that part of the American myth that speaks to a God-led, invincible, democratic, savior nation. The Walt Disney movie *The Lion King* is an imaginative story vehicle for a mythic statement about life as an interdependent web of existence deserving of respect and noble action. Thus, whether or not the vehicle accords with our sense of historical accuracy is immaterial to the myth being conveyed. It is the truth of the myth, rather than the truth of the vehicle, that is at contention. Attempts to discount a myth because its conveying vehicle does not accord with our sense of reality is to miss the point and, possibly, to miss the truth being conveyed. Perceptiveness requires keeping the myth and its vehicle of expression separated. This does not discount our right to make judgments based on our mythic perceptions of fact versus fiction. It only cautions us not to confuse the truth of a myth and its vehicle.

To view a myth as truth and then to demand that its vehicle also be viewed as truth because it is the carrier of truth is a similar matter. It is to weld myth and the story of its expression into a unity. It is to demand that the truth of history be twisted to fit the truth of myth. Thus, it distorts fact to accommodate to faith. It simply does away with any criteria by which fact and fiction are distinguished.

However, answers to life's compelling questions do not require a story vehicle to be a myth. The English word *myth* comes from the Greek word *mythos*, which means "story or word." As in religion, philosophy, or any other instructive discipline, a myth may be stated as a set of beliefs. A myth is a way of seeing, not the vehicle that conveys it. Whether it comes to us as a story or statement, the combined answers to the compelling questions create the mythic eye.

In Reverse

The compelling questions also work in reverse. By taking the meaning given to an experience, story, or statement and pushing it backwards through these questions, the inherent answers will be exposed. The mythic eye will be opened. Tales and declarations always speak to a view of reality standing in background.

While facilitating a workshop on defining personal and community myth, I pointed out the benefit of this reverse process and encouraged participants to apply it to some story or statement of their choice. A therapist in the group chose to translate his perception of Sigmund Freud's views into answers to these questions. The result was a transformation of his understanding of Freudian psychology. During another workshop I suggested parents push the fairy tales their children were reading through the compelling questions. Some found the mythic messages in these tales to be contrary to their basic parental values. Through this process they discovered the real message was often disguised or subtly buried beneath the story action. One or more of the compelling questions serve as the impetus for all influential stories and statements.

The compelling questions work in both directions—either to create a myth or to reveal the answers a myth is designed to transmit.

Meaning Making

The powers of my mind converge to make it possible for me to discern options and make choices. In turn this enables me to create meaning. I can make choices about everything in my existence except one thing. I cannot choose to not make meaning. Even if I declare that life is meaningless, that is a meaning I have made. That my mind cannot stop creating meaning may have been what caused Robert Frost, in his poem *The Clearing*, to wryly comment:

> *Forgive, O Lord, my little jokes on Thee,*
> *and I'll forgive thy great big one on me.*

Although I cannot stop participating in this joke, I can exert some control over how I do it. Such control requires an understanding of how meaning-making happens. This understanding begins with the recognition that meaning is the translation of experience into the language of communication. Translation demands a medium.

The Formula

The life equation for how we create meaning is this:

$$E + M = M^2$$
(Experience plus Myth equals Meaning-Made)

Experience is awareness of happening. It has no meaning until I give it one by pushing it through my myth. There is nothing new about this life equation. It has been recognized throughout history as the way meaning is created. It has simply been stated differently. There is a jaded Western version: "Beauty is in the eye of the beholder." And there is a modern Western version: "Thought is creative." There is an ancient Near Eastern version: "As one thinks in the heart so is one." And in the Far East there is a version in the form of a Zen koan (a teaching story). A religious novice is standing before a Zen Master. The novice points a finger at a flag waving in the wind and asks, "Master, which is waving, the flag or the wind?" To which the Master responds, "Neither! It is the mind that is waving."

Fine, Regular, Perk, or Drip?

Do I create my own reality? In high-energy physics there is an assumption that the very act of observing is, within itself, an act of distortion. Although, in science, this assumption tends to be limited to the particle world, in the world of normal human interaction it translates into a universal principle that governs all meaning-making, as well as all living. Alexander Pope was affirming this principle when he stated: "All looks yellow to the jaundic'd eye." I am also affirming this principle when I state that someone is looking at the world through rose-colored glasses. And both of these statements affirm that people can participate in the same experience, yet give it radically different meanings.

The agent of distortion in human meaning-making is the mythic eye. The mythic eye assigns meaning to experience consistent with its view of reality. To assign meaning is to convert an experience into the language of communication. Thus, meaning-making is a dual distortion. It both reduces the experience to the limits of language and conforms that language to the view of the mythic eye. While the experience remains its own reality, the meaning made becomes the reality of this dual distortion.

All humans live in the same universe and on the same planet. We are exposed to its same phenomena. This is the natural reality we share in common. But the meaning we give to this natural reality and to our relationships within it are created in our minds through myth. In this sense I create my own reality. Or, as the nineteenth-century English novelist George Gissing puts it:

> It is the mind which creates the world around us, and even though we stand side by side in the same meadow, my eyes will never see what is beheld by yours, my heart will never stir to the emotions with which yours is touched.

While in high school I worked in a grocery store and one of my jobs was to grind fresh coffee beans for our customers. As I recall, there were four options on the grinder—fine, regular, perk, and drip. What I did was select the requested setting, pour in the beans, and turn on the grinder. What came out were not the beans, but grounds consistent with the setting.

My mind creates meaning in a way similar to the coffee grinder. My mind is like the grinder. My experience is like the coffee beans. My myth is like the setting. As my experience pours through my mind, it is converted into meaning consistent with my mythic setting. This meaning is not the experience itself. Rather, it is the essence of that experience made to conform to the assumptions of my myth. The primary difference in this analogy is that my mind is not limited to fine, regular, perk, or drip settings. Its capacity for creative variety in mythic settings is limitless. This is why people see differently. This is how we create different stories from the same event.

Myth is the creative link between experience and meaning. This capacity to create our stories rests on three sustaining truths:
- ➢ I am a compulsive and unrelenting meaning-maker.
- ➢ I choose the myth by which I convert my experience into life meaning.
- ➢ The myth I choose determines my relationship to myself, others, and the universe.

My experience in North Carolina underscores these truths. Both black and white majorities were driven by human nature to create meaning from their life circumstance. Both groups chose the mythic eye that converted their experience into different meanings. And the mythic eye each group chose determined the temper of the relationship that existed between them.

Or, consider the September 11, 2001, event. Most Americans viewed it as an unmitigated atrocity and saw the terrorists as nothing more than murderers. The average American could find no justification for this act in respect to their perception of our nation's historical behavior in the world. On the other hand, the terrorists, owing to their radical religious beliefs, undoubtedly viewed what they did as a holy act that would assure them a special place in paradise. They believed that the behavior of the American nation justified the horror that their act invoked. This view seemed to be shared by other terrorists around the world. While the 9/11 experience was a common event, it was given two radically different interpretations. These interpretations are a reflection of differing mythic eyes. And what the morality of the event might be is determined by the mythic eye making the interpretation. Objectivity is in the eye of the beholder and will always be consistent with that eye's answers to life's compelling questions. In the same manner, my personal perceptions about myth and the myths of others will be consistent with my personal myth.

The Bottom Line

Here is the bottom line: It is not love that makes the world go around; it is myth. Myth determines what love is, and what and whom I love. I see through a mythic eye. I think with a mythic mind. I hear by a mythic ear. I feel with a mythic heart. And I speak through a mythic mouth. All of my attitudes and actions are mythically instructed. There is nothing in human experience having to do with meaning that is not the creation of myth. This bottom line is the gage of all truth.

Another way of stating this bottom line is that we are determined more by what we bring to experience than by what experience brings to us. Experience is raw material without the shape of meaning until we mold it into something that contributes to our understanding of the life we are living. This is why it is so critical that we be able to define our myth and the myth of others. Within this definition resides the difference between being in control and being controlled, the difference between being a player and being a pawn.

The essence of all of the foregoing can be summarized in the following historical insights:

It is not seeing which is believing
It is believing which is seeing.

—Anonymous

The mind is its own place, and in itself can make a Heav'n of Hell, a Hell of Heav'n.

—John Milton

We do not see things as they are; we see things as we are.
—Hebrew Talmud

Myth-Applied Meaning
(Pun-dacity)

➤ All truth is a myth-conception of reality.
➤ All values are statements of myth-understanding.

- ➤ All lifestyle is a myth-odology.
- ➤ All living is myth-behaving.
- ➤ All commitment is myth-trust.
- ➤ All differences are myth-takes.
- ➤ All fate is myth-fortune.
- ➤ All change comes through myth-appropriation.
- ➤ All community is myth-alignment, because myth-ery loves company. — *Unless you purposefully choose outside your "comfort" or myth*
- ➤ All children are myth-begotten.
- ➤ All decisions are myth-calculations.
- ➤ All religions are myth-representations.
- ➤ All culture is myth-managed.
- ➤ All government is myth-rule.
- ➤ All justice is myth-carriage.
- ➤ All leadership is myth-direction.
- ➤ All education is myth-guided.
- ➤ All conflicts are grounded in myth-apprehension.
- ➤ All wars are myth-fires.
- ➤ All relationships are engaged through myth-cues.
- ➤ All devotions are myth-matches.
- ➤ All stories are myth-shaped.
- ➤ And, despite what we believe to be real, life remains a myth-tery.

THE MAGICIAN
(A Metaphor of Meaning-Making)

Meaning-making is mental magic. It is sleight of mind. And each of us is a magician who conjures meaning from the hat of myth. If I pull a rabbit from my hat and you summon a bird from yours, can either be denied? The question of mental magic does not concern the reality of the meaning conjured, but what the meaning can do. Is it free to roam or soar? Can it scurry through brambles or fly over mountains? The thing to guard against is the illusion that the hat is the only reality and its conjuring the only truth. The trick of being a magician is not to be tricked by the magic.

The Potter of Me

(The Importance of Myth)

No handy craft can with our art compare,
For pots are made of what we potters are.
   —Unknown (Motto of Eighteenth-Century Potters)

The Potter

My myth is like a potter. It throws my living upon the wheel of destiny and shapes me in the image of its vision. As the motto of eighteenth-century potters affirms: "pots are made of what we potters are." Just so, people are made of what their myths are. My myth is the potter of me. All living is myth-shaped. Following are four ways my myth shapes my living and creates my destiny.

Closedness and Openness

My myth shapes how closed or open my living is to experiences of the new that bring freshness and challenge to the adventure of living.

Potters of Closedness

The closed myth is a view of reality designed to shut down my experience of the new. It shuts down such experience by:
   ➤ declaring itself as the only test of reality
   ➤ declaring all experiences that will not conform to its reality as false

No experience can be new when the meaning given to it makes it adhere to a prescribed reality or be false. This is analogous to locking the picture end of a kaleidoscope so that the pattern of reality that is seen is always the same, irrespective of how it is shaken or twisted.

This locking is a refusal to allow the old to be changed by the intrusion of the new into its pattern. Thus, no matter what the circumstance or other forces of newness seeking entry into the picture, the view of reality remains unperturbed and stable.

The reward offered by the closed myth is profoundly appealing to my human desire to impose upon existence the control of dependable order and expectation. Even when life shakes or twists me with force, the expected pattern of reality will emerge. It is the reward of comfort and security in a world of unending and disturbing change.

But there is a price to be paid for allowing the closed myth to shape my existence. Alan Watts, British philosopher, summarizes the price paid for embracing the closed myth in one of his limericks:

There was a young man who said "Damn,
For it certainly seems that I am
A creature who moves
In determinant groves:
I'm not even a bus, I'm a tram."

Life is intended by nature to be wild. Wild does not mean to be out of control in the environment of living, rather it means to be controlled by a natural response to this environment. This natural response is my desire to enter the surprise of the new and explore the meaning it might offer life. The closed myth seeks to tame this wildness by breaking its spirit in the cage of sameness and by training it to fear the new as a threat to the control of reliable order and expectation. To have my wildness tamed is to have my living domesticated into the security and comfort of sameness.

Yet having my living shaped by the closed myth is not entirely without adventure. It does offer the adventure of parallel challenge. One challenge is defending my myth against attacks on its claim of being the only legitimate view of reality. The other is the challenge of propagating my myth as the only legitimate view of reality. These challenges are the adventure of the true believer—both individually and institutionally.

Participating in the closed myth saturates my living with the satisfaction of knowing that I am right, irrespective of those voices that claim otherwise. It empowers me with the conviction of righteous attitudes and actions. It provides me with definitive purpose for my life. It declares clear boundaries for my decisions.

The adventure of participating in the closed myth is grounded in its refusal to acknowledge any other reality except its own. When I give my life to this myth, it closes my living to all alternatives and shapes my destiny with its closedness.

Potters of Openness

The open myth is a view of reality that welcomes experiences of the new. It welcomes the new by:

> ➢ declaring itself as worthy of commitment while being unfinished
> ➢ declaring that all experience is a potential vehicle of further revelation

The new is an intrusion of unfamiliar insight into living. The posture of openness permits this insight to create a shift in my view of reality. It is analogous to keeping the picture end of the kaleidoscope unlocked so that when it is shaken or twisted by life an entirely different configuration emerges. Each time a new insight enters this viewing end, a shift of the pattern's relationships is made to accommodate its perceived truth. Thus every new circumstance of living with its intrusion of newness may bring about an altered view of reality or, at the least, an enriched pattern of meaning.

The reward of the open myth is its acknowledgment and facilitation of the natural wildness that exists within me as a human. It keeps me available to be surprised by what life can offer at any moment and encourages me to explore the meaning of this surprise.

Emily Dickinson, in her poem *Hope*, describes the posture of openness this way:

The soul should always stand ajar, ready to welcome the ecstatic experience.

But there is a price to be paid for allowing my life to be shaped by the open myth. I must be willing to live with the instability of the awareness that how I view reality today may be different from yesterday and even tomorrow. Therefore, I must have a diligent faith in my personal capacity to make judgments without the comfort and security of an unchanging view of reality. This is profoundly appealing to my desire to live as my own authority and explore the mystery of existence in my own way.

As with the closed myth, the open myth provides two parallel adventures. One adventure is that of the new reshaping the old. With every new revealed insight, my old view of reality is reshaped. With every new reshaping of reality, my old being in the world is transformed. And with every transformation of being wrought by this adventure, my old potential for growth is expanded. The new keeps my living in constant recreation, and excitement permeates existence.

The second parallel adventure is experiencing the new refreshing the old. The new causes the old to be seen in a way never experienced before. This refreshing of the old is described in a song from the Broadway stage production of *Zorba the Greek*. Zorba is trying to persuade his friend, whom he calls Boss, to crawl out of the rigid abstractions of the academic and engage the old with its possibilities of newness. Recounting many of the common experiences of his living he sings these words:

> *I believe in grabbing at life:*
> *every minute a new minute . . .*
> *every second a new second . . .*
> *never happened before.*

And whether it is smelling a woman, pounding on a table, or sniffing at a flower, it is always a first-time experience no matter how many times it has been done before. He concludes the song with these words:

> *I soar like a seagull. I stamp like a bull.*
> *I comb out my whiskers so ladies can pull.*
> *I chew on the mutton until my belly's full,*
> *   but each time—a hat, a dumbag, a*
> *   person, each time is new.*

The adventure of participating in the open myth is grounded in its willingness to risk what the experience of the new might bring to reality. When I give my being to this myth it opens my living to multiple alternatives and shapes my destiny with this openness.

Conclusion

Whether my myth of choice is open or closed, it is a potter that will shape the clay of my living in its own image. Therefore, whichever choice I make, I should make it by deliberateness, not by default.

Seeing and Not Seeing

There is said to have been a tribe of African natives who believed so strongly that reality did not exist beyond the geographic boundaries of their self-proclaimed territory that their physical eyes cooperated in maintaining this illusion. This story is an apt analogy of how myth works in my experience. My mythic eye refuses to see anything as real beyond its self-proclaimed boundaries. This is the case whether my myth's posture toward reality is closed or open. Every mythic eye sees only what it is designed to see. It will distort my vision to conform to its own built-in expectations. Therefore, my myth shapes both what I see and don't see because my myth is the potter of me.

Not Seeing

I was parked at the drive-up window of my bank waiting for the teller to cash a $39 check. She pushed the money through the exchange outlet and I counted it. The amount was a dollar short. I returned the money to the teller. She recounted, indicated it was correct, and pushed it back. Again I counted, indicating she was in error. She laughed and asked if I had counted the two-dollar bill. I had not. Even through I had counted it twice I had seen it as a one-dollar bill because that was what I was expecting to see. My mythic eye works the same way. It sees what it expects to see and its expectation is that experience will conform to its own view of reality.

When the teller asked it if I had seen the two-dollar bill, she was suggesting that I look at the money through different eyes. In doing so, I saw a different reality. Occasionally, others whom I trust may claim to see what I do not. When I become aware that I often miss what is actually there, I may wish to ask myself if the degree to which my myth is myopic is a limitation I am willing to accept.

Seeing

My myth will also cause me to see what isn't there. I can visualize a Pogo cartoon that makes this point. The scene is a baseball diamond. Pogo is batting, Churchy La Femme is pitching, and Albert the Alligator is catching. Churchy winds up and throws an imaginary ball. Before Pogo can blink, Albert goes, "Pow," with a fist in his mitt and yells, "Strike one!" Pogo is still dazed when Churchy hurls the second imaginary ball. "Pow," goes Albert's hand in his mitt as he hollers, "Strike two!" For the third time Churchy winds up and lets the invisible ball fly. But this time, before Albert can slap his fist in mitt, Pogo swings his bat, makes a cracking sound, and shouts, "Home run!"

Mythic living is like playing with an imaginary baseball. Since my myth is my viewpoint, it causes me to see what it is designed to see. And its design is to confirm my answers to the compelling questions as reality. Thus, it interprets all experience as a confirmation. So diligent is its devotion to confirmation it will even see what is not there. This is not willful deception. It is willful envisioning. In the same manner that the tribe of African natives had blinded itself to reality beyond its mythic boundaries, my myth can see within its boundaries what does not exist.

As a professional minister I have lived with this truth throughout my career. Decades ago I became aware that what people heard was a mythic transaction. So I began delivering sermons from a manuscript. In addition, the sermons were audio taped. On occasion someone will want to talk with me about something upsetting that they sincerely believe I had said but which I had not. Usually listening to a copy of the taped sermon resolves the issue. But sometimes it will not. I recall a person who insisted I had made a derogatory remark about her favorite cause. It happened to be a cause that was receiving my utmost positive support.

She read my manuscript. She listened to the taped sermon. She queried members of the congregation. The alleged remark did not show up on manuscript or tape, and no one she talked to had heard it. Nevertheless she said to me, "I heard what I heard, and you said what I heard." Even though what she had heard was not there, faith in her mythic hearing was unshakable. But one does not have to be a professional minister to encounter this phenomenon. It is the stuff of daily existence, whether it be family quarrels, workplace contentions, or any of life's myriad routine negotiations. The insight of American psychologist Lawrence LeShan is apropos:

If all you have is a hammer, then everything is treated as a nail.

When I become aware that I often see what is not there, I may wish to ask myself if I am willing to accept the fantasies my myth creates, because my myth is the potter of me.

Objectivity

Becoming aware that my myth will shape what I see and don't see has taught me a valuable lesson about the role of objectivity in my experience. This lesson is about illusion. It is not my myth that is an illusion. My myth is as real as I make it with my life's investment. The illusion is that my myth sees with an objective eye.

This illusion of objectivity is created by the logic of my myth. This logic comes from the mutually supportive answers I give to life's compelling questions that create my myth. The assumption of these answers is that they see with clarity. My claim to objectivity is nothing more than an appeal to the logic of these answers. This is called circular reasoning. And every myth is subject to this fallacy of objectivity. Critic of urban life Lewis Mumford says it this way:

What was once called the objective world is a sort of Rorshak inkblot, into which each culture, each system of science and religion, and each type of personality, reads a meaning only remotely derived from the shape and color of the blot itself.

The uniqueness of the Rorschach inkblot test is that it is a set of images without a common identifiable form. These blots invite the participants to project onto the images their own peculiar meaning. This meaning derives from the present state of the individual's view of reality.

As an analogy, the inkblot is my experience of existence. The meaning given to that experience is not common to all humans. It is the projection of my myth onto the image of the experience. In making this meaning my myth assumes it has been objective because the meaning it has projected is consistent with the integrated logic of my answers to life's compelling questions.

Thomas Carlyle, eighteenth-century Scottish satirist, expresses this insight in these words:

> *In every object there is an inexhaustible meaning; the eye sees in it what the eye brings means of seeing.*

The only objective experience ultimately common to all humans is that of the natural world in which we reside. But this experience is of nature's function and not of its meaning to my living. That a tornado destroys my house is an experience of nature's function. The meaning I give to this experience is my myth's function. The experience is objectively unbiased. The meaning is unobjectively biased. These are radically different realities. There is objectivity in experience but none in the meaning myth imposes upon experience. Thus, the only objectivity of my myth is its own internal consistency of logic.

As a potter, my myth shapes my sense of objectivity. An awareness that objectivity is only the logic of my answers to life's compelling questions invites my humility and encourages my tolerance toward people who choose a myth of differing logic.

Relationship Meanings

My myth shapes the meaning I give to all relationships. It prescribes whether I like or dislike myself. It prescribes whether I love or hate other people and who the recipients are going to be. It prescribes whether I am empathetic or utilitarian toward the universe. The prejudices I harbor and the companions I desire are myth-defined. Those images that instruct whether my relationships will be of happiness or discontent are conjured by my myth.

Community

The word *community* originates from the notion of holding something in common. Aside from the natural bonds of survival and support of family, all normal social bonding is through myth-affinity. This same truth drawn from nature is that birds of a feather flock together. In the bird world this feather-bonding is biologically genetic. In the human world it is mythically generic. Human community normally grows from myth-alignment. The breakup of a community is normally due to myth-alienation.

Aside from the vague outlines of civilizations, cultures are the largest mythic communities with specific identities. Within a culture are multiple mythic subsets that are social, political, religious, and regional in nature. Against the background of the cultural myth and its subsets, my personal myth tells me if my values are liberal, conservative, or moderate. I seek out smaller communities of love, friendship, religion, and politics based on this mix of mythic meanings. My perception of allies and enemies and my view of harmony and conflict roots in this mythic matrix.

Whatever the size of my communities, from the smallest to the largest, it is mythic attraction that bonds into community. And this attraction is conveyed through the mythic language that reveals its view of reality.

Communion

Communion is my ability to feel a community bond beyond spoken language. The medium of communion is sensory. The intuitive spirit of unity that moves through the medium is a common experience of fear or joy. This common experience permits a bonding that transcends the barriers of mythic differences.

However, despite communion's ability to bond without language, it is still dependent on myth for its triggering. The previous meanings I have given to my relationship with self, others, and the universe determine what is fearful or joyous for me. So although I do not need language to commune, my myth will prescribe the circumstances for its occurrence.

A few years ago I visited Bryce Canyon in the state of Utah. The canyon is a spectacular display of eroded and sculpted columns and walls of varied white and orange limestone and sandstone. In early morning light the patterns of color magically change as sunlight moves across the surface of these columns and walls. Watching this happen is an awesome experience, full of inarticulate wonder.

I stood on an outcrop vantage point with a dozen other people whom I later learned were of different nationalities. As the sun gradually bathed the canyon we were all immersed in a mystical moment of union that demanded a willful reverence of silence. We were a group with kneeled spirits communing with the universe and each other for thirty minutes without the utterance of sound.

The prior meanings we had all given to our relationship with the universe had permitted the common experience of joy to transcend our mythic differences and bond us in a transcendent communion. We sensed it, engaged it, and only later spoke of the experience with common meanings. I have had other similar experiences through different sensory mediums such as music.

Harmony and Discord

Whether it is conflict that separates us, communities that bond us, or communions that confound us, all flow from the mythical meanings we have given to our relationships. Myth harmonizes with myth and myth discords with myth. Birds of a feather flock together and birds of a different sort flock apart. My myth is the potter of me.

Life Focus

My myth shapes my life's focus and I become this focus.

Michael Rogin was a world-recognized distinguished professor of political science at the University of California in Berkley, California, until his death in 2001. Among his myriad publications is a book entitled *Ronald Reagan The Movie*. In this book he analyzes the mythic impact of Reagan's screen roles on his life and career. He asserts that Reagan's life focus was the roles he played in such films as *Knute Rockne, All American* and *King's Row*. Rogin shows how Reagan took on the images of these roles and converted them into his mythic self. Even Reagan's autobiography is titled from the critical line he speaks in *King's Row*: "Where is the rest of me?" In the movie this line is a response to the realization that his legs had been amputated following an accident.

Reagan's favorite character of self-identification was George Gipp, the football hero in *Knute Rockne, All American*. As Gipp is dying in the movie, he says to his coach Knute Rockne, "Someday when the team is in trouble, tell them to win one for the Gipper." Later when Rockne's team is being beaten in a crucial game, he reminds them of Gipp's statement and, inspired, they come from behind to win. "Win one for the Gipper" was Reagan's favorite invocation, merging himself with George Gipp as the hero who inspires victory.

He invoked this line repeatedly during his political career. "Win one for the Gipper," he told the 1984 U.S. Olympic team. "Win those races for the Gipper," he challenged the masses during one presidential election campaign. At the 1984 Republican Convention, a film of Nancy Reagan's life was shown and she spoke. At the end of her speech she turned, raised her arms toward a huge projected image of Reagan, and exclaimed, "Make it one more for the Gipper!" Clearly Ronald Reagan saw himself as the Gipper, the inspiring hero, and identified this self-image as the body politick. He and the nation were one.

Hollywood had come to the White House, and the distinction between real life and movie fantasy was blurred in politics as it was in Reagan's own mind. On one occasion Reagan tearfully told an audience a true story about a Congressional Medal of Honor winner's heroism. In reality the story was a segment of a World War II movie, *A Wing and a Prayer*. Rogin cites other examples of this blurring.

Ronald Reagan was so obsessed by his mythic identification with the hero he played in *King's Row* that he watched the movie continuously year after year. The notion that he was missing a vital support that would make it possible to stand on his own two legs was a life pursuit.

According to Rogin, in Reagan's autobiography, entitled *Where Is the Rest of Me*, he declares that he finally found this missing support— Nancy Reagan and the body politick. Nancy and the nation "won one for the Gipper" by becoming his mythic prosthetic.

The importance of Rogin's exposé is not that it simply enables us to better understand Ronald Reagan. Its greater importance is that it graphically reveals how Reagan became his mythic focus. The only difference between Reagan and most of the rest of us is that no one has exerted the energy required to show how we have become our mythic focus.

I become the focus of my myth and this focus becomes my reality. My myth is the potter of me.

The Potter

The potter is an apt metaphor of the myth that shapes my living and destiny by:

> ➤ determining my openness or closedness to the new

> ➢ determining what I see and don't see
> ➢ determining the meaning of my relationships
> ➢ determining my life focus

The vital importance of this shaping underscores the most critical decision I make about my myth: "Who will be master and who will be servant?"

Master or Servant

There is a story in the Old Testament book of Isaiah about a woodcutter who chops down a tree. He uses part of what he has chopped down to build a fire for warmth. He uses more to cook a meal to satisfy his hunger. Then, with what is left, he carves an idol and falls down before his creation and worships it as a god. Consider the transaction of this story. The wood that provides the means of sustaining life and the crafted idol come from the same source—the felled tree. Yet the woodcutter separates the idol from both its original source and himself as its maker. Elevating the meaning of the idol and lowering the meaning of himself, he deifies his craft. It is a fundamental paradox of human existence that I create the myth that creates me. Inherent in this paradox is an entitlement and an entrapment.

The Entitlement

The entitlement is a gift of birth. It is engaged by maintaining control over my myth. This control is the ability to change my destiny by changing my myth. Essential to this control is remembering that my myth is a creation of the human mind. Remembering this keeps the roles that my myth and I play clearly defined. I am the master and my myth is the servant. Within this entitlement, the paradox that the myth I create creates me remains, but I control its outcome by controlling my myth. I am the master because I choose that myth and maintain the power to recreate my myth at any moment.

The Entrapment

The entrapment inherent in this paradox is a matter of choice. It is engaged by relinquishing my entitlement to my myth. This relinquishment is a reversal of control. My myth becomes the master and I become its servant. Essential to this reversal is canonizing my myth.

Like Isaiah's woodcutter, it is to deify my craft by elevating its meaning above the meaning of myself.

There are two ways I can convert my myth into a deity. One is deliberate and direct. I declare my myth to have been dropped into existence from a source outside the human mind. I view it as a mythic immaculate conception with the human mind as only a conveyance. I sanctify its truth as absolute and irrefutable. I canonize it.

The other way is subtle and indirect. Since my myth provides my living with the sustenance of meaning and illuminates the mysteries of my living it is natural that I should hold it in high regard. However, when honoring my myth, it is easy to forget that it is a craft of the human mind. Such forgetfulness allows my myth to take on a life larger than my own. Such enlargement increases its meaning while decreasing the meaning of myself. Eventually, this subtle process may empower my myth to achieve the stature of deity in my mind. And its perceived truth becomes sanctified as absolute and irrefutable.

The act of deifying my myth is encouraged by rewards. But while these rewards are appealing, they are also trade-offs for some of the privileges most critical to my humanness.

> ➢ Deifying my myth provides me with the comfort of living through unquestioned allegiance. However, it divests me of the privilege of that continued myth craft that controls the answers that comprise my myth.
> ➢ Deifying my myth provides me with the security of unquestioned truth. However, it divests me of the privilege of experiencing one of life's most profound excitements, that of venturing into the insecurities of the mystery of existence.

Deifying my myth, whether directly or indirectly, traps me within the boundaries of its answers. And when my myth becomes my life trap, the trap becomes my life trip. Within this entrapment the paradox remains, but I give control of its outcome to my myth.

So not only does myth shape every facet of my living and destiny, through my personal choice, it can become my controlling master.

A Conversation

Me: It's wonderful. I see colors and flowers and people and stars. I see it all.

Myth: You may see the natural world through your physical eye, but what you see in your mind is through my eye. Don't confuse the two.

Me: There you go again, taking all the credit for what's going on in my life.

Myth: And it's well deserved. I shape your whole outlook. You couldn't get by without my help. So worship me!

Me: You're kidding! Worship is for the most important influence in a person's existence.

Myth: But I am the most important influence in your existence.

Me: I'm influenced by a lot of things in my life.

Myth: True. But I determine how open and closed you are to these influences. Indeed, I determine what will be an influence for you. Your influences await my pleasure.

Me: Don't talk so high and mighty. Nothing is as important to me as my relationships, and you don't fit the category.

Myth: Don't fit the category? I am the category. I am your ultimate relationship. You live me twenty-four hours a day. I determine what all your other relationships will be. Wake up!

Me: Maybe. But one thing you don't do is determine me. I am who I am.

Myth: Oh, but I do! You may be who you are as a human, but I decide the focus of your life and the identity that focus becomes.

Me: You forget one thing. I created you out of my imagination. You are not my god.

Myth: But I will be if you let me! And let me tell you about the rewards of letting me!

Conclusion

My myth is the potter of me. I willingly yield the substance of my living to its shaping. I become its vision of reality. I become its image projected in the world. The only issue is whether I am in control of my myth or my myth is in control of me.

All this of Pot and Potter—Tell me then,
Who is the Potter, pray, and who is the Pot?
                                              —Omar Khayyam

4

Virtual Reality

(Faith and Myth)

Faith is the force of life.

—Leo Tolstoy

Faith and Living

Russian novelist Leo Tolstoy (*My Confessions*) was right in asserting that "faith is the force of life." Without this underpinning force, human existence would collapse. From the mundane to the sublime, faith sustains every facet of my living.

Predictability

My living is sustained by faith in the predictability of nature. I have faith that the sun and moon will rise and set, providing a consistent pattern of light and dark. I have faith that the elements will nourish and cleanse the environment. I have faith that the seasons will continue unfolding in rhythmic sequence. I have faith that the universe will maintain itself in my corner of creation. The predictability of nature is so constant that I often forget I order my life around it through faith in its self-appointed rituals.

Responsibility

My living is sustained by faith in the responsible behavior of society. I have faith that doctors, mechanics, chefs, lawyers, clerks, garbage collectors, and other assorted professionals and workers will perform their socially appointed duties. I have faith that the mail will be delivered, the electricity and water will flow as promised, and technology will behave as expected. I have faith that the vast array of institutions that serve my needs and govern my culture will function as designed.

The responsibilities fulfilled by the entities of the social order are so constant that I often forget I order my life around them through faith.

Reliability

My living is sustained by faith in the reliability of my relationships. I have faith that my loves and friendships will remain true. I have faith that my family will nurture my existence. I have faith that my workplace will remain secure. I have faith that the network of casual associations that ground my living will provide constant stability.

These relationship reliabilities are often sorely tested. Nevertheless, they are trustworthy enough to order my life around them through faith.

Conclusion

From my rising at the morning, through my walk in the day, and until my retiring at night, all the activities of my life, howsoever mundane or sublime, are sustained by the force of my faith in the predictability of nature, the responsibility of society, and the reliability of relationships.

Faith and Reason

Because faith is the habit of my everyday existence, I tend to forget that my life is wrapped in profound mystery. And I plod through life in the illusion that what I am doing is perfectly reasonable. While this is true in some measure, there is a catch. The catch is that this reasonableness is a self-contained box, free-floating within this wrap of mystery.

Limits

Reason is the architect of my living. Its primary purpose is to explain the mystery that embraces my existence. It does this by answering the compelling questions that reside in this mystery. These answers become the myth my reason uses as a blueprint for constructing the meanings of my relationships. And this myth becomes the box whose boundaries protect me from the chaos of meaninglessness that mystery seeks to impose on my living.

But this box simply hangs suspended within mystery because I cannot prove the validity of any of my answers to the compelling questions. For when my reason pushes my answers to the limit of its capacity to verify, they dissolve back into the mystery they are seeking to resolve.

Authority

But my reason remains undaunted because it has great difficulty in abiding its own limitations. It has one more trick up its sleeve to create the illusion of verification. This trick is an appeal to some authority of its choosing. And this choice may be of itself or outside itself. The locus of this authority is inconsequential to my reason.

Whatever the source of this authority, reason must assume that it is ultimate and verifies the validity of my answers to life's compelling questions. So, in finality, in resorting to such an assumption, it has only affirmed that it, too, must operate by faith for it cannot prove the ultimateness of the authority it chooses.

Assumption

The best my reason can do for me in justifying my answers is to appeal to a blended kind of logic. One part of this blend is my accumulated knowledge and the other part is the wisdom of my personal experience. The question of this logic is whether or not my answers jibe with this knowledge and wisdom and feel right. It is out of this jibing-feel-right assumption that my reason builds a supportive logic to validate my answers.

Validity

But however unflawed the logic of this process may seem, it still cannot prove the validity of my answers except to myself. And when I accept this logic I do so as an internal act of faith in my own reasoned judgment and not on external proof. Even if this judgment seems to accord with the common experience of other humans it is an accord of mutual perception and not proof.

Faith

During my late twenties I began struggling with whether or not the conservative Christianity of my upbringing was worthy of my continued devotion. This struggle involved questions addressed to my Christian mentors. When I would ask why a certain belief was true, the answers would be, "Because the Bible says so." When I would ask why the Bible was true to the exclusion of all other sources of truth, the answers would be, "Because the Bible says so." And when I would suggest that appealing to the Bible to confirm itself was illogical, the response would be, "It's a matter of faith." Whatever I questioned, the final response was to circle the wagons of faith around the belief in doubt.

My Christian mentors were right. Irrespective of the authority of my resort, I begin with values in which I have faith and build the logic of my myth upon this foundation. Mystery will not yield answers to the compelling questions except through the preconceptions I bring to it. And reason is the tool I use for guiding and justifying this construction. Norman Friedman says it this way:

Values are the basis of logic rather than its product.

Whatever appeal I may make to my reason and however satisfied I may be with this appeal, it remains an activity of faith that sustains itself without proof. As nineteenth-century American essayist Ralph Waldo Emerson reminds us:

No power of genius has ever yet had the smallest success in explaining existence. The perfect enigma remains.

This does not mean that faith is a denial of reason. Rather, faith is my mind reaching beyond reason's limit to pluck out meaning from mystery and then relying on reason to support what is plucked. Again, American poet Emily Dickinson captures this understanding:

Faith—is the Pierless Bridge
Supporting what We see
Unto the scene that we do not—

The physicist Werner Heisenberg affirms this insight with the notion that what we see depends on how we look.

Servant

Reason is not its own master. It is the servant of faith. In *The Wit* and *Wisdom of Dean Inge*, the Dean of London's St. Paul's Cathedral expressed this understanding in these words:

> *Faith is an act of self-consecration in which the will, the intellect, and the affections all have their place.*

Faith submits my total being in consecration to the myth it has created. No part of my being, including reason, is exempt from this devotion.

As a servant of faith, my reason empowers the mythic assumptions of faith with a supportive logic. Once this is done, reason becomes a defender of the logic it has created. When my faith plunges into a crisis because experience has presented its assumptions with a challenge, my reason comes to the rescue. If this rescue fails and faith revises its assumptions into a new mythic eye, it is my reason that gives support to this revision and becomes as obsessed with its defense as it was with that of my old mythic eye. Reason is fickle to all masters except myself or those I choose.

Conclusion

Reason is the servant of my mythic way of seeing—both in its creation and defense. And in both of these endeavors its final end is to rely on faith. So, however much I would like to believe that my walk in mystery is a walk of reason, it remains a walk of faith.

Blind Faith

My mythic eye is the assumptions of my faith. It is my peculiar way of seeing. This is its purpose. As such, it is not blind. Nor is any mythic eye blind. Since all ways of seeing are sights of faith, if one way of seeing is blind then all ways of seeing are blind. However, we can see nothing without faith providing the eyes.

The notion of blind faith, then, can only have a pejorative meaning. It is an accusation of my mythic eye against another mythic eye for not seeing as mine sees. It is a negative metaphor for condemning the logic that has created a way of seeing contrary to my own.

Every mythic eye is wide open to see precisely what it was designed to see. If there is a blindness, it is in what the eye was designed not to see. Since all mythic eyes are created by finite minds, no mythic eye can see all that is available for seeing. Therefore, while all faith sees by design, all faith is also partially blind by design. The mythic eye, then, while wide open, will always see while not seeing.

Faith and Science

Although scientists will often construct their own myths out of the implications of scientific thought, they will also deny that science proves the validity of their mythic assumptions. They do this for appropriate reasons. These reasons are found in the primary differences between the roles science and myth play in the human venture.

Field

The field in which both myth and science work is universal mystery. Each is concerned with finding answers within this mystery, but there are significant differences. The first is the focus of role:
- ➤ The focus of science is the function of nature.
- ➤ The focus of myth is the meaning of human existence.

The second is the scope of role:
- ➤ The scope of scientific exploration is boundless in its attention to the mysteries of the natural universe.
- ➤ The scope of myth exploration is deliberately limited to the meaning of human existence within the mysteries of the universe.

Describing the function of something in nature is different from giving that function meaning in human relationships. The scientific description of the function of a flower in the natural environment is different from the meanings given to that flower by myth in respect to beauty, romance, and metaphor in human relationships. The scientific description of the function of atomic power in nature is different from the meanings given by myth to this function's use in human experience. That the Japanese cities of Hiroshima and Nagasaki would be destroyed if atomic bombs were dropped on them during World War II was a judgment of science based on the bomb's function. That this result and destruction would be moral or immoral was a judgment based on different mythic meanings.

The implications of scientific findings are available in the construction of myth as are those of any human discipline. However, scientific descriptions of function do not prove the meanings given to them in this myth construction.

Method

Both science and myth approach mystery through intuitive insight and observational methods. But there are significant differences. The first is the validation of assumptions:

> ➤ Science seeks to validate its assumptions through external means such as the logic of mathematics and experimental testing.
> ➤ Myth seeks to validate its assumptions through internal means such as appeals to confirmation in personal experience and self-verified authorities.

The second is the focus of faith:

> ➤ Science posits faith in the external results of its calculations and experiments.
> ➤ Myth posits faith in the internal affirmations of the mind of the believer.

There is a difference between determining the validity of a scientific assumption by mathematical and technological testing and determining the validity of a mythic assumption by the judgments of right-feeling and self-affirming authorities. Faith is always faith irrespective of its focus. However, while faith in scientific assumption can be justified by its method of testing, faith in mythic assumption can only be justified by choosing to justify it.

Absoluteness and Science

While both science and myth often lay claim to absolute truth, neither can find support for this claim in the larger dimension of history. Once new insight has captured the scientific community, it is as prone as any other human discipline to convert it into a final reality. The history of science is one of resistance to new assumptions until satisfactorily validated by its methods. It is also a history of gradual evolutional change in reality views.

The reality view of Ptolemaic science changed to the reality view of Classical science that changed to the reality view of Modern science. This evolution reflects shifts in understanding from an earth-centered planetary system to a sun-centered system, and from the perception of a stationary universe to a fluid universe. It also represents a shift from existence perceived as a series of isolated events to existence perceived as an interdependent web of mutual effect.

In essence, scientific perceptions about the nature of reality continue to evolve from one historical stage of understanding to another.

However, that scientific perceptions are evolutionary rather than absolute does not invalidate faith in their implications. Lack of absoluteness does not necessarily mean falseness. It only means that the truth of the universe gradually unfolds to human understanding and forever remains incomplete. It only means that, even for science, our finite human capacity for knowing is ultimately swallowed in the infinite mystery in which we reside.

Absoluteness and Myth

Myth has an even greater difficulty changing than science because of its focus on human meaning and its methods of internal verification. Despite a natural reluctance to do so, given clarity of explanation, technological application, and the normal evolution of thinking brought about by time, cultures will generally alter their mythologies to accommodate the implications of scientific advance. However, mythologies that lay claim to absolute truth tend to be implacable in their resistance to change because the validity of their existence is challenged when this claim is threatened.

Normally mythic claims to absoluteness rest on sacred texts of authority. If a part of the supposed truth of this authority is shown to be false, then all of it is open to doubt. Thus, to retain unquestioned integrity the myth must successfully ward off any challenge to the absoluteness of this authority. The most serious threat to mythic absoluteness normally comes from science, with its evolving perceptions of reality.

The challenge is not simply the perception, but its seeming validation through the scientific methods of testing and application. It is not surprising, then, that those myths most likely to be in contention with scientific views of reality are those that claim absolute truth. Advocates of absolute truth will inevitably be in hostile conflict with advocates of evolutionary truth.

This conflict is exemplified in the contentions the conservative wing of institutionalized Christianity has had with scientific perceptions of reality. This wing has adamantly maintained that its sacred text, the Bible, is the absolute truth dictated by an omniscient god who, therefore, cannot be wrong.

However, the mythic theology of this text is geared to problematic scientific views. One is the ancient view of a flat, stacked, three-storied universe of heaven, earth, and hell. Beginning in the sixteenth century with Copernicus and Galileo and evolving into the twenty-first century, science has proposed a view of the universe that threatens biblical authority. Conservative Christianity has responded, depending on its social power, with violence, suppression, condemnation, and its capacity to use language to manipulate meaning.

Another threat to the absoluteness of conservative Christian theology has been the scientific proposal of the development of the universe and its inhabitants through a process of evolution. This stands in contrast to the conservative Christian belief in a literal seven-day creation. In the early twentieth century, the famous Tennessee Scopes trial was a social manifestation of conservative Christianity's attempt to suppress the Darwinian theory of evolution. In the latter part of the twentieth century and into the twenty-first century it has sought to either have this theory evicted from the public school curriculum or to have its own sacred text elevated in legitimate scientific contention. Myths that lay claim to absolute truth, by necessity of survival, will either control the assumptions of science or be in battle against them.

Social Relevance

In contrast, myths that are committed to social relevance in their moment in history understand that their answers to the compelling questions of human existence are not absolute. They stand ready to alter these answers to accommodate new perceptions about the nature of reality.

Such myths tend to evolve with advancements in human knowledge. They know their grasp of truth is incomplete, but they are not threatened by this understanding. Rather, they revel in knowing that the mystery of their living is inexhaustible and is always ready to yield new insight into the meaning of human existence. Like science, this lack of absoluteness does not mean falseness nor does it invalidate faith in their answers. It only acknowledges that humans, as finite beings, are incapable of fully grasping the truth of the infinite universe in which they reside.

Meaning

While science and myth use different methods to test their assumptions, both rely on faith that the conclusions reached are valid. When claiming absolute truth, history shows their faith to be misplaced. But neither can pursue their purpose without resorting to faith in assumptions, methods, and conclusions because mystery is their workplace.

Conclusion

Application of scientific discovery impacts the material and social nature of human existence. However, such discoveries do not impact the human mind until translated into mythic perspectives. While science may accurately state the function of something, it is only possible to give human meaning to that function through myth. We may live materially and socially off of the fruits of science, but we can only live spiritually off of the meanings of myth.

Science, despite its difference of purpose, scope, and method, does not exist independent of myth. All scientists bring a mythic view of reality to their work that gives direction to their focus and limits to their vision. Science exists for the sake of the human enterprise and the human enterprise is, above all else, a mythic drama. And science serves no ultimate spiritual purpose unless its findings are integrated into the mythic structures of this drama.

Kinds of Faith

The most frightening thing about human existence is that it is a venture of faith. When I seek to prove the validity of my answers to life's compelling questions I am pushed over the edge of reason to free-fall in mystery. That which sustains me in this free-fall is a conviction of the rightness of my answers. This conviction is the force of faith. As nineteenth century Swiss philosopher Henri Amiel points out in his *Journal*:

Faith is a certitude without proofs...

There are two basic kinds of certitude I can employ to sustain myself within this free-fall in mystery.

Boundaried Faith

Our daily living is fraught with the necessity of countless decisions. Some of these are conditioned mythic responses that require little thought but others require degrees of mythic mental wrestling. Such wrestling can be stressful work. Moreover, once a decision has been made, a cloud of anxiety-producing doubt may hang over its sense of rightness. Decision-making and uncertainty in human experience tend toward companionship. It would be a comfort to forego such daily wrestling and make the right decision without stress or doubt.

Boundaried Faith offers this kind of certitude. In this faith, I assume I have found the once-and-for-all-time answers to life's compelling questions. Philosopher-theologian Walter Kaufmann has coined a phrase that describes why I might choose to participate in Boundaried Faith. He calls it a Decidophobic Decision. *Decido* is deciding. *Phobic* is fear, dread, and apprehension. *Decidophobic* is a fear of decision-making.

In choosing Boundaried Faith, my fear of decision-making is relieved. One grand leap of faith is made into a set of answers that, thereafter, prescribes the ground of deciding. All I need do is apply these answers to the decision to be made and the right choice will be known. Since my answers are absolute, so will be my decisions. Concern over alternative choices is banished. What can be known of mystery is already known and bound up in my once-and-for-all-time answers. All myths that disagree with these answers are false, along with their decisions of choice.

The rewards of participating in Boundaried Faith come from the assurance that the boundaries of my answers are eternally fixed. This fixedness prohibits the intrusion of any further revelation that might question the validity of these answers to the compelling questions or disturb the tranquility of decision-making. This closed system of belief provides the security of absolute truth and the comfort of absolute certitude. In language politically correct for his time, Polish novelist Joseph Conrad summarizes the appeal of Boundaried Faith:

To have his path made clear for him is the aspiration of every human being in our beclouded and tempestuous existence.

Unboundaried Faith

The other kind of certitude to which I can resort is Unboundaried Faith. In this faith, I live my answers to the compelling questions as if they were once-and-for-all-time while accepting them as only temporary. This paradoxical posture toward my answers keeps the option of change open to me. This openness is important because the more I know of mystery, the more I know how little I know. I choose Unboundaried Faith because I willingly embrace the challenge of decision-making with this lack of knowing.

While the boundaries of my answers are real, they are also flexible. I can expand or alter them with every new revelation of truth. Thus, even though my answers prescribe boundaries, my faith is unboundaried because it operates without limit to the new. Certitude is my capacity to rightly choose rather than in having rightly chosen.

The rewards of participating in Unboundaried Faith come from the flexibility of my answers. This flexibility provides openness, excitement, and adventure. I am open to trust my perceptions, test my judgments, make my own decisions, and give direction to my living without prescription. I am excited by knowing that a fresh revelation can fall upon me at any moment and transform my living with new or expanded answers.

I am thrust into the adventure of watching my potential unfold into the reality of growth and the anticipation that tomorrow may be totally different than today. Twentieth century American political commentator H. L. Mencken captures the paradoxical nature of Unboundaried Faith in this insight:

The most satisfying and ecstatic faith is almost purely agnostic. It trusts absolutely without professing to know at all.

There are no alternatives existing between Boundaried Faith and Unboundaried Faith. They are the only options. I am living one or the other. The issue of my existence is never whether I am living by faith or not living by faith. It is always about which kind of faith I am living.

Faith and Authority

The most influential answer I give to life's compelling questions is this: *How do I know what I know?* The reason is that the two most critical choices of my destiny are explicit in this answer. It chooses whether my authority will be internal or external. It chooses whether my faith will be boundaried or unboundaried. These choices are inseparable. If I choose internal authority, I simultaneously choose Unboundaried Faith. If I choose external authority, I simultaneously choose Boundaried Faith. Following is a description of the differences between choosing internal authority and external authority.

Internal Authority

To choose internal authority is to control my mind at my will. In this choosing:

> ➤ I create and alter my myth as I confront experience.
> ➤ I retain the authority of personally answering life's compelling questions. While my mind will be guided by my answers I control how my attitudes and actions will conform.
> ➤ I may grow as fully as I please and can expand the possibilities of my growth by expanding the boundaries of my answers.
> ➤ I choose to live by Unboundaried Faith.

External Authority

To choose external authority is to give control of my mind to a source outside of myself. In this choosing:

> ➤ My myth is created for me.
> ➤ I give permission to this authority to answer life's compelling questions on my behalf. I allow my mind to be contained within the boundaries of these answers and my attitudes and actions to conform to their dictation.
> ➤ I may grow as fully as I please but only within the boundaries of these prescribed answers.
> ➤ I choose to live by Boundaried Faith.

Freedom

The primary distinction between the choice of internal and external authority is that of mind control. My freedom is not at issue. Whether

I choose internal authority and control my own mind or choose external authority and permit my mind to be controlled, I have done so as an act of freedom. Not only am I free to choose my source of authority, I remain free to change my choice. Just as the nature of Boundaried Faith resides in external authority and the nature of Unboundaried Faith resides in internal authority, the nature of my freedom to choose resides in my humanness. I cannot be divested of this freedom without being divested of this humanness. And only death can so divest.

Certainty and Uncertainty

That I can discern options and make choices creates the problem of uncertainty. When I choose between authorities and myths how can I be sure I have chosen correctly? Competing authorities and myths are constantly knocking at the door of my mind claiming to represent the real truth. This competition for my allegiance underscores the uncertainty of my choosing. And I wish for some measure of assurance that I have chosen the right authority and the true myth.

Certainty

The appeal of external authority with its Boundaried Faith is that it provides this measure of assurance. The trade-off is my willingness to give control of my mind to this authority. If I want the certainty of having found the mythic truth, then this is the price. That so many people around the world give their lives to external authority attests to the power that our human longing for assurance exerts. Choosing external authority and its Boundaried Faith dispels the anxiety of creating meaning out of mystery by converting uncertainty into certainty.

Uncertainty

Those who choose their own internal authority and its Unboundaried Faith must learn to be comfortable with this uncertainty. Becoming comfortable is an activity of paradox. Concurrently, there is a certainty about the rightness of their myth and an openness to further revelation of truth that uncertainty promises. Comfortableness is found in maintaining this balance. But uncertainty is always threatening the balance with its desire for assurance. And the devotees of internal authority must be aware of this desire's subtle trap.

A colleague of mine was minister of a religious congregation that

ascribed to internal authority and Unboundaried Faith. The congregation took great pride in this posture that permitted freedom of individual belief. They were very sensitive about any authority issue that
might threaten this posture. A part of this sensitivity was maintaining
that the minister had no greater access to truth than any other member
and, thus, spoke only out of his own internal authority. The minister supported this perspective and had no need for an authority larger
than the influence of his own personhood.

But this minister also had a playful and mischievous sense of humor
out of which he concocted a scheme. Unknown to the congregation,
he invented a fictional author and created quotations from this source
supportive of the themes and major points of his sermons. While the
congregation was appreciative of these sermons, they grew increasingly
enamored of the insightful quotations from this fictitious author. They
began viewing him as an authoritative confirmation of their mythic beliefs. This love affair went on for over a year and the clamor grew from
the congregation for the minister to reveal the source of the perceptive
wisdom of the author.

Finally, the minister confessed that the author was fictional, and
that he had created the quotations all in the spirit of playfulness. But
most of the congregation did not view his confession with good humor.
They responded with a resounding verbal stoning. On the surface, this
verbal stoning may appear to have been motivated by anger over having
been deceived. But it was much deeper than that.

The minister's deception had exposed their desire to have the un-
certainties of truth that flowed from their internal authority affirmed
as certain by an external authority. Moreover, the fictional authority,
with which they had grown so fond, turned out to be only their minister whom they knew to have feet of clay just like themselves. This
exposed another ironical truth. All external authorities upon whom
they might rely for a sense of certainty about mythic beliefs were mere
mortals just like themselves.

The congregation did not see that the small joke by their minister
was only a reflection of the larger joke in which all humans participate,
namely, that there is no ultimate authority to confirm the validity of
the meanings we create from mystery but our finite selves. The congregation was angry at their minister not so much for his deception,
but because their response to the deception had caused them to vividly

illustrate the truth of this larger joke. That is, this playful joke had re-vealed the oxymoron of their posture toward truth. While vehemently avowing that each was their own ultimate authority in ascertaining truth, they, nevertheless, pined for some source that could be used to validate the truth they ascertained.

Those who choose to live by internal authority and its Unbound-aried Faith choose to deliberately acknowledge the uncertainty of exis-tence. If they wish to be comfortable in this choice, they must be will-ing to live with the larger joke of life in good humor.

Faith and Virtual Reality

A technological wonder is evolving that will create a revolution in many areas of human living. It is called virtual reality. Virtual reality is a computerized technology that permits us to experience a reality in which we do not actually exist.

The Technology

How does virtual reality work? Through the use of a special device, the sensory input of our real environment is blocked out and our eyes only see the images created by a computer with corresponding sound. These images and sounds elicit a response from our senses as if we were actually confronting them.

For example, if the created image and sound were of a forest fire being driven by the wind in our direction our senses would cause us to respond with fear and the impulse to survive, as if we were actu-ally experiencing this environment. But we are not. It is only a trick of technological magic. The experience would be similar to the old 3-D movies except our senses would respond as being more fully a partici-pant rather than as partially a spectator. It is not actual reality we are experiencing; it is virtual reality.

Reality is an experience of factual happening. Virtual is an effect without material cause. Michael Heim is an academic who is often called "the philosopher of cyberspace." He has written definitive works on virtual reality that have been translated into numerous languages. He puts the two foregoing notions together in a single definition:

Virtual reality is an event or entity that is real in effect but not in fact.

Fiction is something imaginary. It is a deliberate creation. Fact is an actual happening. It cannot be changed. The virtual reality experience is a fiction responded to as fact. Our emotions and our senses are tied together. The sensing experience of virtual reality causes us to have the same emotional response as if it was real. Thus, VR (virtual reality) could as easily be called CR (created reality).

The Mind

While the scientific capacity to create virtual reality is a major technological breakthrough, the practice of virtual reality is as old as human existence. The human mind is a virtual reality machine. Involuntarily, during sleep, it will dream events that are as real to the person dreaming as any wakeful factual event. This dream, while not a fact, causes an effect with like kind emotional response. Who has not had a nightmare and awakened with heart-throbbing fear and a sweat-drenched body?

While dreaming is involuntary, the mind primarily creates voluntary virtual reality. The ability to imagine and then respond as if what has been imagined is real is the hallmark of being human. Indeed, without this capacity for imagination, there would be no computers or technology to mimic the mind's ability to create virtual reality.

The daily existence of every human is governed by the necessity to create a virtual reality and then live in it as if it were fact. How does the mind do this? It deliberately devises a virtual reality environment by doing two things.

> ➢ First, it creates a mythic vision by answering life's compelling questions.
> ➢ Second, it seeks to block out all input that is contrary to this mythic vision.

The result is a virtual reality that is real in effect, but not in fact. The effect that is real is a meaning imposed on the fact of experience that is not inherent in the experience itself.

The Conversion

What anchors all humans in factual reality is their common experience of the natural world. What causes humans to convert this factual reality into virtual reality is mythic vision. For example, two people are observing a dandelion. The dandelion is a fact of nature. However, they are seeing through different mythic visions. One sees a beautiful flower—an expression of nature's infinite capacity to articulate itself in forms that create awe and a sigh of the human heart. The other sees a noxious weed—an expression of nature's infinite capacity to produce ugly pests that deface a manicured lawn.

While viewing the dandelion is a commonly experienced factual event, the contrasting meanings of beautiful and ugly are products of different virtual realities. The mythic eye of both people experienced the real event of the dandelion and created an effect that was inherent in their respective mythic visions, but not in the fact of the experience.

The Faith

How do I know that the virtual reality my mind creates through its mythic vision is true or untrue? I can never know the answer to this question with certainty because truth and falseness are reflections of the values of my mythic eye. Perceptions of truth and falseness are my myth justifying itself. I may feel that I have evidence from human history to warrant such justification, but such proof is also in the eye of the beholder.

Finally, I must rest my case on faith. Faith has always been the answer to this question and faith will remain the answer because the answer is the meanings I pluck from mystery.

Paradox

I cannot create meaning outside the realm of paradox that makes choice possible. And the paradox of faith is that I know without knowing. I am certain without being certain. To acknowledge this paradox is frightening to a species that craves the security and comfort of assurance. Yet paradox is the natural state of human existence that requires us to live through the creativity of virtual reality. Without this paradox our living would be deprived of the freedom to choose and devoid of any adventure in living.

My Story

My story is two things made into a whole. The first thing is a string of factual events. The second thing is the meaning I give to these factual events by my myth. My story does not exist except in this collusion of event and meaning. Thus, my story is created through virtual reality.

Conclusion

By faith I consecrate my whole being to the virtual reality created by my myth. Every moment of my existence is the activity of this larger faith played out within the smaller daily faith I express in nature's predictability, society's responsibility, and the reliability of my relationships. From the mundane to the sublime, faith reigns supreme in my existence.

> *Faith is to believe what you do not yet see; the reward for this faith is to see what you believe.*
> —St. Augustine (Joannis Evangelical Tract)

Betting My Life

(Lessons from Columbus)

*The passions are the only orators which always
persuade.*

—La Rochefoucauld

*People seem not to see that their opinion of the world
is also a confession of character.*

—Ralph Waldo Emerson

Columbus

From the Winifred Sackville Stoner, Jr., poem *The History of the
United States* come these familiar lines:

*In fourteen-hundred and ninety-two
Columbus sailed the ocean blue.*

This voyage of Columbus, which led to the discovery and exploitation of the Americas by European powers and dramatically altered
history, was a mythic venture. The primary myth that drove Columbus
was a strong messianic belief that he had been chosen for greatness by
God. This greatness, he also believed, would bring him the honor of
fame and the luxury of wealth.

A secondary myth, which opened him to the realization of his messianic vision, was that the earth was round. This concept of globalness
was just beginning to develop in the late 1400s. Some of Columbus's
recorded remarks seem to allude to his possession of a secret document
that supported a round-earth theory. But such a document has never
surfaced in history's archives—possibly because Columbus was para-

noid in his concealment of information or because its possession was a deceit to gain funding for his desired expeditions.

Some evidence implies that Columbus's conception of the earth as a globe was based more on spurious interpretations of biblical texts and erroneous ideas drawn from apocryphal books than any available scientific data. As one historian has suggested, Columbus discovered America by prophecy rather than by astronomy.

However, from whatever the source, Columbus was convinced that India could be reached by sailing due west from southern Europe. But he grossly underestimated the distance of the passage. By remarkable coincidence his calculated distance was approximately that of between southern Europe and the Caribbean Islands.

Columbus was deeply committed to the mythic vision that drove him. And he should have been, for as he set sail on his perilous voyage he was both figuratively and literally betting his life on this myth. He was also inviting those who sailed with him to place a similar life bet. In these two respects, the story of Columbus is a parable of all human stories. Seeing Columbus's venture this way reveals lessons that are applicable to the mythic venture of every human.

The Bet

The first lesson is that, like Columbus, I am a mythic gambler. My gamble is on the rightness of my own view of reality. I may change my bet by changing my myth. However, I cannot exist as human without placing this bet. And the bet I place is my life.

From birth, those in authority over my existence begin training me to wager my life on their myth. Because of my dependency, I am prone to do so without question. Nevertheless, it is my life that is being wagered. But once I learn to discern options and make choices, the responsibility for the wager gradually shifts to me. When the fullness of that moment arrives remains a moot issue in human perception, but it really makes little difference as regards mythic wagering. From birth on, whether by me or someone else, my life is being bet. I am either being wagered or wagering.

The Givens

While the responsibility of choosing my myth eventually becomes mine, there are certain givens of my birth that will significantly impact my choosing. These givens are my time in history, my gender, my geographic location, my family, my genes, my race, my economic environment, my educational opportunities, and my culture. These givens make up the peculiar cradle of my existence. There is no fairness inherent in this cradle. I arrive in it by happenchance, and it may be curse or blessing. Nevertheless, it is my cradle.

Columbus's Givens

The impact of the givens of Columbus's birth is illustrative of this lesson.

> To the best of our knowledge, he was born on the coast of northwestern Italy to merchant parents. Shipping was vital to the area's economy, and under this influence he probably went to sea when still a juvenile. Sailing became his livelihood and his life interest—a vocation critical to his mythic vision and destiny.

> He was a devout Roman Catholic and was enamored of literature with mysterious meanings—which likely accounts for the messianic qualities of his myth and his belief in the earth's roundness.

> The culture of his birth was characterized by attitudes of utilitarianism toward nature, materialism toward living, and militarism toward accomplishment—attitudes that spiced his mythic views and spurred his behaviors.

> He arrived on history's scene with his vision at a moment when the continent's resources were being depleted and interest in exploration was rising—setting the historical stage for the ripeness of his mythic venture.

> Being of male gender, he could envision mythic possibilities that no woman at the time could have dreamed of with any expectation of fulfillment.

None of these givens of Columbus's birth were more or less important than any of the others. Each played its critical role. Together they served as an integrated force that shaped his mythic destiny.

Had he been born a hundred years later along the western coast of Africa, he might have been a slave imported to the Americas rather than the supposed discoverer of the Americas. Alter any of the other givens in his birth potpourri and the difference would have been equally decisive.

The Paradox

The lesson is that, like Columbus, my mythic choices will be impacted by the givens of my birth. This means that I am not totally free in my choosing. However, this truth is forever bound to another. I am born into the limited freedom of my givens with an unlimited inner freedom. This inner freedom is the innate gift of my humanness. Nothing can divest me of its privilege. And its privilege is to freely choose within the options of my cradle of birth.

This tension between innate inner freedom and imposed outer boundaries is the essential paradox of my existence. This paradox defines both the struggle and the meaning of being human. I am free while not being free. My inner freedom remains inviolate while the conditions of my choosing remain boundaried. Within this paradox, I make a mythic wager that will determine my destiny.

The Character

The third lesson is that, like Columbus, my character is shaped by the myth that drives my existence. Character and myth are inseparable. Study the character and the myth will be revealed. Study the myth and the character can be predicted.

Columbus

What we know of Columbus's character is gleaned from sketchy information and recorded action. Together, these sources seem to paint an ambivalent portrait.

On the one hand he was a portrait of disreputable self-centeredness. He was secretive and refused to divulge information about his visions and voyages for fear that others might usurp his glory. He was devious and deceptive in manipulating others to support his desires. He was indifferent to the plight of those who stood in his way or whose mythic views countered his own—often leading him to enact or condone cruel and murderous behavior. And if it served his purpose, he was willing to move beyond fact and create fiction. In brief, he was utilitarian, manipulative, and often unprincipled.

On the other hand, he was a portrait of engaging charm. He was a visionary who perceived possibility beyond the limitations of his time. He was courageous in his willingness to venture into the dangerous unknown. He was clever in his capacity to motivate others. He was passionately convincing about his vision. He was a weaver of fanciful stories. He was doggedly determined when he set his eye on a goal. In brief, he was adventurous, forceful, and undaunted by rebuff.

This mixed portrait often created mixed response. When draped with his mythic vision, some viewed Columbus as comical and pathetic while others saw him as visionary and persuasive. This portrait also reflected his eventual ambivalent standing in history as both bold explorer and brutal exploiter.

Ambivalence and Dominance

Like Columbus, all humans are ambivalent in character. Even those who appear saintly in our eyes admit to such ambivalence. The apostle Paul, in the New Testament, stated this ambivalence as a foible of human nature. He confessed that what he aspired to do he did not do, and what he loathed to do he did. The issue of character ambivalence is not whether we have it, but which side of it will receive the larger measure of our life energy—its light side or dark side.

What determines this measure is whether our natural self-interest is allowed to include a concern for the well-being of others or is permitted to degenerate into the dominance of private concern. It seems clear that Columbus's character was dominated by private concern. This dominance plagued how his messianic mythic vision was processed and caused immense suffering for others.

Española was the original island of Columbus's new world conquests. He was an abysmally inept administrator, and his attempts to shun responsibility and elevate himself above his failures resulted in brutal treatment of those fellow voyagers he supervised. His inhumane policies led to the near genocide of the hospitable and peace-loving natives of the island because of their incapacity to submit to Spanish culturalization and their unwillingness to submit to enslavement.

History may have anointed Columbus with greatness because of his supposed discovery of the Americas, but Columbus anointed the Americas with a barbarous bloodbath because of his character. When the dark side of my myth gets my life energy, the dark side of my character gets my energy's life.

The Tool

The term character derives from a Greek word referring to the mark made by an engraving tool. The myth I choose engraves its image upon my living. The answers to life's compelling questions, which comprise my myth, are the tools of this engraving. The who that I am is the price I pay for the myth that I embrace.

I do not build my character by choosing desired traits and committing myself to their fulfillment. I build character by devotion to a myth that is my answer to life's compelling questions. If I wish to change character traits, I must change my commitment to those mythic answers that produce these traits.

Whatever my character, it is a reflection of devotion to my myth. As Ralph Waldo Emerson once suggested:

> *People seem not to see that their opinion of the world is a confession of character.*

If Emerson is right, then the reverse is equally true:

> *People seem not to see that their character is a confession of their opinion of the world.*

My opinion of the world and my myth are the same. I am my myth.

The Persuasion

No one knew whether Columbus's belief that India could be reached by sailing west was valid. From the time he first petitioned for royal sanction and support for his expedition, it took eight years of dogged persistence before he was successful. During this period he made a number of approaches to Queen Isabella and King Ferdinand of Spain. Following his appeal in 1486, a special commission was established to investigate the feasibility of his proposal. After four years, the commission reported unfavorably.

A part of this negative response was probably due to Columbus's elusiveness regarding evidence supportive of the direction of the voyage. But even more off-putting was the arrogant unreasonableness of his demands. Not only did he want sanction and support, he insisted on being knighted, appointed grand admiral and viceroy with complete authority, and a 10 percent take of all wealth that accrued from the expedition (both immediately and in the future).

In January of 1492, Queen Isabella and King Ferdinand successfully concluded a ten-year campaign to rid Spain of Muslim control over the kingdom of Granada. This campaign had seriously depleted the royal treasury. On the eve of this victory, Columbus again petitioned the court to sanction his voyage. Perhaps he thought visions of riches flowing into the royal treasury from his expedition would cause the court to look more kindly upon a sanction. Perhaps he thought that the substantial funding for the voyage he had already secured from alternative sources would add to his vision's appeal.

However, in light of the prior commission's unfavorable report and lack of evidence of a westward passage to India, Columbus had no valid reason to expect anything but another rejection. Yet, the queen and king gave their sanction. And historians can find no commonly agreed upon explanation for this turnabout.

A factor often overlooked that possibly tipped the scale in favor of royal sanction for the voyage was Columbus's own character. He possessed an uncanny capacity for persuasion that surmounted the most difficult of obstacles. This persuasive capacity was conviction blended of passion and persistence. His conviction was a passionate belief in the rightness of his mythic vision. His persistence was an expression of the depth of this passion. There was no inherent logic in this capacity to persuade; it was unmitigated charm.

Conviction

The lesson is that, like Columbus, I must be convicted of the rightness of my mythic vision if I expect others to invest in its possibilities. And this conviction must be undergirded by passion and persistence.

Persistence

Persistence is a devotion that holds despite adversity. Consider Columbus's three-vessel sailing expedition toward the new world as a metaphor that underscores the role of persistence in achieving mythic vision. Sailing *under* a mythic flag is different from sailing *with* a mythic flag. To sail *under* the flag is to be persuaded that what the flag stands for is right. To sail *with* a mythic flag is to board the ship out of lesser motivations than the rightness of the voyage.

The motivations of those sailing in Columbus's small fleet were varied. Most were sailors who valued the employment opportunity. Some were released criminals. Others represented the interests and official functions of the Spanish court. Those who commanded, aside from Columbus, envisioned rich material reward. None shared Columbus's mythic vision. The irony of merely sailing *with* a mythic flag is that one's life is still attached to why the flag waves from the ship's mast. Thus, when adversity rises that threatens life, lesser motivations may lead to discontent or mutiny that imperils the mythic purpose of the voyage.

This was the situation Columbus faced numerous times on this first voyage. And each new moment of discontent led to the more serious threats of mutiny. To quell these threats and restore commitment to the expedition's mission, Columbus resorted to deceit, reward, and his own threats. He repeatedly falsified the distance yet to be traveled. He offered a hefty reward to the sailor to first sight land. He pronounced severe punishment for disobedience and mutiny. These were the tactics of persistence. They reflect Columbus's determination to overcome even the most threatening obstacle in achieving his mythic vision. And this persistence was a reflection of the depth of his passion.

Passion

Passion is a fervored focus of the total being. It is this passion that lays to rest any doubt others may have that conviction is contrived. It is this passion that captures the attention of others in considering mythic commitment. Francois de La Rochefoucauld, seventeenth-century French writer and moralist, puts it succinctly:

The passions are the only orators which always persuade.

As long as my conviction burns with passion, it is capable of persuasion. When this passion diminishes, so does the power of conviction to dispel doubt and capture attentions. Shakespeare, in *Hamlet*, says it this way:

What to ourselves in passion we propose,
The passion ending, doth the purpose lose.

Passion not only invites others to enter my myth, it encourages them to be equally passionate in fulfilling its mission. To sail *under* a mythic flag is to do so with the passion of its rightness. It is to board the ship motivated by allegiance to the flag's symbolic meaning. Thus, it is passion that inspires the courage necessary to remain true to the mythic vision when circumstances seem to declare it as folly.

Reasoned logic will not sustain courage for it counsels the taming of passion by cool practicality. When confronted with adverse or threatening circumstance, reasoned logic will most likely recommend self-preservation over mythic sacrifice. Columbus, braced with the passion of mythic conviction, determined to persist in the face of survival threats. Most everyone else, motivated by the reasoned logic of survival, wished to cancel the voyage.

The choice to persist despite demoralizing obstacles or even to die on behalf of mythic conviction is beyond reasoned logic. Indeed, conviction does not need such support. It only needs the passion that sustains it. As Alexander Pope, in *Moral Essays*, understood:

The ruling Passion, be it what it will,
The ruling Passion, conquers reason still.

Persistence and passion are the hallmarks of uncontrived conviction. And conviction is the sine qua non of mythic persuasion—that without which it will not occur.

The Worth

The mythic vision that drove Columbus was grounded in a conviction that he had been especially chosen by God for greatness. While this sense of having been chosen did not create humility or a devotion to human service, it did ennoble his perception of self-worth. The lesson is that, like Columbus, the issue of self-worth is critical to my choice of myth.

The Answers

The issue of self-worth is addressed by my answers to two of life's compelling questions. My answer to the question of "*Who am I?*" defines my birthright of worth or lack of worth. My answer to the question of "*What is my purpose?*" instructs me how to invent and/or sustain my self-worth. In regard to my worth, these two answers are inseparable.

Columbus's obvious answers to these questions are examples. His answer to "*Who am I?*" was that he was one chosen by God for greatness. This answer was a statement of perceived self-worth. His answer to "*What is my purpose?*" was to achieve greatness by voyaging from Europe to India via a westward passage. This answer sustained the sense of worth inherent in his identity of having been chosen by God for greatness.

The Need

Fundamental to human existence is the need to feel worthy of being alive. This need is critical to our choice of myth. The logic of this choice is the logic of this need. And reason will be used to confirm this logic of choice, howsoever unreasonable it may seem.

Columbus's choice of myth was totally illogical to his station in life, yet he chose it. The choice of myth does not rest on the mind's capacity to discern the most logical option but on its capacity to discern the option most enhancing to self-worth. The most illogical of myths will be chosen for this reason.

But whether others see my choice of myth as logical or illogical is irrelevant. What is relevant is whether the myth I choose disenfranchises my sense of worth or empowers it. And the quality of all of my social relating will be determined by this disenfranchisement or empowerment.

In no sector of life is the issue of self-worth in myth more apparent than in religion. Indeed, how well this is provided is the primary appeal of any religious perspective. In 1955, James Warren Jones founded a movement which he labeled as Apostolic Socialism. Eventually, his group was called the People's Temple. The focus of the community he built attracted people who were concerned about the abuses of capitalism and the injustices of racial prejudice. Increasingly, the rhetoric of Jones took on a paranoid tone and the tendency was to see communist countries as the model for living. In fulfillment of both this tone and model, Jones took around one thousand children, women, and men to a jungle setting in Guyana, South America, called Jonestown. The purpose was to establish a supposed paradise where racial prejudice did not exist, where fascist capitalism could be avoided, where communist principles could be embodied, and where the group would be free from the critical eye of the American press. Jonestown was to be a place that elevated the self-worth of all of its inhabitants.

However, due to concerned parents who felt that their children participating in Jones's community had been brainwashed and that the community, itself, was being run dictatorially and possibly with a fear orientation and physical brutality, a California politician, accompanied by the press, arrived in Jonestown to investigate. Precipitous acts of murder by the settlement's armed guards inflicted on these visitors and some of those forsaking the community pushed Jones over the edge, and he ordered that the total of the People's Temple should commit what he called "revolutionary suicide." Revolutionary suicide was supposedly an act that denounced the cruelties of the world in favor of the paradise of heaven. It was an act that supposedly underscored the worthiness of those participating. Over nine hundred responded to this order and died as a result of drinking a concoction laced with deadly poison. Parents first murdered their children and then themselves. The date was November 18, 1978.

Keeping in mind that all behavior is done in the service of self-worth, this incident reveals what desperate and outrageous measures people will take in order to affirm their worth in light of a perceived sense of social deficit. Again, such a violent means of affirmation has nothing to do with reason. It is a way of confirming the logic of the mythology being enacted.

The Jonestown incident is only a reflection of the extraordinarily stunning kinds of beliefs and corresponding actions people have engaged in throughout history in order to affirm their sense of personal worth. In brief, people will choose myths that are ruthlessly demeaning, unconcerned with self-preservation, or grossly irrational as long as they sufficiently elevate a sense of self-worth. Self-worth is the primal consideration in the choice of myth.

It must also be stated that there are many myths that appeal to that which is most noble in human living and to the best self the individual can bring forth in commitment. These, too, are approved by those participating as reasonable by virtue of their own self-affirming logic. Again, the bottom line is that our innate human tendency is to choose a myth that we believe best enhances our sense of worth. If we are unhappy with the level of this enhancement, we will normally rebel against the myth involved or seek an alternative that has a higher appeal. If we perceive no convincing alternative available, we will continue to seek ways within this lesser fulfilling myth to affirm our worthiness. Whatever our mythic circumstance, our behavior will be driven by the desire to be viewed as worthy. It is a desire that is initiated by human birth and does not cease except with the advent of death. And whatever its logic, it is the logic of fulfillment.

The Stakes

As a parable of all human stories, the drama of Columbus reminds me that:

> ➢ I am a mythic gambler.
> ➢ My mythic choices will be impacted by the givens of my birth.
> ➢ My character is shaped by the myth that drives my existence.
> ➢ I must be passionately convicted of the rightness of my myth if I expect others to invest in its possibilities.
> ➢ I will choose a myth that enhances my sense of self-worth.

It is obvious that my destiny rides on the myth I choose to give meaning to my life. With so much at stake, it behooves me to be certain that this myth is worthy of my life bet.

I shall the effect of this good lesson keep,
As watchman to my heart.
                                        —Shakespeare (*Hamlet*)

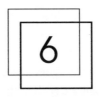

6

The Past Is Yet to Be Determined

(Changing Our Stories)

The past is the present, isn't it? It's the future, too. We all try to lie out of that but life won't let us.
—Eugene O'Neill

Life must be lived forward, but can only be understood backwards.
—Kierkegaard

The farther backward you can look, the farther forward you are likely to see.
—Winston Churchill

The Problem

There is a common wisdom that dissatisfaction is the mother of human change. In my late twenties, spurred by dissatisfaction, I engaged a series of experiences that transformed my life. Spread over a ten-year period, these experiences began with the unsettling exposures of a seminary education and culminated with the shattering insights from a tour of duty during the Vietnam War. This transformation was a radical change of my view of reality. It was the creation of a new mythic eye with a perspective one hundred and eighty degrees from my old one.

This dramatic shift in reality presented me with a problem. What was I to do with a past that now seemed obsolete to the present?

This problem was given perspective by Lionel Johnson's (*Post Liminium*) observation:

We live in time, and the past must always be the most momentous part of it.

Essentially, the past was my whole life, and it now seemed to be a lie. It had been lived in a view of reality that I now rejected as false. It felt like wasted life. Yet, the wisdom of history's sages spoke a different view of such issues. For example, note this comment from Britain's prime minister Winston Churchill:

If we open a quarrel between the past and the present, we shall find we have lost the future.

I would eventually understand Churchill's meaning, but at this particular moment in my life I had decided to open a quarrel with the past because logic seemed to dictate such as the most appropriate response.

The Response

Thus, like so many people presented with this problem, my initial response was reactionary. I rejected my past. This was symbolized in how I treated my library that consisted of several thousand volumes. Since this library was a catalogue of support for a rejected view of reality, I got rid of it. I later regretted this action because in ridding myself of what I considered obsolete I also rid myself of valuable references and resources.

Hindsight showed me this action to be a metaphor of what happens when a shift in reality is made and the past is rejected.

When I throw away my past, I also throw away its references and resources for living the present and future. Simone Weil, in *The Need for Roots*, expressed this understanding:

The destruction of the past is perhaps the greatest of all crimes.

The crime of which Weil speaks is against myself. It is the rejection of my own life. It is the abandonment of personal being.

What, then, do I do with a past that seems obsolete to the present? The answer is that I can recreate it for the present in the same way I created it originally. This is the same as changing the stories that I have already created because my past is my stories.

Following are some insights into how I can be a re-creator of my life stories as well as their creator.

The Past Is the Present

To recreate a story I must recognize that the past is, paradoxically, the present. As Henri Bergon, in *Creative Evolution*, observes:

The present contains nothing more than the past, and what is found in the effect was already in the cause.

The present is only one moment in time that succeeds the total moments of the past. To grasp the significance of this perception, consider the present as one second of time with the past as all accumulated seconds:

1 second = the present
60 seconds = one minute of the past
3,600 seconds = one hour of the past
86,400 seconds = one day of the past
31,536,000 seconds = one year of the past
31,536,000 seconds, times the number of years I have lived, plus the added seconds spent doing the math equals my past.

Imagine a clock ticking away each second. The present is the tick of time I experience now. At the next tick this present becomes the past. The number of moments in my past is so astronomical in comparison to my present moment as to be incomprehensible. While the present is a moment the past is momentous. Twentieth-century English writer G. K. Chesterton recognizes this significant difference:

We live in the past, because there is nothing else to live in. To live in the present is like proposing to sit on a pin.

The metaphor is arresting when visualized. One pinpoint representing the present slightly out front of billions of pinpoints representing the past. It would be impossible to separate that lead pinpoint as a resting place from past pinpoints.

Time

Time is a human invention patterned after planetary rhythms. Its purpose is to artificially divide our existence into manageable proportions. Time marches on, we say, and view its passage as irretrievable. While it is true that time passes it is not true that it is irretrievable. Janet Frame, in *An Angel at my Table*, addresses this distinction:

Time past is not time gone, it is time accumulated.

Time not only accumulates, it condenses. The accumulation is of all the stories of my living. The condensation is the meaning of these stories gathered into my being. As Thomas Carlyle affirms in *Essays: Characteristics*:

The present is the living sum total of the whole past.

My past is my embodiment of time's march. As I march in time, time marches in me.

I not only embody the stories of my past, I embody the impact of these stories on my living. The past has shaped my character. It has nurtured my skills. It has taught me the lessons that guide my decisions. My identity is the incarnation of the meaning of my stories. Mary Antin puts it this way in *The Promised Land*:

It is not that I belong to the past, but that the past belongs to me.

The past belongs to me because we are synonymous. Indeed, the only way the past can live is if I embody it in my story.

Consider the tree as an analogy. A seed falls into the ground and bursts upward into a sapling. It adds new concentric rings of wood each year as it grows. As time passes it is no longer the sapling of its youth, yet it is the same tree. The sustenance that nourishes its growth rises from its taproot flowing through its old trunk and into its new branches and leaves. The old and the new are symbiotic. They depend on each other for life. Both are its identity. If either fails, the tree fails.

As with the tree so it is with me. As my story grows, I change, yet I am the same person. The juices of life that sustain me flow through my old stories to nourish my new ones. These old and new stories merge into my identity. While I may live in the present, I live through the past. Irish novelist James Joyce says it this way:

> *The now, the here, through which all future plunges to the past.*

Because my stories live within me, I can go backward in time and retrieve any I wish. Because they are alive, I can recreate what I retrieve.

The Past and Obsolete

When I rejected my old myth for a new one, my initial reaction was that the life I had lived under the old myth's guidance was obsolete. Reflection caused me to see this as an error in perception. Obsolete means to fall into disuse. An automobile I drive may become obsolete because a newer model offers me greater mobility. So I trade in the old model for the more rewarding car. But in rejecting the obsolete car, I do not reject that part of my life story driving it. All the adventures of driving, all the places it took me, and all the stories it created shaped my living. While the old car is obsolete to my mobility, it is not obsolete to my life story.

In the same manner, the old myth that had driven my life had become obsolete. I traded it in for a more rewarding one. Obsolete meant the old myth no longer gave direction to my living. That it was obsolete in giving direction did not mean it was obsolete as part of my life story, or that the story created while it was giving direction to my life was obsolete. The adventures it provided, the places it took me, and the stories it created remain an alive part of my present. This old myth had happened to me and I had happened through it.

While the reality of my past myth is not the reality of my present myth, it, nevertheless, was a reality that shaped my destiny. Obsolete, then, does not mean that the life lived under the aegis of the discarded myth was wasted. It only means that its shape and direction were different from that dictated by my present myth. My myth may become obsolete, but the past it created remains a relevant part of my current life story.

The Problem

The problem I face in changing myths is that the stories my new myth creates will be out of sync with the stories my old myth created. Indeed, these new and old parts of my story may be so contradictory that the resultant tension and chaos threaten to pull my life apart. The issue is how I bring harmony and order back into my life after changing one mythic eye for another.

Changing My Stories

In *The Speed of Darkness*, Muriel Rukeyser observed:

The universe is made of stories, not of atoms.

That atoms make up the universe is a story that reinforces Rukeyser's point that human living is story living. History is human events interpreted in story form. Individuals, families, nations, and civilizations are collections of stories within stories. And each story revolves around covenants made and broken. As Jewish theologian Martin Buber points out:

We are the promise making, promise breaking animals.

Covenant

Covenant means to meet or agree. It is separate minds meeting and agreeing about purpose and behavior. It involves promises and commitments.

Covenant is the heart of human relating. Without personal covenants, families would dissolve and love and friendships would founder. Without social covenants there would be no governmental order or justice. Covenant is our human acknowledgment that cooperation is the ground of all social unity. Without covenant, the human story would plunge into the chaos of social destruction. Without covenant, the human story would die.

Freedom

Covenant is a cooperative venture. And every choice I make to relate cooperatively imposes boundaries on my behavior. In my choice to be cooperative, these boundaries are self-imposed. Such choices are affirmations of my personal freedom. The marriage covenant is an example. While entering it may abridge certain behaviors, it is entered willingly because the payoff is higher than the loss. And just as covenants are freely bonded, they may be freely dissolved. So whether I choose to enter a covenant or to dissolve a covenant, both actions are expressions of my freedom. This means that freedom is not a commodity to be protected and preserved. It is the privilege to choose the manner and nature of my relationships. It is the right to make and break those covenants that determine my destiny. It is the power to create my own story. Freedom is my human birthright.

Reward

The freedom I express in choosing covenants is grounded in my perception that there will be rewards that are so profound to my living that whatever the seeming losses might be, in terms of abridged behavior, they are minimized in comparison. In brief, the reason humans enter into covenants is because our collective experience clearly shows that the rewards are too generous to ignore. Covenant is the ultimate and infinite well of human blessing.

Myth

Behind every story I create is the shaping hand of my covenant with life, itself. Every morning I wake to this covenant, and every day I live to its heartbeat. This covenant is my myth. It is the answers to the compelling questions of my existence. Again, consider these questions and the promises they invoke.

(1) *Who am I?* When I answer this question, I promise life that I will see myself and other humans a certain way.

(2) *How do I know what I know?* When I answer this question, I promise life that I will appeal to a certain authority in making my decisions.

(3) *Who or what is in charge?* When I answer this question, I promise life that I will give my highest priority to a certain value.

(4) *What is my purpose?* When I answer this question, I promise life that I will invest my energy in a certain way of living.

(5) *What does my death mean?* When I answer this question, I promise life that I will look at time a certain way.

All of these promises integrate into my covenant with life. This larger covenant determines the nature of all the stories I create and all the smaller covenants of my living.

I may grow within the boundaries of this covenant I make with life. But when I change any of the answers, I change the covenant itself. When I do so, I must bring all the other answers of my myth into harmony with this change and, consequently, all the smaller covenants as well. This means I must break those covenants that are in conflict with this change. This means I must make new covenants that are in agreement as well. Until I do this harmonizing work, my living will be a reflection of conflict and turmoil.

Possibility

When I make a new covenant with life, which is the same as adopting a new mythic eye, an extraordinary possibility opens to me. All the stories of my past offer themselves to be recreated. The meanings of these stories were shaped to fit the promises of my old covenant with life. When I broke that covenant in favor of my new one, I also shattered the old meanings of these stories. As a result, each of these stories opens to a new meaning consistent with my new covenant with life. Whenever I make a new life covenant, a special transition occurs. During this moment my past offers itself for reshaping. When I recreate my past, I also create a new future.

How is this possible? Isn't the past unchangeable? It is possible because the events of my past and the meanings I give to these events are not the same. And while I cannot change the events, I can change the meanings I give to the events. Since my stories are these meanings, rather than the events, the stories can be recreated by giving them new meanings. Out of this insight come three life axioms:

> ➤ *There are no obsolete events in my life.* There are only obsolete meanings made from obsolete myths. My past only appears to

be obsolete when I make the event and the meanings I give to the event inseparable.

> *My past is yet to be determined.* When I separate event and meaning, I keep my past alive. I keep it open to be recreated by a new myth and a new covenant with life.

> *I am my life stories.* The meaning I give to these stories is my identity. I can create a new identity by creating new meanings. Because my story remains open to evolutional change my identity remains open as well.

Example

When I was twelve years old, the disease polio threatened my physical existence. I became totally paralyzed and the doctors said I would die. If, by a miracle, I should live, they predicted I would be "nothing more than a living vegetable." In compassion, they suggested my family should pray for the grace of death. But my family lived a different reality. They believed in a god who answered prayers that rose from the heart of faith. And their faith was absolute. They prayed for my complete recovery. They prayed for a miracle.

Coincidental to my physical crisis, an Australian nurse named Elizabeth Kenney had developed a new treatment for poliomyelitis. I was a recipient of this new treatment. My crisis passed and I recovered. The doctors declared that no apparent aftereffects could be detected in my body. This remarkable recovery provoked conflicting interpretations as to cause.

After I left the hospital, I would return periodically to a prescribed medical clinic for checkups. I remember those moments clearly. The doctors would gather and ask me to perform certain physical exercises. As I did so, they would shake their heads in amazement and whisper to each other words about the miracle of modern medicine. But my family did not buy this interpretation. After all, the doctors had predicted certain death. On the other hand, my family and my friends believed that God would spare my life if they prayed with sufficient faith. And I lived. It was obvious to them that faith had been sufficient.

First Interpretation

The values behind my family's interpretation were consistent with the religious environment in which I had been born and raised. I had no reason to believe any interpretation of my miraculous recovery other than that God had been responsible.

This interpretation became focal to my identity and purpose in life. I was one who had been chosen by God to proclaim his power and preach his grace. I became a minister of my denomination. This interpretation shaped the meaning of my story and prevailed in my life until my mid-thirties. At that time, my life underwent a profound transformation, and I adopted a new and radically different myth.

Second Interpretation

Through the eyes of this new myth I began questioning the meanings I had given to those events that had shaped my identity and announced my purpose in life. The cause of my recovery from polio was critical to this questioning.

Eventually I gave this event a new meaning consistent with the new mythic covenant I had made with life. This meaning echoed the whispered words of the doctors about the miracle of modern medicine. God was removed from the equation of cause. The story of recovery had been recreated and with it my identity and sense of purpose in life.

Third Interpretation

But this was not the end of changing the meaning given to this polio event. A number of years later I began to explore what modern physics had to say about the world in which we live. The impact of this exploration caused me to, again, alter my myth and make a new covenant with life.

My miraculous recovery from polio opened itself to yet another twist of meaning. I retained the role of modern medicine while adding a new dimension consistent with my understanding of the physical realities of our world. I acknowledged the cumulative effect of the powerful healing energy released in my direction by the multitudes of people who prayed so faithfully for my recovery. The focus of this acknowledgment was not a god but the energy, itself, that was propelled with my name on it. In this new combination of perceived causes, my sense of having been graced by the caring energy of people and the incomprehensible mystery of life were added to being graced by the saving marvels of medicine.

Event and Meaning

That I experienced a miraculous recovery from polio remains an unchangeable event of my life. But the original meaning I gave to that event has gone through two major transformations. Each of these transformations reflects the changes I have made in my covenant with life. When I acquire a new mythic eye, I also acquire a new way of giving meaning to my stories that is the same as recreation. This perception has enabled me to understand the meaning of Sir Arthur Pinero's (*The Second Mrs. Tanqueray*) insight:

The future is only the past again entered through another gate.

As long as I remain open to changing my mythic covenant with life, the past is yet to be determined. That is, its meaning offers itself as malleable clay to be reshaped according to new life perceptions.

Conclusion

Following are the axioms that govern this possibility:

➤ My *past* is my whole life story. It is the meaning I have given to yesterday's events.

➤ My *present* is only a moment in time during which I create my future through my past.

➤ My *future* is my story I shape by my past meanings.

➤ If I wish a different *future*, then I must give new meaning to my *past* in this *present* moment

➤ I give new meaning to my past by making a *new covenant with life.*

➤ I make a new covenant with life by changing my *answers* to the *compelling questions* of my existence.

➤ I may *recreate* my life's *stories* anytime I *choose* because I am a *free* meaning-maker.

Whatever the meaning of my future, it is under my control. And the path to that future is through my past. That this past is yet to be determined highlights the gift of the universe to humans—that of being meaning-makers.

We live in reference to past experience and not to future events, however inevitable.

> —H. G. Wells

To what a degree the same past can leave different marks—and especially admit to different interpretations.

> —André Gide

The future is purchased by the present.

> —Samuel Johnson

The past is not dead. In fact, it's not even past.

> —William Faulkner

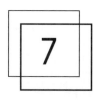

But Does It Sing?

(Testing My Myth)

The song that we hear with our ears is only the song that is sung in our hearts.

—Ouida

Defining My Myth

Since my myth determines the nature of my relationships, the quality of my life, and the direction of my destiny, I will want to be sure it works for my benefit. I can only feel this assurance if I have tested its validity, and I cannot test its validity unless I know what I am testing. Thus the first step is to define my myth by writing my answers to each of the compelling questions. I can give focus to my answers by limiting them to a three- or four-sentence paragraph.

➤ Who Am I?
  (What is my nature?)
➤ How Do I Know What I Know?
  (What is my source of authority?)
➤ Who or What Is in Charge?
  (What is my ultimate value?)
➤ What Is My Purpose?
  (How is my self-worth sustained?)
➤ What Does My Death Mean?
  (How do I view time?)

With these answers before me I am ready to test my myth.

A Metaphor Test

When I buy a car, I test drive it before I make the purchase to be certain it:

> ➢ performs as advertised
> ➢ suits my particular needs

If I want it to remain in good working order after the purchase, I do three things:

> ➢ Place it on a regular maintenance program
> ➢ Have an annual checkup to be sure it's functioning okay
> ➢ Learn its idiosyncrasies and have it checked out when it behaves abnormally

Unlike buying a car, I have no choice about the body I received at birth. Yet I also place it on a regular maintenance program, have an annual checkup, and care for it when it seems to have a need. I do these things for my body because I have a heavy investment in its future, and I want it to behave reliably.

I am born into a mythic environment. Unfortunately I have no choice over what this will be. Fortunately, unlike my body, I don't have to continue living in it simply because I was born in it. Once I become my own person, I can choose a different mythic life. Like purchasing a car, I can shop around for a myth that suits my particular needs. I can even test-drive it before investing it with my life.

And this raises three primary questions:

> ➢ Did I test-drive my myth before its purchase, or did I inherit it with the assumption of it being the only myth worthy of my devotion?
> ➢ Did I know what I wanted in my myth before I accepted ownership, or did I just take the reality that was offered?
> ➢ Did I understand that the purchase price of my myth is my life, or did I assume it was without cost?

Once I decide the myth I am living is the myth for me, I will want to treat it at least as well as I do my car and body. Periodically I will want to ask myself:

> ➢ Is it meeting my expectations of its purchase?

➤ Is it taking me where I want to go?

These two questions are ways of getting at the most important question of my existence:

"Is my myth worthy of my life investment?"

Our culture is awash with books, movies, plays, and television shows that call for us to examine the worthiness of our relationships. But these mediums rarely call for us to examine the worthiness of the myths that shape our relationships. In brief, cultural media normally deals with the drama of symptoms rather than the difficulty of causes.

This reflects the general tendency of most any culture's people to live on the surface of life rather than in its depth. On the surface is the immediate interaction of our relationships. In the depth is the mythic transaction that determines the meaning of our relationships. If I wish to know why I relate as I do, I will only find the answer by allowing my relationship interactions to lead me to the myth from which they spring. If I do not find my relationships worthy of my life, it may be because my myth is not worthy of my life investment.

My life is precious. And, like sand trickling through my fingers, it is gradually diminishing in quantity. What makes this ebbing away bearable is the awareness that I can increase its quality. And the one means I have of doing this is in making sure that my myth is capable of making life better as it gets shorter.

Since what my life is and what it will be is shaped by my myth, it seems imperative that at appropriate moments I should test its worthiness. Some deliberateness in this testing is appropriate, such as setting aside an annual retreat to review how well my myth is working for me. This is for my myth what an annual checkup is for my car or body.

Life Circumstance Test

There are circumstances in my living that naturally prompt on-the-spot testing.

Competing Myth

One circumstance that might prompt me to test my myth is when another myth claims to be more worthy of my life than the one I'm presently living. To be more worthy it must be capable of elevating the quality of my life beyond that of my present myth. To know if it is capable of doing so I do not have to leap out of my myth into its claims, all I need do is take a peek through its mythic eye. This peek requires two things:

> ➤ Defining its answers to the compelling questions
> ➤ Defining how living these answers would shape my relationship to myself, others, and the universe

Once I have taken this peek, I can lay the resultant definitions alongside those of my present myth. This comparison will show me whether or not the competing myth can offer me a greater quality of life.

If I wish a more specific testing I can take a bothersome relationship in my life, apply the definitions from this peek to the scenario of that relationship, and ask how it would be altered as a result. I could expand this testing further by applying these definitions to any scenario of my living.

A challenging myth will offer me the opportunity to test the worthiness of my present myth. Peek before leap is the principle that informs this testing.

Challenging Moment

Another circumstance that invites testing is when my myth does not seem equal to the challenge of some life moment. Existence is full of events that throw down a gauntlet to my myth. Examples are a loved one's death, a shattered dream, a threat to self-worth, or an inexplicable happening. One purpose of my myth is to give me strength, courage, assurance, and insight when confronting such moments. It is to empower me to meet the specific need of the challenge with a sense of being equal to the demand. It is to enable me to make sense of living.

The crises of my life tend to reveal the strengths and weaknesses of my myth. A myth worthy of my life will come through with what I need when it is pushed to the wall by crisis. It will provide those meanings that can convert the crisis into conquest. Here is a checklist of those meanings in the form of test questions:

> ➤ Does it make sense of the crisis?
> ➤ Does it offer me the spiritual tools to fully engage the crisis?

> ➤ Does it empower me to rise above the crisis with a strengthened resolve for living toward the future?
> ➤ Does it translate the crisis into useful lessons for living the future?

For a better look at how well my myth is working for me, I can take any major life crisis (past or present) and ask if it passes this meaning checklist.

What if I am unsatisfied with how my present myth is responding to life's challenging moments? I can take a myth that promises a better response, define its mythic eye, apply it to a personal life crisis, and run it through the meaning checklist.

This should tell me the measure of its promise.

It is the challenging moment that most dramatically underscores the mettle of my myth. Life is too precious to bet on a myth contestable by the trying event.

Daily Routine

A third circumstance that calls for testing my myth is the routine of daily living. Most of human life is routine. The question is what my myth offers me beyond its capacity to meet competitive mythic claims and challenging moments of life crisis. Can it take the humdrum of life and make it feel worthwhile? Can it inspire the insipid and bring blessing to the banal?

Changing diapers and taking out the trash are not particularly festive occasions, yet they are necessities that are symbolic of the routines of daily living. However, it is not the nature of the necessity that offers the possibility of satisfaction; it is the meaning given to why acting on the necessity is important. Satisfaction is not found in changing the diaper. It is found in the meaning of having a healthy and happy baby—to say nothing of the parent's state of mind. Satisfaction is not found in taking out the trash. It is found in having a clean environment for living and the removal of a health hazard.

Acts of drudgery and repetition do not necessarily hold the possibility of great satisfaction within themselves. But fulfilling their purpose does. So it is not the act of engaging the routine that is important; it is the space in between. When this space is filled with the satisfaction of fulfilled purpose, the satisfaction raises the quality of the ordinary.

test my myth for its capacity to raise the quality of the
ask it to answer the following questions:

remind me that acting on the ordinary is what makes
on the extraordinary possible? (No one ever succeeded
in a grand purpose without a devotion to the routines required
of that purpose.)

➤ Do you endow the ordinary with the same sense of sacredness
with which the whole of life is endowed? (Every moment of life
is a gift and therefore a sacred trust.)

➤ Do you place the actions of the ordinary within a larger framework of living? (Knowing the purpose of an act and understanding where that purpose fits in the grander scheme of life
meaning inspires satisfactions.)

The notion of the banal rises from our incessant attempt to divide
life into the important and the unimportant. Ironically, the important
is always dependent on the unimportant for its existence. This irony
is confirmed in folk wisdom by the story of the important race being
lost because the horse threw its shoe because the "unimportant" nail
that held the shoe was lost. The banal determines destiny. If you do
not believe this, then don't change the baby's diapers and don't take out
the trash.

Life Journey Test

One of the most common metaphors for the human experience is
that life is a journey. The purpose of a journey is its destination. Some
have suggested that it's the journey that's important, not the destination—that it's getting there and not arriving that has meaning. While
this sounds like profound wisdom, it is not. It is the destination that
provides both motivation and direction for taking the journey. While
the journey may comprise the bulk of living, it is only a wandering
without a destination. The journey and the destination are of whole
cloth. Rend the cloth and neither has meaning.

My myth provides both the destination for living and the road map
for getting there. My myth *is* the journey. The purpose of the journey is
to arrive at meanings that make living worthy of its gift. This purpose
is captured in the first stanza of a religious hymn entitled "Sing Out
Praises for the Journey":

Sing out praises for the journey, pilgrims, we, who carry on, searchers in the soul's deep yearnings, like our fore-bears in their time. We seek out the spirit's wholeness in the endless human quest.

A journey requires a mode of transportation. Because the automobile is the primary mode of transportation in Western culture, it serves as an apt analogy. Like a car, my myth moves my living toward desired destinations. And like vehicles, myths are unequal in accomplishing this task. So I can test the capacities of my myth by asking it some of the questions I might ask about my car's capacities.

> ➢ Is it reliable, or does it have a history of breakdowns when pushed? (Can I count on my myth to get me there?)
> ➢ Is it fast or slow? (My myth may get me there, but will it waste the time of my life doing so?)
> ➢ Is it powerful or must it creep up a steep grade? (How does my myth handle the demanding challenges of living?)
> ➢ Is it able to navigate the movement of traffic? (Does my myth move me through life with ease or tension? Can it keep up with life's flow, or will I be left behind?)
> ➢ Is it fun to drive or is it tiring or boring? (How much excitement does my myth generate in the journey? Is driving my myth wearing me out or increasing my energy?)
> ➢ Is it old or new? (Is my myth equipped to meet the needs of my time or was it created for time past?)

As with any vehicle, it costs more to drive a myth that is reliable, fast, powerful, adaptable, exciting, and created for today. But what I am willing to pay for a rewarding myth is the measure of how much I value my life. If my myth's performance does not measure up to my expectations of life, I can trade it in for one that does.

Satisfied Dissatisfaction Test

It is possible for me to believe that my myth is worthy of my life yet still feel dissatisfied. The purpose of a myth is to stretch my human possibilities. No one ever lives up to a worthy myth's full capabilities—otherwise it would have no stretching incentive. So my satisfaction in living it is the awareness that doing so has expanded the quality of my life. It is in knowing its incentive that has stretched my being toward my potential for growth. It is in knowing that it still calls for me to stretch beyond where I am at this moment.

If I am dissatisfied despite its stretching incentive, then the question is whether the problem is with the driver rather than the vehicle. Am I committed enough to my myth to derive satisfaction from its possibilities? Here are some questions that probe this issue:

> Do I really believe the answers to life's compelling questions that make up my myth?
> Do the goals of my living measure up to my myth's capabilities?
> What do I fear that retards a full commitment to my myth's capabilities?
> Is this fear worthy of the gift of my life?
> What would my life be like if I gave up this fear?
> What must I do to banish this fear and make a full commitment to my myth?
> Do I need a community of inspiration and support to encourage me in living up to my myth's capabilities?
> If I need such a community, where will I find it?

Fear paralyzes life by sucking its energies into a black hole of despair. Commitment releases these energies toward fulfilling the aspirations of my existence. I am responsible, for I am the chooser between commitment and fear.

There is another choice open to me—that of exchanging my myth for one less demanding of my commitment. I can accommodate my fear by trading in my myth for an economy model. But there is a price to pay for this reduction. First, it shifts control of my life from my hope to my fear. Second, by downsizing my myth, my capacity for quality living is also downsized. The question is if this is too high a price to pay to avoid confronting my fear. The decision is mine.

Compelling Questions Test

I may be fully satisfied with my myth, and I may be devoted to living its capabilities. Things are going well in my life. To assure that it continues this way, I may wish to occasionally fine-tune my myth. Fine-tuning has to do with performing at peak level. It makes whatever adjustments are necessary to guarantee that exerted energy gets maximum benefit.

How Does It Sound?

The first step in fine-tuning is to listen to the sound of my myth.

*Does it have the smooth purr of excitement and hope
or the rough growl of cynicism and despair?*

If I wish to be sure its smooth purr is a maximum performance or I want to eliminate any hint of rough growl, then the adjustments that need to be made will be in my answers to life's compelling questions. Here is a checklist:

Who am I?
➢ Does my myth make me feel worthy and powerful or unworthy and powerless?
➢ Does it assume responsibility for my choices or make me a victim?

How do I know what I know?
➢ Does my myth have the capacity to account for all my experiences of living or must I reject the validity of some experiences to keep my myth from being threatened?
➢ Does it limit the scope of my reality or permit new additions of source?

Who or what is in charge?
➢ Does my myth contribute to brokenness or wholeness in my relationship with myself, others, and the universe?
➢ Does it expand or reduce my ultimate value?

What is my purpose?
➢ Does my myth stir within me an aspiration toward human nobility or does it simply satisfy selfish goals?
➢ Does it sustain and enhance my sense of self-worth irrespective of external social valuation?

What does my death mean?

➤ Does my myth encourage me to look at death as a fear or a fulfillment?

➤ Does it inspire me to live without wasting the life it will conclude?

A fine-tuned myth takes me further on my life journey and uses less of my energy in doing so. It opens me to the fullest range of possibilities that my life represents. It increases the joy of living.

Is It in Transition?

If I am a searching, growing person then there will be occasions when the engine of my myth will sputter. My living will move in jerks and stops. It will seem like I'm exerting enormous energy while making little progress. When this happens, it's time to ask this question:

Do the answers that create my myth harmonize, integrate, and mutually support?

If the answer is no, then I'm probably in transition between myths. I shouldn't worry. It's a good sign that I'm moving to a more challenging and fulfilling level of living. It's what happens when I am leaving an old myth I have outgrown but haven't fully defined the new myth toward which I am headed.

Transitions occur when I change the answer to one or more of the compelling questions and the rest of the answers haven't caught up. There is critical tension between the new answers and the old answers because they are out of sync. I am frustrated because my myth is frustrated. I know what I have left behind but I'm not quite sure where I'm going.

To fix my myth, I must adjust all the answers to the compelling questions so they harmonize and mutually support. It's like remodeling a house. It takes deliberateness, time, and overcoming mistakes. And I will make mistakes. But that's all right because what I learn now will help me make the next transition quicker and easier.

This may sound like transitions are all frustration, but that is not the case. Transitions can also be joyful fun. There is wonderful delight in searching for and experimenting with new answers that will make up my new myth. What I must guard against in the midst of this fun is letting it get out of control. I must keep in mind what I am trying to do. An out-of-control mentality will slow down the process of transition and can even cause me harm in my relationships. I must take care about what mythic changes I am exploring.

However, if I persist with purpose through this transition of frustration/fun, I will end up with one of life's greatest thrills—the creation of a new myth and the exhilarating hope its possibilities announce for my life. I have entered a new life because of a new myth and my journey will move in exciting new directions.

The Singing Test

My minister friend and I were discussing a particular sermon we both had heard. Our individual responses were in agreement. As craft, the sermon was a fine piece of work. It was introduced effectively. It had all the right parts and points. It was articulated with clarity and woven together with apt illustrations. Yet it lacked that essential ingredient that pulls a congregation into its spell and makes its presentation an engaged experience beyond spectator listening. In describing this missing ingredient my friend observed: "It was well-composed but it didn't sing."

A myth that is worthy of my life bet possesses this missing ingredient. This ingredient is more than clearly defined answers to life's compelling questions. It is a singing that rises from mythic synergism. This synergism is created by what my myth brings to me and what I bring to my myth. It sings me and I sing it. This duet blends into a single harmonious song—a vocalized power that is more than the sum of the two voices. It is the music of my answers made incarnate.

We can all witness to some person whose mythic song has cast its spell over our living. Martin Luther King, Jr., is an example of one whose singing has become a part of that vast mythic chorus that makes up our evolving national conscience.

- ➤ It sang of overcoming when the shackles of prejudice clanged the reality of social bondage.
- ➤ It sang of nonviolence when confronted with the demeaning abuse of hate and brutality.
- ➤ It sang of the light of faith in the midst of the darkness of defeat.

> ➤ It sang of dreams of equality and freedom brought down from the mountain of hope.
> ➤ It sang of racial partnership in fulfilling the promises of democracy's grand experiment.

King's singing reminds of Tennyson's words in *The Charge of the Heavy Brigade: Epilogue*:

The song that nerves a nation's heart
Is in itself a deed.

King's myth was singing long before it gained the ear of the nation. It was social circumstance that conspired to bring it to public attention. Most of us will never be presented with such a national hearing. Our mythic song will rise to join the singing throngs that make up the cacophonous symphony of our surroundings. For my myth to infuse my living with worth and blessing, it need not receive acclaim. It need only to fill my own heart.

Ouida, in *Wisdom, Wit, and Pathos*, understood:

The song that we hear with our ears is only the song that is sung
in our hearts.

A singing myth is not one that occasionally bursts out with a brief tune. It does not rise from the surface of living. It is not a temporary response of my spirit to the delightfully superficial. A singing myth rises from the depth of my being where its music is in constant composition by my profound engagement with reality. It is an aria that cannot cease as long as this engagement holds. My myth and I sing because we are mutually enthralled. I, the creator, am being created by my own creation. For humans, this mythic synergism is the music of the spheres.

Evidence that my myth is singing are:
> ➤ a passionate conviction of its rightness
> ➤ a sense of inspiration from its challenge
> ➤ a deep feeling of human worth
> ➤ a joy and elation from being alive

It is imperative that I examine my myth for clarity of answer, integrity of harmony, and power of function. Yet, however high the marks I may give it through this examination, such will not ensure that it is worthy of my life. Worthiness depends on the mutual answer my myth and I give to the question of synergistic incarnation:

But Does It Sing?

If the answer is music, I know my life bet is being well placed.

The fineness which a hymn or psalm affords
Is when the soul unto the lines accord.
                    —George Herbert (*A True Hymn*)

Match the Myth

(Extracting the Questions)

People and organizations are prone to advertise aspects of their myth in a variety of ways. These advertisements are often found on bumper stickers, billboards, marquees, etc. Can you match the statements listed below with one or more of the five compelling questions?

> ➤ I'm out of estrogen, and I have a gun.
> ➤ Truth does not depend on a consensus of opinion.
> ➤ Warning: In case of rapture this car will be unmanned.
> ➤ There is no *away* to which to throw.
> ➤ My kid can whip your honor student.
> ➤ Free trip to heaven. Details inside.
> ➤ Vibrantly flawed.
> ➤ Raise your own dope/Plant a man
> ➤ Psycho Amazon war bitch from hell with an attitude
> ➤ He who dies with the most toys wins
> ➤ He who dies with the most toys still dies
> ➤ My other car is a broom
> ➤ The truth is out there
> ➤ Dog is my co-pilot
> ➤ A dusty Bible leads to a dirty life
> ➤ I don't need to be forgiven
> ➤ What if the Hokey Pokey is what it's really all about?
> ➤ Next time you think you are perfect, try walking on water
> ➤ Bad boys use bad toys
> ➤ Question reality
> ➤ Life, liberty, and the pursuit of all who threaten it
> ➤ Born OK the first time

A Tale of Boxes

(A Metaphor of Mythic Liberation)

I don't know how long I had been in the box, but when I opened my eyes my parents were peering down at me, proudly smiling. Culture must have approved, for it was smiling, too, towering behind them. "Enjoy your box. We made it just for you." This my parents said, beaming down their delight. And Culture nodded assent.

I looked around. It seemed like an awfully small place to grow up in. So I said: "Thanks a lot. But how can I exercise and explore in such a small space? I need room to grow." With that, Culture's face turned into a frown. "Well," replied my father, somewhat displeased, "we were raised in a box just like yours." My mother chimed in enthusiastically: "And look how big we grew up to be!" Then, with stern voices, they said together: "When you get to thinking your box is too small, just remember that!" With this admonition they smiled again and closed the lid.

"Hey," I cried, "open the lid. Give me some light!" "Keep the lid closed," boomed back my father, "you've got all the light you'll ever need in your box." Maybe they were right. After all, I was just a kid. Still, I didn't like feeling so confined. So I banged against the walls to see if they would give. But my mother heard the ruckus and yelled: "Quit testing your boundaries or Mother will have to punish you. Your space is just fine. You'll get used to it." That settled me down for a while. Banging against the walls wasn't helping anyway.

As time passed, I noticed I was getting taller. This gave me an idea. The place to get out of the box was the lid. If I jumped high enough, I could catch the edge of the wall, raise the lid, and peek out. So I began jumping and finally my fingers snagged the edge. I pulled myself up and carefully started to lift the lid. Pow! A stick whacked my fingers so hard I yelped and fell back into the box.

As I whimpered, I heard my father's voice: "Son, that hurt me more than it did you. You know better than to try and crawl out of your box. Remember: you can't hide what you've been doing from your mother and me. Be a good boy. Stay in your box. And don't forget the stick!" I was quiet for a while, nursing my wounded fingers. Then my father spoke again: "You're mighty quiet in there. How are you doing?" With a slight catch in my throat, I replied: "I'm being a good boy." With that the lid opened. My father smiled over me, patted me on the head, and dropped a carrot in my lap. The lid closed and I ate the carrot. It was good.

Every once in a while I would try to jump to the lid and peek out, but each time I was whacked back into the box with a stick. After staying there for a while without fussing, I was given a carrot. When I was away from home and tried the same stunt, it was Culture who whacked me and gave me a carrot when I was good. Soon I had a stockpile of carrots I could eat whenever I wished or trade for something else. I liked that. So I began doing whatever was necessary to get another carrot and every time I did I felt good about who I was.

Years passed and I grew bigger. Finally, I filled up the box. When that happened I stopped growing and didn't have to worry about my box getting too small. I also stopped trying to open the lid. I learned that all I had to do to get a carrot was to stay quietly in my box and soon enough one would be dropped in my lap—sometimes two. It seemed stupid getting whacked for no good reason. Instead, I waited for the carrots. They kept coming and I kept feeling good about who I was. I liked my box more and more. It was cozy and it kept me in carrots.

Sometimes someone would bump up against my box in one that felt different from my own and I would ask my parents or Culture what kind of box it was. The answer was always the same. "That isn't a box at all. It's really an illusion. That person just thinks they are in a box because they are blind. There's only one real box and they all feel just like yours. Don't associate with people who are not in real boxes. You'll become blind, too." This made me like my box even better. I felt virtuous snuggled in its tight realness.

I pondered a lot about why all those people in illusionary boxes didn't see how blind they were. I felt sorry for them. So I tried convincing them to live in a real box just like mine. Sometimes I would meet with my family and friends to discuss the piteous state of mind that would cause people to live in illusionary boxes. We planned ways to lure them into real boxes. We held meetings and implored them to touch our box and feel the difference between illusion and reality.

One day as I was driving down Life's main highway, I turned off down an unfamiliar road. My box seemed to know more about the area than I did because it began shouting: "Danger, danger! Turn back, turn back!" But I was moving fast and, distracted by my box's fear, I slammed head-on into a huge new experience. I tried to hold the road but careened into a ditch and my box flipped onto its side.

When my head cleared, I realized my box was being invaded by light. I tried to push it back with my hands but it slipped around and kept punching me in the eyes. I cowered into a corner to escape it. Then I heard my box saying with exasperation: "Shut the lid, stupid, shut the lid!" I looked up and saw that the lid on my box had been popped half-open by the impact. Not since my youthful attempts to peek out had my lid been unguarded. The light was pouring in. Fearfully, I straightened to my full height and reached to pull it shut. As I did my head extended above the walls. I was stunned by what I saw. There were people in all kinds of boxes. A few, just like mine, were wandering around with their lids partially opened—amazed eyes peering from inner shadows. Obviously, they had been upset by the same new experience I had run into.

I was spellbound by those different boxes. Many were bigger than mine and I was aghast that the people in them were driving with their lids open. As I watched, I noticed some were playfully bumping into each other and holding conversations. And some were zipping here and there at speeds I had never attained in my box.

Most astonishing, all these different boxes seemed to be real. Their drivers didn't appear to be blind. Then I realized I hadn't been whacked on the fingers. I looked around and couldn't see Culture anywhere. Maybe this was my chance. One of these bigger boxes was close by. If I could just touch it, I would know whether it was real or not. I decided to risk it. So I gradually began to crawl out of my box. Alarmed, my box screamed that it was too dangerous and I could perish. Maybe, I thought, but I have to know. And with that I gained the ground and headed for the nearest different box.

My box was right. The ground was treacherous. There were stumbling blocks, quicksand, and bottomless pits. What was I doing out here?! I thought of turning back but noticed I was already halfway there. Surely the ground couldn't be any worse than it had been. I decided to continue on.

As I touched the side of this different box, I was surprised to find it was solid. Even more surprising, it was much larger than it appeared from a distance. It was probably twice the size of mine. Suddenly, a face peered over the side. "Hi! Want to take a ride and see how it feels? You seem to be exploring." Why not, I thought to myself, I've come this far. I can always jump out if it doesn't feel right. So I climbed in. "Go ahead, drive it yourself. The controls are the same. It's just the boxes that are different."

What a ride! It had far more power and was much smoother riding than my box. And it could go over terrain mine would get hung up on. After I drove it for a while I stopped and looked around. I didn't see any carrots. This puzzled me. "Where are your carrots?" I asked. For a moment the reply was only a grin. Then the words came. "You don't need them in the bigger boxes. You can feel as good about yourself as you wish. It's the growing room." "But," I asked, "what if I grow and fill up the box?" "No need to worry. Just get a bigger one," was the reply. I was dazzled. Was this true? I could hardly believe my good fortune in running into that new experience.

"Where do you get one of these? How much does it cost?" I asked. "Well, it won't cost you anything except trading in your old box. They'll put it in Obsolete and give you a new one. There are hundreds to choose from. And they'll even pick yours up out of the ditch. The place is just over that rise ... has a big wide gate that says TRADE-INS on it." That all sounded wonderful. But I had a concern. "Won't Culture get angry? What about the big stick?" This garnered a good-natured laugh. "Don't worry. Culture doesn't carry much weight with big box drivers. Anyway, Culture hardly bothers folks who have their lids open. It isn't worth the effort. Go ahead. You can drive my box to the gate." And that's exactly what I did.

I was so excited about my new box I drove back home as fast as I could to show my parents what I had discovered. But they were not pleased. Said it was an illusion. Said it wasn't real. Said they were ashamed to see me blinded. And they never forgave me for changing boxes. But what's a person to do? I had grown so much while I was exploring that I couldn't even fit back into my old box. Anyway, it was my life!

For the first few years I drove around in my new box like crazy. I played bump box and had a lot of fascinating conversations with other drivers. Went places I never dreamed of. And the more I explored the more I grew. Finally, my new box began to cramp my style. But I knew enough by then to drive right through that big TRADE-INS gate and pick up a new one with room to grow. That was forty years ago. Since then I've traded in for two more new boxes. Each one bigger and faster and smoother riding than the last. Each one able to go over more difficult ground. The one I'm driving right now doesn't even have a lid. I've found I like to drive with the wind in my face. I like to see everything there is to see.

Sometimes I'll drive back to the TRADE-INS place just to look at my first box and remind myself how small it was. When I do, I'm always amazed that I drove it for so long without opening the lid to see what was really out there. I know now that I can keep on growing and exploring and that there will always be another bigger box and there will always be places to go I've never been. If you don't believe me, give it a whirl. It's a thrill a minute. All you have to do is open the lid of your box and you'll see what I mean.

What a life!
What a world!
What a universe!
And it's all there for ————The Opening!

P.S. Try a side road sometime. You might bump into a huge new experience.

Initium est dimidium facti.
(Once you've started, you're halfway there.)
—*Latin Proverb*

PART II

Creating Cultural Stories

We live out our existence within the womb of culture. Whatever this culture, its mythic design is to use our energies to fuel its drama. Even if we control our personal myth, we cannot control our cultural myth. What we can do is understand its drama so we can choose where and how we will give it our energies. This deliberateness of choice is our only measure of influence over its destiny. Yet it is a sufficient influence; for if enough of the citizenry determines a similar influence, then the culture will yield to it with a reflecting change.

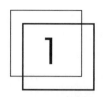

Defined by Heaven and Hell

(The Drama of Culture)

We are bound by the culture we have in common, that culture which distinguishes us from other peoples and times and places. Cultural constraints condition and limit our choices, shaping our characters with their imperatives.

—Jean J. Kirkpatrick

Mythic Character

Everyone knows that national cultures are different. To experience these differences is why we travel to other countries. And such travel experiences make us aware that cultural differences are both obvious and subtle. I was reminded of these differences by a T-shirt that caught my eye on a crowded tourist bus:

(The front)	*(The back)*
Heaven is:	**Hell is:**
French chefs	*British chefs*
British police	*German police*
German mechanics	*French mechanics*
Italian lovers	*Swiss lovers*
All organized by the Swiss	*All organized by the Italians*

Each of these listed national cultures is a perception of certain penchants of behavior that reflect something basic to their character. These are the ground of the humor:

> ➤ French—a penchant for artistic flair

> ➤ British—a penchant for restrained behavior
> ➤ German—a penchant for strict order
> ➤ Italian—a penchant for passionate expression
> ➤ Swiss—a penchant for definitive organization

These character penchants rise from a cultural identity that has essentially developed out of each nation's collective mythic answers to life's compelling questions and the history of these answers within its geographic context.

Excessive Stress

Heaven is a concept of bliss while hell is one of agony. These concepts are polar opposites that define each other. Thus behind every heavenly character penchant lurks the danger of its hellish polarity. When that which is perceived to be heaven is pushed too far, it can lapse into hell. The principle is that even an appealing character trait overdone becomes counterproductive.

One of the basic character traits of American culture is an incessant penchant for personal independence that is translated into the spirit of excessive individualism. This penchant is not only viewed as a desirable personal strength, its attainment is viewed as arrival in cultural heaven. Moreover, it seems perfectly consistent with the democratic vision of self-determination. Arrival in cultural heaven always feels blissfully compatible when it is perceived to be a marriage of individual myth and cultural myth.

The problem with excessive individualism is that it fosters a selfish focus for living that diminishes a sense of moral responsibility for the welfare of the community. Perceptions of individual welfare become the barometer of personal morality. The result is that community habitually becomes the captive of private interest. Two things occur in this captivity that jeopardizes democracy. First, the democratic notion of the common good takes a backseat to the whims of perceived personal good. This jeopardizes the democratic purpose of cultural government and institutions—converting them into instruments for processing private goals. Second, the democratic notion of a community of mutual concern is replaced with a concern for how the community can benefit private goals. This jeopardizes the democratic ideal of equal opportunity for all citizens, and leaves the less fortunate to fend for themselves. The welfare of the part takes precedent over the welfare of the whole.

Become an active member of almost any cultural institution in America and the primary obstacle in fulfilling its purpose will become glaringly apparent: the excessive individualism of its members. Assess the lack of accomplishment for the common good of almost any of the sessions of Congress and the reason will become glaringly apparent: the excessive individualism of its members. Much of the failures of democracy in America are the successes of excessive individualism.

A very concrete example of the negative effects of excessive individualism occurred in 2008. The worst of individualism and unmitigated greed has been wedded on the nation's metaphorical Wall Street throughout its history. But in 2008 this marriage gave birth to a financial crisis that not only brought America to its economic knees but quickly spread across the globe. Its ultimate impact is yet to be known. However, the immediate effect in America was incalculable loss for the general public in every area of economic life. The self-aggrandizing quality of rampant individualism and its lack of concern for the larger community has had devastating consequences. A metaphor for the oxymoronic consequences of this excess is the multimillion dollar golden parachute rewards granted to corporate CEOs who were responsible for the economic meltdown and whose companies went under or were bailed out by the government while average citizens lost their economic futures without any available redemption.

While there is nothing inherently destructive about individualism within itself, its excess makes the very fabric of democracy threadbare.

The opposite of this American penchant of character has historically prevailed in Japanese culture—the excessive valuing of community. The individual is called upon to surrender private goals to the community's well-being. The welfare of the group is the barometer of morality. For example, as long as lying is perceived to be for the good of the community, it is morally justified and not considered deceit. This nuance of cultural character has permeated the social structures of Japan with what has appeared to be admirable results. However, its insidious destructiveness came to light in 1998 when the nation's entire economy almost collapsed under its weight. Like deceiving a patient with cancer with assessments of good health, government and corporate lies about the state of the country's financial health had concealed the truth until its deterioration was nearly past reversal. The consequence of these lies was destroyed careers, bankrupted institutions, devastated individual futures, and a profound negative impact on the global economy.

While there is nothing inherently destructive about community within itself, its excess will spawn moralities that can be destructive to the cultures in which it is cradled as well as other victimized nations.

Tension

A culture is made up of people. These people reflect two innate desires that are tensional in their relationship:

> ➢ The desire to freely express individuality
> ➢ The desire to be bonded in community

This tension cannot be resolved without destroying what it means to be human, because the individual and the community, like two sides of a singular coin, are an inseparable whole. They are inseparable because:

> ➢ they create the need for each other
> ➢ they define the meaning of each other
> ➢ they nurture the life of each other

Thus to value one over the other is like valuing one side of a coin over the other. It is to fail to recognize that the value of both is either mutual or nonexistent.

Basic to every culture's character is how it deals with this tensional relationship. As indicated by the emphasis given to one over the other in American and Japanese cultures, excessive stress can carry its own destructive consequence. Only when an ongoing healthy tensional balance is maintained between these two desires can a culture realize maximum benefit from the life-giving juices they generate.

The issue in this tension is not the wholeness of a culture. The issue is the spiritual health of this wholeness. And whatever the status of this spiritual health, it will find graphic expression in the culture's character. And how the culture gives emphasis to the individual and the community will be a definitive factor in this expression.

Space and Time

As suggested in the aforementioned T-shirt statements, cultures will express their character through the valuing of certain behaviors such as restraint, order, artistry, organization, and passion. There are also character nuances that find expression in some way in all cultures such as space and time. In some cultures, it is appropriate for individuals to crowd the space of other people. In other cultures, space crowding is considered an aggressive act. In some cultures, punctuality is considered a virtue. In other cultures, punctuality has little meaning because time does not control behavior. Whatever a culture's view of space and time, such will help shape the culture's character in the same way as other valued behaviors.

External Contexts

There are also external contexts of existence that operate on a culture's uniqueness of character such as geography and weather. The mountains of Peru versus the sands of Egypt, and the cold of Norway versus the warmth of the Caribbean all affect the economy, music, customs, and lifestyle of their respective people. Thus, geography and weather may not only help shape the moods and celebrations that enrich and define cultural character, they may also contribute to the shape of that character itself.

Holistic

Culture is a holistic package of multiple and mutually effecting influences that shape character. Some of these are permanently external and add unique flavor to this character. However, always fundamental to a culture's heartbeat is its prevailing myth.

Mythic Incarnation

The root meaning of the word *culture* is "to cultivate." Culture is a sphere of cultivated influence. That which is cultivated is a particular myth. The soil of this cultivation is the mind of a particular people. Thus, culture is a boundaried community institutionalization view of reality that involves:

> ➤ a form of government that gives political structure and legal enforcement to the myth's ideal.

> ➤ a system of rewards and punishments designed to discipline conformity to the myth's perspectives.
> ➤ a body of instructive attitudes and actions that support the values inherent in the myth.
> ➤ a core of institutions that preserve and propagate the myth.
> ➤ a set of customs, protocols, and rituals that celebrate the myth.
> ➤ a language that participates in conveying the nuances of the myth.

This boundaried community institutionalization produces a distinctive collective character that is defined as culture. In essence, culture is a peculiar way of life that reflects how a community has organized itself around the ideals and implications of a view of reality.

Geographer Peter Jackson says it this way:

Cultures are maps of meaning through which the world is made intelligible.

The maps of meaning Jackson speaks of are created from the mystery of human experience. And because different myths create different meanings the intelligence embodied by cultures are also different. When we speak of German culture or Italian culture, we are recognizing this definition. The Heaven Is/Hell Is T-shirt is a playful acknowledgment. All culture is mythic community and all mythic community is culture.

Integration

All cultures, then, are living incarnations of particular myths. When a new myth takes over, an old culture it will do two things. It will seek to accommodate those parts of the old that can be remolded in its own image. This is why nations whose cultures have been dominated by a number of past myths may appear analogous to Frankenstein creations. But whatever the appearance, the culture will be an integration of parts that incarnate the synchronizing heartbeat of the new myth.

When the colonists of America sought to establish a form of government for their new independent nation, they used England as a model. But the new myth of self-ruling democracy could not find an accommodation with the old myth of a ruling royalty. So the colonists eliminated royalty and pressed the model to fit a more grassroots democratic mold. Out of this remolding, the American form of government was created.

Destruction

The other thing a new myth will do when taking over an old culture is seek to destroy those parts of the old that cannot be remolded in its own image. During the eighteenth-century French Revolution, peasants sought to destroy the statuary images of royalty that represented totalitarian rule. This was symbolic of the attempt to replace royalty with a more democratic rule. It was a mythic gesture that reflected revolutionary intent.

Such visible destruction of mythic public symbols that paralleled the destruction of mythic social structures was common in cultures taken over by the USSR following World War II. And when the USSR dissolved in the late twentieth century, its own public symbols were overturned and destroyed as an expression of its defeat and incompatibility with the myth of the incoming regime.

Representation

Whether it is the establishment of a new culture, the remolding of an old culture, or the destruction of an old culture, the myth driving the process will find an incarnation that fully represents its own view of reality.

British historian Arnold Toynbee wrote a twelve-volume analysis of the rise and fall of civilizations along with many other publications. Out of this milieu of insight he offers a description of the mythic incarnation of culture:

> *Every historic culture-pattern is an organic whole in which all the parts are interdependent.*

In this description, Toynbee implies that a culture is defined by:
- its patterns of organization
- its boundaries of expression that outline a wholeness of being
- its interdependent and mutually supportive parts
- its organic pulsating aliveness

Culture is the cultivation of a mythic garden in the mind of a peculiar people.

Mythic Boundaries

Myth is a view of reality. A nation's myth creates boundaries of perception that shape the contours of a tunnel vision unique to its cultural existence. This is the nation's way of seeing. And this seeing will interpret events differently from that of other cultures. All history is mythic judgment. This is why the history written by one nation might be unrecognizable as reality by another nation.

Even nations that live next door to each other see with contrary eyes. I lived for a while in Canada. I read both Canadian and American national news magazines. Their respective interpretation of the same world event was often remarkably incompatible. It is not geographic boundaries that separate nations. It is mythic boundaries. There are no reality boundaries without myth and there are no myths without reality boundaries. Every myth imposes a limitation on the nation's capacity to see anything other than what it was designed to see.

If this is true, then the question is what is real and not real. Unnerving as it might be, the answer is that reality is in the mythic eye of the beholder. Every nation is bound into the reality produced by its own mythic vision. What is real to one nation may be illusion to another. But that which is not debatable is the undeniable reality of the behavior spawned by cultural myths. Stanislaw Lec was a Polish aphorist, poet and writer who drew heavily on his experiences during and after World War II. Understanding the role that myth played in human conflict he observed:

When myth meets myth, the collision is very real.

Whether this collision is one of conflict or collusion, it creates a reality that is beyond illusion.

The myth of a culture creates boundaries that:
- determine its peculiar view of reality
- separate its peculiar existence from other cultures
- define its peculiar identity character

Mythic Classes

Economic classes are a cultural prerequisite. British journalist and author George Orwell suggests:

> *Throughout recorded time ... there have been three kinds of people in the world, the High, the Middle, and the Low ... even after enormous upheavals and seemingly irrevocable changes, the same pattern has always reasserted itself, just as a gyroscope will always return to equilibrium, however far it is pushed one way or the other. The aims of these three groups are entirely irreconcilable.*

As Orwell points out there are normally three classes in a culture— upper, middle, and lower. When only two classes exist they will be the upper and lower.

These classes have been defined in numerous ways. At the end of the nineteen hundreds Lawrence Sutton won the contest offered by a British newspaper for the best definition of middle class. Here is that definition:

> *Wearing overalls on weekends, painting somebody else's house to earn money? You're working class. Wearing overalls on weekends, painting your own house to save money? You're middle class.*

To round out Sutton's description we can add:

> *Never wearing overalls because you don't need to save money and somebody else is painting your house? You're upper class.*

Positive

Classes serve contradictory roles in culture. One of these roles is positive. Classes mutually restrain each other from extreme expression. Without this balancing restraint, classes tend to behave in reactionary ways detrimental to a culture's well-being. Greek philosopher Aristotle believed the key to this restraining balance is the middle class:

> *The best political community is formed by citizens of the middle class, and ... those states are likely to be well-administered, in*

*which the middle class is large, and stronger if possible than both
the other classes, or at any rate than either singly; for the addition
of the middle class turns the scale, and prevents either of the
extremes from being dominant.*

As Aristotle implies, the classes with the greatest tendency toward extreme behavior are the upper and lower. Without restraint the upper class, in its arrogance, tends to be brutally exploitative, suppressive of social liberties, and uncaring about the well-being of other classes—particularly the lower class. England's upper class (of its dominant history), America's upper class (especially its first one hundred and fifty years of existence), and the politically dominating Roman Catholic Church upper class (during the Middle Ages) are obvious examples in the Western world.

The lower class, in its anger over being exploited and treated inhumanely, tends to be subversive and revolutionary in response. Liquidating its oppressors, normally the upper class, is viewed as an activity of rightful justice. The lowest economic class that has ever existed in America was that of the slaves. On August 30, 1800, Gabriel Prosser led a rebellion of somewhere between two and three thousand slaves in an attempt to take over the state of Virginia. Their goal was to acquire the arsenal and powder house in Richmond. They were thwarted by a violent rainstorm that inundated roads and washed out bridges, giving Governor James Monroe time to call up the state militia to subdue them.

Marx, Lenin, Stalin, and their successors used the exploited circumstances of the lower classes to stir the communist revolution in Russia and to fan the flames of working-class revolution around the globe. During the civil rights movement of the 1960s and 1970s in the United States, Martin Luther King, Jr., proposed a nonviolent form of rebellion in response to the white population's economic exploitation and social suppression of black lower-class citizens. Other black leaders proposed more extreme forms of violent rebellion. The revolutionary rhetoric and call for aggressive action by black leaders of militant Muslimism is an example.

Also, as Aristotle pointed out, the class most likely to mediate and curb such extremism is the middle. It has the most to lose by extremism and the most to gain by balance. Moreover, it is the class that tends to maintain a closer attunement with the culture's mythic conscience. It sees and protests conscience violations when social liberties permit such expressions. If empowered to do so, the middle class will enact laws and process justice in keeping with this conscience. It is susceptible to having its own conscience raised by examples of violation.

One reason for this middle-class sensitivity is that many have risen into that class from the lower class and hold a sympathy for its plight. A second reason is that restraining the exploitations of the upper class paves the way for its own entry into upper-class privileges. And a third reason is that it has a general focus on information enlightenment that takes the form of education, reading, and news exposure. While the design of this focus is normally for social advancement, social conversation, and informed politics, it also has a consciousness-raising effect that broadens perception of social need.

In essence, economic aspirations, information assimilation, and mythic conscience attunement make the middle class the keeper of cultural values and the arbiter of the status quo. It is the class balancing act.

Negative

The other role of classes in culture is negative. The very classes necessary for a culture's existence militate against the mythic ideals of the culture's government. Consider as examples the two polar options of totalitarian government and democratic government. In totalitarianism, there must be a ruling class to control social liberty and to subordinate other classes for the economic benefit of itself. Yet the class exploitation necessary to the existence of totalitarianism militates against any perceived idealistic benefit for the masses. The notion of a benevolent dictatorship is an oxymoron.

In a democracy, economic classes rise naturally out of the privileges of social liberty and its implied free enterprise. Yet these classes militate against the ideal of social egalitarianism and, indeed, are based on economic exploitation. The equality of the masses is an illusion because people do not begin their existence on an equal level.

It is not possible to have a culture without classes and it is not possible for these classes to not militate against the mythic ideals of the culture in which they exist. At the least, classes dehumanize social relationships by engendering attitudes and conditions of superiority and inferiority. The paradox is that culture cannot exist without classes while culture cannot find complete mythic fulfillment with classes.

Mythic Inconsistency

In all nations there are noteworthy social behaviors that are inconsistent with the cultural myth. For example, throughout most of American history, despite the egalitarianism of the democratic myth, women have been treated as inferiors to men in all areas of living except the kitchen and nursery. Normally, such inconsistencies are practiced mythic views that conflict with a culture's guiding myth. They are permitted to exist because their representatives are socially influential enough to outweigh the conscience of the cultural myth.

Totalitarianism

In totalitarianism, even the grossest of mythic inconsistencies can be openly maintained because the power to control is concentrated in the ruling class. The so-called communist regime is an example. The myth of communism idealizes a culture where a classless citizenry commonly owns and shares the means and rewards of production. Classes are touted as the root of all evil. Yet all attempts to implement this myth have been undertaken by totalitarian ruling classes who justify their existence as an interim necessity for realizing the mythic ideal. But history shows that the temporary is only a label to disguise the permanent.

These totalitarianisms are intentional inconsistencies. They deliberately violate the myth they purport to represent in two ways. First, they use methods of ruthless brutality and suppression that are inconsistent with the goal of achieving a common good. Second, they use a dictating class to impose classless activities on the citizenry. Not only are attempts to implement the myth activities of gross inconsistency, but the label is an oxymoron. No classless society has ever emerged from these attempts (except in some isolated and temporary instances). In fact, they have generated classes. The communist myth remains an unembodied and unrealizable ideal. Thus, all so-called communist cultures are, in reality, totalitarian ruling classes that suppress social liberties and economically exploit their citizenry in the name of a noble but unattainable myth.

Democracy

In a democratic society such mythic inconsistencies can only be maintained as long as permitted by the voting citizenry. In American democracy the cultural myth idealizes the capacity of the people to govern itself. Inherent in this myth is an egalitarianism of civil rights and social liberties. Some of the historically persisting inconsistencies perpetrated by influential segments of the citizenry are:

➤ male gender superiority (over the female gender)
➤ white racial superiority (over all other races)
➤ upper class superiority (over both middle and lower classes)
➤ business management superiority (over both white- and blue-collar workers)
➤ heterosexual lifestyle superiority (over homosexual lifestyle)
➤ the religious truth superiority of Christianity (over all other religions)
➤ the superiority of business interests (over citizenry interests) in politics

Much of the internal energy and drama of American history has revolved around attempts to diminish the level of citizen exploitation that has been perpetrated by these conflicting mythic inconsistencies.

The myth of democracy remains an experiment in government because its success requires that the mythic conscience of individual citizens be in supportive alignment with the nation's mythic cultural conscience. Significant strides have been made legally in requiring that the social behavior of citizens be in compliance with democratic ideals. However, the only real success is evidenced by a willing citizenry compliance that comes from a commonly held mythic conscience. There are at least three gages that measure the degree of this success:

(1) One gage is sociological and political in nature. When civil rights issues cease to dominate social relationships and political concerns then a large measure of success will have been achieved.

(2) One gage is perceptual in nature. Patriotism has traditionally been viewed as loyal support of the policies and actions of

the country's government. When the perception of patriotism shifts to that of loyal support of the country's mythic spirit and conscience then a large measure of success will have been achieved.

(3) One gage is representational in nature. Election to represent a region in government is normally viewed as a responsibility to maximize benefit for that region. When this provincial view of representation by politicians and people is transcended to a manifested responsibility to maximize benefit for the whole nation, then a large measure of success will have been achieved.

In applying these three gages it becomes apparent that democracy in America remains an evolving experiment rather than an achieved cultural performance.

It is not possible for any culture to exist without the inconsistencies produced by internal competing myths, whatever its form of government. The dissolution of the Union of Soviet Socialist Republics in the latter part of the twentieth century shows how these competing myths can drain the power of an economically overextended totalitarian culture's ruling class. The challenge of a democratic culture lies in promoting civil rights and social liberties while limiting the power of internal competing myths to exploit the citizenry and drain its energies. It seems obvious that this can only be done when the personal myths of the vast majority of its citizenry remain aligned with the culture's mythic spirit and conscience.

Mythic Preservation

Since culture is a creation of myth its designs are intended to preserve that which birthed and sustains its existence. At the heart of this preservation is the issue of mythic allegiance. This allegiance is maintained by controlling the social mind and the social liberties of its citizens. The attempt to control the social mind is made through programs of mythic training and propagation. The attempt to control social liberty is made through a system of rewards for mythic compliance and punishments for mythic transgressions. The aggressiveness or gentleness and overtness or subtleness with which a culture pursues its attempts to control depends on the degree to which it leans toward the polar ideals of totalitarianism or democracy. Since the ideal is inherent in the dominating myth the agencies of cultural control will be reflective.

There are exceptions to these principles of preservation that occur because of political revolutions, war, and survival necessities but these exceptions will not prevail unless they succeed in changing the myth that dictates the manner and means of control. Not only is the manner in which a culture pursues allegiance a reflection of its creating myth, so is its primary means of government enforcement. When the myth controls the manner and means of incarnation, it controls the ability to reflect itself in the cultural mirror.

As a rule, the preservation of cultural allegiance is not a difficult task. As Ruth Benedict observes in her book *Patterns of Culture:*

Most people never question the essential myth of their culture. Because they are birthed into and trained into its ways it feels as natural as breathing.

Thus the citizenry of a culture normally gives unquestioned allegiance to the myth that drives the culture and to the attempts to control its own social mind and social liberties.

Mythic Threat

The greatest threat to a culture's social control is for its citizens to show allegiance to a competing mythic vision. In totalitarianism, such threats can be readily squashed by the use of psychological terror and physical violence. These are the primary means by which totalitarian governments remain in power. But in a democracy, where freedom of thought and speech is idealized, such threats pose a special problem. The question of this problem is to what extent mythic deviation can be tolerated without this deviance undermining the myth that sustains its expression. The answer to this question is problematic and is another reason for referring to democracy as a grand experiment.

In American history there have been moments when government has viewed the expression of mythic deviance as a threat that required aggressive response. One major threat came within a hundred years of America's independence from England. Its focus was two issues that eventually became welded together: the indivisible unity of the states and the social liberty of the slaves. The perceived threat of the dissolution of national unity initiated the Civil War with the federal government assaulting its own citizens to preserve this unity.

On December 7, 1941, Japan attacked Pearl Harbor in the Hawaiian Islands, initiating America's official entry into World War II. Immediately, and without collaborating evidence, almost all Japanese Americans were viewed as mythic threats to democracy. The ground of this perception was a racial ancestry different from the European Caucasian ancestry of most Americans. In a shameful manner, these citizens were divested of their civil rights, homes, businesses, and futures and herded into degrading concentration camps for the duration of the war.

During the 1950s the myth of communism was viewed as a significant internal threat to the nation's mythic stability. The government sought to destroy this threat in two ways. It suppressed the civil liberties of the citizenry by outlawing the Communist Party, and it initiated a national witch hunt designed to expose the disloyalty of any citizen whose personal ideology or associations implied support of communist ideology. The instrument of this witch hunt was the Congressional House Un-American Activities Committee chaired by a senator named Joseph McCarthy. The end result was the unjust destruction of the reputations and careers of many citizens and the imprisonment of others who refused to abet the violation of their constitutional rights by the committee.

During the 1960s and 1970s, responses to the Vietnam War divided the citizenry and caused a major questioning of that part of the cultural myth that viewed America as the world's democratic savior nation. Draft evasion, draft card burning, flag desecration, and angry demonstrations were symbolic expressions of this questioning. Government response was to portray the questioners as disloyal Americans and to use law enforcement and troops to curb social liberties. An example was the use of the National Guard to quell an antiwar demonstration at Kent State University in Ohio in 1970 that ended with troops killing four students and wounding a number of others.

The evident truth is that any cultural government, totalitarian or democratic, will do violence to its own citizens when it perceives its grounding myth to be violated or threatened. And the government in power will view any action by its citizens that threatens its own continuing control as mythically inappropriate and, thus, unpatriotic. Actions maintaining mythic stability and control will inevitably take precedent over actions affirming mythic ideals and conscience.

Mythic Enemies

The government of a culture is its mythic protector and perpetuator. No concept has been more useful to governments throughout history in fulfilling this role than that of the enemy. Having an enemy that threatens a culture's well-being galvanizes mythic allegiance and justifies government action.

Credible

Sometimes this enemy is a credible threat. The mythic war machines of Germany and Japan that spurred World War II were legitimate threats to the well-being of all nations. They were enemies that both raised mythic allegiance and justified the sacrifices required for their defeat. Every culture, when threatened by a credible enemy outside its national boundaries, will do what it can to preserve its way of life. The will to fight for survival is innate to human existence and endemic to mythic allegiance.

Concocted

Sometimes this enemy is concocted to hide the real reason for a government's action from its citizens. The ostensible reason for American initiation of the Spanish American War of 1898 was to rid Cuba of suppressive Spanish rule. This published reason gave mythic justification for American intervention and the shedding of American blood. It fit that part of the American myth that perceived the nation as a democratic savior—and particularly in its role as the rescuer of the oppressed underdog seeking democratic self-determination.

However, the real reasons were to exert stabilizing control over Cuba's sugar production, which was important to the American economy, and to secure a greater American dominion over the Caribbean and Pacific areas that were, in measure, controlled by a weak Spanish government. The end result of the war was a stronger American influence over the Cuban economy, the ceding of Puerto Rico and Guam to America, and the transfer of the sovereignty of the Philippines to America—all for the sum of twenty million dollars to Spain.

Cloaking

Sometimes an enemy takes action that is not a direct threat to the mythic well-being of the nation but does, in the eyes of its government, undermine its influence in the world. This undermining may target its foreign policy, its economic goals, or simply its prideful standing. In order to justify an aggressive response of attempted restoration that is worthy of possible citizen bloodshed, governments will cloak their response with mythic morality. Especially is this the case in a democratic nation where citizens do not normally view undermined influence as a moral basis for aggressive action.

A scenario in point was the Persian Gulf War of 1991. Iraq, under Saddam Hussein, had invaded and taken control of Kuwait. President George H. W. Bush initiated an aggressive military response designed to destroy Iraq's war machine. The publicized reason for this response was to restore Kuwait's independence. Again, the democratic savior nation going to the rescue of a distressed nation satisfied the American public's need of a mythic justification for war. But this was a moral cloaking. The American government did not protest when Iraq, in 1980, invaded Iran. In fact, it had tacitly approved and helped arm both parties. However, Iraq's invasion of Kuwait activated the American government's foreign policy of assertive intervention in Middle East politics when any nation's behavior upset balances of power that threatened American attempts to control the flow and price of oil. When Iraq invaded Iran, this balance was not upset. When Iraq invaded Kuwait, it was.

A New York City newspaper cartoon captured this real reason for American intervention with elegant simplicity. President Bush is facing the reader with open hand as he admonishes:

We SHELL not EXXONerate Saddam Hussein for his actions.
We will MOBILize to meet this threat to our vital interest in the Persian GULF until an AMOCOble solution is reached.

John Dryden, in the *Hind and the Panther*, summarizes why governments often cloak their real reasons for action in mythic lies:

War seldom enters but where wealth allures.

Conceptualized

A mythic enemy need not be a person or group in order to serve its purpose of catalyzing mythic allegiance. This enemy may be conceptualized rather than specifically designated. President Lincoln's 1863 Gettysburg Address dedicating the National Cemetery at Gettysburg, Pennsylvania, is an example. There was a convergence of cultural forces focused around the Confederacy that caused the American Civil War to erupt:

> ➤ The economics of slavery and the Southern way of life
> ➤ The issue of national unity and whether a state could secede from the union
> ➤ The moral issue of slavery

In his address, Lincoln, rather than designating the Confederacy as the enemy, conceptualized a viewpoint. The enemy was the view of national disunity and human inequality that betrayed the founding fathers' intention of a united nation "dedicated to the proposition that all men are created equal." In this conceptualization, he lifted the Civil War above economics and politics to the moral high ground of a struggle about national integrity and social liberty. In conceptualizing the enemy Lincoln inferred two things. First, that the unity of the states was fundamental to the nation's being. Second, that social liberty was fundamental to the nation's conscience. These two inferences made the sacrifices and death of their champions righteous.

In similar fashion, Martin Luther King, Jr., and the civil rights advocates of the 1960s and 1970s appealed to the culture's social liberty conscience and conceptualized the enemy as race hate and prejudice. This mobilized the civil rights movement above specific attacks on individuals and local governments.

Clearly Defined

Having a clearly defined enemy strengthens mythic allegiance and opens human resources for both mythic defense and mythic assertiveness. It makes little difference whether this enemy is credible, concocted, cloaked, or conceptualized. It is citizenry belief that the enemy exists and must be responded to that persuades mythic allegiance and action. As Carl Jung (*The Structure and Dynamics of the Psyche*) suggested:

The real existence of an enemy upon whom one can foist off everything evil is an enormous relief to one's conscience. You can then at least say, without hesitation, who the devil is; the cause of your misfortune is outside, and not in your own attitude.

Frederick Nietzsche says it more humorously in *Marching Against an Enemy*:

How good bad music and bad reasons sound when we march against an enemy.

Mythic Flawedness

Every culture is flawed because:
- it is a reflection of myth and all myths are flawed realities.
- it is a community of people and all people are flawed creatures.

Thus every culture is an expression of flawed people organized around a flawed view of reality. This is why all attempts at building utopian communities are doomed to failure. But this is also why cultures are delightfully different as reflected in the humor of the Heaven/Hell T-shirt described at the beginning of this chapter. So while flawedness denies the perfection of cultural utopianism it designs the patterns of cultural uniqueness.

Mythic Impact

Geert Hofstede and Gert Jan Hofstede (*Cultures and Organizations: Software of the Mind*) suggest this metaphor:

Culture is the software of the mind.

Although the human mind is more complicated and creative than a computer or its software, the metaphor rightfully underscores two facts:
- The cultural myth and its attendant applications are programmed into the human mind from birth.
- The cultural incarnation of the myth is the condition of life in which the human mind resides.

Thus culture is both life programming and life context. It is the sine qua non of the mind's function.

Even though, as an individual, I make the choices that determine my personal destiny, these choices are not made within a vacuum. They are made within my culture. Therefore, the mythic character of my culture will impact my choosing with its social instructions and prescribed options. Even if my personal myth is contrary to that of my culture, this very contrariness will give focus to my choosing. In brief, my way of seeing and being in the world cannot be separated from the culture of my existence. As Ruth Benedict (*Patterns of Culture*) puts it, my living is inescapably edited by my culture:

> *No man ever looks at the world with pristine eyes. He sees it edited by a definite set of customs and institutions and ways of thinking.*

Every human is inextricably caught in the drama of their culture; there can be no divorce. Even if people move to live in a different culture, they take the previous culture with them in their mind. This previous culture will constantly interact with the new culture in judging its concept of reality and in assessing what is liked or disliked. The old culture will forever remain a companion of the mind for it is the original mythic imprint that is disputable but not erasable.

> *Cultures are maps of meaning through which the world is made intelligible.*
> —Peter Jackson

2

Uncle Sam Wants You!

(Cultural Mythic Maintenance)

Most people never question the essential myth of their culture. Because they are birthed into and trained into its ways it feels as natural as breathing.

—Ruth Benedict

New York State businessman Samuel Wilson was affectionately referred to as "Uncle Sam." During the War of 1812 with Great Britain, he supplied the American army with barrels of beef. To indicate these barrels as government property he stamped them with the letters "U. S." The transposition of the U. S. label with Uncle Sam is supposedly the origin of the symbolic nickname of the United States. This nickname evolved into a cartoon figure with white hair and goatee whiskers dressed in striped pants, vest, and swallow-tailed coat wearing a tall top hat—all in red, white, and blue.

During World War I and World War II, this figure appeared on posters recruiting citizen support with captions such as:

UNCLE SAM WANTS YOU

The figure of Uncle Sam is leaning forward with arm and index finger extended, compelling the viewer's attention. While this cartoon of Uncle Sam has become a national symbol of American democracy, the forthright beckoning for citizenry support is an apt metaphor of the explicit demand of all cultures. This demand is for the energies of the citizens to be invested in the maintenance of the culture's mythic organization. It is not an idle demand. Without this energy investment the culture would die for the culture is its myth incarnated in its people.

The Question

The question is how a culture ensures that its citizens will heed its demand. The answer is that it does so by immersing every moment of citizenry existence in its all-encompassing mythic propaganda system. This system molds citizenry response into the shape of the culture's demand. There is no escape from this system because it is endemic to the culture. It is the culture modeling itself and modeling is the most powerful form of procreation.

Propagation

The word propaganda comes from the Latin term *propagare*, which means to reproduce by planting. Rather than a seed, this planting is done by taking a more mature element of a living plant, such as a slip, and embedding it in fertile soil. So propagation is not an endeavor that relies on the hope that a planted seed will eventually fertilize and grow. It relies on the direct insertion of that which is already growing into that which is fertile for acceptance.

The word propaganda has drifted into negative meaning because it is often used to imply that which is false or manipulative. But this meaning is a skewed interpretation. Propaganda is nothing more than information proclaimed as worthy of acceptance. Whether it is true or false is determined by the response of those who encounter the information. Propagation is the focus of mythic maintenance in a culture. Unless a living form of the grounding myth is planted in the soil of fertile minds, it will eventually die. Propagating is a description of the act of planting. Propaganda is the mythic information being planted. Mythic maintenance is the result.

Far from being false and manipulative, propagating mythic propaganda is the action that builds and maintains cultures. Without this action and information there would be no human community; it is the glue that binds all social relating. That other cultures might be propagating myths contrary to one's own does not negate the necessity and validity of mythic propaganda and propagandizing. There is no cultural survival without this methodology.

There are five primary propaganda institutions in a culture that make up its encompassing system of mythic maintenance. In combination these institutions shape the social mind and determine social behavior. They keep the myth alive and healthy through social incarnation.

Family

The family institution is essential to mythic maintenance. Parents are mythic tutors and children are the minds fertile for their mythic propaganda. If a culture is to survive, parents must inculcate its grounding myth into their tutoring. Whatever the approach parents might use to describe the process of child-raising, the end result is mythic indoctrination. To indoctrinate is to impress with a specific point of view—which is a definition of the mythic eye.

The desired end of parenting, from the parents' point of view, is mythic duplication in their children. The notion that some parents hold that they do not indoctrinate their children, rather, they educate them to make up their own minds, is an illusion. Whatever beliefs these parents are seeking to instill in their children's mind is indoctrination. That is, it is an attempt to indelibly imprint a view of reality. That it involves becoming comfortable with exploring options and making up one's own mind is irrelevant to this imprinting. Indoctrination is the end result and not the mythic value in question.

The Goal

This desired end is made evident by the consternation parents feel when their children stray from the myth they have sought to inculcate in their minds. I retain the vivid memory of such an experience with my own parents. Although indoctrinating me in the grounding cultural myth was basic to their training, set within this myth was indoctrination in the religious myth of their devotion. Indeed, this religious myth and the cultural myth were perceived as synonymous by my parents. Much of our bonding revolved around a common commitment to these seemingly compatible myths during my early years. However, through a series of life-altering experiences, I forsook both of these myths and adopted others more suitable to my altered perspectives.

When I shared this mythic change with my parents, their repeated response was, "How could you do this to us after the way we raised you?" This complaint was an expression of mythic betrayal and one natural to the expectations of parental training. Mythic community had been lost. Inherent in this loss was a view by my parents that they had ultimately failed in their function as mythic propagators, and that I was a mythic turncoat. My parents were typical of parents everywhere in all cultures. The expectation is for children to reproduce their parental values in unerring fashion. Notions of success or failure are predicated on this expectation. It is the stuff playwrights and movie directors fondle with glee.

The Key

This experience is a metaphor of how vital mythic bonding is for the maintenance of the larger cultural community. And the foundational stage of this bonding is the mythic indoctrination inculcated into children by parents. As all builders know, what is constructed upon a foundation is only as secure as the foundation itself. Thus the key to cultural strength and survival is its mythic propagation through the family unit. The numerical or gender nature of this unit is inconsequential. As regards cultural maintenance, the only important consequence is the result of the indoctrination.

The Lamentation

When cultural leaders lament the dissolution of family values, they are, to a significant extent, lamenting the failure of parents for not properly indoctrinating their children with mythic allegiance. The myth to which they refer, of course, is always their personal perception of what is focal to cultural preservation. Nevertheless, such lamentation is indicative of how crucial the family is to a culture's mythic training system. This is why, when there is a hint of mythic change in the cultural air or of a new mythic interpretation being spoken, the finger of responsibility is usually pointed first at the family.

Summary

The family institution is foundational to the mythic training necessary to a culture's maintenance because it is the beginning point of a mythic indoctrination cycle that ends where it begins. Parents indoctrinate children, and children become parents who indoctrinate their children. Within this cycle culture has established other basic means of mythic propagation to ensure that it remains unbroken. Yet the family remains the beginning and end of this propagation cycle.

Education

So powerful is the educational institution in a culture's system of maintenance that it can often counteract the myths taught in the family. This power does not negate the family unit as the critical stage of a culture's mythic maintenance cycle. It only underscores the susceptibility of youth to propaganda and the impact of time spent in an educational process.

The Control

Awareness of this power has taught cultures to exert as much control as possible over the content of public education. Because of the nature of social liberty in a democracy, its government exerts less direct control than a totalitarian one. Nevertheless, the culture's cycle of mythic maintenance ensures a success sufficient enough to serve its purpose.

The Goal

By definition education is the process of rearing, leading, or towing. Its purpose is to take students to a prescribed destination. In a culture, this goal is exposure to the interpretations of event that inspire mythic allegiance. When this goal is fulfilled, the culture's mythic eye is transplanted in the mind of its youth.

Prior to and during World War II, the Nazi Party took control of Germany's educational system so tightly and effectively that it was able to reproduce its mythic self in the minds of the vast majority of the nation's youth, despite the impact of the family's propaganda machine. While this is a dramatic example, it only illustrates what is common practice among cultures with successful mythic education systems.

Textbooks

The basic textbooks of a culture's education system are written and chosen as agents of mythic enlightenment. And, generally, this aspect of textbooks is only revised when the culture's myth is undergoing revision or to correct perceived mythic distortions and omissions. For example, in America throughout the last half of the twentieth century, such revisions took place in regard to the lives of the founding fathers, the contributions of blacks and women, and the less noble role the nation has sometimes played in world history.

While education involves the learning of basic skills such as language, arithmetic, and science, they are taught in support of cultural necessities and not as ends to themselves—unless such ends are implied in the culture's grounding or supplementary myths.

Power

The power of education as a cultural mythic training ground lies in its expanse and time exposure during a youth's formative years when issues of identity and value development are critical. When this education ceases with what is called high school in America, the recipients tend to more readily retain their grounding mythic allegiance and to adopt the prevailing mythic views of cultural patriotism and nationalism.

The Risk

Participating in educational processes beyond the high school years in a democracy opens students to alternative ways of thinking that pose the greatest threat to the culture's mythic control. While upper levels of education are a necessity in producing leaders of mythic guidance and workers of mythic production, the exposures can also open to mythic deviance and rebellion.

Examples are the civil rebellions of university students in America during the Vietnam War and in China at Tiananmen Square in 1989. Despite the risk of exposures that might cause students to think independently, strong cultures rely heavily on the institution of education to maintain mythic allegiance. And parents with clarity about the myth they are seeking to reproduce in their children will guide these children toward institutions of higher education that reflect their own mythic views.

Summary

While the mythic training that transpires in the family institution is largely hidden and can only be relied upon as an act of social trust, the mythic training of a culture's education institution is open to a scrutiny and control that gives greater assurances of success.

Religion

Depending on citizen devotion, religion can be a strong supportive training institution in a culture's program of mythic maintenance.
Moreover, not only can it contribute to the shaping of the culture's
myth, it can serve as the core of that myth. In America, citizen devotion
to various brands of the Judeo-Christian religion exemplifies religion's
potential influence over both mythic training and shaping.

Civil Influence

Consider examples of Christianity's civil influence throughout the
nation's history:

> ➤ The capacity to have pronounced witches burned at the stake
> and public punishments of moral transgressors and disbeliev-
> ers during the nation's colonial years
> ➤ The capacity to have prayers made in the name of the Christian
> god delivered in government sessions, schools, and other pub-
> lic events
> ➤ The capacity to have legislation enacted in 1919 that prohib-
> ited the manufacture, transportation, and sale of alcoholic bev-
> erages
> ➤ The capacity to have legislation enacted and school boards
> elected denying the right to teach the scientific theory of evo-
> lution in public schools
> ➤ The capacity to have legislation enacted denying certain medi-
> cal procedures to pregnant women
> ➤ The capacity to have legislation enacted denying the gay com-
> munity the same legal and social rights accorded heterosexuals

Moral Influence

Consider examples of Christianity's moral influence throughout
the nation's history:

> ➤ The capacity to ambivalently both justify and condemn slavery
> and maintain both prejudicial and accepting attitudes toward
> black citizens
> ➤ The capacity to sustain male superiority over women in family,
> social, and political relationships
> ➤ The capacity to have legislation enacted and community codes

justified endorsing restrictive puritan morality in both public and private sexual behavior

Mythic Influence

Consider examples of Christianity's shaping and support of the nation's myth:

> ➤ The messianic concept of a universal savior nation
> ➤ The perception of America's invincibility under the leadership of its god
> ➤ The support of capitalism through its perception that the role of humans is to subdue and conquer the earth

Symbolic Imprint

The symbolic imprint of the Christian religion's influence is found:

> ➤ on the nation's coinage: "In God We Trust"
> ➤ in the nation's pledge of allegiance: "One nation under God"
> ➤ in the nation's hymns: "God shed his grace on thee"
> ➤ in the nation's swearing-in ceremonies: "So help me, God"

If America is a more subtle example of Christian mythic influence the Roman Catholicism that dominated centuries of Europe's cultures with its brutalizing and demeaning control over science, politics, economics, beliefs, and living is an obvious one. Equally as graphic are the deep prejudices of the cultural division of Christianity into Protestantism and Catholicism in parts of Ireland that have symbolized deeper political divisions.

Other Religions

But Christianity is only one religious myth that has impacted varied cultural myths. Far East cultures have been influenced by religions such as Hinduism and Buddhism. And the blurring of religion and state exemplified by Islamic cultures such as Iraq, Iran, and the Jewish state of Israel further underscore the profound influence religion can have on a culture's development, maintenance, and destiny. This is to say nothing of the worldwide turmoil created by the radicals and terrorists of Islam toward the end of the twentieth century and the beginning of the twenty-first century.

Summary

If a culture is dominated by a religious focus, then it will play a critical role in mythic training and maintenance. Moreover, its beliefs will find reflection in the primal political myth that is endemic to that culture.

Politics

The political realm is another major institution of cultural mythic maintenance. Politics originally referred to the rights and status of citizens. In present time it has come to designate the management system of government—the making of policy, supportive laws, and their enforcement and the manipulation of economics for mythic benefit. A politician is viewed as one who processes this management.

Control

To be in political control empowers to interpret, sustain, or change the meaning of the prevailing cultural myth. This is done by orating meaning and by contracting, expanding, and regulating the legal boundaries of citizen behavior. These orations and controls address both the social mind and social liberty of citizens for the purpose of mythic maintenance.

Policing

It is instructive that the word politics and the word police derive from the same generic root. To police is to ensure compliance and protect from violation. The purpose of political management is mythic policing. It is to ensure compliance to the nation's myth and to protect this myth from violation.

In what it perceives to be service to this purpose, government will create fiction, hold secrets, manipulate events and their meaning, sacrifice citizen rights, and engage both overt and covert aggressions and wars against other mythic cultures.

In this sense all national cultures are police states. This is the trade-off citizens make for government. And since myths cannot survive unless institutionalized, it has always been perceived as a worthwhile price to pay for culture's benefits. In totalitarian governments this price tends to be higher since policing actions are easily cloaked in capriciousness and secrecy. In a democracy, this price tends to be lower since policing actions must be given rationale and are more difficult to hide.

Mythic Keepers

Political parties in a culture are the keepers of the culture's myth and seek to control how the myth will find economic and policy expression—both domestically and internationally. In a totalitarianism, a single political party is usually in complete mythic control and is able to suppress all competition. In a democracy, political parties tend to focus on those aspects of the cultural myth believed to be most important to its fulfillment and maintenance.

In America, prior to the advent of the twentieth century, political parties were sometimes indistinguishable in their mythic focus. However, since the early part of the twentieth century two political parties have risen to dominance—Republicans and Democrats. Gradually these two parties have developed distinguishing tendencies brought about by their respective mythic focuses.

While these two parties may seem to agree at times on certain issues, their real focus is mythically polar—representing divergent views and goals about what's best for democracy. As such, they provide balance and correction to each other's tendency toward myopic excess and dramatize how politics become the public arena of applied mythic interpretation.

Summary

Politics is vital to mythic maintenance. It keeps the citizenry's eye focused on the practical dimensions of applying the culture's myth to the social drama. Its activities provide citizens with an opportunity to express their individual mythic views in multiple ways. It energizes the management of government. It is the visible arena of both agreement and contention around mythic interpretation and social application.

Media

The media institution is the fifth major player in mythic maintenance. Media is plural for medium, which derives from a Latin word meaning middle. Over time, the term evolved to mean instrumentality and by the mid-twentieth century had become a reference to instruments of communication. Thus media designates all basic agencies of information flow such as newspapers, magazines, books, radio, television, art, and cinema. Media is the primary tool by which:

> the cultural myth is incarnated through words and imagery
> the mythic meaning of human events is disseminated, revised, and preserved
> the conflicting interpretations of the myth's meaning are publicized
> the competing myths are exposed as threat
> the heroines and heroes of the myth are celebrated and its betrayers vilified
> the values implied in the myth and its emotional content is translated into a way of life
> the mind of the citizenry is both reflected and manipulated according to the mythic perspective of the particular media controllers

In brief, the media maintains the myth by creating and cataloguing its drama and history. Media is the theater of the myth. The shallowness and artificiality or the depth and profoundness of how the myth is processed are dependent upon the perceptions and motives of those who control the media.

Control

Thus whoever controls the instruments of media controls the power to influence the citizenry's mind and the culture's destiny. There is no objectivity involved in this enterprise. All who control media instruments are mythic creatures, and their biases are reflected through subject matter selection, editing, presentation, exposure length, censorship, and interpretation. In essence, all media are instruments of mythic propaganda whether they are played out within a totalitarianism or a democracy. The very fact that media are generally labeled as conservative, moderate, or liberal is an affirmation that they are mythic reflections.

Bias

The degree to which any media claims to be unbiased is generally the degree to which:

> the ownership sees itself as the only valid view of reality.

➤ the news it presents will be carefully crafted to fit this view of reality.

➤ the programming it airs will be selected to reflect this view of reality.

➤ its personnel will be hired because they share this view of reality

➤ all other views of reality will be treated as either twisted or false

In brief, all media claims to be unbiased reveal the embodiment of some measure of a view of reality that recognizes no legitimate alternatives. The notion that a media can exist without bias is the product of a mythic bias. History reveals that this claim has minimal support in reality.

Manipulation

The word *manipulation* roots in terms that imply the skillful handling of objects. It eventually evolved as a reference to the clever use of skills or influence. Manipulation is amoral and is inherent in the maintenance of all cultures. The media controllers of a culture create images such as friends and enemies, heroes and villains (of both genders), success and failure, good and evil, justice and inequity, strength and weakness, integrity and duplicity, masculinity and femininity, worth and valuelessness, patriotism and dishonor—all plugged into the culture's grounding myth. These images are then used to motivate citizenry commitments and actions. Thus mythic manipulation is the primary focus of media.

Politicians use media to create mythic images appealing to voters. Industry uses it to manufacture mythic product desire. Educators use it to shape mythic views and attitudes. Publishers use it to mythically titillate the public mind. Television and radio commentators use it to generate mythic feeding frenzies. Artists use it to elicit a mythic response from viewers. Cinema uses it to invent and revise mythic history. In all of this usage the media instrument remains amoral. Like any instrument, it only reflects the morality and purpose of the user.

Cover-ups

Those who control a culture's government will always use media to enhance their power, create favorable responses to their policies, and convert their violations of the culture's myth into images of its maintenance. American interference in Guatemalan politics is an example. The story revolves around the American-owned United Fruit Company.

During a period of history referred to as Yankee Dollar Diplomacy, the United Fruit Company had purchased or leased enormous tracts of land in Guatemala for the growing of crops and served as a major employer in the country's economy. With this economic leverage, combined with monetary bribery, it had acquired a significant hold over the nation's politics. It was often referred to by the country's citizenry as *el pulpo*, or the octopus. Moreover, the UFC was a major supplier of fruits, cocoa, wood, and oils for the American economy, and many Americans made huge profits through investments in the company.

In a country characterized by social and economic inequality, numerous attempts at reform had failed. However, in 1954, President Jacobo Arbenz Guzmán began initiating land and tax reforms that, if allowed to stand, would have significant negative impact on the UFC's political control and enormous profits. But some of America's most respected and highest elected and appointed government leaders were stockholders in the UFC. These leaders, using the Central Intelligence Agency, manipulated the overthrow of Guzman's government and established a new president who was against reform and favorable to the UFC's control over the economy.

Although Guzman was a nationalist, the American government manipulated the media into portraying him as a communist and American involvement as the democratic savior nation once again aiding freedom fighters throwing off the tyranny of communism. A legitimate government was overthrown, nationalist leaders expelled or killed, social and economic reforms squashed, and the exploitative United Fruit Company's profits and control preserved. It was a simple act of greed legitimized in the public eye by the clever manipulation of the media by profiting government officials to appear mythically heroic. It was a clever cover-up of a gross violation of the American democratic myth.

Exposures

There is also the other side of the coin. While media can be used to cover up mythic violations, it can also be used to expose such violations and strengthen mythic maintenance. In 1972 five men were arrested for attempting to burglarize the headquarters of the Democratic National Committee in Washington DC's Watergate complex. Members of this group claimed to be associated with the administration of then President Richard M. Nixon. Nixon denied any knowledge of the group's activities.

Over a period of two years other allegations of misconduct against the Nixon administration emerged—illegal use of campaign funds, campaign "dirty tricks," wiretapping, a secret White House intelligence unit, and the burglary of psychiatrist Daniel Ellsberg's office who had leaked the Pentagon Papers.

Eventually, Nixon's complicity in the Watergate burglary, the truth of other allegations, and his attempts at cover-up were revealed. All of this culminated in the House of Representatives passing three articles of impeachment to remove Nixon from office. Nixon resigned.

Critical to the process of probing these allegations and uncovering Nixon's complicity was the media and specifically the work of several reporters of the *Washington Post* newspaper. Aware of the media's power, at one time during his term in office, Nixon commented, "The press is the enemy." As an amoral instrument, the media can be used to both cover and expose mythic violation.

Prostration

The media, itself, is amoral. It only reflects the morality of the controller. The primal issue in respect to media freedom in American is the ownership of so much of the media by the corporate world. There are two primary reasons that have made this control possible. The first reason is that the corporate world has gained control of the democratic electoral process. This has been a willing subjugation by politicians as a trade-off for the corporate money they feel is necessary to be elected. Politicians, for the most part, have sold their soul to the company store, and the company store wants nothing less in return but laws and benefits that increase the enormity of their profits. And, in respect to media, they wish an outlet for their peculiar mythic views, which is the same as being able to exert control over the public mind.

The second reason is that a large part of the media industry itself has sold its soul to the company store. Specifically, it is that part of the media that the public most depends upon to keep it informed about what is happening in both the nation and the world. These forms of media, primarily reliant on advertising and business sponsorship for their income, prostrate before the corporate world as a subject willing to do whatever is necessary to see that this source of income is not jeopardized. Doing whatever is necessary involves not reporting news that reflects negatively on corporate products, not addressing issues that reflect negatively on corporate motivations, not expressing views that are contrary to the views of corporate ownership, and not airing anything that offends the paying sponsors. In brief, this willing control is more about what the media is pressured to not reveal as it is about what it is allowed to reveal. The reluctance of the media during the last half of the twentieth century to reveal the machinations and lies of the tobacco industry is an example. The tobacco industry was a prime source of media income.

The history of war over the past seventy years is also illustrative. It appears that when an American president decides to take the nation into war that the media rarely questions the legitimacy of this intention. Indeed, if employees of major media question such decisions, they may be in jeopardy of losing their job. Here is an example: Phil Donahue, one of the originators of the successful talk show genre on television, began hosting a program for MSNBC. However, it was a time, following 9/11, when the media was waving the flag rather than investigating reality. Donahue insisted on airing the views of people who were questioning the legitimacy of going to war against Iraq. The show was cancelled in February of 2003.

According to media analyst Rick Ellis, NBC had commissioned a study of the future of the news media. A part of internal communications responding to that report was a memo indicating that Donahue posed a problem because he might present a "difficult public face for NBC in a time of war." This is a peek into the world of media that is minimally driven by its public obligation to investigate and question with maximum objectivity. It suggests literally that showmanship is a higher priority concern than the objectivity provoked by alternative views. Or to say it from another angle, any program that might jeopardize television ratings and, thus, affect product sales, is of greater concern to most media than its ethical obligations to the public. The conclusion is that profit will inevitably trump truth.

Moreover, due to the proliferation of television channels and the intense competition to capture and maintain audience loyalty, the constant invasion of the citizenry's private life and the insufferable and time-consuming feeding frenzies over the innocuous and inane all attest to the fact that this media seems more interested in creating the news than reporting the news. In brief, most anything will be used to invent newsworthiness and sustain a story for the sake of public attention.

The First Amendment

Guidance by the first amendment continues to remain, for the most part, the role of independent media agents who have diligently refused or minimized the influence of the corporate world on their capacity to speak truth to power without being bankrupted. Unfortunately, there are fewer and fewer of these types of media because of both economic pressures and the failure of the public to give due diligence to their own rights to be served by a media that values the first amendment above the bottom line of profit.

No one will deny that the media, whatever its form, resides within a very complicated and slippery world of ethical and moral decision-making in reference to its reason for being. However, this world has been created by the control and greed motivations of corporations and the willing compliance of politicians to permit the public's best interests to be subjected to corporate interests.

Media, especially its visual forms, will cease prostrating itself before the corporate world when it decides that it has a deep moral obligation to democracy to actually serve its legitimate role as the investigator of reality and the reporter of perceived truth and when the American public decides it is preferable to pay for a free press rather than being the pawns of a press in bondage to corporate greed and the reality views of corporate ownership. The trick is how to address this problem when it is the corporate world that largely owns the media. The answer lies in denying the corporate world the opportunity of monetary influence over the election of politicians. When this happens, lawmakers will create laws that protect the public's right to a media devoted to the first amendment.

Revolution

A revolution in communications is taking place around the globe.

Its creator is the computer assisted by the satellite and a growing body of attendant and supportive technologies. The uniqueness of the computer is that while most media information flows one way from source to recipient, the computer transforms the user into both source and recipient. The computer:

> ➤ has opened and generated vast information markets that make it far more difficult to control the social mind through withholding and manipulating material.

> ➤ has made it possible to market mythic views without resorting to permission from established media controllers.

> ➤ has made it possible to cross international boundaries and communicate directly with entities of different mythic cultures.

> ➤ has eliminated time as a consequence in mythic information flow.

> ➤ has transformed the technological means of imaging mythic information.

> ➤ has brought the world of information to the fingertips of the mythic user.

> ➤ has facilitated mythic communication between people who would otherwise never make contact.

These are just a few of its impacts limited to mythic information flow. Other than the depersonalization of human relationships, no one knows what the ultimate impact of computer technology will be beyond its immediate and profound revolution of mythic information flow. And as the twenty-first century begins, no one has a clue as to how to control this information flow in a democratic society or how to regulate its truthfulness or falseness. It remains the unknown factor in media's influence over mythic maintenance.

Summary

The influence of the media over a culture's mythic destiny is summarized by a quotation from Learned Hand, twentieth-century United States federal judge. The statement was made in 1942, prior to the cultural domination of television and the arrival of the computer and other media-enhancing technology. However, its essence remains true:

The hand that rules the press, the radio, the screen, and the far-spread magazine rules the country.

Conclusion

As Ruth Benedict (*Patterns of Culture*) observes:

Culture is not a biologically transmitted complex.

Culture's primary means of transmission are the institutions of the family, education, religion, politics, and the media. These means combine in every culture into some metaphorical Uncle Sam with pointed finger demanding the energies of its citizens for the sustenance of its own life. It is the citizenry's response to this pointed demand that not only maintains the culture but gives it animation of being.

History makes no judgment about the being of those cultures that have inhabited its annals. It only attests to a single undeniable truth:

All culture is of myth, by myth, and for myth.

Most people are shaped to the form of their culture because of the enormous malleability of their original endowment. They are plastic to the molding force of the society into which they are born… In any case the great mass of individuals take quite readily the form that is presented to them.
—Ruth Benedict

Culture is always engaged in a vast conspiracy to preserve itself—at the expense of the new demands of each new generation.
—John Haynes Holmes

3

The Wizardry of Worth
(The Great Cultural Con)

In America, everybody is, but some are more than others.
—Gertrude Stein

Self-esteem isn't everything; it's just that there's nothing without it.
—Gloria Steinem

An Illustration

During lunch hour on April 20, 1999, Eric Harris and Dylan Klebold began a shooting spree at Columbine High School in Jefferson County, Colorado. Armed with an arsenal of guns and bombs, they killed thirteen people and injured scores of others before killing themselves. Their victims seem to have been selected at random.

According to various media reports, this rampage of violence had been meticulously planned for months with expectations of executing a significant part of the school's population, blowing up its buildings, savaging the local neighborhood, and hijacking an airplane to be crashed into a large metropolis. It was a plan of monumental design that reflected the scope of their rage and the depth of their disillusionment.

In the middle of conservative well-off suburbia, the apparent senselessness of their rampage evoked shocked cries of "Why?" Some of the proposed answers have been:
- ➤ the media's posturing of violence as the panacea for every human problem
- ➤ parents who seemed unaware of their children's inner consciousness or outward behavior

➤ a school administration supposedly out of touch with the deeper currents of student hostility running through the school's rosy atmosphere

➤ exposure of youth to antisocial imagery, models of violence, and games of death offered through cyberspace technology

➤ the cruel behavior of cliquish students that encouraged a sense of rejection and alienation from the mainstream of the school's social drama

➤ easy access to guns for use as agents in resolving issues of human conflict and expressing emotions of discontent

Many of these proposed causes reflect social failures in a culture obsessed with the right to ignore the consequences of its lifestyle. And in combination, they create an influence that could foster mindless violence. But no one can say with certainty which are the culprits because such certainty is hidden in the killers' deaths.

However, there is a seedbed from which sprouts everyone's response to the influences of life, however neglectful, degrading, or cruel they may be. This seedbed is one's perception of self-worth. This perception gives meaning to life's influences and translates them into social behavior. A denominator common to the Columbine killers and many of their student predecessors and copycats elsewhere in the nation is low self-esteem that easily converts into views of alienation and a sense of being misfits. Seething beneath the surface of living such views and feelings are either resolved in some way beneficial to social adjustment or they seek to erupt in destructive behavior toward self and others.

The depth of Harris and Klebold's sense of alienation was reflected in their tentative association with a group called the Trench Coat Mafia—a loosely knit community of students who administered mild therapy to each other by using the misfit label as a bond of mutual acceptance. But such mild therapy was obviously insufficient to address their profound self-worth issues. And this profoundness opened them to the dark side of human nature that focused on Nazism, violence, and death. The raw material being shaped in this dark kingdom was hate and revenge—material so often molded by humans into affirmations of self-worth. The plan was to translate this material into celebrative action on the 110th anniversary of Adolph Hitler's birth.

Harris and Klebold felt that they had been denied entry into the school's social world of acceptance. Other students had exacerbated their bitterness by pelting them with missiles of contempt in the form of words and rocks. On April 20, they turned the tables and denied students their lives by pelting them with missiles of their own contempt in the form of bullets and bombs. It was a frenzy of killing done with reveling and gleeful abandon. In wielding the power to grant life or death they took on the superior worth of gods. And finally they carried this worth-inducing power to its ultimate limit and killed themselves. It is irrelevant whether their actions were designed to affirm superiority or uplift inferiority. The bottom line of either motivation is self-worth.

Harris and Klebold are examples of the consuming rage that can be generated in a society that has externalized the social worth of its people and then denied them its access. The broad and bold plan of revenge they had conceived went beyond the students who had taunted them to embrace the innocent of the school, its neighborhood, and the nation. It accused the entire culture—and rightfully so—for their actions were stimulated by something endemic to our society that encourages moral and violent pathologies.

The Principle

There is a principle that has operated in all cultures throughout history that is innate to both human being and human relating:

All behavior is employed in the service of self-worth.

Consider the following examples:
- Friendship and love: We pursue these because they are the human relationships most likely to affirm our worth despite our own views or behaviors (marriage).
- Heroic action: We engage such because our own sense of worth demands it and because its acknowledgment is the ultimate affirmation of our worth that society grants (war and peace).
- Dangerous adventure: We engage such because in overcoming its life-threatening obstacles we affirm our own self-worth (Mt. Everest).
- Social fame: We pursue this because in its achievement society adores us as worthy above itself (Hollywood).

> ➤ Social position: We pursue this because society attaches extra worth to its attainment (presidents).
> ➤ Material wealth: We pursue this because society has declared its amassing as a measure of unusual worth (millionaires).
> ➤ Social power: We pursue this because society looks upon its capacity to influence as worth-affirming (talk-show hosts).
> ➤ The best: We pursue becoming this because in its achievement society will heap upon us accolades of superior worth (sports).
> ➤ Special achievement: We pursue this because society affirms its attainment as announcing elevated worth (Nobel Prize).

There are no exceptions to this principle that all behavior is employed in the service of self-worth. Even what appears on the surface to be an exception, upon examination, will yield itself as an affirmation.

Suicide is an example. In far Eastern cultures, suicide has sometimes been viewed as an act that bestows special worth or that counteracts the loss of worth. In the west, suicide is often an act that is prompted by a sense of self-worth emptiness, as an attempt to avoid the shame of a sense of diminished self-worth, or is utilized because the self is seen as too worthy to endure unavoidable pain. The Harris and Klebold suicides were a statement of worth-affirming control over their existence. Whatever the motivation, the act of denying one's own life is profoundly tied to self-worth as the focal issue of human existence.

Cultural Enticement

The problem inherent in every culture is how to entice its citizens to willfully give their energies to sustaining its existence. The crux of this problem is that citizens do not share equally in a culture's social and economic benefits and, therefore, are not equally motivated. Such inequality of benefit is exemplified in a culture's class system.

The Question

The question is how a culture can motivate its citizens to more freely give their energies to its preservation despite such inequalities of benefit.

The following are all ways a culture's system seeks to entice energy from its citizens for this purpose:

> ➢ Rewards for mythic compliance and punishments for mythic deviation
> ➢ Propaganda maintenance system of family, education, religion, politics, and media
> ➢ Appeal to patriotism
> ➢ Use of the concept of enemy

However, like parents offering various incentives to motivate their children toward supportive obedience of the family's myth, cultures know that these methods are powerful but not foolproof. Such motivational schemes may elicit unpredictable responses. So cultures wish for a more certain guarantee of energy support from their citizens than these motivations can normally provide.

The totalitarian government approaches this problem by drawing energy from its citizens through the power of fear and coercion. But the democratic government, by virtue of its designs of social liberty, cannot successfully rely on such means. However, whatever the form of a culture's government the bottom line remains: the more willingly citizens give their energies to cultural maintenance, the more stable and viable the culture's preservation.

The Con

The dominating answer as to how to gain the willful energy support of citizens seems to be shared by all historical cultures irrespective of their form of government. It is a remarkably clever ruse that has worked like a charm throughout human history. And what makes it so clever is that it exploits the inequality of social benefit a culture metes out by sustaining these inequalities and using them to motivate citizens to give their energies toward the culture's preservation. In brief, the citizenry is conned into cultural support. Here is how the con works:

> ➢ The citizenry's self-worth is externalized and converted into a social commodity for purchase by attaching it to achieved stations of social status.
> ➢ The purchase price of this commodity is the citizen's energy investment in an upward mobility of social status that gradually and incrementally adds to their greater social worth.
> ➢ Since being viewed as worthy is the primary driving force of

human existence, citizens freely give their energies toward this externalized achievement.
➢ Since the possibilities of achievement cannot be exhausted, the motivation for achievement remains high, along with citizen energy investment.

The end result of this con is an enormous amount of citizen energy and resources freely and continuously expended toward maintaining and preserving the culture's viability.

This con initiates a self-sustaining cycle of citizenry involvement passed on from one generation to the next as the normal way of life in a culture. It becomes a part of the culture's system of reality.

Cultural Limits

This con has found obvious expressions in world cultures since the advent of those freedoms characteristic of the twentieth century. However, it seems to have been and is presently exercised in all historical cultures irrespective of existing strictures. Even in cultures where rigid class or caste systems have decreed the starting point of its citizen's social worth pursuit or imposed boundaries on the fulfillment of the pursuit, the con has worked. Citizens simply shift their focus to:
➢ improving or maintaining their worth status within the imposed boundaries
➢ breaching the imposed boundaries
➢ rebelling against the boundaries in an attempt to elevate the social worth of an entire class or caste
➢ recreating an entire cultural government with new structures more favorable to social worth status and achievement

History seems to reveal that strictures imposed upon the achievement of externalized social worth does not diminish the desire or effort of citizens for its fulfillment. Strictures only create the bitterness of deprivation and fuel the determination to thwart the prohibitions. Boundaries only encourage the application of human ingenuity and instill the willingness to die for the sake of their breaching.

Whatever the cost, people will seek the means to be viewed as socially worthy since such is a desire endemic to human nature. It is this desire that has given shape to the entire human drama. And this drama has been directed by perceptions of the inequitable distribution of social worth and the constant attempts at correcting this inequity. And the problem that fuels the drama is that no culture has ever been an equal opportunity employer as regards social worth status.

All Cultural Governments

The cultural con works in all forms of government, albeit in different ways. In a democracy the greater the social liberties of a culture, the greater the appeal of the con. Expanded social liberty means expanded opportunity and easier access to the social worth promise of upward mobility. Thus citizens are more readily enticed to invest their energies in procuring an upgraded worth status. Moreover, expanded social liberty offers unlimited possibilities in this procurement and keeps citizenry vision glued to the prize. The compatibility of social liberty and the con's promise in a democracy creates the illusion of synonymity.

While the con is most enticing in a democracy, it still works in a totalitarianism despite its suppression of social liberty. Those in control invest inordinate amounts of energy in maintaining their status of upscaled worth by suppressing the opportunities of advancement of other citizens. Those out of control invest inordinate amounts of energy in gaining a greater status of worth by seeking to overcome this suppression.

The energy investment by the suppressors is to maintain and preserve the viability of the culture. The energy investment of the suppressed is not to overthrow the culture—although perhaps its government—but to expand their opportunities within the culture to improve their social worth. As history shows, leaders in a totalitarianism can be replaced, and even if a person is on the bottom of the social worth scale, there are ways to move upward toward the top.

Whatever the form of government, a culture can use the con to energize itself with citizen support.

The Key

The key to the con is the creation of an artificial social worth that substitutes for any concept of an innate human worth standing by itself. Divest the con of this substitution, and it collapses from lack of motivating power.

In Western cultures, the dominance of the institutionalized version of Christianity has leant credence to this con because it uses the same ruse to enhance its own preservation. Its key is the declaration that all humans are born sinfully unworthy and are impotent to change this condition. However, it also declares that if people will submit to its scheme of external redemption from this plight, they will be instantly awarded a full worth from the religion's god.

While national cultures, in using the con, normally begin with a zero concept of citizen worth that can be immediately enhanced by privileged birth or built up though accumulated achievement, Christianity begins with a negative concept of human worth that can be wiped out instantaneously. These may appear contradictory but they share two vital similarities:

> ➤ Human worth is a commodity that is imputed from outside the individual.
> ➤ The individual must remain faithful to the imputing agent for this worth to be sustained.

Although gradual realization of worth and instantaneous realization of worth are different methods of attainment, they are mutually supportive in that both educate the citizenry that human worth is a commodity of import rather than an innate endowment of birth. This also leads to a compartmentalization of living where a person can become totally worthy within the religious context while only becoming gradually worthy within the cultural context. These two concepts are not incompatible since the arenas and payoffs are different, as well as the methods of attainment.

Whatever their differences, the key to both is the same and both collapse without this key—the substitution of an imported human worth for an innate human worth.

The American Version

Two social inventions made the birth of America unique in immediate human history. One was the invention of a peculiar form of democracy that recognized the political equality of white male citizens. This was a remarkable evolution in the prevailing standards of political privilege. Not only was royalty eliminated, but a sense of trust in commoners was elevated.

The other invention was the American Dream—a designer label for the great cultural con. While the American Dream embodied this con, it was also remarkable in its innovation of application. As a rule, our national ancestors immigrated from countries where human worth was decreed by the accidents of birth. Tight class systems determined the level of worth accorded to each citizen. Royalty was at the top of the worthometer scale, followed by "those to the manor born." The rest of the citizenry was graded downward from these top levels.

When America was born, royalty was eliminated from the worthometer scale, but class structures of graded worth remained. These structures continued to be tied to status and wealth. However, the founding fathers espoused the radical notion that those on the lower rungs should be able to climb to higher rungs by achieving economic and social success. Thus, the American Dream was born—the prospect of true upward mobility. In keeping with the key of the cultural con, the innate worth of citizens is externalized and converted into a commodity of purchase. The essence of the American Dream is that a greater social worth is available to anyone willing to work for its achievement.

Since American democracy and the American Dream were born of the same revolutionary womb, they have been viewed as synonymous. This has been to the misfortune of democracy because this sense of synonymy keeps the essential problems of the American Dream hidden behind the veneer of democracy's spirit and conscience. There are at least four of these problems.

Problem One: The Lie

The first problem is revealed by separating the American Dream's truth from its lie. Its truth is that American democracy does offer opportunities of economic and social betterment through personal achievement. Its lie is that this achievement confers human worth. That this is a lie can only be affirmed by the acknowledgment that human worth is a confirmation of birth rather than of achievement. But once this acknowledgment is made, then the lie of the American Dream is exposed.

Its Promise

Its promise is exposed as false. The social worth meted out by the

American Dream is geared to one's level of wealth or status. The goal of pursuing the American Dream is a maximum accumulation of social worth. This means getting to the top rung of wealth or status—unless one is satisfied with a lesser worth. But there is only so much room at the top. Everybody can't be a queen bee because it means eliminating the positions of the worker bees that make the existence of the queen bees possible. If everyone was upper class, there would be no lower classes to generate the wealth that sustains the upper class. If everyone was a president, there would be no superior worth to be gained in attaining the position. Thus, despite the American Dream's promise, only a few can ever realize its fuller possibility. For the majority of the population, the promise of the American Dream is false and will remain so.

Its Premise

The American Dream's premise is also exposed as false. This premise is that the culture's democratic structures grant all citizens equal opportunity to move upward in wealth and status. But this premise defies reality. Race, gender, genetics, economics, education, family, life circumstance, and luck all conspire to guarantee that the opportunities of upward mobility will be grossly unequal for individual citizens. To compare the privileges of upward mobility of those born into wealth with those born into poverty is hardly an affirmation of equal opportunity. Because of the gross inequalities of human existence, most citizens will remain in the station of their birth—despite their best efforts to move upward.

The difference in ratio between those who are at the top in either wealth or status and those on the lower rungs has always been immense. This difference speaks to the improbability of the average citizen ever reaching the top. Such an attainment is akin to winning the lottery—it is possible but highly unlikely. Only a few will become millionaires, the country's president, a movie star, a national hero, a famous celebrity, or win the Nobel Prize. If the premise of the American Dream is true then these few are more worthy than the rest of us.

For every success story told to validate the American Dream, thousands of failure stories can be told to invalidate it. No promise or premise can overcome the realities of inaccessibility. The premise of the American Dream is false and will remain so.

The Compensation

When citizens buy into the lie of the American Dream and then realize they can never attain a satisfying amount of social worth through any recognized means of status, they will invent social compensations. These compensations will be external worth declarations designed to mask a sense of internal worth deficit. One of the easiest of these compensations is to invest in some form of social superiority. Such inventions require no justification other than the desire for their elevating support. And they can be created from any perceived value at hand—race, gender, class, religion, nationality, etc. Moreover, as self-perceptions, there is no argument against them except that of an alternative conscience. They are self-sustaining.

These compensating inventions often become so crucial to perceptions of worth that they are converted into crusades intended to heighten social standing by suppressing that of those who do not measure up to its built-in prejudice. This is the irony of all such compensation ploys: in order to increase the social worth of the inventor they must decrease the social worth of others. And this plugs into the irony of all externalized social worth ploys such as the lie of the American Dream—their very endorsement, of necessity, militates against mutual human respect. Thus, in order to affirm one's own full worth, the full worth of others must be denied. They encourage the violation of the democratic spirit and discourage the valuation of civilized relationships. In brief, as long as America subscribes to the lie of the American Dream, it can never attain a true democracy built on the notion of egalitarianism.

Problem Two: Unrealizability

The second problem with the lie of the American Dream is that it can never be fully realized irrespective of its level of attainment. It is a metaphorical carrot extended on a stick dangling just beyond the reach of the goat's grasp. It motivates hunger but never fully satisfies. If wealth is a measure of social worth, then one million dollars is not as good as ten million, and one billion is even better. If status is a measure of social worth, then having a little of it is not as good as having a lot of it, and even better is being famous. The point is that there is no end to trying to find fulfillment because there is always more of both wealth and status to be achieved.

Satisfaction

Moreover, there is always someone ahead who has accumulated a greater measure of social worth and someone behind who is threatening to catch up. One can never accumulate enough social worth to satisfy the hunger as long as there is more available on the table. There can be no ultimate satisfaction.

A Metaphor

Pursuing the American Dream is like investing in the stock market. I trade my life—time, energy, talents—for social worth commodities. These commodities are subject to the whims of the cultural marketplace:

> ➢ My social worth rises and falls with fluctuation of market need.
> ➢ My social worth may be bought or sold by those with greater marketplace resources.
> ➢ My social worth may be manipulated by secret deals.
> ➢ My social worth may drop to rock bottom but has no attainable ceiling.

Because my social worth is external to my being, it is external to my control. I live constantly on the edge of boom or bust. Bears and bulls tromp through my existence with unpredictability. Each morning I awake to the possibility of abundance or bankruptcy. In brief, as long as I rely on fulfilling the American Dream to assure my social worth, its level and retention remain an unpredictable gamble.

Problem Three: Corruption

The third problem with the lie of the American Dream is that it breeds corruption. Since being viewed as worthy is the fundamental desire of human existence, the natural tendency of this desire is to take precedent over all other considerations. Because the American Dream harnesses this desire to its goal of achieved social worth, the ethic of the American Dream becomes a me-first selfishness, and the morality of the American Dream becomes a dog-eat-dog utilitarianism.

The Cesspool

While this ethic and morality may invest the structures of culture with citizen energy and stimulate an increase in the gross national product, it also encourages the cultural drama to become a cesspool of personal, social, business, and political corruption.

> ➤ It corrupts human relationships by viewing people as utilitarian commodities.
> ➤ It corrupts the spiritual quality of living by replacing its necessity with material values.
> ➤ It corrupts the human justice system by dispensations based on wealth and status.
> ➤ It corrupts human integrity by encouraging dishonesty, deceit, and bribery.
> ➤ It corrupts business practice by placing money and status above all other human concerns.
> ➤ It corrupts work incentive by rewarding *quid pro quo* favoritism over actual accomplishment.
> ➤ It corrupts government by converting its function into a status-imaging salon and a representative-for-hire market.
> ➤ It corrupts the democratic process by elevating personal achievement over the common good.

End and Means

In brief, the notion that social worth is an achievement rather than a birthright promotes an attitude that the end justifies the means, and inclines its devotees to operate from the dark side of their human nature.

Problem Four: Trivialization

The fourth problem with the lie of the American Dream is that in its conversion of human worth into an externalized commodity of purchase, it trivializes that which is most sacred in human existence.

It trivializes our most meaningful and life-altering experiences by diverting our energies away from their pursuit. While our deepest values and profoundest connections are tied to our relationship with the inner being of other people, the lie of the American Dream shifts the devotion of our energies to the shallow values of materialism and the superficial connections of status. This shift is from that which gives life to that which mocks life. It gives utility preeminence over spirit. Thus it fosters a life empty of spiritual content and devoid of inner spiritual responsibility. The result is demeaning attitudes and actions reflective of this emptiness and irresponsibility.

In finality, the lie of the American Dream asks us to abandon those meanings that are our grandest affirmation of humanness in favor of an artificial worth geared to the most shallow and superficial of human experiences.

Problem Consequences

The lie of the American Dream trivializes that desire which is the wellspring of human existence—the yearning to be honored as worthy by virtue of being alive. By divesting humans of this innate sense of worth, life ceases to be an inner search for deeper and more satisfying meanings and relationships and becomes an outer search for the elusive worth commodity—a potential soap opera of gains and losses, of acceptances and rejections, all infused with emotional frenzy.

When the losses and rejections are perceived as overwhelming, we are opened to that rage of deprivation that fosters irrational attitudes and behaviors. We become consumed with hate for those who seem to have what we do not. We enter a desperateness that may resort to any means of procurement—no matter how unreasonable, neurotic, or pathological.

The end result can be violence and destruction as is exemplified in the deliberately planned and executed revenge and murder rampage of Eric Harris and Dylan Klebold. One underpinning of such action is believing the lie and accepting its indictment that human life itself is trivial. And one motivation is to leave life in a grand burst of artificial worth glory; to impose an immortal signature upon the culture; to become a legend of the lie. To assume that the lie's trivialization of human worth is a minor matter is to misunderstand the force that has shaped human history.

Evolution

The concept of democracy as a form of government implies a political equality of citizenry self-rule. The ideal of democracy as a spirit of guidance implies a social equality of citizenry status. Government is an embodiment of mythic concept. Ideal is the vision of this embodiment's conscience. While the best of worlds would find a compatible marriage of government and ideal, this is rarely the case in human affairs.

Normally, for a democracy, the conscience of a culture's mythic ideal is far ahead of its government's embodiment and its people's attitudes and practices. To ask for a closure of this gap is to ask for both the government and people of a culture to behave with integrity and nobility. And therein is the crux of the American story—the struggle to rise to the noble claims of the democratic conscience.

Limited Enlightenment

Our founding fathers were representatives of the educated cultural elite of the colonies. When they conceived the American brand of democracy, they were reflecting an enlightened vision. Given the context of the times, it was a bold and scary assumption that the common man could make informed political decisions. To include women, let alone slaves, was beyond the capacities of their level of enlightenment.

Unleashed Spirit

However, once unleashed, the spirit of equality implied in the governance of democracy produces a natural urge toward leveling the political playing field. This urge has created a national drama of continuous conflict intended to legalize the political rights of all qualified inhabitants. This drama is marked with milestones along the evolutional path the spirit of democracy has pioneered. The founding fathers would be aghast at what this evolution has wrought.

It took almost a hundred years and the Civil War in the 1860s to free the slaves and establish the constitutional right of black males to political equality. It took almost a hundred and fifty years and the suffrage movement of the early 1900s to establish the constitutional right of women to political equality.

Despite these legal victories, both blacks and women were denied rightful entry into that true part of the American Dream that offered the opportunities of upward mobility. The American Dream remained the game of a white male clubhouse where women and blacks could do service but not play. It appeared that white males would have to be forced into the nobilities of the democratic spirit's conscience.

This forcing visibly began with the upheavals of World War II and culminated in the dramas of the civil rights movement and the feminist movement of the last half of the twentieth century. Yet even with the clubhouse door ajar, many white males continue to practice blocking actions. Why has it been so hard for white males to engage the spirit and conscience of democracy?

The Corruption of Nobility

The deeper answer resides in the lie of the American Dream. The notion that social worth is acquired, while being incompatible with the conscience of democracy, is not incompatible with the sense of social worth superiority spawned by the American Dream's lie. White males created the American Dream for white males, and inherent in its creation was an automatic status of superiority on the worthometer scale over women and blacks.

Most men, throughout American history, have preferred to give their devotions to the American Dream's lie than to the conscience of democracy. After all, the democratic conscience suggests that they behave toward women and blacks as equals, while the lie of the American Dream suggests they rightfully belong in the catbird seat of superiority. The spirit of white male superiority has been domination and suppression. For those who perceive themselves to be kings of worth, it is a humbling experience to dismount the royal steed and walk with servants as equals. It requires a nobility that denounces the spirit of superiority and affirms the spirit of democracy.

The lie of the American Dream does not encourage such nobility. The spirit of the American Dream's lie is worth-discrimination and assumed superiority. Thus, the lie of the American Dream encourages the same domination and suppression as the spirit of white male superiority. Together they encourage ruthlessness in both gaining and maintaining the status of superior worth. This has guaranteed that blacks and women must wage hard battle in both acquiring the basic right of democratic political privilege and the implied right of honored human worth.

In this battle, it is important to note that the dark character traits that white males have often employed in seeking to maintain their position of social superiority are not peculiar expressions of the male ego. They are human capabilities and not gender specific. When women are given the same upward mobility opportunities as men, many will be equally as ruthless toward their own gender.

Every human is capable of both nobility and ignobility. Whichever gets our energies is determined by the myth that drives our life and the goals it engenders. All behavior is employed in the service of self-worth—whether it be acknowledging it, getting it, or enhancing it. If worth is viewed as a social commodity, then people will pay whatever price is necessary for its purchase—no matter what the cost to self and others. It is the lie of the American Dream that remains the great corruptor of human character and the great destructor of human relationships.

The Specter

Behind every battle for democratic equality in American history looms the specter of this lie. It is the archenemy of the democratic spirit and conscience—eschewing the worth of others in favor of personal status. It is the archenemy of the democratic process—eschewing the common good in favor of personal gain. This lie has created a nation of schizophrenics who on the one hand champion the virtues of democracy, while on the other hand champion a view of socially acquired worth that denies these virtues. While America has been a culture offering its people the social opportunity innate to the democratic process, it has not been a culture offering its people the social worth innate to the democratic spirit.

Conclusion

The assumption behind the great cultural con is that citizens will not freely gift their energies to the culture's well-being without artificial inducement. While this may be true in cultures where social liberties are suppressed, we do not know if it is true in the American culture where social liberties are championed.

And we do not know this in America because the spirit of democracy has never been unleashed from the lie of the American Dream. And we will not know the answer until the lie is killed and replaced with the acknowledged social worth of every citizen.

If the privileges of democracy are not sufficient within themselves to motivate a willful gifting of those citizen energies necessary for its viable preservation, then it is not a myth worthy of citizen devotion.

In brief, if democracy cannot stand upon its own spirit and conscience without the artificial support of the American Dream's lie, then failure will be its eventual destiny.

When America determines to alter its myth by eliminating the great cultural con, then the social context that produced Eric Harris and Dylan Klebold, and their likes, will also be profoundly altered.

[Democracy] is a great word, whose history, I suppose, remains unwritten because that history has yet to be enacted.
—Walt Whitman

All the ills of democracy can be cured by more democracy.
—Al Smith

When we can make democracy work, we won't have to force it down other people's throats. If it is really such a good idea, and if they can see it working, they'll steal it.
—Dick Gregory

ADDENDUM I

Addressing the Columbine Syndrome
(Within the School System)

The issues that have emerged from the tragedy of Columbine cannot be separated from the lie of the American Dream because Columbine is the lie's child. Task forces have reported on what must be done to prevent another such incident. Their recommendations include:

- greater parental involvement in their children's life and the local school's activities
- greater control by teachers over the school's media systems
- a greater attunement of students, teachers, and administration to critical signs of discontent
- hotlines encouraging students to inform on the attitudes and misconduct of other students

> ➤ the presence of more security guards
> ➤ a more thorough security system to prevent the entry of weapons into school buildings
> ➤ availability of trained professionals to aid students with social relationship problems

None of these suggestions attempt to address the profound issues of self-worth inherent in the social makeup of school politics or the subtle provocations of the lie of the American Dream embedded in the school's curriculum. In brief, as is the case of the larger society's response, the focus is on symptoms rather than cause.

If our culture wishes to seriously address the Columbine Syndrome, it must look to two sources:

> ➤ The content of textbooks in schools
> ➤ The atmosphere created by teachers and the administration of schools

Both of these sources carry profound weight in the diminishment of the syndrome. And these sources must look more to a long-term impact than an immediate one. Dealing with symptoms is necessary but will not ensure anything but a temporary decrease of symptoms. Dealing with the cause is essential because it will not only decrease the symptoms but diminish the possibility of event occurrence. The cause is the crucial issue and it is the issue of self-worth from which rises behavior.

Textbooks

Adequately dealing with the cause through textbooks entails separating the true vision of opportunity in the American Dream from its lie of externally achieved social worth. This separation can be promoted by a mandatory school curriculum at every grade level that:

> ➤ acknowledges the innate self-worth of every human
> ➤ recognizes the real meaning and contribution of social achievement to both the individual and nation
> ➤ explores not only the political opportunities of democracy but the necessities of embodying its spirit and conscience in social covenant
> ➤ revises American history and reveals it as a democratic struggle

to overcome the degenerate morality and destructive behavior spawned by the lie of the American Dream

➤ releases students from the programmed schizophrenia of simultaneously supporting democracy while supporting its dream-lie enemy

➤ encourages students to appreciate the necessity of differences and the contribution differences make to a vital democracy

➤ teaches students how to respond to and mediate issues of self-worth that pose a threat to both themselves and a healthy social drama

Atmosphere

But such a curriculum cannot fully achieve its purpose unless it is modeled in the relationship and teaching styles of a school's teachers, administration, and other employees. It is this embodiment that enhances the power of curriculum to shape the attitudes and behaviors of students. Thus it is incumbent upon these models to:

➤ affirm their own personal sense of self-worth despite the demeaning attempts of culture to force them into pigeonholes of downgraded social value

➤ understand the necessity of a system of hierarchical responsibility in the school system while concurrently treating all personnel with the respect of equality of worth

➤ announce the social worth of every student irrespective of race, gender, or class

➤ refuse to confer extra social worth upon students because of innate endowments or extra-curricular achievements

➤ clearly distinguish between dispensing the rewards of academic achievement or failure from a synonymity with adding or subtracting social worth

➤ adequately deal with all attitudes and actions on school property that imply a superior status of social worth

➤ arrange parent-teacher-administration experiences that empower parents to address the self-worth issues of their children beyond the classroom

While such an approach will not satisfy those who wish immediate solutions, it could, given time, produce generations of students who might not succumb to the arrogance that fuels the pathologies of violence. It might, also, eventually produce generations of citizens who will not succumb to the moral degeneration encouraged by the lie of the American Dream.

A Chicago school teacher was told that her class would be host to a mystery visitor. Upon learning the identity of this visitor she was ecstatic:

> *I thought it would be someone like Al Gore or Clinton. But Michael Jordan? This is the biggest thing that's ever happened to this school.*

The perception, by a teacher, that a celebrity visit is the biggest thing that has ever happened in the life of a school speaks to two issues:

> ➤ A value system that reflects the perversions of the lie of the American Dream
> ➤ A desperate need for an event that would externally grace the social worth of both teacher and students

It also underscores the profound necessity for curriculum and modelers that can alter the atmosphere in our schools from that of worth-hunger to that of worth-fulfillment. A celebrity visit is an artificial snack dispensed at random. What is needed is real meals dispensed daily.

Conclusion

The Columbine tragedy is the American tragedy writ small. Whatever may be the legitimate glories of the American democratic culture, a trail of human destruction runs through its history. This trail of destruction is largely the social ruination produced by our cultural devotion to the lie of the American Dream. Until the lie that has created this destruction is unmasked as a causal factor, the destruction will continue. And our school system is both focal and critical to this unmasking.

ADDENDUM II

Understanding Suicide Bombers
(Current World Peril)

Sometimes I wonder if suicides aren't in fact the sad guardians of the meaning of life.

—Vaclav Havel

There are many who dare not kill themselves for fear of what the neighbors will say.

—Cyril Connolly

A Ripe Time

People will believe the most atrocious, abasing, aberrant, appalling, asinine, and astringent notions as long as they affirm their sense of self-worth. Indeed, the greater the self-perceived need for such affirmation, the greater can be the appeal of absurdity. Age is irrelevant to this appeal. It is the level of circumstantial ignorance that informs susceptibility. Thus the isolation of the individual from alternative educational experience creates a highly susceptible state for any form of indoctrination that offers imputed self-worth.

However, while it is ignorance rather than age that is the ground of susceptibility, there is a span of life that is fertile with circumstantial ignorance. It is the age from birth through the twenties. This ground of fertility is so rife with the possibility of ignorance isolation that it will readily entertain notions about self-destruction as a source of super forms of endowed self-worth accompanied by super forms of special rewards. Thus, this age span has been the educating space for extremely radical and grossly antisocial notions about self-worth.

The nature of the educating system being used is irrelevant. It can as easily be a cultural political system such as that which produced the youthful Japanese kamikaze pilots during World War II as it can be a cultural religious system as that producing modern-day Muslim suicide bombers. It is not the system, itself, as much as it is the boundaries of circumstantial ignorance the system imposes on its believers.

The susceptibility of the natural ignorance of this age span is further compounded by an additional susceptibility, namely, that of natural idealism. Idealism is the vision of a flawless paradigm of reality. It is the appeal of a model or archetype that should exist and, in the mind of the holder, could exist if engaged with an equally flawless commitment. Idealism is an inducement in all human socializing. Its vision can be either light or dark. And even though the dark vision is generally recognized for what it is by the majority of humans, if there is no alternative available it will have its appeal. Moreover, even a light vision can immerse the holder in a merciless obedience to demagogueries that actually reflect the human dark side. This can happen when the vision of light is not tempered with the realities of the dark side of human possibility.

The flip side of that self-destruction inherent in the ignoble act of the kamikaze or the suicide bomber is the self-sacrificing hero, the one who gives up life as an affirmation of the self-worth of others. In either case, the issue is that of self-worth. This does not mean that the two are of equal merit. Certainly the self-sacrificing hero can contribute to the betterment of the human enterprise by acknowledging human worth while the kamikaze or suicide bomber inevitably diminishes this betterment by trivializing the worth of others.

The Hero

Taking one's life in order to achieve self-worth is quite different from giving one's life on behalf of affirming the self-worth of others. The first has minimal concern for ultimate social good, while such is exactly the concern of the second. The first is an elevation of the part over the whole, while the second is an elevation of the whole over the part. The first invites fear of one's fellow humans, while the second invites fortitude. The first speaks of indifference for other humans, while the second speaks of compassion for other humans. Thus, the first debases other humans for the sake of imputed self-worth, while the second exalts other humans because of an affirmed self-worth.

All of this underscores the essential truth of human experience, namely, that all behavior is done in the service of self-worth, irrespective of the nature of that behavior. The two natures that have characterized the two basic approaches to addressing the issue of self-worth have been the light and dark sides of human possibility. The battle between these two means of achievement has determined the direction of the entire human enterprise from its inception.

This battle has been between those who have engaged their dark side to attain a sense of self-worth and those who have engaged their light side to affirm a sense of self-worth. It has been between those who have sought attainment at the expense of others and those who have sought affirmation through the honoring of others. It has been between the users and the stewards, between the takers and the sharers, between the self-centered and the other-centered. It has been a battle between those who seek to live out of their ignoble capabilities and those who seek to live out of their noble capabilities.

Of course, there are no purities of behavior. However, there are dominances that characterize human living. And the battle is about dominance of life focus and energy. It has traditionally been viewed as the battle between evil and good, keeping in mind that such concepts are human inventions intended to characterize human behavior as it affects the whole of the social order from one's own mythic view.

Again, this underscores the notion that all behavior is done in the service of self-worth and that self-worth is the focal issue of every human action and of the entire human drama. History has never revealed an exception to this truth.

Why Suicide Bombers?

Where do suicide bombers come from? Suicide bombers are the products of education. Suicide bombers are taught to be suicide bombers. And those most susceptible to such teachings are the experientially ignorant and the worth-hungry idealist. In brief, suicide bombing is a mythic gesture. It is a devout belief in the efficacy of the act and the reward that will ensue from the act. The efficacy and reward are as real in the mind of the believer as that of any other human who believes in the efficacy and reward of their own view of reality. Being convinced that being a suicide bomber makes no sense is a revelation of the judger's myth rather than a negation of the suicide bomber's myth. The suicide bomber is as convinced of the rightness of being a bomb as the social hero is convinced of the rightness of self-sacrifice. Indeed, the suicide bomber will view one's self as a hero.

It might be argued that there is a distinction between the premeditated act of becoming a living bomb and the spontaneous act of self-sacrifice. While this may be true, it does not change the fact that both are reflections of mythic belief. The studied act and the spontaneous act both derive from one's mythic devotion. What others call the studied act or the spontaneous act is a matter apart from why the individual engages the act. Humans are meaning-makers, and they can make whatever meaning satisfies their need for affirmed self-worth irrespective of the manner of its achievement. As the acts of love and self-sacrifice are taught as part of a mythic system of belief, so are the acts of hate and sacrificial vengeance.

The stage play *South Pacific* is about prejudice and hate. One of its songs suggests that you have to be taught to hate before you are "six or seven or eight." This is true in the sense that the ignorance isolation of youth makes them an easier target for all teaching. However, one need not be a youth in order to be taught either love or hate. Whatever one's age, the human mind must have a mythic translator in order to convert experience into meaning. And as long as the mind is alive it can transform itself into any mythic image it chooses or it can give permission to be transformed from any outside source. But whatever the transformation its appeal will always be rooted in the believer's perceived need for self-worth affirmation. It is this appeal that ultimately gives shape to the suicide bomber.

Would Hamlet have felt the delicious fascination of suicide if he
hadn't had an audience, and lines to speak?
                                                              —Jean Genet

Face-off

(The Conflicting Poles of Culture)

I often think it's comical
How nature always does contrive
That every boy and every gal,
That's born into this world alive,
Is either a little Liberal
Or else a little Conservative.

—W. S. Gilbert

Mythic Sacrifice

On the Yucatán Peninsula of Mexico is located the ruins of an ancient Mayan city called Chichén Itzá. It was occupied between 1500 BC and AD 300. The engineering of these ruins is impressive, and the still standing structures imposing—reminiscent of the Egyptian pyramids. These are the artifacts of a very bright and skilled people.

In the Mayan language *chi* means mouth, *chen* means wells, and *Itzá* was the name of the tribe that built and inhabited the city. Thus, Chichén Itzá literally means: Mouths of the Wells of the Itzá. There is a long, dry season in this geographic area as evidenced by vegetation that can survive an arid climate. The most precious commodity is water. So vital is water for survival that the city itself was named for the large open-mouthed wells that sustained the population.

The largest of these wells is really a deep pool, about fifty yards across its circumference. According to local history, this well not only supplied water, it was a focal religious ceremonial site. At a prescribed time of year, when the annual drought and heat most severely threatened the crops and survival of the inhabitants, a ritual was enacted by

183

the priests who ruled the city. On an outcropping of limestone over-looking this pool, a young person, adorned with expensive jewelry, was thrown into its depths as a sacrifice to appease the rain god. Legend has it that this young person was always a virgin.

I once visited this site while exploring the Yucatán Peninsula. As I stood next to this pool, with sweat from the heat drenching my clothes, I tried to crawl into the mind of the people who would have gathered here for their annual sacrifice. I would have been birthed into an envi-ronment where human sacrifice was an essential part of the religious myth. Perhaps, as with all mythologies, there might have been a few who questioned its validity, but they would have been a not-well-re-spected fringe group and one probably holding a life-threatening per-spective.

I mused about my response were I to have been a father designated to give up my unwed daughter as the sacrifice required to bring life-giving rain to the whole city. In all probability, I would have been heart-broken while, at the same time, seen this act as a great privilege. Others had done it before me, and the rains had come. Possibly I would have been elevated to a position of religious nobility with special rewards both now and beyond death. It would have been my time to make the ultimate sacrifice for the sake of the life of my people.

These were not ignorant people. Given their time in history, they were obviously well educated. They were simply born and bound into a religious myth of sacrifice. And, in actuality, this myth is very similar to the one that has dominated Western culture for almost two thousand years—that of Christianity. The prevailing interpretation of this myth is that God, the Father, engineers his only son's death on a cruel cross in order to appease his own wrath against human sin and offer the pos-sibility of human redemption.

Mythic Culturation

This similarity is illustrated in Mexico's history. In the early six-teenth century, the Spanish began their conquest of Mexico. Following the military phase, there was a need to accommodate the native Indian population to the Christian myth as a socializing and subjugating cultural process. The mythic background of the Indian population in central Mexico was the Aztec culture for which blood sacrifice was a focal ritual—and particularly offering the beating heart of their victims as appeasement to the gods. The Catholic religious emphasis on the blood sacrifice of Jesus and the imagery of Jesus with an exposed bleeding heart probably made this accommodation easier for the Indian population.

The Chichén Itzá sacrifices may have been more humane than either the Christian or Aztec. It is said that their victims were drugged to deny the pain and horror of their death. In both the Christian and Aztec myth, the experience of being fully alive to the pain was essential.

As it was at Chechén Itzá, during the Aztec culture and presently in Christian dominated civilizations, the educated serve the role of primary mythic promulgators. Obviously, the impact of education is not necessarily a determinant in accepting mythic persuasions grounded in ancient perspectives and rituals.

Questioning

As Ruth Benedict suggests, accepting the myth into which one has been birthed and raised is as natural as breathing. What is not natural is to question the validity of this myth. To do so normally requires a traumatic experience of self-perceived enlightenment. But for the sake of illustrating the differences between liberal and conservative perspectives, assume a dialogue taking place between two citizens of Chechén Itzá about the mythic validity of this annual ceremonial event of sacrifice.

Liberal: Maybe the sacrifice and the coming of the rains is a coincidence. After all, the rains normally follow the sacrifice. What if we didn't make the sacrifice, and the rains still came?

Conservative: What you say is blasphemy! Our sacred texts tell us to make the sacrifice. It is our tradition to do so, and the rains come. We must not abandon what the texts instruct.

Liberal: But sometimes we make the sacrifice, and the rains don't come. Doesn't that imply that the two may not be connected?

Conservative: It only implies that we have violated other parts of the sacred text and are not deserving of the rain even when we have sacrificed as instructed.

Liberal: But what if the tradition is wrong? What if taking a life every year is needless? Isn't even a single life sacred?

Conservative: What is sacred is our tradition. We cannot afford to offend the rain god. Thousands will starve to death without the rain.

Liberal: But why kill a young person who has their whole life ahead? Doesn't it make more sense to sacrifice an old person who is already close to death? After all, a life is a life? Why should the rain god care?

Conservative: It is clearly stated that the sacrifice must be a young virgin. What makes sense is to honor the tradition that has brought us life and keeps us strong.

Liberal: You make it all sound so simple. Maybe it's more complicated. Maybe there is more to know than our tradition tells us.

Conservative: No! It is simple. It's always been simple. You're the one making it complicated. We know everything we need to know, and you'll understand that when you stop asking questions and accept the truth as it is.

Poles

There are two polar opposites that bracket the range of options open to us in choosing the posture that will characterize our view of reality. We call these poles conservative and liberal. These poles can only be defined by caricature since they represent the extremes toward which we can lean in choosing a view of reality. This caricature can be outlined by sketching the conservative and liberal response to truth, tradition, and time.

There is another consideration in defining these terms. In the political arena, they have been converted into rhetorical weaponry and their meanings constantly twisted and vilified to accommodate this conversion. During one election campaign both terms might be defined one way and in the next campaign defined differently. The following definitions intend to avoid being tainted by this linguistic combat. They are based on the root meanings of the words and seek to draw images consistent with these meanings.

Caricatures

Conservative refers to a posture of closedness. It roots in the Latin term *conservare*, which means:

> ➢ to be watchful
> ➢ to maintain
> ➢ to protect
> ➢ to preserve

Liberal refers to a posture of openness. It roots in the Latin term *liberalis*, which means:

> ➢ to be noble
> ➢ to be generous
> ➢ to be free

Using this framework of definition, following is a caricature comparison of these extremes as they relate to views of reality:

Conservative Pole	Liberal Pole
Truth: ➢ is simple ➢ all that is necessary is known ➢ there is no mystery Posture: closed, affirming	Truth: ➢ is complex ➢ all that is necessary can never be known ➢ all is mystery Posture: open, questioning
Tradition: ➢ is the repository of truth ➢ anchors living ➢ takes precedent over human need Posture: legalistic, prejudiced, pro-status quo	Tradition: ➢ is the cage of truth ➢ confines living ➢ is subservient to human need Posture: permissive, tolerating, anti-status quo

Conservative Pole	Liberal Pole
Time: ➢ the past informs the present and future ➢ the present and future must be bent to conform to the past ➢ change is constructive if it shapes the future into the past	Time: ➢ the present informs the past and future ➢ the present and past must be bent toward the possibilities of the future ➢ change is constructive if it unleashes human potential toward the future
Posture: fights change, reveres the past	Posture: welcomes change, hopes for the future

Both the conservative and liberal poles are models that offer themselves as postures that add definitive character to our view of reality. The conservative posture always regressively invites a return to a former state. The liberal posture always progressively invites an advance to a new state. In every area, each defines the meaning of the other. In defining conservatism, Abraham Lincoln also defines liberalism:

> *What is conservatism? Is it not adherence to the old and tried, against the new and untried?*

In the same manner when British philosopher and Nobel prize winner Bertrand Russell defines liberalism he implies the conservative opposite:

> *The essence of the liberal outlook lies not in what opinions are held, but in how they are held: instead of being held dogmatically, they are held tentatively, and with a consciousness that new evidence may at any moment lead to their abandonment.*

Characteristics

Each of these polarities, with their distinctive postures toward truth, tradition, and time, express certain characteristics when dominantly embodied in a lifestyle. Again, these characteristics are caricature tendencies and not required absolutes.

Conservative Lifestyle	Liberal Lifestyle
TRAIT: Conformity (commitment to causes that uphold tradition)	TRAIT: Compassion (commitment to causes that serve people's needs)
FOCUS: Building Institutions (preserving values by strengthening the value carriers)	FOCUS: Building Relationships (preserving values by surmounting destructive prejudice)
SPIRIT: Cautionary (incorporate by slowing down the process)	SPIRIT: Actualizing (incorporate by speeding up the process)
TENDENCY: Trust (acceptance of external authority)	TENDENCY: Suspicion (questioning of external authority)
ETHIC: Standardized (morality is determined by social prescription)	ETHIC: Situational (morality is determined by circumstantial judgment)
BELIEF: Self-determination (the social good is best served by individual achievement)	BELIEF: Social-determination (the social good is best served by community achievement)
GOAL: Social Control (achieving the security of conformity)	GOAL: Social Liberty (achieving the freedom of toleration)
METHOD: Caging (the solution to social ills is a stringent application of law)	METHOD: Coaxing (the solution to social ills is a serious application of generosity)
CONTRIBUTION: Stability (keeps vision focused on the practical)	CONTRIBUTION: Progression (keeps vision focused on the possible)
WEAKNESS: Loss of Future (a grounding so rabid that there is no movement)	WEAKNESS: Loss of Past (a movement so rapid that there is no grounding)
TRAP: Tunnel Vision (reality is perceived to be so simple that doubt is lost to absoluteness)	TRAP: Cynicism (reality is perceived to be so complex that hope is lost to paralysis)
DYSFUNCTION: Over Guarded (a closedness so restrictive it mistakes liberty for license)	DYSFUNCTION: Under Guarded (an openness so loose it mistakes license for liberty)

Both lifestyles, as caricatured, deny the social merit of the other. However, despite this denial, both conservatives and liberals often share each other's characteristics. That is, there are no purities of embodiment in human lifestyles. Thus, caricature is only a means of arriving at useful definition and indicating usual inclination.

Both/And

These polarities provide a natural tension in cultural life—a dialectic of dialogue and action that offers the possibility of simultaneously conserving the best of the past and stretching toward the best of the future. This dialectic fosters citizen motivation to participate in the cultural drama and to commit energy to its well-being.

While each of these polarities has their vices and curses, they also have their virtues and blessings. And while the goal of the advocates of each is to capture the allegiance of the citizenry, no culture will long endure that does not incorporate the correction of course and balance of focus their mutual tensions are intended to provide. The danger is not that they contend for allegiance but that in this contention one shall overpower the other into excess. It is in excess that virtue is converted into curse.

This does not mean that the aim of a culture is to weigh them equally in its scale of investment. Quite the contrary. The aim of a culture is to know what virtue of either to employ at any given moment and what curse to avoid. The balance to be found is not in parity but in imperative. The course correction to be gained is not in centrism but in necessity.

Metaphors

There are two metaphors that throw light on the dual role these polarities play in the cultural drama.

Roots and Wings

One metaphor is a line from the song *Spirit of Life* by Carolyn McDade: "Roots hold me close; wings set me free." As a preserving view of reality, conservatism is the root that holds a culture close to its past. It gages both present and future against a model of this past.

Thus the primary energy of a conservative is expended trying to reproduce this model for all time. This means that the major battle the conservative engages is with the emerging new. A conservative is preoccupied with roots, and anything perceived to imperil these roots is viewed as an enemy.

As an open view of reality, liberalism is the wings that set a culture free toward a different future. It gages both the present and past against models of perceived progress.

Thus the primary energy of a liberal is expended trying to produce these models for the future. This means that the major battle the liberal engages is with the confining old. A liberal is preoccupied with wings, and anything perceived to imperil free flight is viewed as an enemy.

Without the conservation of the past, there is no solidifying cultural identity. Without the liberalization of the present there is no energizing new future. A culture's roots and wings enable it to embrace all time into its present—to be anchored in the past while soaring toward the future. Without roots a culture's flight is aimless. Without wings a culture's roots atrophy.

Pioneers and Settlers

A second metaphor is that of pioneers and settlers. The spirit of liberalism is to explore new territory—to adventure into the unknown. And for the liberal there is always a different place to go—there is always a discovery that offers enlarged possibilities.

This spirit is the essence of openness that characterizes the liberal polarity. Liberals are the pioneers of culture. They are the risk-takers that infuse culture with the excitement of potential.

The spirit of conservatism is to build on what has been discovered—to consolidate the gains of the known. For the conservative there is no need to go further—what has been already found is sufficient for tomorrow.

This spirit is the essence of that closedness that characterizes the conservative polarity. Conservatives are the settlers of cultures. They are the entrepreneurs of the status quo that infuse culture with the solidity of a firm foundation.

A culture needs both pioneers and settlers for its health. It must build on the territory found while seeking new lands. It is in this ambivalence of energy investment that it creates a dialectic of gradual movement into a new future. To survive it must conserve and be generous at the same time.

Moderation

In between the conservative and liberal poles is a middle ground of moderation. The moderate acknowledges that both polarities hold valid viewpoints. The moderate assumes a freedom to choose which aspects of either polarity are applicable to any given circumstance.

The term moderate derives from a Latin word that means "to regulate." In later years one of its acquired meanings was a reference to presiding over, as in the regulation of a debate. And, metaphorically, this is the role the moderate plays in the cultural debate between conservatism and liberalism.

More than anything else moderating is mediating. So the moderate plays a critical role in helping shape the directions of a culture but is rarely the leader in initiating these directions. The leadership roles are normally taken by conservatives and liberals who propose directions of opposition.

The moderate is not a centrist in the sense of trying to keep culture rolling down the stripe in the middle of the road. The posture of moderation is not tied to the halfway mark between the two polarities. It is only tied to not assuming a permanent allegiance to either.

Depending on perceived need, the moderate may take either a strong conservative or liberal position. If the path of a moderate were graphed as to positions taken on issues, it would be a zigzag of lines of varied lengths extended to the left and right of center. In brief, the pattern sometimes might extend a little to the left or right of center while at other times extending a great deal to the left or right of center.

To use the previous metaphors applied to conservatives and liberals, the moderate may choose a root today and a wing tomorrow or may feel the need to either explore or settle. Moderation is a natural ambivalence that abhors both excess of application and permanency of state.

Views of Freedom

While the choice to assume a posture toward the polarities of life is an act of freedom, the choice itself is a view of freedom.

➢ The conservative fears too much freedom and wishes its restriction.

➢ The liberal fears too little freedom and wishes its expansion.

➢ The moderate fears excess regarding freedom in either direction and wishes its regulation.

All of these fears about freedom find their expression in the cultural environment. They are the tensional spice of social living that both creates the issues of culture and serves as responses to those issues.

None of these three postures is the ideal one for a culture except as perceived by their advocates. To provoke its life, a culture needs the face-off these alternatives provide. It is the drama of this face-off that keeps both the grounding and fluidity of a culture alive.

Pigeonholes

A pigeonhole is a small roosting place. By the sixteenth century it had been converted into a slang expression for categorizing something. The terms conservative, liberal, and moderate are pigeonhole categories. They are useful in identifying basic postures and empowering communication, but they are not absolutes.

The problem with pigeonholes is that the pigeons won't always stay in their appointed roosts. The liberal pigeon may decide to perch for a while in a conservative roost and the conservative pigeon in a liberal roost. The moderate pigeon will roost where it chooses at any given moment and stay an unprescribed period. No pigeon, whatever the self-styled label, can be confined to an appointed roost.

Perch Preference

If people cannot be so conveniently pigeonholed, how then do we arrive at the conclusion that they are conservative, liberal, or moderate? The answer is the dominance of choices made that converts into general lifestyle. To revert to the metaphor, whether it is the right roost, the left roost, or somewhere in between, all pigeons tend toward a preference of perch. It is this preferential pattern that defines the posture of choice.

So it is not the single choice of a perch at any given moment that defines the posture. It is the dominating percentage of choices over a span of time. But while the pigeon can be defined by dominance of perch choice, no pigeon's choices can be confined by a pigeonhole label.

Polar Within

Where are these conservative-liberal poles? They reside within each human. It is precisely because they reside within us that the full range of choice options is arrayed before us for every decision we make.

We may have a self-conditioned mythic response of preference but this does not deny the options or preclude a deviant choice.

Cultures and Institutions

Cultures, and the institutions that give them structure and expression, are made up of people. Because of this human makeup, every culture and every institution within it will be characterized in two ways:

> ➤ It will have a dominant posture of conservative, moderate, or liberal.
> ➤ It will, within this posture, be housed by people of all polar persuasions.

Thus a dominantly conservative culture or institution will have a liberal and a conservative polarity with every possible posturing in between. The same is true of a liberal or moderate culture and institution. While the battles of culture will be between its polar postured institutions, the battle of these institutions will be between their polar postured individuals. People will behave as people whether they congregate as cultures or institutions.

Reciprocal Influence

The polar posture tiers of civilizations begin with individuals, move to institutions, and become cultures. This people makeup of a culture underscores the individual's influence over cultural destiny. But the prevailing myth of a culture will ultimately determine the character of posturing by the individuals within it. This underscores the culture's influence over people's destiny. This duality of influence is illustrated by the differences in the major direction of the influence that dominates a democratic versus a totalitarian culture.

In a democracy, individuals have a broad range of influence over cultural direction. The dominant influence is from the bottom up within the mythic framework. In totalitarianism, the culture has a broad range of influence over the individual's direction. The dominant influence is from the top down within the mythic framework.

Fundamentalism

The term fundamentalist derives from the Latin word *fundamentalis*, which means foundation. A fundamentalist believes with convicted assurance that the foundation of all living and relating has been found. The essence of fundamentalism is an adamant resistance to a change of viewpoint about this foundation. Thus, fundamentalism is not any particular perception about reality but the manner by which this perception is held. It is a dogmatic manner that accepts no alternatives.

Mythic Obstinance

During the nineteenth century in America, the term fundamentalism became a designation for that conservative branch of Protestant Christianity that believed a literal interpretation of the Bible was the foundation of all reality. That designation persists in American culture.

However, it is useful to untie this term from its designation of dogmatic religious conservatism and allow its definition to stand on its own. When freed to be applied where appropriate, it becomes obvious that liberals as well as conservatives can be fundamentalists.

Fundamentalism is a refusal to recognize an alternative to the mythic reality being held. And the liberal can be as adamant and unyielding in this refusal as can a conservative. Conservatism and liberalism are polar opposites of choice. Fundamentalism is not the choice but the manner by which the choice is held. Fundamentalism is mythic obstinance.

Reasons

What is it that drives people to embrace fundamentalism? There seem to be at least two primary and often related reasons.

One is a belief perceived to be so foundational to living that it has become indispensable to existence. A liberal example is a belief of Patrick Henry of the Virginia Colony in early America. Henry was one of the first colonialists to invoke the doctrine of natural rights that asserted that humans were born with certain inalienable rights. He was also a prime mover in having the Bill of Rights added to the United States Constitution as a protection of these inalienable rights.

In 1775, in a speech supporting the taking up of arms against the British, he declared:

> *I know not what course others may take, but as for me, give me liberty or give me death.*

No belief is more fundamental in terms of indispensability to existence than one for which there is willing forfeiture of life on its behalf.

A conservative example is the belief of Barry Goldwater that militant excess is indispensable to safeguarding democratic social liberty. He was particularly adamant about dealing harshly with communism in this safeguarding. As the United States senator from Arizona he was nominated at the 1964 Republican National Convention to be that party's presidential candidate.

In his acceptance speech he declared:

I would remind you that extremism in the defense of liberty is no vice. And let me remind you also that moderation in the pursuit of justice is no virtue.

Goldwater was decisively defeated by Democratic incumbent Lyndon B. Johnson, not simply because of the country's high level of prosperity, but because of the country's fear that his extremism might lead to war with the Soviet Union. Throughout his career as a politician, Goldwater remained an unabashed conservative political fundamentalist.

In Patrick Henry's case, the fundamental cry for going to war to acquire social liberty was heeded in the American Revolutionary War of 1776. In Barry Goldwater's case, the fundamental cry for extreme measures to protect social liberty was rejected in the presidential election vote of 1964. The lesson about fundamentalism in this comparison is that heeding or rejecting its cry is not based on its extreme belief but on the circumstance to which this belief is applied.

Patrick Henry's and Barry Goldwater's fundamentalism of belief are bookends of American history, spanning its inception to the end of the twentieth century. In between those bookends are volumes of stories about the clashes of fundamentalism that comprise this history. Examples are:

> ➢ Manifest Destiny: A phrase that captured the fundamentalist belief that Americans should occupy the continent "from sea to shining sea," and that led to aggressions that divested Mexico of half of its territory, the Louisiana Purchase, and the near genocide of the Native American Indian population.
> ➢ The Civil War: A clash of fundamentalist ideologies over the

political issue of national unity versus state's rights, and the moral issue of pro-slavery versus anti-slavery.

➤ Women's Suffrage Movement: A clash of fundamentalist beliefs about the superiority of the male gender over the female gender.

➤ Civil Rights Movement: A clash of fundamentalist beliefs about the superiority of the white race over the black race.

➤ Religious Right Movement: A clash of a fundamentalist branch of Christianity with advocates of social liberty and constitutional rights over control of education, information, morality, lifestyle, and government.

Nowhere on the globe is a citizen more free to espouse and behave a fundamentalism of indispensable belief than in American democracy. This fact underscores the ultimate irony of a true democracy wherein the cultural championship of egalitarianism permits a fundamentalist ideology bent on the destruction of egalitarianism to survive and flourish along with a fundamentalist ideology bent on the defense of egalitarianism.

The bottom line is that fundamentalisms of indispensable belief have always driven human history—both conservative and liberal brands. And whether such fundamentalisms are good or bad depends on the interpreter of history. America was birthed of fundamentalisms, and its history thereby shaped.

The other closely related reason why people embrace fundamentalism is a need so foundational to living that it has become consuming of existence. This need is to feel worthy of life. While all humans have a profound need for a sense of self-worth, its fulfillment is usually found in non-extreme beliefs.

What attracts people to fundamentalisms of belief is that such fundamentalisms generally offer instantaneous or easy paths of fulfillment. In any culture where the innate worth of citizens has been denied and attached to some form of social status, the sense of social failure and worth deprivation can be keenly felt. Fundamentalisms flourish in this environment because they:

➤ provide a sense of self-worth by endowing life with an absolute correctness—by being one of the chosen

➤ provide a sense of security within this self-worth by framing reality with absolute boundaries—by living within sanctified beliefs.

Any fundamentalism will supply these provisions of fulfillment whatever its social nature. However, those that tend to be most appealing are religious, because they are easily accessed, elevate one to the immediate status of ambassador, and offer a mantle of divine sanction. Moreover, their natural militancy of cause strengthens the sense of the sanctity of the worth and security they provide. And, further, they can only be questioned by an alternative faith expression which means that they reside outside the realm of reason.

Morality

When entering fundamentalism, the rules of morality are changed. Moral conduct is gaged by interpretation of the mythic belief around which the fundamentalism has been built. If this interpretation permits, then oppression and violence toward others is sanctioned as holy activity.

The histories of the fundamentalist branches of Christianity and Islam with their Crusades and Holy Wars are obvious examples in Western culture. Ironically, such moral sanction, by giving the believer power over the lives of nonbelievers, tends to increase the sense of self-worth of the believer. This elevation may be so radical that it leads to a sense of superiority and self-righteousness.

Boundaries

Fundamentalisms have no social boundaries. They can be found in every arena of living. And whatever the arena, they attract people because they readily fulfill the consuming need for a source of self-worth.

Firebrands

Whatever the fundamentalism, it will reflect the character of the polarity it represents. The more conservative it is, the greater will be its emphasis on purity. The more liberal it is, the greater will be its emphasis on diversity.

Because of these emphases, fundamentalism is the firebrand that ignites the drama of history. It creates the tensional conflicts of culture that shape human destiny. This fact is easily seen when reviewing the impact on history of the tensional conflict between the political fundamentalisms of communism and democracy during the last half of the twentieth century.

It is also seen in the tensional conflicts between the ideologies of the political parties that dominate American culture.

Capacities of Freedom

Humans are creatures of innate freedom. There are at least three components to this freedom.

Creating

The first is the capacity of the human mind to create. There is no limit to this capacity to create except that imposed by imagination. There is no confinement of this capacity to create except that imposed by will. Myth is the most intimate form of human creation and the highest form of human art because it creates its creator. And it is an activity of self-creation because it is an activity of self-freedom.

Choosing

The second component of this freedom is the capacity of the human mind to choose. The scope of this choosing is polarity. If freedom is innate to being human, then polarity is innate to being free. There are hundreds of polarities that create the options and choices of freedom in defining the character of myth. But basic to this character is the choice about openness and closedness offered by the liberal-conservative polarity.

Every myth will reside somewhere along the scope of this continuum. This requirement of residency is not a confinement of freedom. The distance between the conservative and liberal poles is established by the mind just as is the choice of where the myth will reside on the continuum.

Changing

The third component of freedom is the capacity of the mind to change. All humans are conditioned, beginning at birth, to accept the myth of their authority figures as the reality of existence. But the confinement of this conditioning can be broken by choice. As well, the self-imposed confinement of any choice made can be broken by the mind that chose it.

The freedom to choose is the freedom to change any choice I have made as well as the freedom to make new choices. This freedom remains, irrespective of its choice of confinements. Thus, all choices are subject to change at the will of the chooser.

The Part and the Whole

The individual's capacity to create, choose, and change myth is reflected in the institutions and cultures into which humans organize. The difference between the part and the whole is the pace of applying these capacities. The larger the group, the slower the pace. That history is simultaneously a cultural birthplace and graveyard attests to this reflection. Human freedom is the caretaker of this birth and death.

This is illustrated by even a brief period of history. The American myth of democracy birthed a culture in the late 1700s that is still thriving. The Russian myth of communism birthed a culture in the early 1900s that died in the late 1900s. The life span of a culture will reflect the health of its social incarnation.

Conclusion

Here are four conclusions:

> Every culture will reside somewhere on the conservative-liberal continuum as determined by the social incarnation of its myth.
> The internal drama of every culture will be determined by a face-off between its conservative and liberal constituency.
> The external drama of every culture will be determined by a face-off between the world's conservative and liberal cultures.
> The life span of a culture will be determined by the health of its social incarnation.

All cultures are dramas of a dialectic between their liberal and conservative polarities. Without these polarities this drama would not exist, nor would there be humans to fuel the drama.

The radical invents the views. When he has worn them out the conservative adopts them.

—Mark Twain

He was learning for himself the truth of the saying: "A liberal is a conservative who has been arrested."

—Tom Wolfe

Soul Force and Social Change

(Making Cultural Change Permanent)

*Again and again we must rise to the majestic heights of
meeting physical force with soul force.*
                                    —Martin Luther King, Jr.

Every act of creation is first of all an act of destruction.
                                    —Pablo Picasso

The Irony

World War II was America's great moral battle to help secure
freedom from the forces of tyranny and make the world safe for democracy. Here is one of the ironies of that victory. Those in the U.S.
military whose skin was black fought for this international liberation
while coming home to a cultural bondage devoid of the freedoms of
democratic privilege.

This bondage reflected not only the white American population's
blatant and demeaning attitudes and actions of discrimination, but
the harsh realities of rock-bottom economic and social status. Aside
from a limited freedom of geographic movement and despite the 1865
constitutional amendment granting it equal rights, the general black
population, for all practical purposes, remained in slavery to the white
population's naked contempt.

The Change

In the 1950s and 1960s, two events of great consequence occurred
to change this reprehensible violation of civil rights and to permanently
alter the democratic conscience of the nation.

The Supreme Court

The first was a change in the composition of America's Supreme Court. Up until the 1950s the majority mythic conscience of this court had remained sympathetic to the white population's prejudices against blacks and had accorded these prejudices and their violent expressions the protection of its decisions and shunnings. But the new composition changed this sympathy and tipped in favor of constitutional rights for all citizens—viewing blacks as real Americans with real grievances to be addressed.

With this mythic change, in 1954 the Supreme Court ruled in Brown v. Board of Education of Topeka (Kansas) that racial segregation in schools violated the Fourteenth Amendment of the Constitution and reversed the 1896 Supreme Court ruling (Plessy v. Ferguson) that permitted so-called separate but equal school systems. This ruling opened the door for the black population's grievances about civil rights to be addressed.

The Civil Rights Movement

With this decision arrived the second culture-shaking event— the spearheading of black grievances by that vague coalition called the civil rights movement symbolized in the leadership of Martin Luther King, Jr. This movement, aided by the exposures of the advent of national television, revealed the grim realities of how far unprincipled Americans were willing to go in expressing their prejudices and hatred toward blacks. As a result, the conscience of America as a whole was raised, laws guaranteeing civil rights were passed, and the assimilation of blacks into the democratic process started to take place.

Moral Revolution

Beginning with the altered composition of the Supreme Court and finding focus in the civil rights movement, a moral revolution in the nation's conscience had begun.

Although this revolution did not signal the end of racial hate and prejudice in America, it did signal the end of those laws and customs that upheld this hate and prejudice and the diminished power of public officials who supported violation of the law. While racial hatred and prejudice continue to flourish among those untouched by the democratic spirit and conscience, these people are no longer a force that can live above the Constitution with impunity. And while there are those who decry the impurity of this revolution, its realities, both morally and legally, persist evidentially.

Examples of Change

Following are examples of the realities of this change.

War Heroes

During World War II there were 433 soldiers presented the country's highest award for bravery—the Congressional Medal of Honor. Although over a million black soldiers served in this war and many were conspicuously and sacrificially heroic in performing their duties, not a single one was among this list.

In January of 1997, after a Pentagon investigation and a congressional waving of the statute of limitations, President Clinton presented this medal to seven black World War II veterans—all posthumously, except one.

It could be said that this belated event was too late to have significance. But this would be uninsightful. It was very significant in that it revealed an elevation of democratic conscience that sought to correct a past wrong. This evidenced that over the forty-plus years since the end of World War II, a permanent change of attitude had taken place in the cultural mind toward America's black citizens.

Aside from civil rights, a part of this attitudinal change was an admission that blacks had played major roles in the country's history. The granting of the Congressional Medal of Honor was a later example of a revision that had been taking place since the successes of the civil rights movement. This revision has been an attempt to correct the lies of both omission and commission of bigoted historians. Essentially, it is a mythic revision of American history that has sought to include the contributions black citizens have made to American life.

Roy Smith

The second example also took place in January of 1997. Roy Smith was a longtime resident of Gilpin County, Colorado—a rural mountain area immediately west of the capital city of Denver. According to the *Denver Post*, Mr. Smith had complained to the Gilpin County

Sheriff's Department of being attacked by his neighbor's dogs, "shot at, run down by a Toyota 4-Runner, beaten with a rake, and tortured while hanging naked, upside down." With obvious contempt for Mr. Smith, the complaint form had listed him as "Nigger Roy" and the complaint itself had been ignored.

Mr. Smith did not take this ignoring of his complaint lightly. He sued for racial discrimination against the Gilpin County Sheriff's Department. The same month and year that black World War II heroes were given their due awards of the Congressional Medal of Honor, Roy Smith was given his due award of a $700,000 lawsuit settlement.

The Gilpin County Sheriff's Department was rudely reminded of something that any informed American should have known—this was no longer the immediate post-World War II era where blacks could be treated with legal contempt. This was the near twenty-first century where a permanent attitudinal change had occurred in the nation's democratic conscience and a similar accord in the upholding of civil rights for blacks.

A Different Nation

In 1945 no one was concerned about war heroes with black skin and Roy Smith would have taken his abuse and kept his place—knowing that pushing the issue could have brought with it far more serious consequences than he had up to that point experienced. But this was 1997 and not 1945. It was a different nation ruled by a different conscience and a different attitude toward the law. A major mythic shift had taken place and it was permanent.

A Presidential Election

In the year 2008, another event took place that was a culmination of all the changes that had begun with the mythic shift of the 1954 Supreme Court makeup. A biracial candidate (generally referred to as African American) for the President of the United States won the Democratic party's nomination. Even more socially astounding, that candidate, Barack H. Obama, was elected the forty-fourth president of the country. In a bit over fifty years the attitudes of the nation had shifted in such consequential fashion as to see happen what would have been viewed as impossible in post-World War II society. Certainly racial prejudice reared its ugly head during this political campaign; however, the democratic attitudes of culture had grown so pervasive as to have demanded that racism be wrapped in a soft rhetoric or stated in more guarded venues. A monumental social revolution had taken place over a fifty-year period of time. The mythic face of the culture had been transformed. Democracy had become color-blind for a majority of voting Americans. Egalitarianism had achieved a major triumph.

The Key

For almost one hundred years the civil rights of black citizens had existed in the United States Constitution. Yet with the blessing of Congress, the courts, law enforcement officials, and the general white population, these black citizens had been inhumanely treated, exploited economically, refused justice, barred from participation in white society, and murdered at whim without democratic recourse.

The Question

All of that had dramatically changed by the turn of the twenty-first century. The question is what created this shift of attitude that all of a sudden enfolded the black citizenry into the democratic process? The answer to this question is the key to how change is made permanent in a culture. Change seems impermanent and fleeting, so the issue is how to capture it as an established cultural resident.

Principles

There are two principles that govern law in a nation's cultural existence. The first is this:

The civil rights of a nation's citizenry cannot be guaranteed by law.

In brief, the law can instruct its citizens as to appropriate behavior but it cannot ensure compliance to this instruction. All that is needed in American history to make this point is a review of how the nation's black citizens have been treated by the nation's white citizens between the Civil War and the 1950s.

The second principle is this:

Only when the conscience of a nation's citizenry accords with the laws of the nation will these laws be fully honored.

Aside from black civil rights being violated by the white population, this point is made by the history of professional criminals in American history. The reason why such criminals consistently violate the laws of the land is because their conscience does not accord with these laws. This is why they break these laws without pang of conscience. This so-called lack of social conscience is usually given psychological labels such as that of sociopath. But criminal behavior, in this respect, is not simply a psychological aberration. It is a cultural conscience miscue. It is rooted in mythic differences that create diverse consciences.

If this were a mere psychological issue, then most white Americans living between 1868 (the year the Fourteenth Amendment guaranteed civil rights for black citizens) and the 1950s have to be labeled as sociopaths due to their lack of conscience compliance to the nation's democratic Constitution and Bill of Rights.

But they were not sociopaths. They were citizens whose mythic conscience did not accord with the apparent conscience of their own national myth. They were mythic rebels in the same manner that their forefathers were mythic rebels against the mythic national conscience of England in 1776. The difference is that the mythic conscience that created America rebelled against the restriction of freedom while the mythic conscience beyond 1868 rebelled against the giving of freedom.

Clearly, the violations of a culture's law are not answered by simply applying psychological labels that imply mental illness. They can only be answered adequately by investigating the issues of conscience. And the issues of conscience are inseparably tied to the issues of myth.

Permanent Change

The points of these two principles converge into a third principle that governs the creation of permanent change in a culture:

Only when the heart of a culture is changed to accord with social change will that change be made permanent.

The heart is a metaphor of those values implied in a myth that make up its conscience—its sense of right and wrong that affirms or disaffirms guilt of violation. Thus, until the mythic conscience of a culture's people is altered to accommodate whatever change is occurring in its midst, that change will only be temporary. Only the mythic conscience accommodation of the citizenry makes for permanent change.

Robert Browning (*Sordello, II*) expressed this truth poetically when he proclaimed:

> *Would you have your songs endure?*
> *Build on the human heart.*

And Martin Luther King, Jr., applied this principle to the civil rights movement's goal in this affirmation:

> *Desegregation will break down the legal barriers and bring men*
> *together physically, but something must touch the hearts and souls*
> *of men so that they will come together spiritually because it is*
> *natural and right.*

This was a constant theme in King's remarks—that only the culture's change of heart could sustain the legal changes the civil rights movement promoted. All he had to do was look backward in American history for confirmation of this truth.

Risky Business

But raising mythic conscience is risky business. People who are bold enough to proclaim either the wrongness of a culture's value conscience or draw attention to the hypocrisy of a culture's citizenry when its behaviors do not accord with its announced value conscience will inevitably become targets of reprisal.

The suffragettes of the women's movement, demanding an entry into the democratic process, had heaped upon them the scorn, wrath, and abuse of white male citizens. One of their leaders, Susan B. Anthony, was thrown into jail for attempting to vote. Had they not been women they would have experienced far greater abuse. Being both male and black, Martin Luther King, Jr., suffered the more horrendous fate of assassination.

The Humane Version

There are two primary ways to bring about social revolution that constitutes a change in the nation's conscience. Both of these ways involve the use of force. But there are dramatically different kinds of force that can be employed.

Technological Force

One of these kinds of force is the use of technological weaponry that intends the physical destruction of enemies, or at least their containment, to assure the institution of laws that affirm new values for a culture's conscience.

An example is the Bolshevik Revolution of 1917 in Russia that created a new mythic cultural conscience reflective of communist values for that nation. In world history, this kind of force has been favored by those who wish to alter cultural conscience. It tends to be quicker and more obvious than other slower and more subtle forms of conscience change.

One of the major problems with the use of technological force to effect a cultural value conscience change is that the change may be by law or force without being by heart and will. Thus, it is susceptible to constant undermining by the citizenry. And this is usually the source of its ultimate downfall if such occurs.

Moral Force

The other kind of force was dramatically modeled by the leadership of Mohandas Gandhi in seeking to overthrow British colonial rule and establish the independence of India. His method was that of a nonviolent activity that maintained respect for the life of his independence movement's enemies. This kind of force infuriated the British who retaliated with violent technological force, but could not stop the spirit of Gandhi's movement. Begrudgingly, the British granted India its national autonomy in 1947.

Martin Luther King, Jr., found Gandhi's concept of nonviolent force to be compatible with his personal perception of the Christian myth. This was to be his weapon of choice as a leader in the civil rights movement of the 1960s. King called this approach "soul force." As he admonished in 1963 at the Lincoln Memorial in his "I Have a Dream" speech:

Again and again we must rise to the majestic heights of meeting physical force with soul force.

Soul Force

What did King mean by the phrase "soul force"? Since some form of weaponry is the issue of all cultural revolutions, it serves as an appropriate metaphor to illustrate King's meaning.

Consider a gun. A gun is a technological instrument that propels an object toward a target. The purpose of that which is being propelled is to impact with force upon the target. Normally, the intention of this impact is to harm or take life. However, in the case of soul force, the intention is to preserve and give life. This is what makes soul force so unique and powerful as a social weapon. As King stated in his 1964 Nobel lecture:

Nonviolence is a powerful and just weapon.... which cuts without wounding and ennobles the man who uses it.

The Gun

The instrument for propelling soul force to the target is nonviolent protest. As to why nonviolence is so vital for the delivery of soul force, King made these comments:

➤ "*... nonviolence is not a method for cowards: it does not resist. This method is passive physically but strongly active spiritually; it is nonaggressive physically but dynamically aggressive spiritually.*" The intention of this spiritual aggression is to deliver a moral bullet to the conscience of the opponent and those who might be observing. The intention of the physical passivity is to make this moral bullet highly visible and impactive.

➤ "*... nonviolent resistance does not seek to defeat or humiliate the opponent, but to win friendship and understanding.*" The purpose of this moral bullet is to open the conscience of the opponent or observer to change—either bringing to life a deadened conscience or altering the character of a contrary conscience.

➤ "*... the attack is directed against forces of evil rather than against persons who are caught in these forces. It is evil we are seeking to defeat, not the persons victimized by evil.*" The spirit of nonviolence is a recognition that humans are worthy even though they choose to empower evil in their attitudes and actions. While pointing out the unworthiness of this evil, nonviolence simultaneously affirms the worthiness of those empowering the evil. This opens the opponent to viewing the nonviolent activist as also a worthy human toward whom evil attitudes and actions are unworthy. It encourages the opponent's conscience-raising.

➤ Nonviolence *"avoids not only external physical violence but also internal violence of the spirit. The nonviolent resister not only refuses to shoot his opponent but he also refuses to hate him."* As a method of protest, nonviolence helps keep the activist from succumbing to the disease of hate that is corroding the spiritual integrity of the opponent. In so doing, it also highlights the redemptive quality of nobility over the destructive quality of ignobility.

Obviously, nonviolence as a form of weaponry to bring about social change requires an unusual level of sustained courage and a persistent sense of nobility of spirit.

The Bullet

The next question is what is the nature of the bullet that soul force delivers which makes it so powerful? Again, Martin Luther King, Jr., defines this bullet's ingredients. The first is love. By love, King directs us to the Bible's concept of *agape*, which refers to a spiritual connection that is more profound than sexual attraction or friendship. As he suggests:

When I speak of love I am not speaking of some sentimental and weak response. I am speaking of that force which all the great religions have seen as the supreme unifying principle of life.

The importance of this love is its capacity to transcend the barriers of race and religion to create a bonding of mutual humanness. Thus, it is the only empowerment that is able to rise above the evil act and to forgive and convert the enemy into a friend.

The second ingredient of the soul force bullet is the combination of a tough mind and a tender heart. King suggests that the soft mind embraces stereotypes, jumps to conclusions before examining the facts, accepts falsehood as a support of self-worth, fears the insecurity of the new, and wishes to freeze life in the status quo.

On the other hand, the tough mind breaks through the crust of legends and myths to discern the truth, examines the facts before reaching a conclusion, welcomes the new, affirms their own self-worth, and looks to change as redemptive. Soft-mindedness is cowardice. Tough-mindedness is courage. While the tough-minded will take a stand on the difficult issue the soft-minded will take the easy way out.

However, tough-mindedness without tenderheartedness is cold and detached—without empathy. Tenderheartedness embraces the person in need and becomes the Good Samaritan, whereas the hard-hearted, like the self-righteous priest, walks by the suffering person. The tenderhearted see their resources as an expression of values that empathize with the unfortunate and disenfranchised. The hard-hearted focus their resources on self-centered purposes.

Only the tough mind, in league with the tender heart, is capable of spiritual love and the promotion of social redemption.

The third ingredient of the soul force bullet is the willingness to die for what one believes. As King says it:

> *The ultimate measure of a man is not where he stands in*
> *moments of comfort and convenience, but where he stands at*
> *times of challenge and controversy. The true neighbor will risk his*
> *position, his prestige, and even his life for the welfare of others.*

And at another moment, King suggested that a person who was not willing to die for something was not fit to live. In modeling this conviction, King understood the danger inherent in his leadership in the civil rights movement and reaped his own death.

It is this last ingredient of the willingness to die—added to love, tough-mindedness, and tenderheartedness—that is the measure of the ultimate power of soul force. In brief, all soul force is not equal. It is possible to exhibit some measure of soul force by modeling love, tough-mindedness, and tenderheartedness. But its ultimate power to transform the heart of the opponent is the opponent's knowledge that the activist will endure abuse, pain, or even death for the sake of the cause being espoused.

Power

This is why martyrs become the most aggressive expression of the power of soul force in the human drama. This is why the last thing an opponent wishes to do is create a martyr for the other side. Heroes, who exhibit their willingness to die for a cause but survive, are living martyrs. They inspire the possibilities of change inherent in soul force only a little less than the dead martyr.

This is one reason why black World War II heroes were not acknowledged at the time of their actions. Such recognition would have been tantamount to equating their worth with white Americans. And this would have provided impetus toward white citizens having a change of heart about racial bigotry.

The Bullet's Purpose

Soul force is the entire transaction of active resistance that has one straightforward intention—the delivery of a moral bullet to the heart of the opponent that emphatically states:

> ➢ I love you even though you might hate me.
> ➢ I will not harm you physically even though you may intend harm to me.
> ➢ I am willing to die for what I believe to be right and just.

The purpose of this bullet is to inflict a sense of profound moral guilt that might lead to a change of heart that will find a reflection in attitude and behavior. (The essence of the foregoing sentiments can be found in King's book: *The Power of Love*.)

The Desire

In the fall of 1983, a host of people gathered at the Lincoln Memorial in Washington DC to commemorate the twentieth anniversary of Martin Luther King, Jr.'s "I Have A Dream" speech. An editor of the *New Yorker*, after reflecting on the meaning of this event and reviewing the speeches of King, made this observation:

> *...far more than he wanted the freedom to eat at dime store lunch counters, far more than he wanted black elected officials, King*

wanted the change of heart of individual Americans which would make those political changes possible.

It is the heart—the value conscience—that both creates change and sustains the change created. What King wanted was for the American white citizenry to live up to the nation's democratic conscience. What King wanted was a change of the cultural heart that would make concerns about the mixing of blacks and whites in the public arena an irrelevant issue. The goal of the civil rights movement was to give white America a powerful moral shove in this direction.

Exposure of the inhumane treatment of blacks by the white population and the pictures of blacks willing to take this abuse without violent physical retaliation was a soul force bullet to the nation's heart. And the white population, as a whole, took a giant step toward embracing the democratic ideals it had, up to this point, only given lip service.

Backlash

The tendency in the social process is to rest in equilibrium—to enjoy the status quo. Thus, whatever upsets the status quo is generally looked upon without favor and becomes the recipient of negative social energy. Change generates an inevitable backlash—the attempt to eliminate the challenge of change by restoring the status quo. The normal cry of this backlash will be that those values the nation cherishes and that have kept it strong are being violated by the intended change. But, whatever the rationale, the values cited will somehow correspond to those that protect and sustain the status quo.

Value Focus

The issue of sustaining change or eliminating the threat of change will be fought over perceived values. This public battle is likely to involve one of three possible venues of conflict:

> **Same Value Conflicts:** Conflicts over the interpretation of meaning given to the same value. An example is the value of the family fought during the last quarter of the twentieth century and into the twenty-first century under the rubric of family values. While this conflict is made to appear to be one of valuing the family versus disvaluing the family, it is in reality a

conflict over interpretations about what constitutes a real family. Can a real family exist without a male overlord? Can a real family exist with only one parent? Can a real family exist with gays or lesbians at its head? Can a real family exist without submission to orthodox Christian values? The conflict is over such interpretational questions and not the value of the family itself.

> **Weighed Value Conflicts**: Conflicts over whether one mutually accepted value weighs more than another mutually accepted value. An example is the 1950s McCarthy era campaign to rid the nation of communist influence. The values in conflict were national security versus civil rights. The tact taken by his Senate investigating committee was that national security outweighed civil rights. In this purging, civil rights were grossly violated by legal authority.

> **Adverse Value Conflicts**: Conflicts over values with opposing mythic messages. An example is the women's suffrage movement of the 1800s and early 1900s. Pitted against each other were two mythic viewpoints: one that women were politically equal to men and the other that women were politically inferior to men. The conflict was over which mythic view was right, since they were totally incompatible.

Whatever the nature of the values in conflict, a backlash to retain the status quo will occur. One of the more graphic examples is the sexual freedom revolution initiated in the 1960s and 1970s and the hard-hitting backlash that followed in the subsequent decades to restore the more restrictive puritan values this revolution challenged.

The Principle

Here is the principle therein illustrated that governs the challenge of change to the status quo:

Like the reverse swings of a pendulum, the status quo backlash tends to be equal in force to the challenge of the threatened change.

This punch and counterpunch of change and the status quo create a dynamic in cultural life that makes full restoration of the status quo a near impossibility without resorting to legal and technological force.

Impact

The culture will feel the punch of change and inevitably imbibe some of its impact, depending on its strength. Despite the severity of the status quo backlash against the 1960s sexual revolution, Americans remained far more free to express their sexual proclivities as they entered the twenty-first century than in the years prior to 1960.

And even when the status quo backlash deals a crushing blow to intended change, the taste of the value change will remain on the cultural tongue—being savored and awaiting a more opportune moment of expression.

The reverse is also true. When change has dealt the status quo a crushing blow, that status quo will remain below the cultural surface awaiting an opportunity to reassert itself. For example, despite the permanent changes in the nation's democratic conscience wrought by the civil rights movement, social groups espousing white race superiority and racial hatred continue to pop to the culture's surface.

Principle

Here is another principle that governs cultural change interactions:

The essence of the human drama is change and no amount of status quo can stop its inevitable progress.

All major cultural change challenges will bring about some measure of cultural alteration, no matter how subtle or overt. In brief, change can be slowed down, but it cannot be stopped.

Thus, the wise nation learns how to determine which change is consistent with its mythic conscience and how to channel the change constructively in that direction. Cultures that do not learn this lesson do not survive. History is a record of this.

Change and Law

The laws of a culture are its mythic instructions to the citizenry. Law-abiding citizens will generally observe the laws of the land unless they feel such laws either violate their own conscience or the mythic conscience of the nation. However, laws cannot guarantee that the citizenry's attitudes, and actions will accord with its instructions.

All social action endeavors with the limited goal of simply changing the law to correspond with cherished values will also find that, even if they succeed momentarily, they may also fail eventually. Unless such endeavors are just as aggressive about securing a change in the social heart that corresponds to the change in law, the law may either be ignored or repealed. Sustained law abidance depends on sustained heart abidance. Thus,

> No change of the law is permanently sustained without a corresponding sustained change of the social heart.

While all the foregoing is true, it must also be admitted that changing the law can have far-reaching positive consequences. Despite where a citizen's heart might lie, the law can be a deterrent to behavior that is adverse to the nation's mythic covenant and can serve as a tool to instruct citizenry conscience. As King also suggested:

> It may be true that the law cannot make a man love me, but it can keep him from lynching me, and I think that's pretty important.

However, King's manner of death instructs us to be cautious about both the deterring and teaching capacity of law. So the bottom line remains that the heart sustains the law's power to influence and deter behavior. Thus, the goal of all social action should be a change of the social heart. Otherwise, the energy of social action may simply bounce off of an unperturbed wall of prejudice.

Conclusion

The word soul roots in the Greek word *psyche*, which means breath, spirit, or essence of being. It is a metaphor for the core of being, for the profound, for the dynamic of life itself. Soul force is the impact of this dynamic of life upon that of another being; it is to address this other being with the full power of one's own inner self.

Martin Luther King, Jr., understood the meaning of this word when he coined the phrase soul force. He was saying to those invested in the civil rights movement that to make a difference in how people live, you must crawl into their innermost being with the message of your action so as to alter their way of looking at reality and relating to that reality. Only when the way of being in the world is changed, will the attitudes and actions that being expresses be changed.

In his book *The Broken Covenant*, Robert Bellah says the same thing:

> *No one has changed a great nation without appealing to its soul, without stimulating a national idealism.*

While the use of technological force can create or alter the political and social structures of a nation, only a sympathetic national soul can guarantee the permanency of the creation or alteration. There is no grander example of this truth than the birth of America and the vicissitudes of the maturing of its democratic conscience.

The key to making cultural change permanent is a resonance of the citizenry's heart with the values the change proclaims. Here is the final governing principle of permanent change in the life of a culture:

> *Cultural change is only sustained when the culture's heart corresponds to the intention of that change.*

This is not a new insight. It has been said by both activists and poets of times past.

> *A nation's culture resides in the hearts and the soul of its people.*
> —Mohandas Gandhi

> *Would you have your songs endure?*
> *Build on the human heart!*
> —Robert Browning

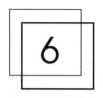

Frolicking in Mystery
(Choreographed by Obsession)

—how fortunate are you and i,
whose home is timelessness:
we who have wandered down from
fragrant mountains of eternal now
to frolic in such mysteries as
birth and death a day (or
maybe even less).

—e. e. cummings

The Critical Issue

In this poetic comment, e. e. cummings puts his finger on the critical issue of human existence—our inability to penetrate the mystery that birthed and sustains us. Nevertheless, as compulsive meaning-makers, we are driven by our nature to know this mystery. Thus, our human frolic in time has been choreographed by two obsessions.

The Secret Obsession

One obsession is to reach into the heart of mystery and extract the secret of the universe. Primarily, this has been the frolic of science.

A Metaphor

The 1998 movie *Pi* (π) is a metaphor about this obsession. The movie's focus is Max Cohen, a computer wiz blessed with unusual mathematical talent. Cohen believes that everything in the universe is revealed in patterns and that these patterns can be reduced to numbers. The key to unlocking the secret behind these patterns is the mathematical symbol pi. The problem is that pi's exact mathematical value defies calculation. Cohen's obsession is to produce the key by giving pi this value. So profound is his obsession that he isolates himself from other human relationships for the sake of this singular focus.

The metaphor in Cohen's life for this pursuit comes from an experience in his childhood. His mother had admonished him to never look directly at the sun. But as children are prone to do in defiance of parental instruction, he looks directly at the sun and is temporarily blinded. Pure light is more than the naked eye can handle. The finite eye was not made to penetrate the infinite. And the attempt to penetrate is rewarded, not with insight, but with blind sight. The secret is further concealed rather than further revealed. Oxymoronically, too much light creates darkness.

Despite his grasp of this metaphorical truth, Cohen persists with his obsession. When his supercomputer seems to have unlocked the secret, it experiences meltdown. Cohen's mind runs a parallel course. Each step toward the solution of pi brings on a new experience of mental meltdown, of increased blinding pain, and convulsive delusion that drives him deeper into insanity. Trying to discover the exact value of pi is like gazing directly into the sun. The longer he gazes, the deeper his darkness becomes.

Cohen has one friend, an older scientist named Sol Robeson. Their bond is a shared obsession to find the exact value of pi. Robeson, overstressed by this pursuit, has suffered a stroke and presumably retired. After Cohen's mental meltdowns, he visits Robeson for advice. But Robeson will only suggest two things. One is that he relax his reason and visit his intuition. The other is that he relax his isolation and visit his human world.

Secretly, Robeson is still seeking the exact value of pi. The stress brings on another stroke and he dies. While rummaging through his apartment, Cohen finds a piece of paper on which he believes Robeson has revealed the exact value of pi. He memorizes the figures and burns the paper.

During the unfolding plot of the movie it becomes apparent that other people besides Cohen and Robeson want this secret. An unscrupulous Wall Street firm wants it. The exact value of pi will unlock the mystery of the stock market and present the holder the key to control and wealth. The leader of this firm, Marcy Dawson, hounds Cohen for the secret and is willing to deceive and brutalize him to get it.

A religious group of Hasidic Jews into cabalistic theology also wants the secret. They believe Hebrew can be translated into math and the mystery of God's name in the Torah can be unlocked by applying pi's exact value. Like releasing a genie from its bottle, knowing this name would unlock the power of God to the user. They, too, are not above intimidation to lay hands on this secret.

Cohen's obsession to find the secret is scientifically motivated. He is repulsed by the profit motive and refuses to divulge what he believes to be pi's exact value to the Wall Street money mongers. He is also convinced that even if the secret could reveal the name of God, God would not reside in the numbers but in the space between the numbers. He refuses to give religion its longed for genie.

Cohen is beginning to glimpse some light in his growing darkness. If the world had the secret of the universe, it would only induce a greater madness. Moreover, his own mind was approaching permanent meltdown. Salvation lay in purging his mind of the pi obsession. So he drills a hole in his head to let it out and returns to sanity.

In one of the first scenes of the movie, Cohen is looking at the leaves of a tree backgrounded by a sparsely clouded sunlit sky. His focus is on the mathematical patterns that compose this scene. It fuels his obsession. In the movie's last scene he is sitting on a bench looking at a similar vision. But this time his focus is on the mystery it represents. Sitting beside him is a young girl whose friendship he had earlier rejected in his isolation. Now he is relating to her.

Purging himself of the obsession to reduce the mystery of the universe to a mathematical formula has opened him to enter that mystery and create a relationship with its human and material expressions. He has not found the key to the universe, but he has found the key to living within it.

He now knows that the universe will not yield its ultimate secret to humans. He understands Russian writer Ivan Turgener's insight:

However much you knock at nature's door, she will never answer you in comprehensible words.

The finite eye cannot penetrate the infinite light. To stare into it is only to be blinded by this infinity. Whatever we can know of the universe's mystery will be revealed indirectly—by viewing it through a filter of clouds, leaves on a tree, or a friend sitting beside us. We cannot explain this mystery. We can only relate to it. We can only know the infinite through the finite the infinite reflects.

Scientific Purpose

The purpose of science is to explain the function of those parts of the nonhuman universe that are accessible to its methods. The problem is that the secret of the universe is locked in its synergistic being. And understanding the function of the universe's parts will not unlock the secret of its synergistic being any more than understanding the function of the human body's parts will unlock the secret of the synergistic being of human. Try as science may with all the keys it can create, the mystery of the universe will remain locked within the nature of its own being. If humans could unlock the secret of the universe, they would be master of that which is their birther and sustainer. They would be greater than that which is their creator.

Three Reasons

Why should science pursue an elusive carrot that dangles from the stick of mystery forever beyond its grasp? There are three reasons. The first is that the impossibility of achieving its ultimate goal of unlocking the mystery of the universe is beside the point. Our inquisitive human nature demands that we seek answers to the mystery of life. And plumbing the mystery of our universal womb is integral to this search. Thus, this search is as natural as breathing, and science is our surrogate self searching into this part of life's mystery. Impossible or not, science, as a reflection of an insatiable human curiosity, must engage the universe's mystery and seek its key.

The second reason is a fruit of the first. In seeking the key to the universe's mystery, science has unlocked many secrets of nature's function. These secrets have been translated into technologies that have revolutionized the quality of human existence. Whether it be construction, transportation, communication, or medicine, the fruit of scientific seeking continues to transform our physical and material existence with consequent social impact. It would be against our nature to not continue pursuing that which adds to the quality of our physical existence.

The third reason is also a fruit of the first. Scientific inquiry into the function of the universe's parts has required us to rethink the meaning of our human relationships. At the root of this rethinking is the notion of the interdependent web of existence. This notion is generating a shift in mythic perspective from seeing ourselves as utilitarian consumers to seeing ourselves as ecological stewards. So even though the purpose of science is limited to describing the function of nature, the implications of these descriptions are having a profound effect on the mythic meanings we are giving to our relationships with ourselves and nature. Thus, without intention, science continues to be a profound mythic instructor.

The Meaning Obsession

The other obsession of our frolic is to reach into mystery and extract the meaning of human existence. While extracting the secret of the universe is the obsession of some humans, extracting the meaning of our existence is the obsession of all humans. We can relate without knowing what makes the universe tick, but we cannot relate without answering the questions that give our existence meaning. It is our frolic in the mystery of meaning that we cannot escape. Again, consider the questions at the heart of this frolic:

➤ Who am I?
The answer to this question becomes the ground of my human identity.

➤ How do I know what I know?
The answer to this question specifies the authority that governs my beliefs.

➤ Who or what is in charge?
The answer to this question defines the ultimate value of my devotion.

➤ What is my purpose?
The answer to this question gives direction to my living and sustains my sense of worth.

➤ What does my death mean?
The answer to this question establishes the boundaries and meaning of time in my existence.

These answers determine the meaning I give to my relationships with myself, others, and the universe. I cannot exist as human without the meanings they create.

The Problem

The problem we confront in answering these questions is that the mystery of human existence is buried in the depth of the mystery of the universe, and it is beyond the grasp of our comprehension. Its infinity is bottomless to our finiteness.

A Metaphor

A number of years ago an item appeared in a newspaper about a man who purchased a house in one of America's southern states. A major appeal of the purchase was a new back porch, included in the sale at no additional cost to the new owner.

Several weeks after moving in, the new owner removed the side boards of this porch to store some seldom used items. He discovered a hole. He threw in a rock and heard no sound. He pitched in several old tires but there was still no sound. He collected all the old junk he could find and tossed this into the hole. Yet no sound emitted. He had purchased what appeared to be a porch built over a bottomless sinkhole.

This story is a metaphor of our human venture in seeking answers to life's compelling questions. We stand on the edge of the universe's abyss and throw our questions into its mystery. But the bottomless universe answers not a sound. In this act we participate in the paradox of our human relationship with universal mystery: it is accessible without being plumbable.

A Reflection

In actuality, what we can know of this mystery comes to us not as a sound but as a reflection. This reflection is a blend of our perceptions of its nature and the assumptions we make about the implications of these perceptions. Thus, mystery only speaks to us as a reflection of the assumptions we make about its nature. What we believe to be its answers to life's compelling questions are only the echo of our own beliefs off of its surface.

Our frolic in mystery is choreographed by these answers. Yet, because we can only access the mystery of human existence by our echoed assumptions off its surface, we can never be certain that our answers are right. Therefore, we are forced to do what we humans most loath to do—to live our answers through faith.

Affirmation

The next best thing is for other humans to affirm our choice of answers. Out of this desire for social affirmation is born communities of faith. Such communities may or may not be institutionally organized. But there are communities of faith that have deliberately institutionalized themselves for the explicit purpose of socially affirming certain answers to life's compelling questions. Some of the most powerful of these institutions, we call organized religion. Within these institutions, the individual can find a security of affirmation that cannot be found alone. It is the security of a common set of answers in our mutual frolic in mystery.

Religion

Whatever conclusions we might come to about organized religion as we review its history, it began with a valid social purpose and continues in an attempt to fulfill this purpose despite the shortcomings of its methodologies and conclusions. This is not to justify any of its institutionalized actions in history; it is only to acknowledge that it was created to fill a valid human need that has not disappeared with the passage of time.

Need

Humans create institutions to fill their social needs. These institutions are organized to pursue the mission inherent in this need. Those institutions that endure represent enduring social concerns. One of history's oldest institutions is organized religion. It was created out of one of humankind's oldest and most pressing concerns—to understand the meaning of human existence within the mystery in which it resides.

Over eons of time the essential questions religion has addressed to this mystery have remained the same. The five compelling questions are a digested version. Answers to these questions become a mythic eye—a view of reality. Religion was created to provide a way of seeing within the darkness of life's mystery. As Zsuzanna E. Byudapest, in *Herstory*, points out:

Mythology is the mother of religion, and grandmother of history.

As the need for mythic answers created the religious institution, the myths created by religion have profoundly influenced the directions of history. Religion is not some irrelevant enterprise seeking to contain people within ignorance. It is the focal enterprise society has created to squeeze meaning from the human ignorance of mystery. And its enormous capacity to exert control over human living only underscores its critical shaping of history.

That some of these religions may seem antiquated, absurd, and even dangerous, yet still enthrall masses of people only further underscores the need they seek to fill and the power of their influence.

Whether the institutions of religion live up to our personal expectations or not is irrelevant to why they exist. They exist because the basic pursuit of every human and every community of humans is to find answers to the mystery of existence. Organized religion is society's most visible social expression of this pursuit. Thus the very reason for the existence of organized religion is to satisfy this innate need that defines us as human beings. To reject the social institutional expressions of this innate need will not cause the innate need to disappear. The need transcends all of its social expressions.

As long as humans exist there will be institutional expressions of this need for meaning. Thus, the real issue is not whether religion is a valid social enterprise but in what directions this social enterprise instructs the larger cultural community. The judgment about the success or failure of institutionalized religion is in the degree to which it has instructed the community with enlightened answers to the compelling questions of existence. That is, to what extent has religion kept up with the rest of society's social disciplines in ferreting out the truth of the human frolic in mystery?

Influence

Extract the influence of religion, as exemplified in Judaism, Christianity, Islam, Buddhism, Hinduism, etc., and human history will appear rudderless. The issue of religion is not the validity of its mission but the profound social influence its resulting visions have on giving direction to human history—both explicitly and implicitly. As Annie Besant observes in *Esoteric Christianity*:

> *A myth is far truer than history, for a history only gives a story of*

the shadow, whereas a myth gives a story of substances that cast the shadows.

While religious myths are not the only myths that have dramatic impact on creating history, they are integral to this impact and will remain so.

Purpose

The purpose of all religion is the same. It is to create a mythic eye that gives meaning to human existence. This mythic eye:

> ➢ instructs about how to relate to self, others, and the universe
> ➢ bestows identity, worth, and purpose within the impenetrable mystery of life
> ➢ saves from folly in the frolic

As an institutional expression, religion becomes a community of faith that organizes itself around the mythic eye it has created. Its purpose is to affirm, celebrate, protect, and proclaim the answers that make up this mythic eye and the values these answers imply.

That the mythic eyes invented by various religions may be radically different only reflects the radically different environments of their creation. These differences provide multiple options for choosing a community of faith that might affirm the individual's personal myth.

The Cultural Eye

At the center of a culture is its own mythic eye. The drama of national life is built around this eye's envisioned view of reality. It is the focus that drives its destiny and the conscience that inspires its morality. When a particular religion dominates a culture, it will find an accommodation of power with this secular mythic eye. It will influence this secular myth's focus and conscience.

An example is American culture, where institutionalized Christianity's mythic concepts of human conquest over nature and a chosen messianic people found a blissful marriage with secular mythic concepts of utilitarian capitalism and a democratic nation. This marriage took place at the altar of the nation's birth, where the old and new vowed mutual allegiance. And while internal forces of mythic change developing over the past hundred years appeal for an annulment of this marriage, the mutually empowering relationship remains strong.

Dangers

Such mythic marriages of the religious and the secular have their dangers. Over time their respective ideologies become merged in the culture's consciousness. When one is threatened so is the other.

This was the case in Russia where the religious myth of Christian Russian Orthodoxy had achieved a long-term accommodation of power with Russia's secular royalist myth. With the 1917 Bolshevik Revolution, the communist secular myth came into control of Russian culture. In its attempt to reorganize the culture's consciousness, it not only sought to destroy the old secular mythology embodied in the tsarist government, it also sought to destroy the old religious mythology embodied in the Russian Orthodox Church. This old secular and religious alliance that had dictated the former cultural consciousness also dictated a common fate.

The Necessity

Whether a culture is dominated by a secular myth, a religious myth, or a marriage between the two, it must have a mythic eye that provides a focus of action and a moral conscience. Without this center, the culture will gradually, over time, disintegrate from within and either develop a new internal mythology or fall prey to the mythic designs of stronger nations.

Surrogate

The primal concerns of the human drama have always been surviving and making meaning of life's mystery. But the work of survival has left minimal time to focus on the compelling questions whose answers create meaning from this mystery. So, from the beginning of history, the social tribe has appointed special elites whose function was to make sense of mystery on its behalf. Members of this elite have been given various titles: witch doctor, shaman, medicine man, priest, pastor, clergy, minister, etc.

Over time this elite evolved into a trained leadership that organized its mythic answers into systems employing the use of sacred names, symbols, rituals, buildings, and places. These systems became powerful forces that give bonding and direction to the life of differing societies. Eventually, in recognition of their focalizing social power, these systems were called religion—a word that means "to bind together."

Institutionalized religion began, evolved, and exists as a surrogate for the individual's search for answers to life's compelling questions and as a means of giving celebrative community focus to these answers. Through most of history, the individuals of a culture have normally subscribed in undisputed fashion to the answers the prevailing surrogate religion gave to these questions. In today's world, such undisputed allegiance to the religious institution's authority no longer exists in many cultures. This is another fruit of science. Its resultant technology has liberated some people to focus on issues beyond physical survival. The input of media has made it possible to consider the merits of their answers to life's compelling question as compared to that of other religious mythologies. Many people in the world have been freed from reliance upon the institutionalized religious surrogate that has dominated their culture.

However, much of the world's population remains poised on the edge of physical survival, not being privy to the liberating impact of technology. And the power and authority of traditional religion remains the caretaker of the individual's need to extract meaning from life's mystery. However, as the impact of technology continues its march around the globe, institutionalized religions will be required to ponder the adequacy of their myths for a modernized citizenry. They will also be required to create new myths that account for the new meanings emerging from scientific exploration. If they do not, they will become obsolete and eventually perish from lack of social sustenance. Moreover, they will become retardants to human progress rather than hubs of enlightenment. In many respects this obsolescence and retardation is in full swing on a global basis. That is, organized religion as a whole has become more harmful than helpful.

Religious Impulse

Essentially, the word religion has come to denote the innate human impulse of this need to find mythic meaning in mystery. In this sense, all humans are religious because all humans must exhibit a mythic eye through which to create meaning. But the term used to describe this

impulse is irrelevant. What is relevant is that the search is at the heart
of every individual's existence.

Humans have lived and can live without institutionalized versions of religion. What they cannot live without is the mythic eye that
explains the mystery of existence, guides their individual living, and
bonds their social relationships.

Lifestyles

There are two basic derivative lifestyles produced by our response
to the mystery of our existence.

Myth within Mystery

One is to hold our myth within mystery. This lifestyle acknowledges that our answers to the compelling questions of existence are
assumptions—that they are echoes of our own faith off the surface
of the universe. In this acknowledgment, our myth remains saturated
with the mystery of the universe. This saturation proclaims an allegiance to a myth that remains open to further revelation.

To hold our myth within mystery affirms the limitations of finiteness and the humility of ignorance. It is acknowledgment without assurance, a conviction without certainty. And its consequent social response is a tolerance that permits others to respond to mystery as they
choose. However, this is not a spineless tolerance. It will fight and die
for the freedoms and privileges of the lifestyle. While it will tolerate
alternative choosing, it will not tolerate the destructions or bondages
of such choosing. This is the lifestyle of personal and social liberty.

Mystery within Myth

The other basic lifestyle is to hold mystery within our myth. This
lifestyle asserts that our answers to the compelling questions of existence are The Truth—that the universe has yielded the answers from
its depths. In this assertion, our myth has squeezed the mystery from
existence. This squeezing proclaims an allegiance to the closure of revelation.

To hold mystery within our myth affirms that infinity has been
delivered into the hands of the finite. It is a knowing with complete
assurance, a conviction with absolute certainty. And its consequent social response is an intolerance that demands unquestioned allegiance.

It will allow no alternatives. It will fight the holy war. It will destroy for the sake of its absolute truth. This is the lifestyle of personal and social bondage.

Choices

These lifestyles are created from our response to mystery and the necessity of making meaning. This mystery is inescapable, as is our response. We can either hold it within our myth or let our myth be held within it. And we can live our choice within an affirming community, or we can live it within our aloneness. If we choose aloneness, we are maximally free, yet we are also maximally alone. If mystery is anything, it is vastly expansive. This is why most humans choose the companionship of a community of faith, whether that community is institutionalized or not, and irrespective of its size.

Art

To imagine is to create a picture of meaning in one's mind. This is the mind's power and the source of all art. Art is the attempt to shape such meaning in tangible form. Whatever the tools used and however crude or elegant the outcome, the shaping of meaning from mystery is the highest art form in the human venture.

It requires the most acute of the mind's imaginative power, for it is a shaping in darkness. It asserts the most impact, for it invents the creator and influences the participants. It provokes humanity's greatest blessings and curses, for it ennobles or degrades their relationships. It choreographs the entire frolic of humans in mystery. The creation of meaning out of mystery is not only the art of arts, it is the only art.

Conclusion

The word mystery refers to something that is hidden beyond human understanding. The mystery that births and sustains us is impenetrable and indomitable. It will not yield any meaning except what we bring to it. Despite this veil of infinity, we must pursue the meaning that lies behind. This is the paradox of our venture—we are compelled to seek while being condemned to fail. It is within this paradox that we create, sustain, and define the meaning of both our individual stories and our cultural stories.

Our human chant forever has been and will be to reduce this mystery to dimensions that are acceptable to the limits of our sensory and mental capacities. However, this paradox also defines the nature of our humanness and the quality of our living. Our nature is not only to reduce the mystery of our existence to proportions manageable by our limitations, but to seek to know more than we can know. This, too, drives the facets of our existence. Our quality of living is sustained by the wonder of what we cannot know. This keeps us open to the promise of the new.

In essence, it is the mystery we so desperately wish to solve that shapes the meaning of being human, both in our attempts to reduce it to boxes of meaning and to open these boxes to more than can be contained.

The amusement of it all is that were we to solve this mystery, what makes us human would be undone as well. The infinite reality of the universe would shrink to the size of the reality in our finite mind. In a sense, the universe has graced us with the limitations of the unknown. Harry Emerson Fosdick, in *The Mystery of Life*, captures the meaning of this gracing in this affirmation:

*I would rather live in a world where my life is surrounded
by mystery than live in a world so small that my mind could
comprehend it. That we cannot achieve that which is our most
compelling motivation is our greatest blessing.*

Unless the universe changes itself, the following perceptions will continue to apply to our human drama:
- ➢ We can never unlock the secret of the universe or plumb the mystery of our existence within it, yet we are compelled by our nature to seek and plumb.
- ➢ We must assume our answers to life's compelling questions and live them through the uncertainty of faith.
- ➢ We can find social affirmation of our particular answers by entering a community of common faith.
- ➢ We have been gifted by the universe with the art of meaning making that defines us as human within its mystery.
- ➢ Through this art of meaning-making we create ourselves and the cultures in which we live.

Shall any gazer see with mortal eyes
Or any searcher know my mortal mind?
Veil after veil will lift—but there must be
Veil upon veil behind.

—Edwin Arnold

7

Having Old Eyes

(The Destructive Myths of Western Culture)

As man is, so he sees.
—William Blake

The Problem

The article claimed that frogs and toads are dying in massive numbers around the globe. But why should anyone care what happens to ugly little creatures like frogs and toads? What makes their death front-page news? The answer to both questions is that frogs and toads are an important part of the balance in the planet's ecology system. Their absence would be another step toward wrecking this system. The bottom line is that nothing is unimportant in the earth's ecology.

Open a newspaper, read a national magazine, or watch television and somewhere will be another warning about human actions that are decreasing the planet's capacity to sustain life as we know it. It may be about the effects of destroying the rain forests and other plant and animal life. It may be about the depletion of the ozone and changes in weather patterns and ocean currents. It may be about global warming and the meltdown of the planet's ice caps. It may be about increased levels of pollutant poisoning and its relation to people's health problems. It may be about the inability to contain hazardous wastes and other contaminations of the environment.

Whatever the focus, the problem is that human destruction of the earth's ecological environment continues unabated. Why is this the case? A digested answer to this question is a natural desire by humans for improved quality of living driven by the guidance of unnaturally bad myths.

Natural Desire

Humans have always applied their creative genius to their natural desire for improved quality of living. In Western culture, this application has translated into two sequential industrial-technological revolutions. The first revolution began in England during the eighteenth century, and the second began emerging in the late nineteenth century, evolving out of the first. These revolutions spawned all manner of inventiveness that has elevated the possibilities of life quality to unimaginable levels.

But for all of their life-quality blessings, these revolutions have also brought their planet-destroying curses. These curses derive from the requirements of industry and technology—the massive input of natural resources and the massive output of consequent pollutants.

Over time the cumulative effects of ravaging nature for materials, manufacturing products, product pollution, and product waste have mounted exponentially. The natural human desire for an ever-increasing quality of living continues to alter nature's natural environmental balances and wreak havoc on the earth's capacity to sustain itself in its current manner.

The Ecology Movement

In the 1950s there began a growing awareness of an old ignored truth—*you cannot do just one thing.* This truth is explicit. Every human action on the globe has a consequence. We began looking at this principle in terms of the whole planetary system of earth, water, air, plants, and animals. And we looked at the utilitarian destruction we humans had wrought on the planet's ecological balance and its capacity to continue sustaining life, and we became disturbed. This disturbance organized itself into what became known as the ecology movement—an effort to address and correct our abusive tendencies toward the natural environment.

Head of the House

The word ecology derives from the Greek word *oikos*, which means household. The ecology movement forced us to begin seeing our planet and ourselves as a family of mutually affecting relationships. This new vision created concern for how human actions were beginning to have a negative effect on our future.

But while this concern caused us to start taking much needed corrective action toward how we treated the environment, it remained utilitarian and stopped short of curbing those actions that provided improved quality of living. We still saw humans as the head of the household and all other members as servants to our needs. Our concern was over destroying the domestic system that provided humans with an abundant future.

Issues

Although the impetus of the ecology movement has placed restraints on environmental exploitation, it has not managed to control this exploitation. The reason is tied to its inability to address the fundamental issues of worth from which this exploitation rises. It is this inability that enables the attitude of utilitarianism to dominate human behavior toward the rest of the planet's ecological household.

The Issue of Worth

The issue of worth in utilitarianism finds expression at two different points of entry in human relationships.

Worth and Creation

Inherent in utilitarianism is a hierarchy of worth. The user is always more important than the used. The utilitarian attitude proclaims humans as more worthy than any other member of the planetary household. Therefore, everything else that exists does so to serve human whim.

This utilitarian attitude is given both sanction and support in Western culture by the myths that have dominated its history over the past two thousand years. The Judeo-Christian faith is primary to this domination. In its sacred texts are found two explicit affirmations:

> ➢ Humans, in the hierarchy of worth in the universe, are superior to all that exists other than the angels and God.
> ➢ Humans, in their function as superior beings, are to subdue and conquer the earth.

This sense of superiority and this attitude of utilitarian subjugation are not only compatible, but this union has been given mythic divine blessing and encouragement to exploit the planet's household.

Although there is debate within institutionalized Christianity about these perceptions and there is a beginning stage of their modification, nevertheless their residual influence remains paramount.

Classical humanism, the second most influential myth in Western culture, also abets a utilitarian encounter with creation. With its focus on the superior value of humans and its insistence that human need comes before all other needs, it explicitly infers that the rest of creation stands ready to serve what's best for humans. If humans are the top value, they are also the top priority on the scale of hierarchical relationships. Again, classical humanism has sought to adjust its mythic perspective to accommodate environmental need, but it remains captive to its own essential notion of the centrality of the human enterprise above all else, as its very name implies.

With the explicit beliefs of these two myths firmly embedded in the social fabric and instructing the psyche of Western culture, it has been near impossible for the truth of ecology to get a hearing sufficient to be given serious consideration. Indeed, on the larger social scale, more often than not, while ecological truth has been given verbal acknowledgment, it has also been ignored with disdain and even contempt by a vast majority of humans.

Worth and Culture

Even more insidious than the Judeo-Christian and classical humanist myths in the validation of utilitarian attitudes in Western culture has been the great cultural con. While these prevailing myths have instructed a hierarchy of worth among the beings of creation, the great cultural con has instructed a hierarchy of worth among humans themselves.

By externalizing human worth and converting it into a product of social purchase, the great cultural con has placed at center stage in the human drama one of humankind's most utilitarian vices—that of greed. If the desire is for a greater social worth the motivation for more is greed. Such greed has no concern except fulfilling its purpose of acquisition. And its utility takes no care for the cost of this pursuit. Moreover, it diligently invites all the other dark-side vices of humankind's nature to join it at center stage in creating the human drama.

In his book *The Dream of the Earth,* Thomas Berry translates utilitarian greed into its economic dimension. He calls it the economics of destruction—the willingness to burn the wood of our own lifeboat for the sake of profit. Berry's metaphor is blatantly obvious in Western culture. Our natural desire for improved quality of living calls for the exploitation of the planet's life-sustaining environment to make this possible. When this is coupled with the pursuit of enhanced social worth through material acquisition, this call becomes a demand. The end result is the destruction of our own environmental lifeboat. And this is the most profound oxymoron of human existence.

This oxymoron is further deepened by the more subtle and less obvious ways we are captured by utilitarian greed. Like most human vices, greed is adept at masquerading itself as a virtue. For example, it sounds very much like a virtue to assert that we must preserve the earth's environment for the sake of its beauty. Such a notion rings with nobility. But as noble as this may sound, its goal is to preserve nature as a playground for human pleasure. It is still a utilitarian motivation.

However, it is possible that utility can unwittingly play into the hands of nobility. Yet even with this admission, it is equally important to admit that when human worth is externalized and reflected in acquisition, the preservation of natural beauty becomes far less motivating than the exploitation of natural beauty. Beauty beheld is less appealing than beauty acquired. The economic capacity to acquire the scenic becomes an affirmation of social worth.

As long as we subscribe to the great cultural con's premise that social worth is a commodity acquired by purchase, the dark side of our humanness will dominate our actions and environmental exploitation will take precedent over environmental preservation.

Double Bind

We humans find ourselves in a double bind: we wish to preserve the planet's ecology while simultaneously exploiting it in pursuit of the good life. We may wish to find a way out of this double bind. But rather than confronting the issues of the bind that are inherent in the destructive instructions of our driving myths and the great cultural con, we look for a miracle of deliverance.

Ironically, for this miracle we look to the very tool we use to destroy the environment—technology. We assume that if technology can create the good life, it can save us from the destruction of its requirements.

But this assumption is false because it overlooks two fundamental truths. The first is that technology relies on the exploitation of resources for its success. To lend itself to an ecological solution would require that it cease its reliance on that which is a prerequisite for its existence. The second truth is that technology is a tool, and tools will only do what the hand that controls them demands. Even if we possessed the technological power to refurbish the planet's ecology, this would not happen unless demanded by the controlling hands. And as long as the perceived masters of the household are invested in a squabble about who is most worthy by playing acquisition show-and-tell, the fate of the rest of the ecological household will remain a secondary concern. This is especially so when the rest of the ecological household is the resource for the game of show-and-tell.

Finally, the hope that technology will save us from our environmental folly only hides us from the responsibilities of our destructive actions and defers their consequences to future generations.

A New Mythology

The ecology movement remains impotent to address the profound issues inherent in why we humans insist on destroying the very womb of our existence. The reason is that it lacks motivational power equal to its task. What is required for this address is a new mythology that affirms three fundamental truths:

> ➤ The quality of living for humans is found in its manner of relating rather than in its modes of acquisition.
> ➤ Every human is socially worthy by virtue of birth.
> ➤ All of creation is worthy by virtue of kinship of being.

A Clue

Jewish religious philosopher Martin Buber published a book in 1923 entitled *I and Thou*. In it he asserts that genuine dialogue comes through a relationship where one being encounters another being in fullness. He calls this kind of encounter an I-Thou relationship. Encounters that do not involve this vis-a-vis fullness of being he calls I-It relationships. Buber's primary concern is that humans develop an I-Thou relationship with God. He suggests that humans sometimes have an I-Thou encounter with each other and cites great friendship and great love as examples. However, since I-Thou relationships require full openness of being, Buber asserts that humans normally relate to general humanity and the rest of creation through I-It encounters.

Buber's notions of I-Thou and I-It encounters are useful in understanding how humans in Western culture have traditionally related. The great cultural con encourages humans to relate to each other through I-It encounters. The Judeo-Christian and Humanist myths have encouraged humans, for the most part, to relate to nonhuman creation through I-It encounters. Since these primary ways of looking at reality dominate Western perceptions it is not surprising that humans and the rest of the ecological household are more often than not treated as objects of utilitarian manipulation. Humans and creation are both depersonalized and demoted in worth.

A Seed Form

Our myth determines how we will relate to ourselves, other humans, and the universe. The myths that presently drive Western culture were created for times past, which were uninsightful of the realities of the interdependent web of existence. Unless these myths are transformed to accommodate new perceptions of reality they will remain enemies of both humans and the universal womb that births and sustains life.

Fortunately, a new mythology is emerging in Western culture out of the perceptions of the ecology movement and new insights into the nature of reality. This emerging myth is independent of old Western views of reality other than echoes of Native American mythology. It promises a different way of relating to self, others, and the universe. This is its vision of uniqueness.

The seeds of this myth are found in the perceptions of all manner of cultural institutions. It is a pervasive grassroots creation. And it is precisely this cross-cultural origin that gives it power and generates hope.

This power and hope lie in its recognition that I-It relating leads to destruction while I-Thou relating leads to preservation. In brief, it embraces the earth's entire ecosystem in a way that cares not only for humans, but equally for the frogs and toads of the household.

Dreaming

Archie Belaney was born in England at the turn of the twentieth century. His childhood was consumed with exploring the culture of the native Indians of the Americas and fantasizing about their lifestyle of wilderness living. As a young man he traveled to Canada to pursue his fantasy. Falsely claiming to be of Indian heritage he was adopted by the Ojibway Indian tribe in Ontario and became known as Grey Owl. He made his living hunting, trapping, and serving as a wilderness guide.

Belaney began writing articles about his wilderness ventures and eventually had a book published that brought him to public attention. People were intrigued by his Indian heritage and capacity to articulate the ecological message. He was persuaded to tour and lecture on the necessity of preserving the wilderness. His message was applauded and in the course of time he became known as one of Canada's leading conservationists.

While playing out the events of being a celebrity, Belaney was also plagued by his deceit about his Indian heritage and fears of exposure. In Richard Attenborough's movie version of his life, Grey Owl is confronted with this deceit in a unique manner while meeting with a gathering of Canadian Indian chiefs. This confrontation is in the form of the group's uproarious laughter upon meeting him that perceptively viewed the deceit as a clever joke, while at the same time appreciating the message the joke was delivering. After this bout of laughter the spokesman for the gathering says to him:

A man becomes what he dreams. You have dreamed well.

The double entendre in these words acknowledges both his dream to be an Indian and his dream of ecological preservation.

Our myths are our ultimate dreams of destiny and when we act them, we become their reality. In Western culture we have dreamed and behaved myths that have translated into an ecological nightmare. To escape the destiny of this growing nightmare, we must create a new mythic dream that honors the womb that births and sustains us. And we must behave it with the same devotion as we have the old dreams.

We evolve into the images we carry in our minds. We become what we see.

                                                                —Jerry Mander

8

Having New Eyes
(The Emerging Myth of Spirituality)

The real voyage of discovery consists not in seeking new landscapes but in having new eyes.
—Marcel Proust

Different Answers

There is emerging in Western culture a new mythology. This new mythology is a response to the failure of old myths and the ecology movement to address the pressing needs of the modern world. At present it is being called spirituality. That title is as good as any since the basic meaning of the word spiritual captures the essence of the myth.

Spirituality is a way of looking at reality through new eyes. It envisions a nonutilitarian way of seeing both humans and creation. It seeks to relate, as much as possible, in an I-Thou fashion. As a mythic eye, it sees human relationships with a vision that is radically different from most Western views of reality. This different vision rises from a different set of answers to life's compelling questions.

Following are my personal perceptions about the assumptions behind these different answers. The eventual shape and formulation of the myth will be created by the larger social mind. At present, it is an evolving creation.

Who/What Is in Charge?

The key to the spirituality myth lies in its answer to the question of *Who/what is in charge?* This answer roots in both ancient wisdom and perceptions about the implications of modern science. This wisdom and these perceptions reflect on:

> what the universe is—its nature
> how the universe works—its dynamic

The nature and dynamic of the universe are an indivisible whole. And whether the assertions of support for this view are ancient or modern, this wholeness is implied.

Ancient Wisdom

An example of ancient wisdom comes from the *Aratamsaka-sutra*, a Buddhist text that grossly predates Christianity:

In the heaven of Indra, there is said to be a network of pearls so arranged that if you look at one you see all the others reflected in it. In the same way each object in the world is not merely itself but involves every other object and in fact is everything else.

The Paradox

This ancient wisdom captures a paradox fundamental to understanding the existence of humans within creation. We are both apart from and a part of the universe at the same time. Being apart from the universe, we have a distinctive identity among creation's forms. Being a part of the universe, we are an expression of its seamless fabric of being.

The Same Stuff

The paradox of this ancient wisdom is grounded in the perception that everything in the universe is made of the same stuff. It is this common clay that makes it possible for the universe's forms to be molded into distinctive identities while being made of the same thing.

You Cannot Do Just One Thing

The English poet Francis Thompson (1859–1907) penned these words in *The Mistress of Vision*:

All things by immortal power
Near and far
Hiddenly
To each other linked are

That thou canst not stir a flower
Without troubling of a star.

Long before the ecology movement and the notion of the inter-dependent web of existence came into vogue in the Western world, Francis Thompson said with poetic grace: "You cannot do just one thing." If you pluck a strand in the web, it will reverberate throughout the system, however distant and seemingly imperceptible. Humans do not live a life isolated from their environment. They are one part of a living whole.

In Thompson's poem, everything that exists is irrevocably linked in a manner of interrelationship that permits the smallest stirring of one form to create a troubling effect on another form, even when the distance between these forms is of a staggering magnitude. In the Buddhist text, the metaphor of this interrelating is a network of pearls. This is not a single strand of sequential relationships as in a necklace, rather it is a complexity of relating that reflects a mutuality of nature and effect.

Both the Buddhist text and the Francis Thompson poem express an understanding of the nature of the universe before the advent of modern science. And it was not that their authors had powers of perception that other humans do not possess; it was because the revelations of the universe have always been available to whomever is willing to be observant long enough to receive them.

Modern Wisdom

The modern version of these insights comes to us through the science of high-energy physics. The purpose of science is to describe the probabilities of nature's functions. In physics the major tool used to confirm intuitive speculation is mathematics, and the endeavor in this usage is to reduce reality to formula of explanation. It is a realm of abstraction that, in its attempt to make the universe simple to understand, has instead accomplished the opposite. It has shown us how incomprehensibly complex and paradoxical reality is.

Implications

Science does not prove the assertions of mythic faith. It deals with the functions of creation and not the meanings of human existence.

However, science does enable us to grow in our perceptions of reality and any myth that seeks relevance to its time will pay attention to the implications inherent in its findings. And there are implications that correspond to those of the Buddhist text and the Francis Thompson poem.

The Same Stuff

The most well known of these is the implication of Albert Einstein's famous equation $E=MC^2$. Heinz R. Pagel, one of history's foremost theoretical physicists, says in *The Cosmic Code*:

Einstein discovered that the postulates of relativity theory implied that the distinction between energy and mass and the notion of their separate conservation had to be abandoned. This shattering discovery is what is summarized in his equation $E\text{-}MC^2$. Mass and energy are simply manifestations of the same thing.

This implies that everything that exists is either energy or some patterned form of energy (mass). All that we humans can sense in our environment—ourselves, trees, rocks, light, water, air, stars, clouds, flowers, etc.—is energy made apparent in specific form. Everything that exists is made of the same stuff, whatever the label given to this stuff.

You Cannot Do Just One Thing

Modern physics also affirms the ecological principle of the universe as an interdependent web of existence. This web is a holistic and complex set of relationships that mutually affect and depend on each other for sustenance and survival. In his book, *The Web of Life*, physicist Fritjof Capra says:

Ultimately—as quantum physics showed so dramatically—there are no parts at all. What we call a part is merely a pattern in our inseparable web of relationships.

This patterned web of relationships is bound together as energy. My physical body has special energy receptors called senses. These receptors are deliberately designed by evolution to pick up certain kinds of energies that my brain translates into the experience of seeing, feeling, smelling, hearing, and tasting. These energy translations make creation available to me for living as a human in my peculiar environment. However, the energy of creation manifests itself in ways far too profound for my physical senses to comprehend. As focal as my physical senses are to my survival and enjoyment, they are small stuff in comparison to the larger energy realities of my environment of living.

An Example

For example, my body is made up of energy organized into different parts that create a self-sustaining system which exists by living off the energy of its environment. The same is true of a tree that might stand ten feet away from me. What appears to be empty space between the tree and me is not empty at all. It is billions of organized patterns of energy. My senses can pick up some of these patterns such as the energies we call light, air, moisture, heat, or electricity. But my senses cannot pick up more profound patterns such as the gaseous energies we call oxygen, nitrogen, and carbon dioxide or the particle energies we call atoms, neutrons, protons, and electrons. As American theoretical physicist John A. Wheeler observes:

> *No point is more central than this, that empty space is not empty.*
> *It is the seat of the most violent physics.*

In brief, that ten feet of so-called space is a teaming mass of energy patterns that, like an indivisible web, connects me with the tree and ultimately to the entire universe. If I move toward that tree, I must literally swim through these patterns. And this swimming will always be mutually effective as a disturbance and a nurturance. The universe is both immensely beyond me and immediately within me. We are different as regards breadth of being while being the same as regards essence of being.

Nature of the Universe

Everything in the universe is made of the same stuff with all its expressed forms woven into a complex web of interdependent relationships. The actions of these forms have mutual effect. Everything that exists is in a constant state of change. This is the nature of the universe.

Premise

From this perception of the universe's nature, the myth of spirituality draws a fundamental premise:

Everything in the universe is part of an interrelated cosmic family, having been birthed of the same womb and made of the same stuff.

This premise implies an equality of all the universe's forms. The least this equality demands from humans is respect. But it is deserving of something more profound. If humans, as one form in creation, deserve to be treated as sacred, then all the forms of creation deserve to be treated as sacred. Whatever is pervasive of the part is pervasive of the whole.

Therefore, that spirit of contempt that views the nonhuman forms of creation as mere utility is an affront to the very nature of the universe. It is the attitude of a form gone insane with self-importance and irresponsible behavior toward the womb that birthed and sustains it. The folk wisdom that captures the absurdity of this attitude is that of biting the hand that feeds you.

The Dynamic

The energy that makes up the universe cannot be destroyed. It is in a continuous state of transformation from one expressed form to another. While some forms remain in existence longer than others, nothing remains the same forever except energy itself. The dynamic of the universe is in constant change.

The Rhythm

The universe cannot create new forms without the destruction of old forms. Nor can old forms sustain themselves without the destruction of other existing forms. Creation-destruction is the rhythm of the universe's dynamic.

The Illusion

The human notion that some of the forms we encounter in our experience are inanimate or dead may be useful in describing our small human world but such a description is an illusion produced by the limited capacities of our physical senses. There is nothing inert in the universe. Beginning with energy and expanding to the forms into which it patterns itself, everything is alive with motion and transformation.

Even what appears to be unchanged is always in a state of change. We humans are one example. Whatever we breathe, drink, or eat is transformed into the energies required to keep us alive. While our bodies appear to remain the same, they are constantly cloning themselves. Without the daily transformation of this creation-destruction we would die.

Other Examples

When a tree dies it begins to decay. Decay is a synonym for transformation. The energy that made up the pattern of the tree is reorganized into other forms such as earth, mushrooms, plants, insects, worms, birds, etc. The process we call photosynthesis is how green plants transform the energy of light into the chemical compounds that facilitate their growth. A flower transforms its nourishment into pollen that is transformed into honey by bees, which is transformed into fat by bears. A log burning is transformed into gases and ashes by fire.

What we call quality of modern living is the result of applying technology that deliberately induces energy transformations with desired outcomes. Steel, nylon, plastic, pavement, paper, glass, paint, and electricity are a few examples. Technology is dependent on the built-in capacity of nature to transform itself. The blast of a gun and whine of a jet engine are the sounds of such transformations.

Food Chain

All of existence, human and otherwise, is an endless process of the universe's energy recreating its patterns of form. Thus, existence is an interdependent web of transforming relationships. The less poetic phrase is food chain. The web is constantly changing itself by consuming and reorganizing the patterns of its own being. Not one single form in the universe can exist except through the sacrifice of other forms to its creation and survival. The mystery in which we humans frolic is the magical quality of the universe to be tomorrow what it is not today, yet remain the same.

Answering the Question

With these perceptions in background, the myth of spirituality would answer the question of *"Who/what is in charge?"* in some way reflective of the following assumptions:

> ➤ The universe is, within itself, the ultimate value. Therefore, the value of its expressed form is derived from being part of a synergistic whole.
> ➤ The universe is authored by its own living stuff. Therefore, every expression of its authorship is equal in nature of being and sacredness.
> ➤ The universe is a constant process of transformation. Therefore, every form within it will eventually cease to exist and become a part of something else.
> ➤ The universe's dynamic of creation-destruction involves cause and effect. Therefore, no form within it can initiate a cause without initiating an effect.
> ➤ The universe, as an interdependent web and a metaphorical food chain, is no respecter of its forms. Therefore, essential to its nature and dynamic is a neutrality of creation-destruction that is unconcerned with human concepts of morality and fairness.

If this universe were given the label of "God," then God is a dynamic power that is paradoxically ordered and chaotic, creative, and destructive, changing and unchanging, and randomly dispensing of the consequences of its actions without regard to form. In brief, God neither favors or disfavors humans, or any of its other member forms, either within its nature or its dynamic.

Who Am I?

The answer to this question is determined by where in the universe one chooses to look at the human enterprise. Almost exclusively, humans in the cultural West have chosen to see themselves as the center of a universe swirling around their peculiar concerns. Thus, they are the ultimate value for which the rest of the universe was created. This is the part converting itself into the ultimate value within the whole.

Metaphorically, this is like a single grain of sand assuming it is the reason why the entire beach exists. It is this kind of self-centered identity that has encouraged humans to relate to the planet with exploitative violence.

Cosmic Perspective

As has been observed, the most profound consequence of the space program is not its technological fallout, as valuable as this has been. Rather, it is the encouragement to see humans and the earth from a cosmic perspective. Actual views of the earth from space invite us to visualize its significance from the standpoint of a grandly larger whole.

If we could launch a spacecraft beyond the Milky Way and view the earth from that perspective, its visible significance would totally dissolve within the immensity of the universe. If humans disappear from the earth's surface when viewed from the moon, the earth itself disappears when viewed from the galactic dimension. I, a single form, am lost within the universe's countless billions of forms.

When I ask *"Who am I?"* from the perspective of this universal whole, I am submerged in an overpowering sense of humility. Out of this sense of humility two exclamations rise that bracket my living. What a miracle that the earth and humans even exist! How immeasurably blessed I am to be a part of this miracle!

Yet even with the understanding that I am one infinitesimal part of a boundless and infinite interdependent web of universal existence, I am a unique being whose living affects this whole. I am important despite my perceived insignificance. This is another profound paradox of human existence. Or, at least, it is an affirmation that our human sense of self-worth demands of our view of reality.

Answering the Question

The myth of spirituality would answer the question *"Who am I?"* in some way reflective of the following assumptions:

- ➤ I am made of the same living stuff as the universe itself is dynamically composed. Therefore, I am worthy.
- ➤ I am birthed and sustained by the womb of the universe. Therefore, my first allegiance is to this cosmic parent.
- ➤ I am blessed by evolution with an intelligence that functions beyond instinct. Therefore, I am free to discern options, make choices, and create meaning.

> ➤ I am a being who chooses how I relate to myself, others, and the universe. Therefore, I am responsible for the nature and quality of my relationships.
> ➤ I am a partner with the universe in its transforming dance of creation-destruction. Therefore, I am responsible for the survival and well-being of both my species and its planetary home.

As a human, I am a being who creates my own view of reality and conforms the meaning of all my experience to this view. Or, as Lawrence Sterne, sixteenth-century English novelist, suggests:

It is the nature of an hypothesis, when once a man has conceived it, that it assimilates everything to itself as proper nourishment, and, from the first moment of your begetting it, it generally grows the stronger by everything you see, hear, read, or understand.

What Is My Purpose?

Just as the clue to human identity is found in the answer to the question *"Who/What is in charge?"* so is the clue to human purpose. Any logical answer to why the part exists derives from the perceived purpose of the whole. But it seems that we humans have been rarely impressed with this apparent logic. Normally, we have preferred to imagine the whole to be extraneous to our perceived purpose other than to be its servant.

If human behavior throughout history is a clue to this perceived purpose, then, it has been to gain power and exercise this power for the sake of goals that are heedless as to how the social or environmental whole is affected. As a result, it has only been the constant restraint exerted by those with more noble mythic views of how humans should relate that has saved us from our own genocidal and global-cidal insanities.

Necessity of Destruction

The universe has, through its evolutionary drama, endowed humans with the unique capacity to discern options, make choices, and create meaning. It is this capacity that enables us to live with deliberateness. This places us in a position to creatively or destructively manipulate our relationships to self, others, and the universe. Because of the very nature of existence, we cannot avoid being destructive. As the Spanish artist Pablo Picasso understood:

Every act of creation is first of all an act of destruction.

Lifestyle

To survive requires that we destroy. However, our capacity for deliberateness makes it possible for us to offset this destruction by creatively replacing and maintaining social and environmental ecological balance. In brief, deliberateness empowers us to determine which side of the creation-destruction equation gets the focus of our energies and, therefore, which side characterizes our lifestyle of existence.

Intrinsic to this deliberateness is the choice of attitude we select as our response to the gifts of life and unique capacities. More than anything else, it is this choice of attitude that determines our choice of lifestyle. There are two basic options of attitude open to us.

Hubris

One attitude is hubris. This term derives from the Greek word *hybris* which refers to arrogance, overbearing pride, insolence, and calculated maliciousness. The attitude of hubris responds to its relationships with a disdaining I-It utilitarianism. Its view of self is that of a superior. Its priorities of concern begin with self at the top, the universe at the bottom, and selected useful others in between. The end result is a lifestyle of destructiveness both socially and environmentally that feels no sense of responsibility about the effect of its utilitarianism.

Humility

The other basic attitude option is that of humility. This word derives from the Latin term *humilis* and refers to modesty, unpretentiousness, meekness, and, by inference, gentleness and peacefulness. It is a refusal to exalt one's self—as in refusing to permit one's feet to be higher than the ground upon which they stand.

The attitude of humility inevitably responds to its relationships with an I-Thou sense of having been gifted with undeserved favor. Its priorities of concern are determined by what seems necessary in balancing the well-being of self, others, and the universe. The end result is a lifestyle of stewardship creativity.

This stewardship is more than a mere caretaking of relationships. It is a deliberate attempt to multiply mutual benefit. The attitude of stewardship creativity is grounded in an awareness that essential to the uniqueness of our humanness is the ability to create a mythic conscience with values that demand caring. If the universe as a whole is indifferent to the human drama in that it dispenses its favors and disfavors indiscriminately, then stewardship creativity endows this drama with a caring that pervades the entirety of human relationships.

It is only because of my discerning and choosing nature that I can create principles to guide life and ethics to define relationships. It is this nature that brings into existence the notion of caring and insists that choices be made about its application in my relationships.

Dominance

Since there are no pure humans, there are no pure attitudes. All humans live somewhere on a continuum between these two basic attitude options. Lifestyle is determined by which attitude gets the dominance of our energy.

Answering the Question

The myth of spirituality gives a primary focus to the stewardship creativity attitude of humility. Thus its answer to the question *"What is my purpose?"* will be reflective in some way of the following assumptions:

> ➢ The universe composes itself of the same stuff. Therefore, human purpose involves treating everything else in the universe with the same sense of sacredness that humans endow upon themselves.

> ➢ The universe has gifted humans with the unique capacities of deliberateness and conscience. Therefore, human purpose involves using these gifts in the creative stewardship of all human relationships.

> ➢ The universe is the whole that births and sustains humans. Therefore, human purpose involves an obligation, to whatever extent possible, to live in ways that enhance the well-being of

the universe and specifically to the immediate planetary context of our living.

➤ The universe has graced humans with an evolved intelligence
beyond that of other known planetary species. Therefore, human purpose involves a response of willful gratitude rather
than assumed superiority.

These assumptions imply that human purpose in relating to self,
others, and the universe should be characterized by a deep sense of
sacredness, stewardship, obligation, and gratitude. When the human
conscience is fused by the values inherent in these assumptions of purpose, then human relating will reflect the highest possibilities of human nobility.

Nobility is a vision of the most morally inspiring and courageously
enhancing behavior within human grasp. It implies the will to sacrifice
for the sake of achieving this vision. It implies the motivating thrill of
living on the edge of the best that is possible in human behavior.

What Does My Death Mean?

This is the question about the nature of time in human existence. Is
our frolic in time boundaried by the events of our birth and death? In
answering this question there is a temptation to fall prey to two of the
most pervasive presumptions of human myth-making.

Presumptions

One of these presumptions is that humans, superior to the rest of
creation, are too valuable to simply cease to exist. The other presump-
tion is that human life is too important to be so full of unfairness and
injustice without redeeming correction. Both of these presumptions
draw the same conclusion, namely that physical death cannot possibly
be the end of human existence.

The unwillingness to accept human mortality and life's inequities
continues to spawn myths that, in one way or another, extend human
existence beyond death and correct life's maltreatment.

Problem

The problem with these mythic conjectures is that they seek to
posthumously alter the realities we know of our existence. Human

experience confirms that when we die we cease to exist as definitive creatures.

What we know of planetary life strongly suggests that death begins a process of energy transformation that distributes our physical remains into the ecological environment. While the energy that composed our peculiar form continues, the form itself is reabsorbed into the universal womb from which it came. Experience affirms that humans, then, are eternal only in that the stuff of their creation is eternal.

Food Chain Inequity

Moreover, the notion of correction of inequities is an idealistic product of human consciousness. There is no evidence that such exists for any form in the universe, including humans. The food chain is not into equity. Its very nature as process is inequity. And given the disdainful destruction heaped upon the rest of nature's forms by humans, it is fortunate for us that there is no built-in system of ultimate justice within the interdependent web.

As much as we humans would like to be viewed by the universe as special, preeminent beings exempt from the principles that govern both its nature and dynamic, there is no evidence that this is the case. Ridding ourselves of this desire would be a major step toward accepting the reality of our existence and creating myths within this reality that encourage nobility and stewardship in our immediate relationships.

Every particle of evidence that we humans can muster all converge toward a single conclusion, namely, that we are time-bound creatures who are derivative of other forms of creation and who return to other forms in the same derivative manner upon our death. We, by virtue of being human meaning-makers, may believe otherwise if we so choose. However, such belief must, of necessity, be constructed contrary to all historical and scientific evidence.

Answering the Question

Assuming an approach free of the speculations of human exemption, the myth of spirituality would answer the question *"What does my death mean?"* in some way reflective of the following assumptions:

➤ The universe is a living phenomenon that continuously transforms itself by creating and destroying those forms that express its being. Therefore, humans, as one of the patterned forms of its energy, live their span of existence and are reabsorbed into its transforming drama.

➤ The universe expresses itself in myriads and varieties of forms that survive by consuming each other. Therefore, humans, as one of these forms, participate in a food chain whose nature guarantees a reality of perceived unfairness that is persistent and without correction.

➤ The universe is an interdependent web of mutual effect. Therefore, the actions of individual humans will have an immediate effect on their social drama and ultimate effect on the universal whole.

The Realities

If we accept these assumptions, then logic encourages us to accept the following realities:

➤ The boundaries of human existence in time are birth and death.

➤ The life humans live within these boundaries will be impacted by nature's functional indifference.

➤ The actions of humans profoundly influence their own destiny and that of other forms.

These realities will not change unless the nature and dynamic of the universe changes.

The peculiar gift of humanness is the ability to create meaning. This ability rests on two capacities.

➤ The capacity to discern options, make choices, and thus live deliberately.

➤ The capacity to invent a mythic conscience that gives guidance to this choosing and deliberateness.

Out of these capacities rise human concepts of caring, fairness, and justice—concepts that further define human uniqueness. The catch-22 of human existence is that these concepts must be played out in a universe that is naturally indifferent to human moral and ethical concepts.

Instructions

Therefore, the meaning of human death implies these instructions:

> ➤ Whatever care, fairness, and justice exists in the human drama will be because humans so determine.
> ➤ Whatever contribution a single human makes to this determination must be initiated within that individual's earthly lifetime.
> ➤ Whatever the individual's contribution, positive or negative, its influence will become embodied in the universal, planetary, and human drama and continue beyond the boundary of that individual's death.

Whatever might be eternal in human existence is eternal in human influence. The interdependent web is one of mutual effect. The most notable effect is on those forms that make up the immediate environment of our living.

How Do I Know What I Know?

Every time we confront life's mystery with one of life's compelling questions it simply echoes our assumptions back to us off of its surface. Mystery's refusal to answer the most critical issues of our living leaves us flushed with vulnerable uncertainty and longing for the security of assurance.

The Key

Whatever security exists for us comes from the assurances of the authority which we finally choose to answer these questions. This is why the answer to the question *"How do I know what I know?"* is the key to living. This answer not only invents our myth by instructing the answers to the other questions, it assures us of its own validity and caresses our spirit with security.

Authorities Drama

So vital is this authority to our sense of well-being that we build our community life with people who share a similar authority, and we do verbal and physical battle with those whose authority is threateningly different. In a real sense, the drama of history is a drama of contentions and consensus around the authorities chosen for the creation and incarnation of myth.

Answering the Question

The myth of spirituality would answer the question *"How do I know what I know?"* in some way that reflects the following assumptions:

> ➤ The universe is made of and continuously creates and recreates all that is within it from the same stuff. Therefore, humans, despite their peculiarity of form, are made of the stuff of the universe.

> ➤ The universe's constant self-transformation is a dynamic process of energy exchange between and within its forms. Therefore, the path of all communication in the universe is the energy stuff of which it is made.

Out of these assumptions spirituality takes its cue for its perceptions about the source, authority, and path of knowing in human experience.

Source

Most major religious myths that have dominated Western culture over the past two thousand years claim to have received special, exclusive, irrefutable revelations of truth. These revelations are viewed as sealed from further intrusion because they are understood to answer the compelling questions of human existence once-and-for-all-time. Thus, these external authorities limit the scope of knowing to these answers and require that the meaning given to all human experience must conform to their implications in order to be true.

In addition, these answers are always anchored in the culture and knowledge limitations of some historical moment of the past. Thus, the requirement is that the believer either disavow the knowledge accumulated since the authority's advent or rationalize how this knowledge is irrelevant to accepting the authority. Examples of such religions in the Western culture are Judaism (the Torah), Islam (the Koran), Christianity (the Bible), and Mormonism (the Book of Mormon). These sealed revelations are the final authorities of these religions.

They are the ultimate source of knowing truth about human living. There is no appeal beyond their authority and scope except authoritative official interpretation.

The myth of spirituality is a study in contrast to these historic religions. The entire universe, and all that is within it, is its source of revelation. This includes accumulated human wisdom. The only limitation imposed on this revelation is the finite human mind seeking to penetrate the infinity of mystery. Thus, every moment of existence is ripe with further revelation. As physicist Emil Wiechert suggested while addressing a group of colleagues and economists in East Prussia in 1896:

The universe is infinite in all directions.

Individual humans cannot live long enough and human history cannot unfold into the future far enough to even begin to comprehend the scope of this potential revelation. We live within this infinity and this infinity lives within us. We are the same stuff. We are the pearl of Indra that reflects the whole. This revelation is, at the same time, out there and in here. And any new perception of truth about out there is also a perception of truth about in here.

For spirituality, all of creation is its Bible and the scope of this revelation is infinite.

Authority

In the ancient Jewish Temple in Jerusalem there was a special room called the Holy of Holies. In this room dwelt the Ark of the Covenant, supposedly containing the stone tablets upon which the Hebrew God Yahweh had written the ten commandments given to his prophet Moses.

This ark represented the presence of this God and the Holy of Holies was his symbolic dwelling place. So sacred was this place that it could be entered only once per year during Yom Kippur (the Day of Atonement). Moreover, the Hebrews, as a whole, were too sinful to enter this space without violating its sanctity. Only the High Priest, ritually cleansed, could enter it on behalf of the people.

Spirituality asserts that the universe is the Holy of Holies and every form within it, including humans, is a microscopic replica. Spirituality asserts that humans are their own High Priest and need no one to enter the Holy of Holies on their behalf, because they exist within it and it exists within them.

Thus, the mind of each human is its own ultimate authority for determining the truth encountered. And every individual is capable of receiving truth directly from the universal Holy of Holies without mediation.

This capability is evidenced in the history of human perception. Long before Einstein pronounced $E=MC^2$, the same truth existed in the Buddhist pearl of Indra insight. And long before the modern ecological notion of the interdependent web of existence, Francis Thompson had penned his poetic insight that one could not stir a flower without the troubling of a star.

Whether one is a religious philosopher, a poet, a physicist, an ecologist, or any other social persona, perceptions of truth are drawn from the same infinite universe. No one stands as an authority above another in garnering such perceptions. The universe is open to all. And each person's final authority for determining the steps of their frolic in its mystery is their own mind.

Path

The other issue of knowing is how the information inherent in the universe is accessed. What is the path of knowing? How can I have an I-Thou relationship with those things of creation that supposedly do not possess a human consciousness? The answer to this question by most major Western religions is an artful form of reductionism.

➢ The possible revelations of the universe are reduced to the text of an exclusive unchangeable and sacred manuscript.

➢ The ultimate value in creation is reduced to a being given human qualities and human consciousness so humans can have a personal relationship and conversation with this being.

➢ To assure that humans understand and do not deviate from the message of the sacred manuscript, special mediums reduce the text to appropriate meaning. These mediums are taught to interpret by interpreter trainers and are called by various names such as teacher, professor, priest, rabbi, minister, imam, etc.

The individual believer is allowed to personalize a relationship with this reduced god that is made known in this reduced revelation and explained through reduced interpreted guidance. A personal conversation can happen in this relationship that is normally called prayer on the believer's side and answering on the god's side. But whatever the descriptions of this process, they are framed within the boundaries of these prior reductions.

The myth of spirituality is, again, a study in contrast to such traditional Western religions. It asserts that our everyday existence is dependent on direct access to the energy revelations that make up creation. And the capacities with which the universe has endowed us are evolutionally designed to enable us to plug into these energy revelations on different levels, depending on our needs of survival and connection.

Physical Senses

One of these capacities is our ability to relate to the universe through special energy receptors called the physical senses. Our ability to see, hear, touch, taste, and smell are all ways that empower our direct communication with the environment of our living. Through these senses, messages are passed back and forth between the environment and ourselves.

For example, when I walk through a forest, all the forms of creation communicate their presence to me through my physical senses. The stuff of this communication is the energy of which everything is made. Our physical senses are designed to pick up the energy transmitted by our environment and send them to our brain where they are translated into images of identity. Each of our senses is designed to pick up certain kinds of energy vibrations. Everything our physical senses perceive is an energy transaction. This is absolutely amazing, yet so common is it to our experience that we take it for granted.

Human survival is dependent on how alert we are to these transmissions. Whether the threat to our well-being is the falling tree we see, the gas we smell, the roar we hear, the poison we taste, or the heat we feel, if we do not heed the message we will be harmed. Beyond surviving, the most basic information of everyday living is communicated through the energies of our environment along with what we call beauty. Far from being a novel idea, the essential purpose of our physical senses is to keep us in unceasing communication with the energies of the universe—from the rock on the ground to the star in the sky.

This communication is a way of knowing the universe directly. And my senses need no interpreter other than myself to make meaning from this experience. I do not need someone else to tell me the meaning of a sunrise or a flower.

Reason

Our other capacity for relating to the universe is our mind. Our mind is composed of two integrated abilities.

One of these abilities is reason. Reason enables me to think. Through reason I can add, subtract, multiply, and divide my experience into manageable proportions. This enables me to discern options, list consequences, and make choices. With this ability I can take the chaos of experience, create meaning, and invent reality. This is a way of knowing myself, others, and universe.

For example, I can take the jumbled experiences I have with another person and construct an image of that person's identity through reason. This construction is an act of creation, for others may know that same person differently by constructing an alternative image. I know the other forms of the universe the same way. Reason is my mental creator. It is the architect of my experience. Spirituality recognizes that reason is essential to both being a human and knowing as a human. Spirituality recognizes that not only survival but creativity are reliant upon our reasoning capacity.

Intuition

The other genius of my mind is intuition. Intuition is my way of connecting directly with the energy of whatever exists. Everything in the universe is made up of spinning vibrating energy. This energy transmits itself through signals. Through technology we have invented ways to harness and translate the meaning of some of these signals. This is what radar, sonar, radio, television, telephones, cell phones, and all cyberspace technologies are about.

The human mind that made these inventions has a far greater ability than the inventions it manufactures. Intuition is a profound energy antenna of the mind. It is designed to pick up the signals transmitted from all the universe's forms.

Intuition empowers me to bypass the limitations of my physical senses to experience and relate to the energy that is the essence of something. It empowers me to know without engaging the mathematical logic of reason. With this power I can sense the energy information that makes up the vast majority of my environment.

For example, as I listen to someone speak, my reason enables me to make logical sense of the words. However, intuition enables me to move behind this reasoned logic to connect with the energy mood of the speaker. This sensing communicates to me what the words do not tell. Does the mood of the speaker support or contradict the logic of the words? Is the speaker's mood pleasant or angry? Is the speaker complacent in attitude or convicted?

We assume such a dependence on the logic of reason to the extent that we fail to realize how little we would know if this logic were stripped of the input of intuition. Living would be a colorless, sterile, and dangerous experience without the input of intuition. Spirituality recognizes that intuition is vital to human reality, for it is a way of knowing what my physical senses and my reason cannot grasp.

The Problem

The problem we humans have in the Western world is the tendency to deny the potential of half of our mind. We are taught from birth to both disregard and distrust intuition in favor of reason. Yet, evolution has given us both abilities and these abilities are an integrated and synergistic whole.

Mindfulness is when both are working in mutual affirmation and appreciation. Either without the other is a crippling of our capacity to know. This mutual enhancement of reason and intuition is not only critical to my survival, it is critical to realizing whatever fullness of knowing I am capable of as a human.

We are fond of asserting the need to use our reason to correct our supposed highly fallible and often misguided intuition. There is a legend that gives a more accurate picture of the corrective process of those who have become comfortable with what intuition does for knowing (one version recorded in Blue Jacket Naval Support Activity, mid-south).

Early in the last century, in the days when the great fleets of sailing ships went out of New Bedford to scour the oceans of the world for whale oil, the most famous skipper of them all was Eleazer Hull. Captain Hull took his vessel into more remote seas, brought home greater quantities of oil, and lost fewer crewmen in the process than any other master of his time. And all this was the more remarkable, because he had no formal navigational training of any kind. When asked how he guided his ship infallibly over the desert of waters, he would reply: "Well, I go up on the deck, listen to the wind in the riggin', get the drift of the sea, and take a long look at the stars. Then I set my course."

One day, however, the march of time caught up with this ancient mariner. The insurance company whose agents covered the vessels of Captain Hull's employers declared that they would no longer write a policy for any ship whose master did not meet certain formal standards of education in the science of navigation.

Captain Hull's superiors could understand this new rule. But they were at a loss to know how to approach the proud man whose life had been spent on the bridge and tell him he must either go back to school or retire. After some consultation they decided to meet the problem head-on. Three of the company's top executives waited on Captain Hull and put their dilemma as tactfully as possible.

To their amazement the old fellow responded enthusiastically. He had, it appeared, always wanted to know something about science, and he was entirely willing to spend several months studying it. So the arrangements were made. Eleazar Hull went to school, studied hard, and graduated near the top of his class. Then he returned to his ship, set out to sea, and was gone for two years.

When the skipper's friends heard that he was putting into port again, they met him in an informal delegation at the docks. They inquired eagerly how it felt to navigate by the book after so many years of doing it the other way. "It was wonderful," Captain Hull responded. "Whenever I wanted to know my position, I'd go to my cabin, get out all the charts, work through the proper equations, and set a course with mathematical precision. Then I'd go up on the deck, get the drift of the sea, listen to the wind in the riggin', and take a long look at the stars. And correct my computation for error."

With the acknowledgment that the capacities of reason and intuition are an integrated whole and that favoring either over the other is always a detriment to full knowing, come these understandings:

> ➤ Without intuition I cannot commune with the energies of my environment, and without reason I cannot communicate about the energies of my environment.
> ➤ To experience profound meaning, I must relate through intuition. To communicate profound meaning, I must relate through reason.

Attunement

What do we mean when we say we are in tune or on the same wavelength? What does it mean when we say we feel good or bad vibes? What does it mean when we say we sense the spirit of a crowd or event?

Attunement, wavelength, vibes, and spirit are simply different choices of words to describe our intuitive connection with the spinning and vibrating energy of our environment. Every form in creation exudes energy consistent with its being. When groups of these forms are gathered, they combine their exuded energies and create a field of energy that characterizes their essential and dominant mood that is accessible to humans.

A simple human illustration is the mood of a crowd gathered for an explicit purpose. Animals, trees, plants, flowers, insects, and all the other forms of creation do the same. We just seem to be more adept at picking up the energy humans exude than other forms. But all beings in the universe are surrounded by the energies flying off of their being.

Spirituality is a term that implies both an awareness that everything is energy being and a deliberate willingness to be attuned with this energy. It could be called essentiality or energyality or stardustality. The term is less important than the notion that through the gift of intuition, we humans can break the barrier of form and commune directly with the form's spiritual, essential, energy, or stardust being.

Spirituality as Interface

Religious philosopher Friedrich Schliermacher once observed that the spiritual is the interface between the infinite and the finite. Interfacing is to be together, one with the other. It is to mingle, enmesh, and mix. A spiritual relationship is to interface with another of creation's beings. It is to touch and embrace with mutual essence. We humans tend to accept this possibility with other humans, but tend to reject it as a possibility with nonhumans.

The myth of spirituality invites us to rise above this cynicism and enter the realm of relating opened to us by the intuitive pathway. It invites us to acknowledge our full mind abilities by heeding the insight of Jacquelyn Small as she expressed in *Awakening in Time:*

We are not human beings learning to be spiritual. We are spiritual beings learning to be human.

Spiritual is not something we catch or try to be. Spiritual is what we are. Indeed, the most profound of human experiences are spiritual. Love is an example. Love is an opening of self to another person that invites a knowing beyond the verbal and physical. It is an attempt to enter the essence or spirit of that person and commune with the energy of their being. It is an intuitive connection which breaches the barrier of individual form that allows a bonding that anchors in mutual depth. Poetry is reason's imaginative attempt to articulate this experience.

Spirituality invites us to enter such holy communion with the other forms of creation on whatever level is possible. In so doing, we find that the negative epithet of "tree huggers," often thrown at environmentalists, becomes a metaphorical reality with stupendous relationship consequences. One comes to see divinity in the tree and all else in creation. A world of reality is opened that totally dwarfs the miniature reality of those who see nothing important in living except subduing and conquering the earth for human benefit. The ecology movement is transformed into a relational movement by endowing creation with a soul of being. And one of Albert Einstein's comments takes on profound meaning:

To teach a child not to step on a caterpillar is as good for the child as for the caterpillar.

Spirituality as Relationship

Spirituality is not a practice or religious ritual, although such may facilitate our capacities. Spirituality is a way of relating. And while this relating is highly personal, it does not require that the forms related to be personalized by reducing them to human characteristics because it is a relation of essence to essence. And rather than reducing what can be known in the universe, it expands the possibilities of knowing beyond human capacity to articulate. And rather than forcing a reliance upon external authority and interpreters of authority, it posits sovereignty in the mind of the individual.

Here is a summary of spirituality's view of knowing:

> ➤ The individual human mind is its own ultimate authority of knowing.
> ➤ The universe of our human dwelling is the source and scope of knowing.
> ➤ The human body's senses and the human mind's reason and intuition are the paths of knowing.
> ➤ We may know other forms of creation by relating to them spirit to spirit or essence to essence because everything is made of the same stuff.
> ➤ How we know other forms is limited to both our human capacities and our will to open ourselves in communion to these forms.

Responding

As with any new emerging myth, spirituality will find itself being expressed through all manner of speculative applications. The primary error that will be made in responding to spirituality is judging the core of the myth by its most radical expressions. This is normally the response of those who are less interested in what the myth is about as a new way of seeing, and more interested in what it is about as a threat to old ways of seeing. Such responses reflect a need for mythic security and tend to judge the new with negative defensiveness.

For those with more openness to the possibilities of what the new might offer, spirituality holds forth a promise. This is not a promise to resolve the mystery of the universe or to give proof beyond faith to our answers to life's compelling questions. Rather, it is a promise to transform the steps of the human frolic within this mystery by choreographing answers that envision a new relationship of humans with the universe.

So shall we come to look at the world with new eyes.
—Ralph Waldo Emerson

A human being is part of the whole that we call the universe, a part limited in time and space. Humans experience themselves, their thoughts and feelings, as something separated from the rest—a kind of optical illusion of their consciousness. This illusion is a prison for us, restricting us to our personal desires and to affection for only the few people nearest us. Our task must be to free ourselves from this prison by widening our circle of compassion to embrace all living beings and all nature.
—Albert Einstein

PART III

Creating America's Story

Every possible adjective, both negative and positive, that humans can use to describe the human drama must be applied to the transaction of the birth and development of the American experiment. The political expression of this mythic drama can be subsumed under the label of democracy.

We must continue to call the application of this myth an experiment because the essential covenant and spirit that imbues democracy with its meaning has yet to be fully realized. Indeed, there is every reason to believe that the outcome of the experiment hangs in balance, awaiting the actions of the citizenry. These actions have to do with seriously applying the process, spirit, and conscience of democracy to cultural living, and recognizing and disempowering the true mythic enemies of democracy that limit this application.

This segment of the book takes a cursory look at how the American political myth might be given translation and a brief look at those myths that have aligned themselves against its viability and perpetuation.

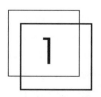

The Government of the Vision
(Map and Steering)

Government, like dress, is the badge of lost innocence.
—Thomas Paine

To govern means to rectify.
—Confucius

Government

The word government is from old French and originally meant to steer or pilot a ship. Thus it is to give direction toward a destination. Such directing involves both the knowledge of how to arrive at the destination and the authority to steer the course. Whatever the culture, the knowledge for arriving is a mythic map. And that same map will announce the authority for steering. Government is a culture's political organization designed to fulfill its mythic promise. Its intention is to serve as a pilot toward mythic fulfillment. This mythic intention is wholly apart from the actual realities involved in mythic application and realization.

Mythic Map

The founding fathers of American democracy were a fearful bunch. And given political history up to their time, along with their new-world experience with England, they had a right to be cautious. They were creating a new mythic map based on history's short-lived previous voyages. Democracy was where they wanted the map to guide them.

The primal issue of fear was the authority for taking them to this destination. They knew this authority must exist because the voyage necessitated a pilot. What they wanted to avoid was an imperial au-

271

thority. And what they wished to accomplish was a mostly all-hands-on-board participation in this authority, as in qualified white males. This desired participation was not a consensus agreement, rather a majority wisdom. In brief, the issue was how to design a government with enough authority to benefit and honor the democratic goal and process but without the capacity to become despotic.

Government Authority

The end result was a three-headed pilot—the legislative, the executive, the judicial. This trinitarian head was deliberately juxtaposed in authority and function to provide checks and balances in piloting and to slow down the process of decision-making so as to preclude hastiness and unilateral leadership. While these three heads of authority were intended to be permanent, the citizenry, through representative government and the democratic voting process, could give them new faces of wisdom.

Citizenry Authority

Thus, while the immediate authority for governing rested in this trinity of heads, the ultimate authority for governing rested in the citizenry's electoral choosing. While the citizenry could not change the form of government with ease, they could change the face of government at will.

Balanced Tension

It is only natural that given the ambivalent desire for freedom and wariness of government that could make that freedom possible, the founding fathers would have created an organizational Frankenstein of caution, contention, and competition. The genius of this organization of authority permits citizenry freedom and government conduct to coexist in balanced tension. However, it must be affirmed that the design of this government was to give the citizenry the final word in direction and the ultimate control of power as understood by some of the nation's early luminaries:

The people's government made for the people, made by the people, and answerable to the people.
                                                        —Daniel Webster

Why has government been instituted at all? Because the passions of men will not conform to the dictates of reason and justice without constraint.

—Alexander Hamilton

2

The Covenant of the Vision
(The Heart of Democracy)

We may be tossed upon an ocean where we can see no land—nor, perhaps, the sun or stars. But there is a chart and a compass for us to study, to consult, and to obey. That chart is the Constitution.
—Daniel Webster

A constitution is a thing antecedent to a government, and a government is only the creature of a constitution. The constitution of a country is not the act of its government, but of the people constituting a government.
—Thomas Paine

Social Conviction

The essential truth of the American democratic myth is that its political expression derived from a social conviction. Political structures are birthed and sustained by social desires which were what the originating conventions, debates, and declarations were all about on the part of the revolutionary and constitutional congresses. The politics and government of such a democracy are only tools for processing social convictions. The governmental structures and political processes of democracy can only fulfill their purpose when informed by a social spirit and conscience. Thus, before democracy can be vital, applied politics, it must be vital, affirmed mythic covenant.

A covenant is an agreement among a people about how they will behave toward each other. There are no deliberate, lasting, and consequential human relationships formed outside of explicitly stated or implied covenants. This is so whether such relationships be of individuals or cultures.

Without social covenant, the politics and government of democracy readily make themselves available to serve private agenda. Before democracy is embodied, political and governmental expression, it is convicted social ideal. This social conviction roots in a perception once expressed by the Greek philosopher Aristotle:

> *Democracy arose from men thinking that if they are equal in any respect they are equal in all respects.*

Indeed, the critical struggle of the founding fathers was how to most effectively translate this social ideal into political covenant and governmental organization within the context of their existing prejudices and fears.

Declaration of Independence

Behind the American Constitution (mythic covenant), stands the Declaration of Independence (mythic ideal). Note these words in its preamble:

> *We hold these truths to be self-evident, that all men are created equal, that they are endowed by their Creator with certain unalienable Rights, that among these are Life, Liberty, and the pursuit of Happiness.— That to secure these rights, Governments are instituted among Men, deriving their just powers from the consent of the governed ...*

This declaration affirms human equality in those rights that affirm life, liberty, the pursuit of happiness, and the function of government in securing these rights through self-rule. This is a view of social covenant with government as the fulfilling agent of the covenanted people.

American Constitution

The American Constitution fleshes out this concept of social covenant. Consider the stated purpose of the union of states:

> *We the People of the United States, in Order to form a more perfect Union, establish justice, insure domestic tranquility, provide for the common defense, promote the general Welfare,*

and secure the Blessings of Liberty to ourselves and our Posterity, do ordain and establish this Constitution for the United States of America.

Union, justice, tranquility, defense, general welfare, and the blessings of liberty are social goals. While the means of achieving these goals is political, the purpose of politics is fulfillment of a democratic social covenant.

Amendments

The first ten amendments to the Constitution are the Bill of Rights, with others being added when deemed necessary. Some of those addressing democratic rights include:
- the right to freedom of religion, speech, press, assembly, and petition
- the right to bear arms (to create a militia)
- the right to be protected against unreasonable search and seizure
- the right to due process of law including Grand Jury indictments and forbiddance of double jeopardy
- the right to a speedy trial by public jury with defense counsel
- the right to be protected from excessive bail and unusual punishments
- the right to refuse slavery and involuntary servitude
- the right to vote when of legal age
- the right to sell and consume alcoholic beverages

These amendments primarily process a social covenant.

The Declaration of Independence, the American Constitution and the Constitution's Bill of Rights amendments are clearly an announcement of a social covenant designed to promote equality of human liberty and civil rights with government as the agent of this promotion. The individual vote of qualified males was viewed as the political tool that assures the covenanted community will remain in ultimate authority.

The Imperative

It is not simply the privilege of voting which is symbolized in the concept of democracy that defines the American social covenant, it is equally the aforementioned documents that define the goals and nature of this democracy. The imperative of the covenant is the purpose of the vote, namely, to process the desired end of the covenant. Thus, in making any judgments about the historical successes or failures of the American brand of democracy, this wholeness must be kept in mind. The vote is the method and the goals are the motive. All references to democracy that follow are references to this wholeness within the American social drama.

Process, Spirit, and Conscience

Democracy, then, is a covenanted mythic social transaction that works itself out through the political and social institutions of the culture. Informing this transaction is:

- ➤ a process of democracy—a means of dialogue and vote that assures citizenry direction and rule
- ➤ a spirit of democracy—a relational egalitarianism that instructs citizenry attitudes and behaviors
- ➤ a conscience of democracy—a nexus of purpose that instructs citizenry decisions and judgments

In 1939, President Franklin D. Roosevelt affirmed this meaning:

Democracy, the practice of self-government, is a covenant among free men to respect the rights and liberties of their fellows.

Forms

Derivative of this covenant and its process, spirit, and conscience are various forms of the American version of democracy that declare themselves as stated or implied character traits:

- ➤ As Covenant: Democracy is a form of government in which the citizenry lives out a social promise to pursue the goals of its grounding documents.
- ➤ As Vote: Democracy is a form of government in which ultimate power is granted to the citizenry by virtue of equality of vote.
- ➤ As Reciprocity: Democracy is a form of government that seeks to maximize the values and benefits for both the individual and the community.

> ➤ As Dialogue: Democracy is a form of government in which the merits of both the lone decision-making of the individual and the companioned decision-making of the community are honored through open dialogue.
> ➤ As Representation: Democracy is a form of government in which the citizenry is represented by duly elected officials who, in trust of their office, make decisions and institute laws that are designed to reflect citizens' desires and benefit the nation as a whole.
> ➤ As Sacrifice: Democracy is a form of government in which, oxymoronically, the part is expected to sacrifice for the sake of the whole so that the whole can create a greater blessing for the sake of the part.

While these forms are ideal ways of viewing democracy, it is the extent to which they are both acknowledged as character traits and acted upon as imperatives that the spirit and conscience of democracy can be embodied by the citizenry.

It is this embodiment that is the measure of the power of democracy to overcome its avowed enemies and model its transforming capacities, whether that power is internal within the nation or external among the nations. Thus, if these forms are at least partial expressions of the true character of American democracy, when engaged with serious commitment by the population, both the individual and community will flourish with mutual blessing and a larger majority of the citizenry will feel enfranchised in some consequential measure. And equally important, it will not be possible for any part of the private sector to hijack the democratic apparatus and process from citizenry control.

It has been said that democracy is the worst form of government except all those other forms that have been tried from time to time.

—Winston Churchill

Reflection

American democracy is an egalitarian social covenant that express-es itself through political organization and social means. This percep-tion finds ample verification by noting that the definitive moments of social conflict in American history all address a hypocrisy of the democratic spirit and a violation of the democratic conscience—with a consequent alteration of political process and privilege. Politics reflects the covenant, not vice versa.

The reason for this is fundamental to the success of American democracy. The politics of this democracy will always fail its mythic goal without an empowering and sustaining sense of social covenant by the citizenry. The principle that informs this is that the heart is the user. That is, behavior will conform to what the heart believes to be imperative. Social covenant (written or unwritten) is the heart's avowal of imperativeness. The unfolding of American history has been an attempt to bring the politics of democracy up to speed with the covenant of democracy. And it has been a cruel and bloody process.

Covenant and Evolution

There are three essential things to note about American democracy as a social covenant:

➢ It is fixed on social ideal.

Equality is the result of human organization. We are not born equal.
—Hannah Arendt (*Origins of Totalitarianism*)

Our democracy recognizes the innate unfairness of human existence that underscores the inequality of social living. It attempts to surmount these inequalities with attitudinal, relational, organizational, political, and legal structures. The spirit and conscience of this democracy accepts this challenge as an imperative while knowing it as an impossibility. It is the citizenry's energy invested in this challenge that empowers the democratic myth with its life and success.

➢ It is founded on social trust.

Government is a trust, and the officers of the government are trustees; and both the trust and the trustees are created for the benefit of the people.
—Henry Clay (1829, Speech, Lexington, Kentucky)

The people rely on the politicians they elect and appoint to be honest, ethical, and true to the spirit and conscience of democracy. In brief, the sole function of the politician is to honor their election or appointment with trustworthiness in respect to democratic spirit and conscience. The frustration of democracy is the violation of this trust. Fortunately, in the past, there have normally been just enough trust-worthy trustees to make democracy viable. It is the waxing and waning of this trust, based on trustee behavior, that will contribute heavily to the fate of America's democratic experiment. And although that fate is not sealed, there are sufficient negative phenomena to invite a measure of skepticism. Trust defies such skepticism. Thus, there is a measure of willful blindness in the expression of trust that sustains hope for suc-cess and anticipates a better future.

> ➤ It is forged on social change.

Democracy is not an easy form of government, because it is never final; it is a living changing organism, with a continuous shifting and adjusting of balance between individual freedom and general order.
—Ilka Chase (1942, *Past Imperfect*)

Former president Jimmy Carter compares democracy to the expe-rience of life in its constant social testing and change. Since its incep-tion, the structures and politics of American democracy have grown increasingly burdened as it has adjusted to the ever increasing com-plexity of social need. Thus, while it is legitimate to appeal to the na-tion's grounding documents, it is also valid to rely on the spirit and conscience of democracy for guidance. After all, it is this spirit and conscience that not only created these original documents but has also provoked their amendments.

The government is us; we are the government, you and I.
—Theodore Roosevelt (Speech, 1902, Ashville, North Carolina)

Every government degenerates when trusted to the rulers of the people alone. The people themselves therefore are its only safe depositories.
—Thomas Jefferson (Letter, 1820, to W. C. Jarvic)

3

The Tension of the Vision
(Freedom and Equality)

*Whatever America hopes to bring to pass in the world
must first come to pass in the heart of America.*
—Dwight D. Eisenhower

*Freedom exists only where the people take care of the gov-
ernment.*
—Woodrow Wilson

The Paradox

In American democracy there is an essential paradox that provides
constant tension in both its philosophy and practice. In a 1940 speech
entitled *The War and the Future*, Thomas Mann insightfully defined
this paradox:

*It is a strange fact that freedom and equality, the two basic
ideas of democracy, are to some extent contradicting. Logically
considered, freedom and equality are mutually exclusive, just as
society and the individual are mutually exclusive.*

In a real sense, the historical struggle of American democracy
has been the tensional conflict between the perceived right of self-
determination (freedom) and the perceived responsibility of public
obligation (equality). This struggle is grounded in grave questions of
concern:

> ➢ To what extent does the majority owe its minority?
> ➢ To what extent are the enfranchised responsible for the welfare
> of the disenfranchised?

281

> To what extent does the democratic conscience act in outlaw-
ing the expression of undemocratic ideals and behavior?

> To what extent is the application of perceived democratic ide-
als permitted to expand beyond the limited and biased perceptions of America's founding fathers?

> To what extent does government interfere in the private sector
to secure public good?

> To what extent does government subsidize business and indi-
viduals without violating democratic principles?

> To what extent do appointed and elected representatives advo-
cate for the concerns of part of America over concerns for the
whole of America?

> To what extent is unregulated capitalism an expression of un-
democratic privilege?

There has always been a rift in American opinion over answers
to these questions because they represent some of the paradoxical
tensions of democracy. This rift can be summarized in the meanings
given to one phrase in Abraham Lincoln's famous 1863 Gettysburg
Address:

... of the people, by the people, for the people ...

The phrase in contention is "for the people." The question is the
meaning of the phrase as it relates to the tensional paradox of freedom
and equality.

The Parties

While the tension of this phrase finds reflection in every corner
of American culture, it also finds symbolic expression in the political parties that have dominated the culture's political life. Throughout
American history there have been various political parties with various names and platforms. Despite different names, it has sometimes
been difficult to distinguish between the platforms of many of these
parties. This started to change in the early part of the twentieth century with the emergence of two fairly distinct political parties claiming to champion the true meanings of democracy—the Republicans
and the Democrats. These two parties exhibit some clarity in regard

to their respective views about the meaning of the phrase "for the people." These views are apparent in their policies, platforms, and voting practices.

Republicans

Republicans tend to come down on that side of the paradox that underscores freedom. This focus is generally on the freedom of economic self-determination. It would not be fair to say that Republicans are more concerned about business than people. It is more accurate to say that they believe unfettered business is what's best "for the people." This view was summarized by the president of General Motors Charles Erwin Wilson in 1952 when the auto industry was bourgeoning:

> *What is good for the country is what is good for General Motors, and what is good for General Motors is good for the country.*

Inherent in this philosophy is the tendency to view capitalism and democracy as synonymous—the notion that free individuals and free enterprise are inseparable.

It finds a broader summarizing expression in the rhetoric of the following 1908 Republican Party Platform Plank:

> *The trend of democracy is toward socialism, while the Republican Party stands for a wise and regulated individualism. Socialism would destroy wealth; Republicanism would prevent its abuse. Socialism would give to each equal right to take; Republicanism would give to each an equal right to earn. Socialism would offer an equality of possession which would soon leave no one anything to possess. Republicanism would give equality of opportunity.*

The stress in this platform is individualism and the right to earn wealth and not have it taken by government taxation and gifted to others or applied to socialistic enterprises. It is an advocate of that part of the American Dream that offers the opportunity of upward mobility of wealth and the worth-inducing social status of procured wealth. Underneath this philosophy is the conviction that people are responsible for their own economic plight since anyone can achieve wealth by pulling up on their own bootstraps. This conviction is the legacy of pioneering America's philosophies of rugged individualism and self-determination.

A second major part of the Republican political equation is that the wealthier the wealthy, the greater the benefit to all the nation's citizens. A late twentieth century example is Republican president Ronald Reagan's trickle-down economics policy—the assumption that those at the bottom of the economic pile will eventually profit if those at the top of the economic pile profit now. Thus, the function of government is to abet the profits of an unfettered free enterprise so that wealth will increase for those at the top of the economic ladder and eventually benefit those at the bottom.

A third major part of the Republican perspective is that government must be kept limited if individual freedom is to be kept safeguarded. While a part of the concern in this view is that the government should minimize its interference in the private lives of the citizenry, its focus is that government should back off of anything that might negatively affect or curb business profits. That is, the government should approach the business world with little or no regulations as to how business operates in the social environment. Personal freedom and business freedom are seen as synonymous.

Consistent with these three perspectives, a fourth characteristic of the Republican political posture becomes apparent. This characteristic is a posture that inevitably favors management over labor. Votes and positions taken over the past hundred years show this to be a firm posture, irrespective of the issue. The wealth and political clout of the Republican Party had been so powerful in earlier American history that it was able to enlist both law enforcement and the military on its side in suppressing the interests of labor. In today's world it has the backing of a corporate-controlled Congress and does not need force of arms to impose its will.

In whatever way the Republicans' view of the meaning of the phrase "for the people" is given interpretation, it will evoke the notion of an economic freedom that favors business and its management with minimal interference by government regulation. If the reference is to that part of the American Dream that refers to the possibility of upward mobility, then each citizen is responsible for creating their own opportunities.

Democrats

Democrats tend to come down on that side of the paradox that underscores equality. They focus on the public obligation to reduce the level of social inequality. It would not be fair to say that Democrats are more concerned about people than business. It would be more accurate to say that they believe that social programs that enhance the opportunities of egalitarianism are what is best "for the people." Inherent in this philosophy is the tendency to view the common good and democracy as synonymous, and the belief that the function of democratic government is to process the democratic spirit and conscience.

The presidential initiatives of the New Deal (Roosevelt), the Fair Deal (Truman), and the Great Society (Johnson) symbolize this philosophy. All of these initiatives assume an obligation on the part of the government to uphold and promote the equality of opportunity of citizens irrespective of their economic or social status. Attendant to this focus is the notion that the function of inequitable taxation is an equitable distribution of benefit to the whole nation. Thus, citizens with maximal wealth should be willing to share this wealth through tax-supported programs with those citizens who have minimal wealth so that all can participate equally in the blessings of democratic living. It is assumed that the wealth of the wealthy is generally accrued at the expense of those who are economically deprived. Thus, sharing the wealth speaks to visibly enhancing the egalitarian spirit and conscience of democracy.

A second major focus is the protection and processing of citizenry civil rights. Again, the government is viewed as the primal instrument of this goal. When there have been consequential cultural corrections and uplifting of civil rights, it has usually been under the advocacy of some element of Democratic party leadership whether that leadership is elected or has risen from other ranks. Prime examples of this advocacy were the late twentieth century feminist and civil rights movements.

A third major stress is that the government has an obligation to protect the citizenry from the machinations of business through a regulation that honors both the right to a fair profit for business and the right of the citizenry to not be economically victimized by business. This is a stress that has essentially come into its own following the first third of the twentieth century when big business, in consort with government, behaved so brutally toward labor, and when lack of governmental regulation set the stage for that national disaster called the Great Depression.

It should be no surprise, given these perspectives, that Democrats will inevitably favor labor over management when it comes to disputes about fair remuneration and safe working conditions. This is their fourth party stress.

The essence of these Democratic perspectives finds expression in the rhetoric of Abraham Lincoln. While Lincoln was a Republican in his era, his views about the role of government seem more consistent with that of twentieth-century Democrats:

> *The legitimate object of government is to do for the community of people whatever they need to have done, but cannot do at all, or cannot do so well, for themselves, in their separate and individual capacities. In all that the people can individually do as well for themselves, government ought not to interfere.*

While citizen responsibility to care for itself is affirmed, the stress in this statement is on a democratic government that takes up the cause of the citizenry where individual circumstance and capacity find their limits. It is an advocate of the democratic conscience that asserts the social worth of all citizens. Underneath it is the conviction that the government should be proactive in helping those who cannot help themselves. The assumption is that bootstrap individualism is neither up to handling all life circumstance, nor matching individual capacities. If the reference is to that part of the American Dream that opens all citizens to the possibility of upward mobility, then the role of government is to help equalize the opportunity for all citizens.

In whatever way the Democrats' interpretation of the phrase "for the people" is given expression, it will impinge on those notions that government action should reflect the spirit and conscience of democracy and that the maximally blessed have a primal obligation to contribute to raising the quality of living for the minimally blessed. That is, the part does not exist for the sake of itself, but for the sake of the whole of which it is part. Moreover, the obligation of the whole is to enhance the quality of existence of the part for not only the sake of the part but for the sake of the whole.

Caricatures

All descriptions of groups of people must, of necessity, be carica-
tures because within such groups people run a gamut of viewpoints
from conservative to liberal. Thus all who claim to be Republicans and
Democrats may not agree with the brief foregoing analysis. They may
hold a mixture of party views while claiming the party label of only
one. Or they may reside at one of the radical polarities. This is why
the terms moderate and independent are useful. Both Republicans and
Democrats would assert strong interest in both economics and people.
However, there is a stress of both rhetoric and vote that distinguishes
them sufficiently as to elicit a sense of clarity about what meaning they
each give to the phrase "for the people."

Corrective Dialectic

There is in the American democratic process a kind of historical
zigzag of corrective political decisions that has kept it from the act of
self-destruction. In the last half of the twentieth century and the beginning of the twenty-first century, this process of correction is vividly dramatized by the platforms and value contentions between the
Republican and Democratic parties. They have decidedly exemplified
the tug-of-war in the tensional democratic paradox between the notions of freedom and equality, self-determination and public obligation, and economic opportunity and social vision.

Enigma

There seems to be some innate sense in America's democratic conscience that perceives when enough is enough—although awakening
this sense has often required the deafening roar of excess. Nevertheless,
the answer to the meaning of the phrase "for the people" remains enig-
matic because the paradox of democracy can never be ultimately resolved without dissolving the very tensions that make humans who
they are and which gives democracy its appeal.

The stakes ... .are too high for government to be a spectator sport.
—Barbara Jordan

He serves his party best who serves his country best.
—Rutherford B. Hayes

Thus the most democratic country on the face of the earth is that in which men have, in our time, carried to the highest perfection the art of pursuing in common the object of their common desires and have applied this new science to the greatest number of purposes.
—Alexis de Tocqueville (a reference to America)

The Illusion of the Vision
(Capitalism and Democracy)

*History suggests that capitalism is a necessary condition
for political freedom. Clearly it is not a sufficient condition.*

—Milton Friedman

The Enemy

Business is a necessity of economic health for any nation, regardless of its form of government. Business has never been the enemy of
democracy. The enemies of democracy are:

➤ those who use business as an instrument that corrupts the
democratic process, spirit, and conscience
➤ those who convert the democratic process into a means of
swelling their business profit
➤ those who abuse the citizenry for the sake of economic gain
➤ those whose only sense of principle and business morality is
the bottom line
➤ those who believe and practice the notion that government exists for the sake of business

When "big business" is mentioned in the comments that follow, it
is a reference only to those operators who fit the foregoing descriptions
of enemies.

A host of American businesses are driven by the democratic spirit
and conscience, both small and corporate. However, there are enough
that are driven by unmitigated greed as to poison the entire system and
unduly influence American economics in grossly negative ways. Greed
is the desire for more so acutely fixated that it is unable to perceive the

boundaries of principle or the honor of integrity. Greed is the essential nemesis of capitalism. No one objects to business making a fair profit; that is its primal purpose. However, the tendency of capitalism is to exceed fairness in profit taking. It is to maximize profit irrespective of possible harm. Such a tendency has no moral or democratic perspective. It exists for the sake of its own fulfillment.

Power lust is another major reason for abusing both business practice and the citizenry. However, in the business world it is difficult to separate such lust from greed because the acquisition of wealth is so often the path of acquiring power. The obverse is equally true. The primary reason for seeking positions of power is that of being able to manipulate its responsibilities and authorities for the sake of acquiring greater monetary gain. While the nuances of power lust and greed may have different faces, they are generally siamese.

Capitalism

Capitalism is an economic philosophy that espouses the belief that a free marketplace should and will regulate itself to the benefit of all concerned. American history shows this belief to have minimal ground in reality. This is why a multitude of government agencies and laws have been created to regulate capitalism and keep the marketplace under some measure of control that reflects an ultimate concern for the nation's economic health.

Moreover, this belief in the efficacy of capitalism to regulate itself does not account for the havoc created by the manipulations of the marketplace of those driven by greed and power lust, disrespect for human life, and disregard for the democratic spirit and conscience of the nation's covenant. As American history progresses, the negative consequences of such ill-motivated manipulations seem to find greater public expression. It has only been the intervention by strong government and its capacities that has placed any restraining curb on such manipulations. However, even restraint has not been sufficient to contain the damage done by these manipulations to the nation's economy.

It is obvious that capitalism is not a pure self-adjusting economic mechanism. It responds to quirks of production and consumption, as well as to lustful manipulations. It is grossly sensitive to the inexplicable mood shifts of both investors and consumers. Thus, it seems that capitalism is far more responsive to unnamable forces and the dark subtleties of human nature than it is to visible economic indicators. The debilitating and downward plunge of the market in the first decade of the twenty-first century illustrates how little even the experts can exert control over a system that seeks defiance of control and has a minimal sense of self-regulation.

The history of capitalism in America clearly shows that, when unregulated, it easily becomes a brutalizing and antidemocratic force in social life. And its unrestricted excesses can help to bring down a nation's economy as illustrated in the Great Depression that swept through both America and Europe during the 1930s. Ironically, out of this depression rose World War II which contributed to the salvation of capitalism. But this salvation was more than a shot in the arm provided by stimulated war production. It was equally the regulating interference of strong government, whether that government was despotic or democratic.

Democracy and Capitalism

In 1961, as President Dwight D. Eisenhower gave a parting speech as the outgoing president of the nation, he issued a warning. He suggested that America must guard against the military-industrial complex that had emerged from World War II. That complex was about a power that could endanger both civil liberties and the democratic process. While this may have seemed a rather shocking insight coming on the heels of a military-industrial cooperation that stood behind the American success of World War II, it was not a new insight except in reference to this peculiar partnership complex in America.

In the early part of the twentieth century, social activist Eugene V. Debs had stated:

The class which has the power to rob upon a large scale has also the power to control government and legalize their robbery.

Debs was referring to an economic class influential enough to exert control over a society's existence—namely, the upper class. However, his insight equally applies to any powerful controlling group in a nation's life. In America, it was the industrial robber barons of the late nineteenth and early twentieth centuries that filled this role by controlling government and legalizing their systematic robbery of the citizenry. It is the modern corporate robber barons of the last half of the twentieth century and the beginning of the twenty-first century that have assumed the same prerogative.

What Eisenhower did not perceive in the early 1960s was that this body of industrial corporations did not need the participating intrigue of the military to accomplish a national takeover. It only needed to control the government. And the government, as exemplified in its elected politicians, has been a willing coconspirator. It is the corporate-congressional complex that is the current threat to democracy. Indeed, it is this complex that poses the most dangerous internal threat to democracy that has ever risen out of the nation's history.

The power and enduring nature of the corporate-congressional complex lies in the fact that it is a willing partnership of complicity. It is an association of mutuality that has only one objective—namely, the profit aggrandizement of its respective parties. And since elected politicians are the face of the citizenry, then this congressional part of the complex is the face of the nation. That is, the corporate-congressional complex is as much the creation of the citizenry as it is of the corporations and Congress. Permission to exist without challenge is affirmation of acceptance, as well as willful collaboration. If the citizenry wished the dissolution of this destructive complex, it could make that wish come true through its ultimate power of the vote. The citizenry is responsible for the well-being of democracy. It is the owner.

Franklin D. Roosevelt, in a message to Congress in 1938, warned Americans about permitting ownership of the democratic process to be taken over by a power other than itself:

> *The liberty of a democracy is not safe if the people tolerate the*
> *growth of private power to a point which it becomes stronger*
> *than their democratic state itself. That, in its essence, is fascism—*
> *ownership of government by an individual, by a group, or by any*
> *other controlling private power.*

It seems obvious that the American people have been negligent of their privilege and responsibility as the owner of democracy and permitted their ownership to be hijacked by the corporate world with a self-centered acquiescence by Congress.

Purpose

The purpose of this control by the modern robber barons is to fulfill corporate aspirations of materialistic greed. The purpose of collaboration by the Congress is a *quid pro quo* accruement of both personal benefit and political election funding. And the obvious price the citizenry is paying for successful fulfillment of this collaboration is an erosion of its civil liberties and a submission of the democratic process to corporate control. This takeover of the government clearly shows that industry can be totally committed to capitalism without any concurrent evidential commitment to the spirit, conscience, or processes of democracy.

It also avows that maintaining their elected status, whatever the cost to the nation, is the paramount concern of the consistent majority of congresspeople. This indictment does not lump all politicians into the same mold. There are those who champion the cause of the people and democracy, and remain staunch in this posture. However, they are the decided minority and are often not only chastised by the majority for not playing the games of trust betrayal, but also deliberately marginalized in their capacity to influence the directions of Congress.

Those who consistently betray the trust of the electorate through their submission to corporate interests will vow that they have no other choice, given the financial necessities of gaining and holding public office. However, to say that Congress is caught in a financial circumstance that it cannot change is to admit to both a lack of courage in confronting a dysfunctional system and a failure of imagination as to how this system can be corrected in favor of democratic fulfillment. It is also a statement of what is of ultimate concern to the electing citizenry—namely, its own private goals over the goals of democracy. Given the continued attitudes of the corporate world, Congress, and the citizenry, the corporate-congressional complex is a fail-safe system of democratic mythic destruction.

Conclusion

American history favors the conclusion that capitalism is not synonymous with democracy. While it may have an affinity to the liberties implied in democracy as an economic philosophy, when turned loose without moral and legal control, it tends toward a form of totalitarianism that cares little about its effect on a nation's economic or social health. In brief, capitalism is unconcerned with either the democratic spirit or conscience. It is only concerned for the profit outcomes of its own economic motions. It is an amoral tool of its user.

Not a Naturally Occurring System

In a September 27, 1989, *Newsweek* editorial on Russia's downward spiral into economic chaos and corruption during the last years of the twentieth century, Fareed Zakaria cites the advice of Western government for Russia to simply adopt "a free and floating currency" (unrestrained capitalism) as the panacea for the country's ills. But the Russian government did not have the authority, trust, or will to engage this advice and make it happen. As Zakaria concludes, "Capitalism, it turns out, is not a naturally occurring system. It requires rules, laws, and customs to protect private property, enforce contracts, and ensure fair play."

It seems that for capitalism to work there must be regulation, constraint, and an authority to impose such by an entity which the people trust. Ultimately, only a strong government appears to be able to provide such a cultural need. Only strong government seems capable of a power greater than self-serving capitalistic oligarchies. Capitalism may find a consistency with the unrestrained spirit of free individualism, but it does not find a consistency with civil rights and the democratic spirit and conscience. To say this another way: Capitalism may have a natural affinity with the spirit of excessive individualism, but it does not have a natural affinity with the spirit and conscience of democracy because this spirit and conscience, above all else, is devoted to the welfare of the total community (*a more perfect union, promote the general welfare*).

Prior to the 1930s, capitalism worked well for the benefit of those who controlled the marketplace; but it did not work well for the benefit of the whole citizenry because the government did not have the will to exert itself on behalf of this citizenry. It was not until capitalism excessed into the collapsed economy of the Great Depression that the government mustered the will to regulate capitalism and exert control over the economy on behalf of all the citizenry. The production needs of the World War II solidified both the economy and government regulation. Strong government had been born and neither capitalism nor government would ever be the same. Capitalism had been saved from its own destructive libertinism. However, the future threat of excessed capitalism only awaited a moment when the government would unleash the reigns on economic libertinism by relaxing its regulatory control and oversight.

The Problem

Part of the problem of capitalism in America is that the more powerful advocates of its equation with democracy tend to elevate its stature as the measure of democracy, when the opposite should be the case. That is, democracy should be the measure of capitalism since democracy is the goal of the culture's myth. Here are three of the problems that ensue from this reverse equating and elevation:

(1) These advocates tend to insidiously measure democratic success by monetary achievement and announce accumulation as a prime virtue over the spirit and conscience of egalitarianism.

(2) These advocates tend to justify all manner of undemocratic behavior, no matter how unprincipled and brutalizing, for the sake of the economic aggrandizement of business.

(3) These advocates tend to condone the replacement of the American democratic tripartite form of government, designed to maintain the stable tension of mutual checks and balances between its branches, with an economic oligarchy that permits corporations to control the nation's vision and destiny for the sake of big business.

These advocates are usually also the champions of what can be called *Libertine Capitalism*. Libertine refers to an insistence on being totally unconstrained in behavior. The posture of *Libertine Capitalism* is an absolute lack of responsibility to the society that makes its existence possible. Its view is that it exists for the sake of itself rather than for the sake of the mythic purpose of the nation in which it functions. Its devotees are modern robber barons who are epitomized by the chief executives of the defunct Enron Corporation. These executives destroyed the livelihood and retirement future of thousands of people, wreaked havoc on the nation's economy, and nearly brought the state of California to its economic knees, profiting billions for themselves in the process. The practice of *Libertine Capitalism* is a primal bane of American democracy. It undermines the democratic spirit, violates the democratic conscience, and mocks the democratic process.

The word most adored by its practitioners is freedom because it so easily masks the irresponsibleness and unprincipledness that non-regulation opportunes. And its false postulate is that lack of restraint is the very essence of democratic liberty. The word most abhorred by its practitioners is socialism because such is the hidden cost required of any government that permits *Libertine Capitalism* to exist as part of its economy. Its trump card in times of trouble is an insistence that it must be rescued from the devastating consequences of its own behavior lest the nation's entire economy fail with it. Both freedom and socialism reside on the tip of the *Libertine Capitalist's* tongue awaiting vehement expression.

The essential attitude of *Libertine Capitalists* is contempt for those who seek to constrain their economic maneuverings, and for the general public which is the inevitable victim of their insatiable greed. Its practitioners are strangely moved to behave this contempt in any available symbolic manner. Flaunting the visible rewards of their mode of capitalism is a common symbolic expression. Golden parachutes, opulent transportation, exotic junkets, and office carpets that cost more than most of the citizenry's housing are typical examples. At the beginning of the twenty-first century the American and world economies experienced a devastating meltdown. An unregulated and unsupervised Wall Street was largely responsible for this fiasco. Yet, when rescued by the government with billions of taxpayer dollars, it simply expressed its contempt by continuing to feather its own nest and ignoring the needs of the nation.

In effect, some of the most powerful advocates of the equation of democracy and capitalism are more interested in the use of the liberties of democracy to enhance business profit than they are in business practice modeling the spirit and conscience of democracy. The intent of the myth of democracy as a cultural guide is to instruct the attitudes and behaviors of its parts. The strong advocates of the equation of capitalism and democracy have reversed this rule of culture. They believe capitalism should dictate national attitudes and behaviors. It is the tail wagging the dog. It is the part defining ethics for the whole. It is capitalism controlling American democracy and determining its character.

An Example

In the late nineteenth century, a reporter of the *Chicago Daily News* interviewed William K. Vanderbilt of the New York Central Railroad. The reporter asked if Vanderbilt ran his trains for the benefit of the public. The reply was, "The public be damned!" Further remarks from Vanderbilt indicated the view that his railroad was run for the sake of corporate interests and if the public benefited it was secondary to this goal.

Libertine Capitalism is alive and well in the twenty-first century. Certainly it is true that the purpose of business is to create profit. It is also true that the mass production of big business displays an efficiency that produces cheaper products and increased employment which are benefits to the general public. However, it is equally true that such efficiency, when authored by greed, also places profit above public interest and treats employees as impersonal tools to be picked up or discarded at corporate whim. Moreover, the primary concern of this authored greed is the use of government to increase profit and the attitude toward the cost of this corporate utilitarianism to the citizenry is, "The public be damned!" The apparent implication is that business has no obligation to the people of the mythic covenant that created its freedoms and potentials. It seems that little has changed in big business attitudes since the 1800s.

Capitalism, in a democracy, is not simply a moral free agent for profit taking. If it is not endowed with a morality that supports the egalitarian spirit and conscience of democracy, then it easily becomes a liability to democracy rather than an asset. It seems that the volunteerism of the majority of corporate executives in respect to observing the democratic spirit and conscience has been a failure. Indeed, what American history shows with unrelenting clarity is that the only force that holds corporate greed in check is imposed through law and regulation that guarantees severe monetary and legal penalties for violators. And even such penalties, at times, seem insufficient because the very notion of freedom in the American corporate world appears to be understood as freedom from restraint and morality rather than freedom to align with the goals of America's democratic mythic covenant.

The Illusion

That democracy and free enterprise seemed to have worked well together in the last half of the twentieth century created the illusion of synonymity. What is not recognized in this illusion is the regulatory role of strong government that made this compatibility possible. In brief, strong government restraint has been successful capitalism's greatest ally in the same manner that lack of government restraint has been its worst enemy.

Capitalism and Mythic Morality

There are those who advocate that capitalism, if it is to work, must exist within the context of democracy without principled restraint. They say that the corporations that symbolize capitalism cannot be treated as a person and that the executives that head corporations should not be held accountable for capitalism doing what it is supposed to do. In brief, they suggest that capitalism should not be faulted for being capitalism and its entrepreneurs should be viewed with the same amoral lack of judgment. These advocates also tend to see capitalism and democracy as synonymous.

However, if capitalism and democracy have any synonymy, then the principled restraints and moral perspectives of democracy must apply equally to the purveyors and the mechanisms of capitalism. Indeed, any economy functioning within American democracy must accommodate itself to the implications of the democratic process, spirit, and conscience irrespective of synonymy or lack thereof. There can be no legitimate systems sustained by democracy that do not contribute to democracy's mythic goals and that are not judged in their effect on these goals. The attempt to separate the functions of capitalism from the purposes of democracy is an exercise in ludicrous logic and has shown itself to be an impetus toward social disaster.

Covenant Goals

The documents that constitute the democratic covenant define the nature of mythic goals and the basis for all judgments of legitimacy. The Declaration of Independence states that among these goals are:

> Equality: all citizens, symbolically, being of the same rank, degree, merit, and political empowerment
> Life: the right of each citizen to the full benefits of human existence
> Liberty: the right of every citizen to be as free as permitted by the boundaries of community well-being
> Pursuit of Happiness: the right of all citizens to engage the fulfillment of their dreams

The purpose of democratic government is to create a cultural context in which these goals can be achieved to whatever extent the well-being of the entire nation permits. The well-being of the entire nation is the key to all government actions.

The Constitution states the characteristics of community life in which these mythic goals can be prosecuted. These characteristics are:

> A More Perfect Union: the individual states working cooperatively to strengthen the union toward a greater synergistic power
> Justice: the government holding the citizenry accountable for any behavior that discounts or violates civil rights and the spirit and conscience of the mythic covenant
> Domestic Tranquility: the government insuring that law and order prevail in such a fashion as to create a sense of internal citizenry well-being
> Common Defense: the government providing, by whatever means are necessary and consistent with its democratic covenant, protection for the nation's mythic and geographic boundaries
> General Welfare: the government maintaining the people's mythic covenant in a manner that maximally benefits the whole nation
> Blessings of Liberty: the government assuring that citizenry liberties are upheld in ways that provoke national good fortune

The Bill of Rights is a reminder of some of the various rights that are necessary to insure that these characteristics are observed. These rights also limit the freedoms of both the government and the citizenry for the sake of fulfilling the mythic covenant.

That which is most obvious in these covenantal listings is the intent that the whole nation be the recipient of its benefits and that anything that threatens or obstructs this holistic payoff should be suppressed or eliminated.

This covenant also implies the following:

- ➢ The process of Democracy is grounded in the common rights of the people.
- ➢ The spirit of Democracy is a devotion to that which benefits the whole.
- ➢ The conscience of Democracy is an attitude of equality that acts with the blessings of social reciprocity in mind.

The Obligations of Capitalism

All of the foregoing means that capitalism is wrapped in the decisive intents of the democratic myth that dictates its goals and defines its limits. The obvious goals are to maximize public good as opposed to private good. The obvious limits are behaviors that would inflict harm upon this common good. And, equally important, the entrepreneurs of capitalism are bound to the processes, spirit, and conscience of the democratic mythic covenant. These entrepreneurs do not operate outside these boundaries, except in violation of their right to be citizens of the nation. To operate in violation is to be both unpatriotic and un-American. Indeed, all such violations should be subjected to the nation's system of justice since that system exists to enforce the intents of its mythic covenant.

The regulatory restraints placed on capitalism designed to ensure the fulfillment of the nation's covenant in the mid-twentieth century began to be dismantled by both Democratic and Republican political administrations during the latter half of the twentieth century. Whatever the other factors involved, this avid deregulation helped facilitate the movement toward the collapse of the nation's economy during the initial decade of the twenty-first century. That is, those regulations that were enacted to safeguard the intents of the nation's democratic covenant were removed for the sake of an unfettered capitalism and both political parties were responsible.

Whatever objective the keepers of democracy had in this rampant deregulation, inherent in it was the implication that corporate executives have no moral or principled obligation to run their businesses according to the nation's mythic covenant. A tragic outcome has ensued. And the paramount lesson for the governmental keepers of democracy is that they have a primal obligation to see that the nation's economic system functions in ways that enhance the goals of democracy's mythic covenant. Their first obligation is to the well-being of the nation's economy rather than to the well-being of the entrepreneurs of capitalism. The two are not necessarily synonymous. Indeed, American history shows that, at critical times, they may be diametrically opposed.

To say that capitalism is an amoral system is the same as saying that a gun is an amoral tool. That capitalism or a gun are amoral instruments does not excuse their handlers from whatever harm may come to the citizenry from use of the tool. Such usage takes place within the purposes of mythic community and those purposes define the morality of all tool usage. The first obligation of all handlers of instruments is to the well-being of the myth that drives the society in which the tool is wielded.

Duplicity

Despite the clear judgment of history to the contrary, the more vociferous advocates of capitalism continue to equate democracy with unfettered business. However, to maintain this position, they must respond with duplicity toward strong government. On the one hand, big business consistently and stringently opposes the regulations of strong government that protect the citizenry from the abuses of big business. On the other hand big business applauds strong government when it becomes a welfare agent for big business.

When strong government enforces laws of collective bargaining, that gives labor the clout to ensure decent working conditions and benefits, big business is outraged. When strong government saved the Chrysler Corporation from financial disaster in the 1980s through secured loans, big business was pleased. When strong government subsidizes the farm industry, bails out financial institutions (Savings and Loan scandal, mortgage agencies, banks, Bear Sterns failure, Fannie Mae, Freddie Mack, etc.) or gives special tax breaks to oil companies that are already making billions of dollars, big business applauds. When strong government places restraints on the capacity of big business to rape the environment, big business yells violation of freedom.

When big business takes itself to the brink of economic collapse because of a consuming greed that has disregarded all considerations for the welfare of the nation (the 2008 economic meltdown) and appeals to the government for economic rescue, the expectation is a willing and positive response. But when strong government taxation subsidizes disenfranchised individuals or groups, this is viewed as abetting social irresponsibility.

The duplicity of big business is an attitude that government socialism expressed toward business is good while government socialism expressed toward individuals is evil.

Economist John Kenneth Galbraith addresses this attitude of duplicity in this observation:

> *The contented and economically comfortable have a very*
> *discriminating view of government. Nobody is ever indignant*
> *about bailing out failed banks and failed savings and loan*
> *associations ... But when taxes must be paid for the lower middle*
> *class and poor, the government assumes an aspect of wickedness.*

The fact is that the economy of a democracy in today's world can neither survive nor thrive without the interference of strong government to regulate according to the egalitarian spirit and the conscience of its grounding myth. The duplicity of big business is an unwillingness to recognize this fact that has emerged out of the traumas of American history—possibly because big business's use of unregulated capitalism has participated so heavily in creating these traumas. Indeed, issues of big business regulation (lack of regulation, deregulation and unenforced regulation) have been consequential contributors to the greatest threats to the health of America's economy and of immeasurable economic harm to the citizenry.

Particularly has this been the case throughout the twentieth century and the beginning of the twenty-first century. The year 2008 is instructive. Wall Street threatened to crash and propel the entire nation into another Great Depression. The George W. Bush political administration that encouraged this disaster through eight years of deregulation and lack of regulatory oversight demanded that Congress award it with billions of dollars for the correction of its own failure and to do so without oversight. In brief, the deregulators wished for the government to bail them out with an unprecedented monetary scheme that would be processed without regulation. And Congress, in a natural fit of incompetency, complied. Thus, through gross neglect to public responsibility, the money thrown at the financial industry would not be accompanied by accountability and the "stop the bleed" purpose of the bailout became a "feed the greed" gifting.

Not only did this entire economic fiasco prove that capitalism is not a naturally self-correcting system, it also proved that capitalism cannot survive in a democracy without constant and often massive welfare from the government and certainly not without persistent regulatory oversight.

What the advocates of an unfettered capitalism have desired is a freedom to do as they please without the constraints of democracy's spirit and conscience. They have wanted freedom without a corresponding responsibility. And they have refused to account for the result that is inherent in such a view. Edith Hamilton (*The Lessons of the Past*) says it well in her comment about the same issue that existed in the life of one of history's earlier experiments in democracy:

> *When the freedom they wished for most was freedom from responsibility, then Athens ceased to be free and was never free again.*

Socialism

The wide streak of government socialism that runs through the American democratic experiment is a statement about the inability of capitalism to either regulate itself or bring balanced economic health to the nation. The relentless monetary subsidizing of both small business and corporations are graphic examples of how important government intervention in the nation's economics are to its well-being and to capitalism's inabilities to address the issues of required balance, mutual reciprocity, and visionary need. So even if there is a measure of compatibility between democratic freedoms and capitalism, there is an equal measure of compatibility between democratic responsibilities and socialism. If capitalism speaks to freedom then socialism speaks to responsibility.

Socialism, as used here, is defined as government abetting the survival and profit of business through financial services such as bailouts, loans, subsidies, grants, and of addressing the profound economic needs of the citizenry such as Social Security, Medicare, Medicaid, certain guarantees of bank deposits, highway systems, national defense, etc. And these are only a few examples of thousands of other socialistic services the government provides that protect and secure the well-being of the citizenry.

As previously cited, in the early twenty-first century, when appropriate governmental agencies failed to regulate and corporations pursued profit by unprincipled and irresponsible means, a mortgage meltdown and the failure of banks and Wall Street posed a serious threat to the economic health of the nation. In confronting the threat of the nation's economic collapse posed by this scenario, the government became a welfare agent to those who were responsible for its creation. While this bailout and incentive program initially amounted to around 800 billion dollars, its ultimate estimated cost is in the trillions.

It is possible that the financial industry of Wall Street is more a con artist than a need agent. Consider their use of bailout money to care for their own concerns and to feather their own monetary nests, rather than to do anything that might open the public to financial assistance or to restore the economy. Add to this their lack of any assumed responsibility for the nation's economic meltdown and their obvious unconcern for the tragic consequences of this fiasco. Together, these expressions suggest an attitude of contempt for both the citizenry and America's democratic covenant.

However, this seeming contempt is beside the point when it comes to acknowledging that a healthy capitalism cannot exist without being subsidized by the government's economic socialism. Capitalism may prevail as an economy of choice in America because of social liberty, but it cannot survive without government regulation and massive economic applications of socialism.

Only when the American public recognizes and accepts the fact that capitalism must be supported by its twin socialism will appropriate oversight and regulation take place and the economic health of the nation be stabilized. The notion of a capitalism standing on its own is a con big-business entrepreneurs and their congressional supporters use to sell deregulation, hide their scams, and justify their bailouts. The real enemy of the American public is not the government socialism that keeps capitalism from failing, but the big business advocates that use capitalism to suck the economic life from the public. Big business will inevitably claim that its problems are caused by either "forces beyond its control" or having made forgivable "mistakes." Normally big business is responsible, in consequential measure, for these so-called "forces beyond its control," and "making forgivable mistakes" is only a euphemism for the disastrous results of incompetent, unprincipled, and greed-oriented management.

It must also be admitted that the citizenry is equally responsible in that it has swallowed the lies and submitted to the cons of both corporations and politicians about the so-called threat of socialism to democracy. One of the presidential election candidates in 2008 used the specter of this threat as an appeal to voter fears and as a negative attempt to tarnish his opponent as a proponent of undemocratic programs. Oxymoronically, this same candidate dropped his campaigning and rushed back to the nation's capital to give strong support to the largest economic socialist bailout of American business in the nation's history. The Republican party that began the multibillion dollar bailout of failed corporations in 2008 railed against the Democratic party as being socialists for doing the same thing in 2009.

The Truths

The international economic depression of the 1930s and the global economic meltdown of 2008 clearly affirm four truths:

(1) Capitalism is not a naturally self-correcting economic system.

(2) Capitalism must be deliberately and diligently regulated by government if the general citizenry is to benefit.

(3) Capitalism can only fulfill its democratic goals when strongly supported by programs of socialism.

(4) Capitalism must be endowed with a democratic morality if it is to overcome the intentions of greed and fulfill the intentions of the nation's mythic covenant.

These historically grounded truths show that while capitalism may have an affinity with the liberties of democracy, it does not have an affinity with the spirit and conscience of democracy. Thus it must be strongly contained on all sides to fulfill the egalitarian goals of a democratic society. Without this containment, the democratic enterprise will always be seriously harmed. Where the ethics of democracy are not willingly complied with, they must be demanded by law and enforced with regulatory diligence. That such a sad state exists is the direct fault of the entrepreneurs of *Libertine Capitalism* that seek to function without any restraining principles or concern for the myth of the nation that makes their existence possible.

The Responsibility

While it is true that strong government can be abusive, corrupt, inept, and self-serving, this is only a sign that it is run by people and not a sign that it is evil within itself. Like capitalism, it is an instrument that mirrors the myth and behavioral morality of its keepers. This is the problem of all governments whatever their strength of influence and of all economic systems whatever their compatibilities of relationship.

Thus the bottom line in assuring that capitalism is a tool of democracy and not the reverse, remains as the same solution to all of democracy's ills—namely, a citizenry that assumes responsibility for making sure that their government reflects the spirit and conscience of the American democratic myth. Whenever the government defaults on democracy, it is only a mirror image of the citizenry. The elected are the face of the electors.

In public services, we lag behind all the industrialized nations of the West, preferring that the public money go not to the people but to big business. The result is a unique society in which we have free enterprise for the poor and socialism for the rich.
                                                              —Gore Vidal

The Ship of Democracy, which has weathered all storms, may sink through the mutiny of those on board.
                                                              —Grover Cleveland

*I believe that, for the rest of the world, contemporary America
is an almost symbolic concentration of all the best and the worst
of our civilization. On the one hand, there are its profound
commitment to enhancing civil liberty and to maintaining
the strength of its democratic institutions, and the fantastic
developments in science and technology which have contributed
so much to our well-being; on the other, there is the blind worship
of perpetual economic growth and consumption, regardless of
their destructive impact on the environment, or how subject they
are to the dictates of materialism and consumerism, or how they,
through the omnipresence of television and advertising, promote
uniformity and banality instead of respect for human uniqueness.*
—Václav Havel

The Fear of the Vision

(Government without Government)

It is perfectly true that that government is best which governs least. It is equally true that that government is best which provides the most.

—Walter Lippmann

The Fear

The fear of government held by the founding fathers created an illusion that persists into the twenty-first century. This illusion is that there can exist a successful form of democratic government that is blasé enough and weak enough to pose no threat to the citizenry's private goals yet alert enough and strong enough to maintain a beneficial social cohesiveness and control. This illusion was called least government.

The Meanings

Least government is a reference to a style and expression of government that exerts minimal influence over a nation's internal drama. It is an appeal for legal and social weakness. It is an idealized desire for unrestrained citizenry freedom, for libertinism.

At the end of the twentieth century, its evolved internal national meaning included a focus on minimal taxation and hands-off policies in the life of the citizenry, except when necessary to grant protection from terrorism or whatever might threaten a free and open marketplace. The advocates of least government are generally those who also advocate for a free and unfettered capitalism and notions pertaining to citizenry economic freedoms. There seems to be no evidence of a corresponding advocacy of social responsibilities toward the whole of the citizenry, the nation's democratic covenant, or demands of account-ability toward those who abuse the privileges of democracy.

The opposite of least government is strong government. Strong government is one that exerts major influence over a nation's internal destiny through the scope and power of its actions. Organizationally, it may or may not be big in size. It is its actions and the influence of those actions that announce it as strong. It is inevitably involved in protect-ing the civil rights and addressing the social needs of the citizenry. For whatever the reasons, the advocates of strong government are generally those who also advocate for government responsibility toward citizenry well-being and issues of equality along with a citizenry responsibility to exert a control over government in the direction of what is beneficial for the whole nation.

Irony

An essential irony is that those who advocate for least or limited government internally are generally advocates of that same government operating with great strength on their behalf externally. That is, within the nation they wish for a government that interferes minimally with their "freedoms," but internationally they wish for that same govern-ment to exert great power to enhance and protect their "freedoms." This enhancement and protection normally includes international agree-ments that favor business profit and political actions that interfere in the affairs of other nations on behalf of their own economic interests, usually referred to as the nation's best interests. In brief, the advocates of least government are generally hypocritical in their application of this sentiment. They advocate for a government of least interference at home while advocating for a government of maximum interference abroad.

Morality

The issue of morality, of good and bad, is not inherent in terms such as least or strong. Morality is what users bring to mythologies, technologies, and processes. Morality reflects the purpose of the user and the judgment of the assessor. Thus, least or strong are descriptions within themselves without moral weight. They simply characterize the nature of influence.

Social Genetics

The fear of a strong internal government with a tangible scope of influence seems to be a genetic social response in American history passed on to succeeding generations from the colonists and the founding fathers. Thomas Paine, revolutionist and pamphleteer, captures the simplicity of this fear in these words:

That government is best that governs least.

This sentiment found a heavy voice in the 1800s from thinkers such as Ralph Waldo Emerson, who was a strong advocate of individual freedom. It has also found heavy voices in the twentieth century—notably in the cryptic pronouncements of twentieth-century journalist and satirist H. L. Mencken. Toward the end of this century, presidential voices took up the cry, though with a political agenda in mind:

A government big enough to give you everything you want is a government big enough to take from you everything you have.
—Gerald R. Ford (1974)

I hope we have once again reminded people that man is not free unless government is limited. There's a clear cause and effect here that is as neat and predictable as a law of physics.
—Ronald Reagan (1989)

Whatever the motivations of those who have articulated and advocated for least government over the past century, there are two factors about their perspectives and behaviors that usually become apparent. The first is that if they achieve public office, they will generally maintain the rhetoric of this posture while, oxymoronically, leaving behind a legacy of increased government influence. This legacy is often most visible in government spending for their programs and initiatives as exemplified in mounted national budgetary deficits. Aside from this discrepancy between pronouncement and behavior, the second factor reveals an essential failure on their part to appreciate the negative historical consequences of this vision of least government as revealed in American history. They are imperceptive historians.

Evil

Such advocacies do not account for the human tendency toward evil that history shows is encouraged by forms of least government. There is a principle that emerges from the attempts to civilize human action within free societies:

Without the moral constraints of strong government, human evil tends to capture the structures of a society.

A trek through American history is all that is needed to validate this principle. Examples abound.

- ➤ During the Industrial Revolution, when the power of management thrived under the minimized constraints of least government, labor was held in a contemptuous, dehumanizing, and suppressive bondage that rivals the worst of a totalitarian collective.
- ➤ During the almost hundred-year period between the time when slaves were freed with full constitutional rights and the mid-twentieth century, least government permitted white racists, and the nation in general, to grossly abuse and violate the civil rights of black citizens.
- ➤ During the country's westward expansion, the mayhem and murder of lawlessness ruled under the aegis of least government.
- ➤ Sporadically, during the latter part of the twentieth century and the first part of the twenty-first century, the unrestrained greed of big business continuously undermined the welfare of the citizenry through a variety of financial institution machinations and corporate CEO intrigues that left large portions of the citizenry bereft of their life savings, retirement futures, jobs, homes, and even threatened the economic well-being of the nation as a whole. Least government authored this lack of restraint.

It has only been since the advent of strong government during the middle of the twentieth century that the violations of the democratic conscience by free enterprise and its abounding greed have been brought under any measure of lawful constraint beneficial to the American citizenry. Both instituting and continuing this restraint has been an ongoing battle. The plunge toward an economic depression in the first decade of the twenty-first century shows how fragile this restraint is when the government is dominated by the advocates of unfettered enterprise.

The Question

A critical question behind the notion of least government is whether such a government can fulfill its constraining, yet liberating, purposes while playing a hands-off role in the private lives of its citizenry.

Because the liberties of democracy favor evil as well as good, the answer to this question, at least from the perspective of American history, seems to be that the well-being of democracy requires the government to play some kind of hands-on role. The issue then becomes the wisdom of:

> ➤ Knowing the difference between the need for a light hand or a heavy hand
> ➤ Remembering that the goal of government is to facilitate the democratic covenant
> ➤ Understanding that individual liberty is a social exercise that demands responsibility to the whole
> ➤ Keeping the reciprocal benefits of social health and economic health in mutual constraint
> ➤ Advocating the spirit and conscience of democracy as the measure of all views and decision-making

Both/And

The liberty to create democracy is also the liberty to destroy democracy. The liberty to expand human action is also the liberty to deny human action. The liberty to give is also the liberty to deny. The liberty to behave nobly is the liberty to behave ignobly. Liberty works in both directions. Only a sense of moral responsibility grounded in the culture's mythic spirit and conscience can guide democratic government toward applying these wisdoms. In their wise application, strong government becomes big benefit, and in their unwise application, strong government becomes big deficit. The difference in these applications is both by those who govern and by those who choose who shall govern.

Lesson

The lesson of American history is that the capacities of least government to exert any measure of control over those forces that would limit and destroy the promises and potential of democracy reached its capacities by the end of the first quarter of the twentieth century. If the nation was to survive the complexities and threats that awaited it in the wings of both its national and international future, a government with greater power to influence its destiny was required. Fortunately, that government emerged out of the forge of history. The current question is whether that government will be controlled by the corporate world or by the people for whose benefit it was created. The answer to this question will be provided by the people. And the answer will determine the nation's destiny.

> *Nothing turns out to be so oppressive and unjust as a feeble government.*
> —Edmund Burke

> *And that government which governs least governs not at all.*
> —Henry David Thoreau

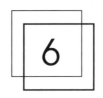

6

The Necessity of the Vision
(Saving Democracy)

That government is strongest of which every man feels a part.
— Thomas Jefferson

The punishment which the wise suffer who refuse to take part in the government, is to live under the government of worse men.
— Plato

Challenges

Factors in American cultural life and world history began to converge by the end of the first quarter of the twentieth century that called for a government with a strength commensurate to the enormous challenges these factors represented.

The Travails of Democracy

Consider the travails of democracy and the need for accommodation inherent in some of the revolutions that had and were about to plow through American history. These were primarily either sociologically or technologically based with mutual effect.

Sociological (Views)	Technological (Means)
➤ Race (blacks)	➤ Industrial (convenience)
➤ Gender (women)	➤ Transportation (movement)
➤ Labor (rights)	➤ Medical (health)

Sociological (Views)	Technological (Means)
➢ Government (influence)	➢ Diet (lifespan)
➢ Sexuality (lifestyle)	➢ Communications (knowledge)
➢ Ecology (relationships)	➢ Economics (classes)
➢ Art (expression)	➢ Time (leisure)

Together these revolutions represented demands for profound lifestyle shifts. Some of these were a shift from:
> ➢ a rural to an urban national lifestyle
> ➢ a provincial isolationism to a national homogeneity
> ➢ simplicity to complexity in every area of living
> ➢ general knowledge ignorance to general knowledge overload
> ➢ a spirit of rampant individualism to a spirit of community obligation and back to a spirit of rampant individualism
> ➢ polar class extremes to a more balanced economic social structuring and back to polar class extremes
> ➢ early death issues to prolonged life issues and consequent economic issues
> ➢ extended family focus to nuclear family focus to fractured family focus
> ➢ moral censorship to moral freedom and constant battles between these poles
> ➢ dawn-to-dusk labor to disposable free time for the middle class and some of the lower class

And pushing these revolutions from beneath was:
> ➢ the explosion of population and all its attendant problems
> ➢ the loss of geographic frontiers and a search for social and scientific frontiers
> ➢ the shrinking of the planet into a global community

As a result, American democracy had already been and was about to be assailed from every angle of social and political existence to respond in application of its spirit and conscience. While these demands genuinely taxed its capacities, the democratic experiment has managed to learn its own meaning and to grow in that meaning. As the nation has evolved, so has democracy. And up to this point in time the experiment has proven John Adams, second president of the United States, wrong (1814):

Remember, democracy never lasts long. It soon wastes, exhausts, and murders itself. There never was a democracy yet that did not commit suicide.

The Necessity

Because of the sociological and technological revolutions previously mentioned, the continuing population increase, the loss of geographic frontiers, the inability of individual states that constituted the Union to adequately respond to the needs of their constituencies, the demands of international conflicts, and the growing complexities of the global community, the government of American democracy was gradually forced to take on increased responsibilities and increased powers to cope on behalf of the citizenry. It was only these increases of power that kept American democracy viable and held the nation together as an organic mythic expression.

The Second American Revolution

This major shift in both governmental scope and responsibility began its visible expression during the Great Depression of the 1930s. At that time, a revolution began taking place that was as dramatic in its ultimate impact as the original American Revolution. While the American Revolution of 1776 established the nation's special democracy, the one that began in the 1930s expanded the philosophy and scope of this special democracy's government.

The signal spirit of this revolution was President Franklin D. Roosevelt as epitomized in his New Deal program. This program was a response to the inability of capitalism to raise itself out of that national destruction called the Great Depression which capitalism, itself, had helped create through its unregulated excess.

The Redemption

The view behind Roosevelt's New Deal was that the government had a responsibility to the general citizenry to make democracy work in its favor. The New Deal was designed for that purpose. It initiated strong government involvement such as:

> creating public works programs to relieve joblessness
> regulating financial institutions, industry, agriculture, and housing to reinstitute financial health
> formulating labor laws and collective bargaining to aid labor in its fight for decent wages and working conditions
> establishing the Federal Deposit Insurance Corporation to safeguard the public's money
> granting business subsidies and installing price controls to stimulate and protect the economy
> inaugurating the Social Security system
> initiating a pervasive modernization of American industry through dam building and water control programs that supplied electricity and transportation as well as halting flood devastation (although the seed of this developed during the Hoover administration, its flowering took place under the aegis of the Roosevelt administration)

Without these kinds of initiatives and interventions of strong government during this critical time, it is possible that democracy, as we know it, might have failed. Further, it is more than likely that World War II would have been lost to Germany and Japan due to a lack of American industrial power that was initiated during this period by America's electrification (a strong government activity). In brief, the advent of strong government saved the nation from mythic failure and foreign conquest.

The Irony

Ironically, while initially attacked as socialism, communism, and fascism by conservative politicians and big business advocates, these practices by strong government of regulating capitalism, stimulating the economy, and provoking modernization programs were so beneficial that they became a permanent part of the philosophy and scope of America's democratic government function.

In the 1950s, under the leadership of President Dwight D. Eisenhower, the federal highway system began, which provided consequential impetus toward the modernization and homogenization of America. Strong government became the force that engaged the subtle battles that composed the Cold War with the Soviet Union. In the decades that followed, strong government played an important role in building national infrastructures and facilitating and protecting the civil rights of the citizenry.

In brief, the blessings and benefits of American democracy, beginning in the second quarter of the twentieth century, have been both processed and preserved by strong government. Strong government has been American democracy's salvation, the sine qua non of its continued viable existence.

Strong and Size

Strong refers to attitude and role and not necessarily to size. It symbolizes the will and the means to make something happen. In American history, the Civil War that preserved the Union and legitimized the black citizenry, the construction of the Panama Canal, the granting of voting rights to women, and involvement in World War I are examples of small-in-scope government acting as strong government.

However, there comes a time when small-in-scope government is simply insufficient to confront and solve immense problems. When the Great Depression threatened to swallow America it became obvious that saving the country required more than a strong attitude and role by government. It required an expansion of the scope of focus and the size of management of government to save the nation from its own unregulated capitalistic excesses.

World War II increased this requirement. The Korean War, the Cold War, the civil rights and feminist movements, along with democratic social programs, business regulation, and other commercial progress required a continuing increase in the scope of government function.

The Rhetoric

The problem inherent in this increase in the scope of governmental influence and power is a lack of responsible congressional oversight in limiting the bloating and proliferation of those bureaucracies necessary to administer adequate government function. During the 1980s, these bureaucracies were made the scapegoat of this congressional failure and their existence made synonymous with large-in-scope government. Thus, through political rhetoric, the citizenry began viewing strong government, mismanagement, and waste as the same. Moreover, certain influential politicians made strong government to appear as synonymous with the ominous image of Big Brother totalitarianism.

Rather than holding politicians accountable for their irresponsibility, the citizenry began viewing large-in-scope government as the enemy of democracy and the suppressor of freedom, rather than its caretaker. Spurious political rhetoric had created a circumstance where the very agent that had secured the freedoms and blessings of democracy during the twentieth century was made responsible for its more obvious failures.

The Problem

American democracy cannot survive in today's complex world without large-in-scope government. But this necessity is difficult to admit by those politicians who stake their claim for election on the negative image of large-in-scope government that they helped create. The problem for these politicians is how to retain the necessary benefits of large-in-scope government by sidestepping its image as the enemy. The answer to this problem began to emerge in the late 1980s. This answer had three components.

This first component is a legitimate attempt to downsize the bloatedness of government bureaucracies. This creates a favorable image with many citizens that the waste of bureaucracy is actually being addressed. But these attempts have been feeble and more showcase than real progress. However, it appears that it is only necessary to minimally address this issue to satisfy a public image of concern.

The second component is an attempt to lift as many regulations as possible from the business world. This creates a favorable image with many citizens that the power of Big Brother is being diminished. But it also gives big business a greater latitude to exploit the citizenry, abuse trust, and violate civil rights. While government is less powerful, the citizenry is more vulnerable. Corporate failures of the last quarter of the twentieth century, such as Enron, are examples of the unprincipled management that emerges from lack of regulation and the negative impact on the economy and the citizenry's future that are the result.

The third component is an attempt to reduce the image of the government from that of a controlling giant to that of a concerned facilitator. The means of this language reimaging is through a seeming shift of responsibility. The federal government passes on the responsibility for managing many of its programs to lesser agents of power such as state governments. This shift of responsibility to middle management creates a favorable image with some citizens that Big Brother is willingly relinquishing power in the best interest of democratic process by assuming the role of concerned facilitator.

However, the use of a less controlling language to describe government function and an emphasis on middle-management does not lessen the power of strong government to create, fund, and regulate its proposed initiatives. The label and manner of delivery does not change the role and necessity of large-in-scope government in processing the issues of democracy on behalf of the citizenry.

The only goal this political sidestepping manages to accomplish is to hide the legitimacy and necessity of the scope of government in processing, protecting, and preserving democracy as a viable way of life. The meaning of the word strong in the present complex world is a description of both scope and action.

Public Susceptibility

The American public seems to have a determined susceptibility to any political utterance that blames government for their private ills. Politicians rely on this distrust to skew the citizenry's perceptions in order to win votes and process their agendas. An example is the 1980 Republican campaign slogan:

GET THE GOVERNMENT OFF OUR BACKS

This slogan was in keeping with the persistent Republican Party agenda of deregulating big business for the purpose of accruing financial and political support. However, its appeal was designed to plug into public distrust by imaging government as the citizenry's enemy.

Politicians, whether Republican or Democrat, will continue this ruse as long as the citizenry chooses to remain willfully ignorant of the history of government in America as it affects the social benefits of democratic living.

Two Clarities

Two things are infinitely clear from American history. The first is that big business, without government regulation, can be brutally dehumanizing to workers, unethical in practice, and generally aims to control government for its own benefit. Its tendency has been to suppress the conscience and spirit of democracy as regards civil rights, social equality, and concern for the egalitarian health of the nation.

While this is certainly not an accurate description of all American business, it is of the larger and more influential parts of the business world. The bottom line for big business remains profit and it has dramatically shown that it cares little about the negative fallout that it may create for the American public in this pursuit. But why should it be concerned? After all, the citizenry will always bail it out when it excesses, despite the harm it causes. And the public will do so because of the image that big business creates for itself—namely, that the whole democratic enterprise will go down the drain without big-business health. Economic blackmail is the final resort of those business CEOs who refuse to assume responsibility for their own failures.

The second clarity is that the only force large enough and powerful enough to confront the controlling machinations of big business, guarantee the civil rights of the citizenry, and uphold what is in the nation's best interest, is a strong government with a wide scope of influence and power. Indeed, it is such government that has protected democracy, up to this moment in history, from the unrelenting destructive forces of both private and corporate interests.

The question is whether or not government has the will to continue this role with any real sense of responsibility toward the citizenry who pay the bills. Another way of asking this question is to wonder when Congress will step up to the plate and bat on behalf of the citizenry that elected it rather than continuing to bat for the sake of its own economic aggrandizement.

Dispensing with America

To "get the government off our backs" would be to dispense with modern America, its maturing progress in civil rights, and its myriad of benefits to living for both individuals and society. Indeed, the truth of life in America is the reverse of this slogan. It is the citizenry that lives on the back of strong government. It is strong government that carries the burden of implementing and sustaining the democratic spirit and conscience. It is strong government that guarantees the economic health of the nation. And the citizenry, while unwilling to acknowledge this truth publicly, does so through its continuous actions of encouraging strong government to rescue it from all that threatens its health of being.

Vilification

In America, large-in-scope government is often made the scapegoat for democratic ills. There are three problems that are used to give credence to this vilification.

Wasteful Bureaucracies

The word bureaucracy seems to have derived from the French language and refers to a desk with separated compartments—as in a bureau. Applied to government, it is the varied departments organized to fulfill its functions. As government grows out of necessity, so do its bureaus. There can be no effective government without bureaucracy. Since bureaucracies are established to meet certain needs, the ultimate issues of their existence have to do with competency of performance and continuity of need rather than their existence.

Incompetent bureaucracies tend to bloat themselves in compensation for their failure. This bloating squanders public resources. The only efficiency of an incompetent bureaucracy is in producing waste. The solution to incompetency is a management that knows its task, tracks this task, and eliminates unwarranted activity.

Few would deny that the American government is full of wasteful bureaucracy. But the fault is not with the scope of government. It is the fault of congresses and administrations who are more concerned about the self-interest of politics than about the welfare of the nation. When governmental bureaucracies are incompetent, it is because Congress and the administration are incompetent. When there is insufficient supervision, it is because Congress and the administration are insufficient supervisors.

Obsolescence is the second problem with bureaucracies. Unless a bureaucracy is established to fulfill a continuing need, then when its purpose is fulfilled that bureau should be terminated. Indeed, bureaucracies should be established with an ending date as part of their life structure. However, they represent jobs and power, and politicians will seek to preserve them for the sake of their own existence. As Brooks Atkinson (*Once Around the Sun*) observes:

> *Bureaucracies are designed to perform public business. But as*
> *soon as a bureaucracy is established, it develops an autonomous*
> *spiritual life and comes to regard the public as the enemy.*

Again, the politicians who create bureaucracies have a public ob-ligation to terminate their existence when their purpose becomes ir-relevant. But the people employed in irrelevant bureaucracies repre-sent jobs, votes, and campaign contributions. And politicians devoted to self-service will not risk such potential losses in the interest of public good. This is not the fault of the scope of strong government. When bureaucracies are obsolete but still in existence, it is because politicians are obsolete and still in office.

Pork Barrel Politics: The Earmark Scandal

The phrase "pork barrel politics" is a long-in-use euphemism for political patronage and bribes that disregard the public interest. The term currently being used is "earmarks." Here is an example. In the fall of 2005, congressional leaders from Alaska secured 223 million dollars in federal funding for a bridge from Ketchikan, Alaska (population less than 9,000), to its airport on the Island of Gravina (a ferry ride of only a few minutes). Because of the outrageous costs for a totally unnecessary project, it became known as "the bridge to nowhere," a label of ridicule. Sarah Palin, while running for governor of the state, strongly supported this earmark. Projects of a similar nature are common in Congress. In prior years, this would have been referred to as "pork barrel politics."

Whichever term is used is irrelevant, though the meaning is per-tinent. It is legislation passed to benefit a person, group, or region de-spite its inappropriateness or wastefulness. This is inevitably done for the sake of quid pro quo among politicians—the philosophy that I will vote for your earmark if you will vote for mine. At the heart of such leg-islation is a willing violation of citizenry trust by politicians. Moreover, politicians are open and blatant about this violation, actually flaunt-ing it in the public face. In 2008, the U.S. Senate (Democrats and Republicans) openly refused to pass laws that would curb this abuse of trust. In brief they said to the American people that continuing to violate the trust of their office for the sake of personal gain was not an issue of their concern because they knew the citizenry would reelect them anyway.

One typical way quid pro quo works is to hide the dishonest transaction in the fine print of other legislation that is extraneous to its purpose. An example is found in an article entitled "How the Little Guy Gets Crunched," by Donald L. Barlett and James B. Steele in the February 7, 2000, issue of *Time Magazine.*

They report that in Congress's 1999 District of Columbia Appropriations Act, Senator Trent Lott of Mississippi buried in this legislation a section 6001, a measure that would largely exempt the nation's scrap-metal dealers from superfund cleanup liabilities at toxic-waste sites. Both political parties supported this hidden benefit. The end result is that while politicians receive financial contributions from junk-dealers, the American public picks up the tab for potentially millions of dollars in damages done by this industry. Barlett and Steele estimate that when combined with other quid pro quo legislation, such measures cost the taxpayer countless billions of dollars. Lott's story is only one example of what is common practice by politicians across the nation.

Pork barrel/earmark legislation is done with obvious deceit and unethical intent in total disregard to the trust of public office. Its existence as an accepted way of life in both federal and state government attests to the depth of political corruption in American democracy. This corruption is further defined by the attempt of politicians to blame the waste of corruption on large-in-scope government. But large-in-scope government is not at fault. The fault is that of corrupt politicians who pass such legislation and corrupt citizens who elect these politicians because they profit from the corruption. Earmark politics exist because earmark politicians exist because an earmark citizenry exists. When the corrupt are elected by the corrupt the elected corrupt will act corrupt.

Campaign Funding

Politicians wish to be both elected and reelected, but unless they have enormous personal wealth they must rely on outside monetary contributions. Benefits from pork barrel/earmark legislation are one source. However, the largest source available is campaign contributions from private enterprise. But private enterprise wants a quid pro quo arrangement—decisions and legislation that increase their business profit. This encourages politicians to deregulate controls on private enterprise, grant unwarranted tax benefits, and pass even more pork barrel/earmark legislation in order to accrue greater campaign contributions.

The end result, in practical effect, is:

> ➤ circumvention of regulation constraints by free enterprise
> ➤ backstage influence over government by free enterprise
> ➤ politicians advocating what's profitable for free enterprise above what's in the best interest of the citizenry
> ➤ corruption of politicians and abdication of public trust
> ➤ a serious wounding of the intents of the democratic process

Honest politicians feel forced into the double-bind of either permitting their ethics to be compromised or risking election and reelection failure from lack of sufficient campaign funding. Such was supposedly the case for Senator John McCain from Arizona who, in 1999, began campaigning for the Republican presidential nomination. He found himself in what appeared to be a compromised position. While chairing the powerful Senate Commerce Committee, he was taking campaign contributions from industries that had business before his committee.

McCain was breaking no laws, but he freely admitted doing what he knows corrupts politics.

Political cartoonist Luckovich of the *Atlanta Constitution*, in a 1999 cartoon, dramatizes where campaign finance corruption ultimately leads. It is the picture of an individual with hands on a keyboard, peering into a computer screen. With a smile on his face he is thinking to himself: "Shopping online really takes the hassle out of buying a senator..."

In the late twentieth century, some states instituted term limits in an attempt to curb this form of political corruption. But this was naive because all that term limits manage to do is cut short the service of honest politicians along with the dishonest ones. It also causes competent and dedicated people to think twice before making politics a career option because of its short-lived nature.

The ultimate corrupting factor in American governmental democracy remains the financial control big business exerts over the elective process via campaign contributions and their expected quid pro quo payoff. In order to secure sufficient funding for their campaigns, politicians are pressured to become government prostitutes for corporate powers. Lobbyists are the pimps of the relationship. Until the citizenry demands complete reform of campaign financing, this game of prostitution will continue to corrupt and undermine the democratic process. There is no alternative solution. It is the citizenry that is ultimately responsible.

It is common to sidestep this obvious truth and seek to lay the blame for the resultant political corruption at the doorstep of a large-in-scope government. But this is a false indictment. Politicians were being bought long before the advent of large-in-scope government. The fault of corruption in American government lies in a combined mutual support of politicians who thrive on the dynamics of corruption and the general citizenry that is unwilling to change the system because it derives residual benefits from the corrupting process. The only other remaining interpretation is that the general citizenry prefers to ignore the corrupting processes of government, lest they be forced to assume responsibility for their own electoral failures.

The Real Problem

The problem with democracy has never been that of strong government. It has always been that of weak citizens. As Scottish satirist Thomas Carlyle points out:

> *In the long-run every Government is the exact symbol of its People, with their wisdom and unwisdom; we have to say, Like People Like Government.*

The bloated and obsolete bureaucracies, the pork barrel/earmark legislations, and the prostituting method of campaign funding that wastes resources, corrupts politics, and diminishes benefit for the citizenry all reflect the citizenry's own self-interest. Citizens get that for which they vote. John F. Kennedy put his finger squarely on the issue:

> *We, the people, are the boss, and we will get the kind of political leadership, be it good or bad, that we demand and deserve.*

The real problems with any democracy lie within its citizenry. These problems inevitably flow from three losses.

The first is a loss of the sense of democracy's sacredness that seriously commits to the use and protection of its processes. Theodore M. Hesburgh underscores this necessary conviction in observing:

Voting is a civic sacrament.

This loss signals the onset of an indifference to the abusers of the democratic conscience and is identifiable in statistics that reveal lack of voter participation in the voting privilege.

The second is a loss of citizenry trust in itself as the agent of democracy that empowers action on behalf of public benefit. This trust is grounded in the conviction that democratic government exists to create a social drama that is:

… of the people, by the people, for the people.

This loss signals the onset of a paralyzing cynicism toward the purpose of democracy and is identifiable in a citizenry that complains without taking action.

The third is a loss of personal responsibility as regards the outcome of the democratic process. This sense of responsibility is a conviction that the success or failure of democracy is self-directed rather than directed by others. As Marian Wright Edelman puts it:

Democracy is not a spectator sport.

This loss signals the onset of democracy's control by private and business interests and the citizenry's willingness to accept this control as an excuse of their supposed impotence.

Twentieth-century educator and philosopher Robert M. Hutchins summarizes the potential outcome of these losses of sacredness, trust, and responsibility:

The death of democracy is not likely to be an assassination from ambush. It will be a slow extinction from apathy, indifference, and undernourishment.

On the other hand, when a democracy's citizenry views its self-rule as sacred, trusts its own capacities, and assumes responsibility for its decisions then that democracy can fulfill its promised purpose and yield its promised blessings. At least that is the assumption behind citizenry control of government. That the citizenry, as a whole, has never exerted this kind of ultimate control is a moot issue.

Benefit without Government

Behind these losses exists a more subtle and pervasive problem. There is in the American cultural psyche, rooted in the attitudes of colonial discontent, a peculiar and contradictory mentality—the desire to have all the benefits of government without being governed. This mentality finds both specific and general expression in the nation's culture.

A specific expression is entrepreneurs and political representatives who wish for the benefits of government (tax incentives, bailouts, etc.) while working diligently for the invisibility of government (deregulation, no pollution control, etc.). A general expression is the public who wants the benefits of government (highway system, crime control, public education, disaster relief, safety regulations, national security, etc.), while resenting and resisting government taxation and controls that makes these benefits possible.

When the American citizenry can lay aside this twisted mentality and recognize that the real issue is not whether government is good or bad but which kind of government is good or bad, then its energies will be released from debilitating ambivalence to focus fully on creating a beneficial government guided by the wisdoms of the democratic spirit and conscience. It is not possible to have the benefits of government without having government. And it is not possible to maintain the benefits of a democratic government without having a strong government. And it's not possible to have a strong government without a strong citizenry. And its not possible to have a strong citizenry without that citizenry assuming its rightful ownership of both the vote and those for whom they have voted.

Democracy's Keeper

The nation's democratic spirit and conscience has had to drag the American citizenry into its bosom kicking and screaming. These fights the citizenry has had with its mythic spirit and conscience have usually been about the paradoxical issues of freedom and equality. A further step is needed in this maturation—accepting not only the legitimacy but the necessity of strong government as democracy's keeper.

On September 11, 2001, when the twin towers of the World Trade Center collapsed and the Pentagon suffered major damage from terrorist attacks, that which become most obvious was that only strong government had the capacity to respond in respect to seeking justice and protecting the citizenry from similar future attacks. And despite the Democrat and Republican contentions in the political arena over how this event and the nation's responses should relate to the meaning of the phrase "for the people," no one denied this necessity of strong government response.

When Hurricane Katrina struck the southern coast of America in August of 2005, the immediate cry from the citizenry was for a strong government to step in and provide necessary aid. When the government apparently and essentially failed in its response, the citizenry was chagrined. In addition, when the government did step in with aid and this aid was primarily usurped by corrupt politicians and unprincipled big business interests, the citizenry blamed the government. In brief, whether it was success or failure, the expectation on the part of the citizenry was that strong government should and would take care of the mess created by this catastrophe.

Even more recently in 2008, when the financial industry, through questionable and devious business practices, induced both the financial and housing industries to take a nosedive and threatened the economic well-being of the entire nation, it was both citizen and politician raising a wail about the responsibility of the government to do something that would restore the economy to a positive state. While a few Republicans, traditionally opposed to any kind of government interference in the nation's economy, objected to congressional response, no one posed the specter of a too large-in-scope government becoming a totalitarian Big Brother by taking such powerful action. Indeed, Congress granted certain arms of the government unprecedented power to administer billions of dollars to this ailing economy in an attempt to resurrect it from what appeared to be certain death.

Interestingly, the bitterness expressed by the citizenry was toward the greed-oriented and unprincipled big business that was the cause of the near collapse and not the strong government that might save the public from potential disaster. Perhaps this was because it was simply too obvious to ignore in favor of again investing in illusions about big government oppression. It must be admitted that the citizenry, in general, began developing a distaste for further bailout investments. But this was not because strong government was at fault. It was the fault of a Republican administration leaving office that had no interest in accountability, either from the big business it was bailing out or to the nation.

The notion that the government that governs least governs best is both historically false and politically naive. Franklin D. Roosevelt, in a 1939 radio address, understood this in reference to a democracy when he observed:

> *The only sure bulwark of continuing liberty is a government strong enough to protect the interests of the people, and a people strong enough and well enough informed to maintain its sovereign control over its government.*

Only strong government can provide the influence necessary to take care of the demands of democracy in today's complex world. That strong government is synonymous with despotic government is not a historically insightful perception. Strong government is as easily democratic as despotic. The issue, in this respect, is not scope of influence, but the guidance of mythic spirit and conscience. This is the same as mythic purpose. Strong government in America is better government because it is the only agent of the people that has worked in giving balance to the tensional democratic paradox of freedom and equality. Strong government is never a threat to the goals of democracy when it is controlled by a strong and informed citizenry that is willing to assume responsibility for holding up its end of the democratic process.

The founding fathers built into this process the power of the citizenry to exert whatever measure of control over government that it needed in order for government to yield to its will. That power is both the social covenant that states the purpose of democracy and the vote which makes the citizenry the ultimate authority within that democracy. Thus, the government can only overwhelm the citizenry if the citizenry permits. And it makes no difference whether this permission is by deliberate vote or apathetic indifference, it is still citizenry choice.

In the design of American democracy, the citizenry remains the master of its own fate. Until the citizenry rises above the mythic illusion of the virtue of least government and determines to exert control over strong government for the sake of the democratic spirit and conscience, democracy will languish in its path toward maturity. It may even die from the insidious activities of its internal enemies.

Nothing in all the world is more dangerous than sincere ignorance and conscientious stupidity.

—Martin Luther King, Jr.

Liberty is not the mere absence of restraint, it is not a spontaneous product of majority rule, it is not achieved merely by lifting underprivileged classes to power, nor is it the inevitable by-product of technological expansion. It is achieved only by a rule of law.

—Robert H. Jackson

The deadliest foe of democracy is not autocracy but liberty frenzied. Liberty is not foolproof. For its beneficent working it demands self-restraint.

—Otto Kahn

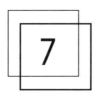

7

The Maturing of the Vision
(Loss of Innocence)

Vietnam was our longest, costliest, and, as it went on, our least popular war; it was also the least understood. And the more attempts were made to explain it the more puzzling it became.

—Merle Miller

Everything in war is barbaric…but the worst barbarity of war is that it forces men collectively to commit acts which individually they would revolt with their whole being.

—Ellen Key

Vietnam

Vietnam is a Southeast Asian country about the total square-mile size of the state of Missouri. It is bordered on the north by China and, like a slim, slightly crooked finger, extends south for 850 miles along the Gulf of Tonkin in the China Sea. Laos and Cambodia concavely rim its western edge.

National Culture

As a distinctive national culture, Vietnam dates backward to around 200 BC. Its history is of feudalism, political intrigue, foreign occupation, and war. The focal issue of Vietnam's existence has been the struggle to achieve an independent national unity. In this struggle it has repulsed the Mongol hoards, expelled Chinese invaders, driven out French colonists, and defeated America's attempt at mythic imperialism.

This deep sense of nationalism has characterized Vietnamese

history. Thus, events that dramatize the expulsion of foreign powers have often taken on mythic qualities in expressing this nationalistic spirit. An example is the first major expulsion of Chinese occupiers in AD 40 through an insurrection led by two sisters named Tung (Trac and Nhi). These sisters took on the aura of goddesses in Vietnamese folklore. It is this unrelenting nationalistic drive toward independence that is the key to everything one might wish to know about this small country.

American Involvement

In the late 1800s, the French colonized Indochina, of which Vietnam was a part. During World War II, the Japanese conquered and occupied the entire region. In order to expel the Japanese, the United States enlisted the aid of a Vietnamese nationalist leader by the name of Ho Chi Minh. The U.S. promise that bound this alliance was that of national political self-determination for Vietnam. Following victory in the war, the United States reneged on its promise to Ho Chi Minh and France reestablished its colonial presence. Ho Chi Minh and his communist, nationalist followers persisted in their insistence on political self-determination and defeated the French in 1954, ending almost seventy years of brutal colonial occupation.

At that time the country was partitioned at the seventeenth parallel by world powers. The northern half was governed by Ho Chi Minh-led communist nationalists with the backing of Russia and China. The southern half was governed by a series of corrupt self-serving administrations backed by the United States.

Beginning in the late 1950s and extending forward, the United States government began sending military advisors to train the South Vietnamese in the art of war.

Why the Involvement?

Given the French defeat, why had America become involved in a second attempt to thwart Vietnamese political self-determination? There were two major factors. The first was the convergence of a messianic mythic view that had gained prominence following the allied victory of World War II and the concurrent emergence of the United States as a world superpower. Briefly, the essence of this messianic myth is:

> ➤ America is God's chosen people
> ➤ America is on God's side
> ➤ America is always right
> ➤ America is invincible
> ➤ America's purpose is to save the world for democracy

The next chapter will constitute a larger review of this messianic myth and its threat to democratic maturity. Suffice it to say that it is so wound around the mythic justification of America's presence in Vietnam as to be inseparable from the second major factor of our involvement.

The second factor was America's foreign policy aimed at containing the Red Menace. The philosophy behind this containment policy was the Domino Theory which asserted that if one country of a region fell to communism all the surrounding countries would topple in turn like pushing over a row of standing dominos. However, rather than providing a legitimate justification for the war, the theory's usage revealed the basic historical ignorance of those politicians and military leaders who led the nation into this conflict. This historical ignorance rooted in disregarding the history and essential political dynamics of the region and a knowledge of the enemy that are fundamental prerequisites for determining the engagement of any armed conflict. Whatever political myth the Vietnamese preferred, they were, first and foremost, nationalists who eschewed any other nation dictating their destiny, including China and Russia. Applying the Domino Theory to Vietnam by American political and military leaders was a perspective grounded in historical ignorance.

The failure to consider the foregoing realities was rooted in a blindness fostered by the messianic myth. Thus, whatever the role of the Domino Theory, the seduction of the messianic myth grounded its usage as a justification for war. In brief, the Domino Theory was simply a camouflage for investing in the messianic myth.

Why the Loss?

Despite our government's justification for engaging this war, why, given the superpower status of the United States, was it lost? Why could America not win a war in a country the geographic equivalent of the state of Missouri when it had employed itself worldwide during World War II and won?

There are interrelated and complex reasons.

➤ The U. S. government never understood, and ignored as irrelevant, the history of Vietnamese politics and the nuances and intricacies of its nationalism, religion, culture, and geography. It believed that all that was necessary to win the war was to "Americanize" the South Vietnamese and supply them with superior arms.

➤ The U. S. government never sold the American people as a whole on the mythic validity of its involvement. This lack of a sale made the horrendous people, material, and monetary cost of the war increasingly unacceptable.

➤ The U. S. government was never willing to use its full power to deal with North Vietnam in an effective military fashion. It feared Russian and Chinese intervention and did not have the mandate of a congressional declaration of war to risk a larger-scale conflict.

➤ The U. S. government's political administrations most invested in the war (Johnson and Nixon) could not make clear decisions due to egotistical posturing. These administrations feared the historical legacy of being labeled as losers in the war and this fear took precedent over all other considerations in interpretations and decision-making. An example is Nixon's declaration: "I'm not going to be the first president who loses a war."

➤ The U.S. government was unable to instill a national mythic reason for dying in the mentality of the common soldier. The goal of most American troops was to survive and go home, while the goal of the communist troops was to win no matter what the cost.

➤ The U. S. government never fully understood the nature of the war it was fighting until it was too late; a guerrilla war could not be won by conventional means and America, as a foreign invader, was incapable of winning a psychological war for the hearts and minds of the Vietnamese people.

➤ The U. S. government, so tightly focused on its own invincibility, never fully comprehended that the South Vietnamese government—riddled with moral corruption, self-interest, and Machiavellian political machinations—was as much its foe as the North Vietnamese communists.

These combined reasons practically guaranteed that South
Vietnam, despite American support, could never prevail over the ideological and sacrifice-driven government of North Vietnam.

Given these converging factors, it is not surprising that the U. S.
government arranged a cease-fire agreement in 1973 and withdrew
its troops. Internal national hostilities began again in 1974 and South
Vietnam easily fell to North Vietnam in 1975.

The Perspectives

My personal tour of duty in Vietnam started during the 1968 Tet
Offensive that signaled the beginning of the end for American involvement. As a chaplain, I had a unique position that exposed me to a wide
variety of information. Both enlisted men and officers confided in me
their experiences, impressions, and moral perceptions about the war. I
had very reliable contacts in the military's communications and intelligence branches. All of this information influx, combined with a military preparatory course in Vietnam's culture and history, prompted the
following perspectives:

> ➢ The notion that America was involved to save Vietnam for de-
> mocracy was a mythic cloak designed to justify its bloodshed
> and expense. Our real reason was the heady stuff of the messi-
> anic myth that was cloaked in our foreign policy of communist
> containment.

> ➢ The Domino Theory, as applied to Vietnam, was spurious. A
> national historical enmity existed between Vietnam and China
> that would have made Vietnam, as an independent communist
> state, a natural buffer between China's political aspirations and
> Southeast Asia.

> ➢ The U. S. military and political representatives in Vietnam, for
> most of the war, were constantly creating bogus information,
> manipulating statistics, and deliberately brainwashing visit-
> ing Washington dignitaries in order to create the illusion that
> America was winning the war. The U. S. government, desper-
> ately wanting to believe this information, passed it on to the
> American public as truth.

> ➢ America was backing a South Vietnamese government that
> was immersed in political intrigue, unstable, and constantly
> shifting. This government was unreliable in its word, untrust-

worthy in its aims, unabashed in its corruption, uninspired in its leadership, unconstrained in its brutality, unprepared militarily, uninterested in democracy, unable to win the allegiance of the populace, and unaccountable to anyone. In brief, it was totally incompetent and incapable of winning a war against the North Vietnamese.

> American soldiers were involved in atrocities. The nature of the war made it impossible to distinguish between friend and foe. While the My Lai Massacre was not a normal occurrence, neither was it an isolated exception to the rule.
> America's presence in Vietnam was grounded in an ignorance of the nation's politics, culture, and history. It stepped into the fray for politicized mythic reasons with an assumption of invincibility that never considered the possibility of losing.
> There is some evidence, as was inferred in U.S. national news magazines at the time, that the potential exploitation of the natural resources of Southeast Asia was also a factor that contributed to the desire to have an American presence in the region.
> From its beginning, the war was not winnable and inconsistent with democratic ideals.

By the time I left Vietnam, the myth that posed America as the world's messianic democratic savior was revealed as a product of self-delusion, willful ignorance, and brash arrogance. This myth epitomized those characteristics that had created the deplorable and negative international epithet "the ugly American." In addition, the Domino Theory also proved itself to be without historic justification.

Loss of Innocence

These perceptions constituted a loss of innocence for me as an American. My tour of duty had been a behind-the-scenes experience that had revealed America's complicity with evil. I was a member of the nation, and thus participated in this complicity. It did not matter that this complicity may have been born of a mythic belief that had intended perceived good. The end result had been the gross destruction of life and the attempt to deny a lesser nation's right to political self-determination.

When I returned to America, I found a multitude of people who had experienced a similar mythic shattering and loss of innocence. The desire of these people was to create a change in American behavior by showing the inconsistency of our involvement in this war with the American version of the myth of democracy.

The critical lesson I learned from the scope of this experience is that mythic shattering and loss of innocence constitute a singular event that is usually called consciousness-raising—the dual sensing that some behavior-inducing perspective does not accord with conscience and needs to be changed so that it does accord. Here is the principle:

> *Loss of innocence, which is the recognition of complicity with evil, is the prelude to consciousness-raising and the impetus for all deliberate change that is necessitated by mythic inconsistency.*

While there are always multiple forces pressuring cultures toward change, all deliberately designed change that is directed toward the correction of mythic inconsistency is created under the governance of this principle.

Complicity with Evil

It is a difficult thing for people who believe they are doing right to acknowledge that they are actually complicit with evil. And the question this reluctance raises is, what makes for such complicity?

Complicity is a collusion, conspiracy, or collaboration. Evil is the harm that human attitudes and actions inflict upon others. Complicity with evil is when attitudes and actions cause this infliction. The intention of the attitude and action expressed is not relevant. It is the end result and not the desired end that is at issue. Whatever the intention, when the attitude and action results in inflicted harm, a complicity with evil has occurred.

Hendrik Hertzberg, commentator for *The New Yorker* magazine, suggests:

> *In war the moral question is always the same: does the end justify the means?*

However, as regards complicity with evil, it doesn't make any difference whether the end justifies the means or not. War, for whatever reason or goal it is fought, is always complicit with evil. It is not possible to fight a war without inflicting great harm on countless numbers of children, women, and men who have no voice in it. During World War II, the allies unleashed a bombing frenzy on German cities that killed hundreds of thousands of civilian occupants of all ages. The justification behind these bombings was that, being citizens of Germany, the occupants were as morally responsible for Nazi atrocities as were their leaders. However, while the infliction of harm during a war might be viewed as morally justified by its perceived goal, it can never be untied from complicity with evil. All wars involve both combatants and noncombatants in atrocity. Three-year-old children are hardly responsible for the actions perpetrated by their elders.

Moreover, the thrusting of soldiers into war tends to not only bring out their most noble qualities, it equally tends to bring out their most ignoble traits. The atrocities committed by American soldiers at the Abu Ghraib prison in Iran during 2003 is an example. According to the *New Yorker*, it had come into possession of a document by U.S. military authorities that described the actions of these soldiers as "… sadistic, blatant, and wanton criminal abuses." All wars invite all sides to behave from their darkest motivations because all wars are inevitably acts of atrocity. And some groups, no matter whom they represent, will succumb to this invitation.

As regards complicity with evil, metaphorically, no one wore a white hat in Vietnam. All hats were black. Consider the estimates of cost:

America

> 58,022 dead and over 300,000 wounded and maimed
> Possibly an average of $2,000,000 per day in expenditures during most of the involvement
> A nation internally divided
> Military returnees vilified despite the fact that most were draftees and were in Vietnam because they were forced to be there

South Vietnam

> An estimated 1.9 million South Vietnamese dead and over 4.5

million wounded and maimed (over six million combined ca-
sualties)
➤ Nine million refugees
➤ Ecological devastation

North Vietnam

➤ No known accurate figures, but estimates range in the millions
killed, wounded, and maimed

Of the foregoing estimates, a large number of the Vietnamese, both
North and South, were civilians of all ages.

During the war, over 7,000,000 tons of bombs were dropped by
American forces—over three times the total dropped in World War II
and the Korean War combined.

Internal Division

The national solidarity that came out of the morally perceived
black and white World War II was broken in Vietnam. America became divided.

The Morally Outraged

At one end of this division were those who were morally outraged
at losing the war. This group was a blend of two perspectives. One
perspective, represented by certain pragmatic politicians and military
strategists, viewed the morality of the war as hinging on whether or
not America did whatever was necessary to win what it had begun. The
other perspective, represented by "true patriotic believers," viewed the
morality of the war as the force of democratic good defeating the force
of communist evil.

For both perspectives, Vietnam was seen as a moral tragedy because the nation failed to win the war and defeat the communists when
it possessed the military capability to do so. Both the nation's pride and
messianic mission had been violated by loss of nerve.

The Morally Disillusioned

At the other end of the division were those who were morally disil-
lusioned by the war. They also saw our involvement in Vietnam as an
exercise in national shame. However, this shame had nothing to do

with winning or losing. It had to do with motivation and conduct. It focused on the use of American power to promote undemocratic interests and its inhumane and destructive consequences.

These people believed the nation was violating its mythic conscience and assaulting its moral character. They perceived the war to be sustained by lies and prosecuted by men whose egos were more important in decision-making than what was right or realistic. Vietnam was seen as a moral tragedy because it was pursued with immoral intent and conduct compounded by undemocratic purpose.

The Ambivalent Majority

In between these polar responses of moral outrage and moral disillusionment were the majority of American citizens—a majority tyrannized by its internal ambivalence of response to the conflicting polarities that besieged it.

On the one hand, this majority deeply wished to believe the Vietnam War was a noble cause. On the other hand, it was deeply suspicious that the cause was both immoral and futile. The end result of this ambivalence was a traumatizing paralysis that gathered momentum in its desire for the war to just go away—to have it end in some way that might retain a vestige of national dignity.

The Scapegoats

Those who suffered most from this division were the returning veterans of the war. Most of these were people who had been drafted into participation. They were immersed in the horror and atrocities of the war and, upon returning home, were generally ignored or berated with disdain and contempt.

They were the scapegoats of a divided and ambivalent public opinion that left them suspended by the thread of unrelieved guilt and a sense of futile sacrifice—bitter and alienated.

Ex-marine and one-time president of Vietnam Veterans of America Robert O. Muller spoke for so many of these returnees:

Because I lost the use of three-quarters of my body, I would want there to be a reason for the war to have been fought. What I'm saying.... is that what happened to me and what happened to my friends was for nothing. It was a waste.

National Inability

The treatment of veterans became a graphic symbol of the nation's inability to deal with either the mythic meaning of the war or the lessons of these mythic meanings. Because there was no general accord, there was no united opportunity to acknowledge the nation's complicity with evil. Whatever loss of innocence occurred as a result of the Vietnam War was experienced by individuals and groups rather than by the nation as a whole.

History of Complicity

Loss of innocence is a major milestone in the evolution of human growth and maturity.

The Individual

For the individual, it is a rite of passage that normally occurs in Western culture during the teens or twenties—a moral rite of passage that marks out the ending of adolescence and the beginning of adulthood. This opportunity to lose innocence is wrought out of interactions with people and events. Without this loss of innocence, the individual either becomes subject to grand illusions about the nature of life or becomes a defensive idealist. In either case, the maturation process is denied or put on hold, perhaps indefinitely.

The Nation

Because a nation is made up of individuals, its maturing movement from adolescence to adulthood also awaits its loss of innocence. As a collective, the process normally takes decades and centuries rather than months and years. But, as with the individual, the opportunities always present themselves with the process of time and the events of interaction with both itself and that of other nations. While the events of interaction will always occur, that which is unknown is how a nation will respond to the opportunity.

Internal Opportunities

Consider some of the internal events that have offered themselves as moments for the American nation to admit its complicity with evil and lose its innocence:

> The mass murder of the Native American population during the nation's westward expansion.

> The inhumane use of blacks as social slaves for close to a hundred years, and the deliberate denial of their civil rights almost a hundred years beyond their legal emancipation.

> The subjugation of women as de facto slaves to white males for almost one hundred and fifty years until granted the constitutional right to vote in the democratic process.

> The continued subjugation of women as de facto slaves of white males for another fifty years until the feminist movement of the 1960s and 1970s.

> The rampant, contemptuous, and brutal treatment of labor by industrial management, with the concurrence of government and law enforcement, until the nation's consciousness was raised and unions organized and the federal government stepped in to regulate fairness in the twentieth century.

> The depriving of Japanese citizens of their civil rights, businesses, homes, and futures and their subjugation to abusive and degrading internment in camp life during World War II without any legitimate justification.

> The government-sanctioned communist witch hunt of the 1950s that destroyed multiple lives and careers of patriotic citizens.

While the nation, from the standpoint of historical hindsight, has admitted these complicities with evil and lost its innocence in these areas of cultural life, it has taken over two hundred years for this maturing to take place and there are still some who wish to have no part in this progress toward national adulthood.

External Opportunities

Consider some of the external events that have offered themselves as moments for the American nation to admit its complicity with evil and lose its innocence:

> The forcing of Japan to open itself to American economic exploitation through the use of military threat.

> The devious political and military conspiracy that wrested California and the Southwest from Mexico, incorporating them into American territory.

> ➢ The contrived Spanish-American War that gained the United States dominance over Cuba and the acquisition of Puerto Rico, Guam, and the Philippines.
>
> ➢ The agitation for and support of Panama's ceding from Colombia with the expressed stipulation of an agreement for recognizing the Panama Canal Zone and its complete American control.
>
> ➢ The continued interference in Latin American politics, support of ruthless dictatorships, and the quelling of legitimate nationalistic uprisings for spurious political purposes and economic gain—as exemplified in the CIA-led suppression of a democratic reform revolution in Guatemala to protect the economic exploitation of that country by the American-owned United Fruit Company.
>
> ➢ The firebombing of German cities during World War II that led to the incineration of countless thousands of innocent children, women, and men.
>
> ➢ The mass death and destruction that resulted from dropping atomic bombs on Hiroshima and Nagasaki in Japan.

Whether admitting these complicities with evil were simply more than the American public could handle, or whether the media posed them in ways hidden from moral implication, or whether there was national disagreement over their character, all of these historical incidents have been refused as touchstones for accepting the nation's complicity with evil and, thus, remain inert possibilities for its maturing.

The Vietnam Opportunity

While most of these examples of forceful antidemocratic international activities could be kept from the American public through media manipulation, the media was not as easily shut out in Vietnam. Despite military and government deception, the facts of the conflict began invading the nation's living rooms. The public was no longer entirely subject to mythic control. People began to see a complicity with evil in the nation's involvement. This was preluded by questions about both the purpose and the legitimacy of our presence in this small, seemingly inconsequential country.

Because of its imposing visibility, the war in Vietnam became a wide open opportunity for America to see that its mythic imperialism was just as complicit with evil as was the colonialism of France. That is, Vietnam become the most compelling occasion of the twentieth century, on an international level, for America to mature into its democratic myth through acknowledged loss of innocence. But it was not to be, except for a minority of the citizenry.

Resistance to Opportunity

Why would America refuse an opportunity to mature its culture through a further loss of innocence on an international basis? Why deny complicity with evil when others in the international community could see it and were announcing it so clearly?

Self-Image

The self-image of America following World War II was of the God-led, always-right, invincible nation that had saved the world for democracy. Moreover, it saw itself as the most powerful nation on earth. Combined, these two facets of imagery were very heady stuff that tended to instill the cultural psyche with messianic arrogance and bravado. The nation's sense of its superior worth among the other nations of the world was grounded in this self-imagery and physical power.

Mythic Violation

The civil rights and feminist movements of the 1960s and 1970s did what they were intended to do—mirror the nation's gross violations of its democratic conscience. As a result, these violations were confronted and addressed toward correction to the extent of significant social progress.

In this process the democratic myth that grounded the nation's being was affirmed rather than threatened, and its democratic conscience avowed rather than denied. The identity of the nation—its self-image and self-worth—were strengthened. The trauma of these two decades was the shame of acknowledged mythic hypocrisy.

Mythic Validation

The issue surrounding the nation's involvement in Vietnam was the opposite. The very myth that had fueled that involvement was under question. Was America God-led? Was America always right? Was

America invincible? Was America the world's democratic savior nation? These facets of the myth are interrelated and mutually supportive. They are a holistic nexus. And the issue was not their violation but their validity. The focus of shame was not hypocrisy but world venturing under a false mythic flag and, specifically, a flag that had seemed synonymous with the nation's democratic flag. To question the validity of the messianic flag seemed to question the validity of the democratic flag. Such questioning was beyond comprehension for the average American.

Mythic Threat

While confronting and correcting violations of the nation's democratic conscience was an affirmation of mythic identity, the questioning of this messianic myth was a direct threat to that mythic identity because the myth of democracy and the myth of messiahship had become fused in the cultural psyche.

This is why the nation's internal confrontation over Vietnam was ultimately polarizing while its internal confrontations over violations of its democratic conscience have been ultimately uniting. In its external confrontation in Vietnam, the democratic myth was viewed as synonymous with the messianic myth while its internal confrontations have normally focused on the conscience and spirit of the democratic myth alone.

The Issue

The issue of Vietnam focused on a part of America's mythic identity being played out on the world stage—the God-led, always-right, invincible, democratic savior-nation part. To admit to the invalidity of this mythic component was the same as admitting that:

➤ America's initiative in Vietnam was based on a delusion.
➤ America's rationale behind its international political maneuvering was spurious.

Such an admission was beyond the psychological capacity of most Americans for it required a corresponding acknowledgment of complicity with evil on the world stage.

Moreover, such an admission would also require that the nation rethink its self-perceived messianic identity and reformulate its mythic role in world politics. The effect of its failure in Vietnam on this re-thinking could only lead to a more humbling self-perception than that generated by the grandeur of the messianic myth.

Humiliation

To perceive the international democratic savior becoming an international democratic servant was easily viewed as humiliating rather than humbling. And the idea of bowing before the world's nations was too much for prideful Americans to swallow. This pride was another component of the nation's psychological incapacity to squarely face the meaning of Vietnam. The opportunity of loss of innocence that could lead to a maturing of American democracy yielded to these incapacities.

Democratic Maturing

The process of maturing is a lifelong endeavor. But its most dramatic possibilities often present themselves during the malleable years of adolescence and young adulthood. The same is true of nations that are made up of individuals. The process is simply slower due to the necessities of collective persuasion. And, similar to the individual, nations tend to learn their lessons the hard way and may have to be pushed by circumstance to confront those most difficult to learn.

The internal battle to mature the democratic experiment in America has been long and socially brutal. Each step has been a confrontation with the nation's behavioral violation of its democratic conscience. Each success in these confrontations has required a confession of complicity with evil, a raised consciousness regarding the violation, and appropriate corrective measures. And on the other side of each success has come a heightened awareness of how a democratic nation behaves toward its own citizens; this is a growth in maturity, whether it has been:

- ➢ how the nation's unity is treated
- ➢ how minorities are treated
- ➢ how women are treated
- ➢ how laborers are treated
- ➢ how citizenry civil rights are treated
- ➢ how the poor are treated

As a rule, the nation has ultimately responded and dealt in some visible way with its internal violations of democratic conscience. All of these confrontations have strengthened both the nation's mythic conscience and an awareness of the social implications of this conscience. In brief, all have culminated in some significant and permanent measure of change in the nation's attitudes and actions toward a greater internal maturity.

Unfortunately, there is no similar evidence that America has matured through loss of innocence in its dealings on an international basis. We remain perpetually adolescent in this sphere of cultural interaction.

Conclusion

Since the inception of America, the perception of democracy's depth of meaning has been evolving internally and, with it, the nation's mythic conscience. This internal evolutional maturing has been bloody and culturally difficult, yet it has progressed in significant fashion. However, one of the primary forces most resistant to this maturing on an external basis has been America's refusal to acknowledge its complicity with evil in the international arena. Until this acknowledgment is both forthcoming and accepted, America will remain schizophrenic in the maturing process of its brand of democracy.

Folly and Innocence are so alike,
The difference, though essential, fails to strike.
                                                    —Cowper

I'd rather see America save her soul than her face.
                                                    —Norman Thomas

The Capturing of the Vision
(The Messianism and Democracy)

...a trait no other nation seems to possess in quite the same degree that we do—namely, a feeling of almost childish injury and resentment unless the world as a whole recognizes how innocent we are of anything but the most generous and harmless intentions.
—Eleanor Roosevelt

Innocence itself hath need of a mask.
—Thomas Fuller

Innocence involves an unseeing acceptance of things at face value, an ignorance of the area below the surface.
—Eugenia W. Collien

The Experience

Without sound the flashes of bursting enemy rockets were surreal—a silent film of explosions pelting the South Vietnamese landscape below. A time-warp image invaded my mind. I was watching a John Wayne, World War II movie dramatizing the ultimate triumph of good over evil—growing my teenage identity from the pap of the invincible hero who never dies. The plane jolted as it descended toward the darkened runway and fear purged my ego of the cavalier image. This was no movie where the hero goes unscathed. This was real life, where death lurked for me down on that explosion-pelted landscape.

With this awakening I began a romance with mortality that demanded an answer to the question screaming in my mind: "What the hell am I doing here?" During the following months, the demand of this question broadened to embrace my country as well. The war in Vietnam presented me hard answers that shattered the cultural myths of my upbringing like a rock against plate glass. These myths became a pile of shards at my feet.

When I arrived home in 1969, I found America in a similar turmoil of mythic crisis. As with mine, this crisis was triggered by a questioning of those myths that seemed endemic to democracy. Critical to this mythic shattering for me was that of the messianic myth.

The Messianic Myth

Where did this messianic myth come from? There are two primary sources.

The Democratic Myth

The first is the foundational perception of America's citizenry that its brand of democracy as a political process and cultural style of living is vastly superior to that of all other nations. This perception took on an edge of celebrative arrogance after America's victorious emergence from World War II as an industrial superpower. Whether this sense of superiority is valid or invalid is irrelevant. It is the attitude itself that spawns perceptions and actions on the world stage. Moreover, the arrogance of the perception is an invitation for collusion with any mythic element that might lend support to its validity, irrespective of the truth or falseness of that element. The messianic myth was made for this collusion since it was a bridesmaid standing in the background at the wedding between America and democracy.

The Judeo-Christian Myth

The second source is the religion that has dominated American life since its inception—the Judeo-Christian myth. The concepts of this religion are deeply embedded in the culture's psyche. Endemic to these concepts are the following:

> ➢ A God-chosen people
> ➢ A God-led people
> ➢ A people who play a messianic role in God's plans
> ➢ A people whose mission is to establish God's Kingdom on the earth

> ➢ A people who are invincible except when they break their covenant with God

Amalgamation

Given the profound impact of the Judeo-Christian religious myth upon American culture, it was inevitable that these concepts would become amalgamated into the nation's self-identity and imposed upon the political myth of democracy. This mythic fusion is symbolized in the nation's slogans:

> ➢ In God we Trust (inscription on its coins)
> ➢ One nation under God (acknowledgment in its pledge)
> ➢ So help me God (oath by its politicians)

These slogans speak to America's cultural submission to Judeo-Christian mythology. And up until the mythic questioning of the 1960s and 1970s, the practice of invoking the leadership of the myth's god through prayer in Congress, schools, and other national and public events dramatized the depth of this religious and political fusion. Moreover, it is a standard benediction of almost all politicians to conclude their remarks with the phrase: *God bless America!* This benediction is the ultimate acknowledgment of the infused power of the messianic myth in the cultural psyche. It is the afterthought of the myth's profound influence.

Emerging from this fusion was a mythic view of the nation as a specially chosen, God-led, always-right, invincible, democratic savior.

This mythic view was voiced anew at the beginning of the twentieth century in the political arena by Senator Albert Beveridge of Indiana:

> *God has marked the American people as His chosen nation to finally lead in the regeneration of the world. This is the divine mission of America, and it holds for us all the profit, all the glory, all the happiness possible to man.*

It was again voiced toward the end of the twentieth century by presidential hopeful Ronald Reagan:

> *I have long believed there was a divine plan that placed this land here to be found by people of a special kind, that we have a rendezvous with destiny.*

Complicity with Evil

Judeo-Christian is a phrase disputed by some scholars. It is deliberately retained in these remarks and is intended to imply an inseparable continuity of mythology as indicated in Christianity's authoritative texts—the Old Testament (Judeo) and the New Testament (Christian). It is also an acknowledgment of the impact of the notion of a chosen people following the leadership of a supreme god with an intended special destiny as epitomized in the religion of Judaism. The messianic myth derives from this continuity and has been playing itself out in near Eastern and Western history for thousands of years.

A reading of the New Testament version of this text reveals the Christian belief that every human is born sinful (in total complicity with evil). There is only one redemption from this plight—the external imputation of goodness from the religion's god. This imputation cleanses from an original complicity with evil endemic to birth. This dual action brings one into covenant with God. Thereafter, complicity with evil is determined by whether or not one is doing or is not doing God's will rather than whether or not one's attitudes and actions cause harm to other humans. This distinction is vital to understanding why the larger Christian community in the nation did not see the Vietnam debacle as an opportunity for loss of innocence, but as a demand by their god for recommitment of the nation to its covenant with this god.

Rule of Thumb

Thus, one can do war or wreak havoc and destruction upon other people and nations without being in complicity with evil, as long as it is God's will. One rule of thumb for such judgment is whether the people or nations under consideration are flying the Judeo-Christian flag of allegiance. If they are not then they are "Godless" and deserving of their fate at the hands of God's people.

Judeo-Christian history is a testament to this mythic view as exemplified in the destruction of life and living wrought through their religion's conquests, crusades, inquisitions, and witch hunts—all of which were viewed as enacting God's will rather than as complicities with evil. The point is that the biblical message, particularly that of the Old Testament, is that God often desires destructive justice to be imposed on enemy nations. This justice is to be acted out on his behalf by his covenanted people.

America Justified

Therefore, the destructions wrought by Messianic America during its Native American purge (Godless pagans), its interference in Central American nationalist movements (Godless Communists), its war in Vietnam (Godless Communists), and the Persian Gulf War and the Iraq War (Godless Muslims) were as righteously justified as World War I and World War II (Godless fascists and Godless imperialists, respectively).

America remained compatriots of European colonial powers because the destruction they heaped upon other nations was also upon Godless cultures that they sought to convert to the Judeo-Christian religion. There can be no complicity with evil as long as battles of destruction are fought against the Godless embodiments of evil. Complicity with evil is converted into a denial of America's god and a refusal to do this god's will.

Allegiance

While many branches of institutionalized Judeo-Christian religion in America have drifted away from any profound allegiance to this messianic myth, the more conservative and fundamentalist right wing has maintained a strong allegiance. These latter are the self-proclaimed flame-keepers and have aggressively entered the political arena to reinstate its validity in the nation's identity perception. For these citizens, the democracy of America and the theocracy of Judeo-Christianity are an inseparable unity as affirmed by this slogan: "One nation under God." Thus, when the messianic myth is violated so is democracy, and vice-versa.

However, that a significant part of the institutionalized Judeo-Christian religion might have forsaken a stress on the messianic myth does not lessen the myth's insidious pervasion of America's general culture. Several hundred years of influence has insinuated the myth firmly in the cultural psyche. And it is far easier to diminish the influence of a myth on an individual by individual basis and on an institution-by-institution basis than to do so on a cultural basis.

Even amongst those whose commitment to the expressions of

Judeo-Christianity are mild or nil, commitment to mythic messianism in democracy remains high. The family, educational, political, and media myth carriers remain enamored of the messianic myth's wedding to the democratic myth. Every major crisis America confronts is witness to the invocation of the messianic god's blessings and aid in confronting the perceived enemy. To fail this invocation is to draw political suspicion because, for most of the population, the very notion of God in American culture and messianic images are synonymous. Even in the 2008 presidential political campaigns, politicians were still ending their speeches with the invocation of "God bless America." The major 2009 events installing the newly elected president were blessed by messianic representatives called ministers, and the politicians involved in the newly installed government repeatedly invoked the blessings of the Judeo-Christian god upon the nation. The messianic myth remains hearty and hale in American politics.

Mythic Testing

How is it possible that a God-led, always-right, invincible, democratic-savior nation could be defeated by a grossly inferior and ungodly communist foe in Vietnam? The explanation for advocates of the messianic myth is simple. When God's people do not keep their covenant, then God abandons them to failure as a punishment for their sins. Thus, the call, on the downside of such defeat, is for a recommitment of the nation to God's will. Examples are:

> ➢ Restoring family values (acknowledging the legitimacy of the Judeo-Christian notion of male cultural dominance)
> ➢ Invoking God's leadership through public prayer (acknowledging the nation's dependency on Judeo-Christian divine leadership)
> ➢ Using the Ten Commandments as guides in public education (acknowledging the nation's commitment to Judeo-Christian morality)
> ➢ Deleting the concept of evolution from school curriculum (acknowledging the supremacy of the Judeo-Christian biblical authority)
> ➢ Denouncing gay, lesbian, and alternative sexual lifestyles (acknowledging the singular validity of a Judeo-Christian heterosexual lifestyle)

All of these activities are viewed as symbolic gestures by the nation that affirms its renewed covenant with the Judeo-Christian god. Without these gestures, it is assumed that the nation remains unrepentant of its sins against God's will. These symbolic gestures address the family, feminist, sexual, and knowledge liberation revolutions that began their social expression in the 1960s. The Vietnam debacle is easily viewed by devout believers in the messianic myth as God's punishment for these violations of covenant.

The submission of politicians to the conservative and fundamentalist religious right's attempt to reinstill the messianic myth as an inseparable component of national identity during the last two decades of the twentieth century and the first part of the twenty-first century attests to both the power of these advocates and the deep-rootedness of the messianic myth in the culture's psyche, despite the political ramifications. And the resort to God's blessings and leadership in the defeat of America's enemies following the September 11, 2001, terrorist attacks and the continued appeal of politicians to this blessing and leadership underscores the undeniability of how deep-rooted the messianic myth is. It is so culturally embedded that it no longer needs the support of the people's belief in either the Judeo-Christian faith or the bible of that faith. It stands apart from either this religious faith or its scripture as a cultural phenomenon. It is programmed into the consciousness of the citizenry through politics, family life, the educational process, the media and the ceremonies of cultural life. In almost imperceptive ways, the messianic myth has converted American democracy into a theocracy.

Messianic Myth

The Judeo-Christian religion's messianic myth has been very elusive of recognition, both in its identity and its complicity with evil. It is possible that the blending of the democratic myth and the messianic myth in the nation's pride are so finely woven that their distinctions are imperceptible to the average American citizen. This imperceptiveness suggests that, despite education about the nature of democracy and political hoopla about its benefits, America as a nation has never considered the primary questions its cultural democratic incarnation raises.

> ➢ What is the true mission of America's version of democracy in the world?

> What behaviors would characterize a true democratic model for the international community?
> Is the attempt to force other cultures into a democratic mold an oxymoron?
> Can a true democracy ever be a world policeman?

Further questions are raised from the potential answers to these questions about democracy.
> How do answers to these questions fit the messianic myth?
> Is the messianic myth the antithesis of a true democratic myth?
> Are a democracy and a theocracy incompatible?

Failure to both raise and respond to these questions has left America susceptible to control by the messianic myth in its international relations and subject to the charge of hypocrisy by the international community. But such control and charges are hard to accept if the nation has not done its homework. That America, as a whole, was incapable and unwilling to recognize its arrogant and undemocratic behavior in Vietnam evidences ignorance of the profound meanings of its own myth in relating to the world community.

Messianic Myth Restoration

For decades following the debacle, America's political leaders deliberately hid from the meanings of Vietnam and instead sought to restore the pride of the messianic myth in national behavior.

The first opportunity following Vietnam occurred in Grenada. Grenada is an independent self-ruled island of the West Indies in the Caribbean Sea just north of Venezuela. It was taken over by a left-wing group in a bloodless coup in 1979. It leaned politically toward communist Cuba. In 1983, the U.S., under the pretext of rescuing American medical students, invaded Grenada and, for all practical purposes, deposed the government and remained until 1984 elections established a democratic government. But Grenada was too inconsequential on the world stage to restore American messianic pride. It was only a momentary hot flash.

The real opportunity finally afforded itself in the form of the 1990 Persian Gulf War that was precipitated by Iraq's invasion of Kuwait under the leadership of Saddam Hussein. Because the event was about the instability of oil prices, it became a world stage affair. However, American actions of response were cloaked in the messianic myth. The factors of restoration of American messianic pride inherent in this event were these:

> ➤ The enemy was a "Godless" Islamic nation (no matter that Kuwait was also a "Godless" Islamic nation).
>
> ➤ The Hitler-like imaging of Saddam Hussein provided a mythic cloaking of rightness about American interference akin to the nobility of American's participation in World War II (no matter that the real issue was the threat to American influence over oil prices).
>
> ➤ The coalition support of other nations broadened the moral appeal that the U.S. was not acting alone (no matter that this support was also due to concerns regarding production, pricing, and control of oil).
>
> ➤ The perception was that America's overwhelming military would assure its invincibility of outcome (no matter that Iraq was a dwarf being smote by a giant).
>
> ➤ America's role in the affair was that of the democratic savior nation (no matter that America had not intervened to save Iran when Iraq had previously invaded it aggressively).

As a world stage event, the importance of the outcome was that America's victory was an antidote to the loss of messianic pride announced in its failure in Vietnam.

The wildly enthusiastic and grossly overdone reception of the Persian Gulf War's returning soldiers as national heroes, all out of proportion to the scope and meaning of the event, attests to the enormous investment in wished for pride the American public had in its outcome. Essayist Peter Marin was a member of a forum discussion about the consequences of the Vietnam war held at the Harvard Club in New York City a number of years after that military debacle. During this discussion he observed:

[W]hen Americans are confronted with the reality of defeat, they tend to reassert their old myths.

The splendor of the messianic myth had finally been restored and the failure of Vietnam could now be swept under the nation's historical rug as an aberration. So, Vietnam, America's most potent opportunity to confront its complicity with evil on the external world stage, was lost in the backwash of the Persian Gulf War.

The Vietnam Mistake

Since the Persian Gulf War, it has been popular for politicians who were involved in the Vietnam War to admit that it was a "mistake." However, such euphemisms do not necessarily reveal that any lessons were learned about America's complicity with evil that might lead to a loss of innocence and a step toward democratic maturity.

It seems that the only lesson learned was to not get involved in a major war that America could not win and to not permit the media to have a free hand in covering America's future wars. The messianic myth would be enacted with greater caution of outcome but it had, in reality, survived the death that threatened it in Vietnam. While Vietnam may have left the nation a bit politically wiser, it did not leave the nation any mythically wiser.

And while the internal maturing of democracy in America continues its slow but steady progress, its external maturing in the world's international affairs remains retarded.

That the majority of Americans easily succumbed to the contrived and spurious justifications given by the George Bush administration for the Iraq War following September 11, 2001, shows that the American psyche continues to be susceptible to the political use of the messianic myth.

Internal/External Schizophrenia

This internal/external dichotomy of maturing is evidence of a dichotomy of mythic conscience—a double standard of national and international dealings. While gradually listening to its mythic conscience when applied to its own internal affairs America has ignored this same conscience when applied to its behavior among nations. The culture is a democratic schizophrenic. And one of the primary agents of this schizophrenia is the messianic myth.

Until the cloaking of the messianic myth is lifted from the democratic myth the nation will remain schizophrenic and confused about the role a true democratic nation plays in the international world drama and its further maturing of conscience will remain retarded. Meanwhile, the messianic myth continues to offer its renewed self as a blueprint for national tragedy.

The Insight

In very disguised and insidious ways, the messianic myth of the Judeo-Christian faith has infiltrated the American myth of democracy to such an extent that the populace is unable to distinguish between the two. This swaddling of the democratic myth continues to influence the nation in becoming involved in international incidents that are counterproductive to both the good of American's well-being and the good of democracy as a model of government. Until the two are separated and our version of democracy can stand alone as its own model of government and culture, America will continue to behave in the world community in ways that draw the epithet of international hypocrite, and the myth of democracy, per se, will be tainted by the association.

Without unspotted, innocent within,
She feared not danger, for she knew no sin.
 —Dryden

The knowledge that makes us cherish innocence makes innocence
unattainable.
 —Louis Mumford

Of all the forms of innocence, mere ignorance is the least
admirable.
 —Sir Arthur Pinero

9

The Threats to the Vision
(Confusing and Disguised Myths)

If you know the enemy and know yourself, you need not fear the result of a hundred battles. If you know yourself but not your enemy, for every victory gained you will also suffer a defeat. If you know neither the enemy nor yourself, you will succumb in every battle.
—Sun Tzu, Fifth Century

Our greatest foes, and whom we must chiefly combat, are within.
—Miquel De Cervantes

There is no little enemy
—French Proverb

Threats

There is much that threatens the spirit and conscience of American democracy. These threats are both external and internal. Yet, as history reveals, the greatest threats to any mythic system are inevitably internal.

Apparent internal threats usually have to do with rebellious questioning and growing dissatisfaction that encourage a withdrawal of citizenry energy allegiance necessary to sustain cultural health and strength. However, there are also unapparent threats that insidiously diminish the health and drain the strength of any mythic system. The capacity of these unapparent threats to continuously debilitate in unopposed fashion lies in their skill at confusion and disguise. This skill often permits them to appear as either an ally of the mythic system or as its synonym. Allies and kin are welcome to feed at the mythic table unchallenged.

Since the advent of American democracy, there has been an array of such mythic enemies feeding at the national table. They have generated sufficient confusion and remained so well disguised that their destructive effect on the democratic experiment has also remained unopposed and unabated (there is one glaring exception that will be addressed as the first mythic enemy). The irony of this scenario is that the American citizenry, without awareness, willingly nurtures those myths that are the persistent and avowed enemies of the democratic myth. It is the fabled story of the house divided against itself except, in respect to America, the house does not know that it is abetting its own destruction. It is a scenario where the house unwittingly diminishes itself at the invitation of its unrecognized enemies by sustaining them with its own vitality.

Unfortunately, these mortal enemies of American democracy exist in almost every cultural dimension and form a web of mutual support that further camouflages their real nature and intent. Unless recognized for what they are and deliberately dealt with, they may eventually precipitate the fall of American democracy.

The Superior White Male Myth

As previously mentioned, there is one mythic threat to American democracy that has never needed to resort to confusion or disguise. It has always been a cultural "in your face" confrontation of mythic posturing. It is the superior white male myth. Indeed, this myth was the most apparent "on top of the table" competition with the democratic myth at the birth of the nation.

The Fear

At the nation's advent, the fear in this myth was that anyone other than the highly educated white male would make decisions disastrous to the democratic experiment. Its immediate context was the very difficulty the highly educated white male founding fathers were having in even agreeing among themselves over its rudiments and framework. If such agreement was so difficult for the creators of American democracy, how could the uneducated possibly choose wisely? The founding fathers feared ignorance of knowledge and its normally accompanying imperceptiveness.

Beyond this wariness, it was scary enough to risk democracy to the care of uneducated white males. To include uneducated white women was beyond the scope of their vision.

Racial Superiority

The white part of this myth spoke to racial superiority. White was viewed as superior in both intellect and insight over all other skin pigmentations, whatever their hue. The general one-down economic, social, and educational status exhibited by people of other skin pigmentations was both deliberately maintained and used as a confirmation of white male superiority. Cause-and-effect relationships were conveniently ignored.

Even into the last half of the twentieth century publications were still proclaiming the superiority of the white male intellect over the black intellect (and by extension all other skin pigmentations). These claims were supposedly based on unbiased scientific studies done by white males. However, beginning with World War II and culminating in the civil rights movement, opportunities were opened to the black population to exhibit intellectual equality with whites in every area of cultural life, and the black response clearly showed the white male superiority myth to be totally false.

Male Superiority

The male part of the myth spoke to gender superiority, that of male over female. Gender superiority justified the continued utilitarian attitudes and behaviors of men toward women as essentially child-raisers, housekeepers, and general social servants of male need. Keeping women ignorant, pregnant, and weary were tactics used to abet their inferior social status. However, this all began to change in the latter part of the nineteenth century.

The first step in overcoming the myth was the legal right to vote gained through the women's suffrage movement. The second step was the World War II experience when women demonstrated that they could capably inhabit so-called exclusive male work and social roles. The third step was the rise of the feminist movement that successfully demanded that women be viewed as the legal equals of men in the marketplace. With these three steps women bounded into the twenty-first century, leaving behind the male gender superiority myth in a state of emaciation.

Male Keepers

At the inception of American democracy, white males announced themselves as the only worthy keepers of the democratic experiment. It has taken over two hundred years of bitter and violent contention to remove the white male superiority myth from the social catbird seat. Yet, despite this removal, its advocates continue to espouse its legitimacy. One reason for this continued espousal is that it is a prejudice that can be held simply because one wishes to hold it. Another reason is that it offers an artificial prop to the male ego in a social environment of self-worth deprivation. A third reason is that it has been given support by the nation's adopted religion, institutionalized Christianity. And a forth reason is that it can easily be justified by the encouraged self-centeredness of most every facet of the American culture. Whatever the reasons, the white male superiority myth remains alive, despite its emaciation, and continues to exert its weight against all that is democratic. And its every expression, from whatever sector of social life, weakens the possible maturation of democracy as America's covenanted myth.

The Externalized Worth Myth

From its inception, the nation's devotion to the profoundly artificial myth of externalized self-worth has grossly retarded its capacity to develop the profoundly democratic myth of internalized self-worth. This externalization is epitomized in that part of the American Dream which is a lie. The truth of the American Dream is that it is possible to move upward relative to material gain and social status, although this possibility decreases measurably with the lowering of economic class. The lie of the American Dream is that such upward movement incrementally confers a corresponding increase in self-worth. Read self-worth and social worth as synonymous.

The Lie of the American Dream

It is the lie of the American Dream that has anchored the citizenry in the limited vision of the founding fathers and the shallow equality perceptions of the eighteenth century. And it is to this anchor that all other myths inhibiting democracy attach themselves for sustenance and lend their weight to further retardation. Every attitude and action of buy-in to this anchor myth by the citizenry drives it deeper and encourages the selling of the national soul to the empty promise of inane artificiality.

Part II, Chapter 3, The Wizardry of Worth, is a broader rehearsal of this mythic lie. However, following is a recap of how it works:

> The citizenry is taught that self-worth is an external commodity acquired by gaining social status.

> This status comes in the forms of wealth, position, fame, and ethnicity. It may be achieved by birth, work, or accident. The means of attainment is irrelevant to the state of being.

> While birth may immediately endow one with a socially measurable status of self-worth, that worth can always be incrementally increased by further achievement or decreased by some negative act of fate.

> While there is a bottom to the social order of worth merit, there is no ceiling on the garnering of self-worth increments.

> There are always others who, presumably, possess a greater measure of self-worth.

The nation's external productivity and its energy vitality are supposedly stimulated by the citizenry's investment in the superficial (although generally debasing) upward mobility games designed for the procurement of additional increments of self-worth. It is tied directly to the economy of acquisition.

This is the great cultural con, the social game that motivates the lifestyle of the average American.

The Price of the Lie

The end result of selling its soul to the lie of the American Dream is a citizenry that assesses the value of democracy in terms of self-aggrandizement. That is, democracy becomes a utility to garner a greater social worth rather than a covenant that enhances the quality of relating. This assessment leaves the citizenry easy prey to all forms of demagoguery and social shamming. In brief, the citizenry's obsession with whatever immediately gratifies its need for another increment of achieved self-worth leaves it susceptible to any ruse of conceit, howsoever inane or empty and howsoever debasing or destructive to self or others.

A product-obsessed society easily comes to see all its relationships in terms of self-elevation. Other humans become product images and, thus, useable commodities. The end result of this dehumanization is a society that treats its neighbors as things. Things are utilities rather than honorees. Things are to serve rather than to be served.

In the immediate aftermath of the 2008 financial meltdown in America there seemed to be an increasing tendency to place significant blame on the average citizen for the consequences of this disaster. The blame focused on out-of-control consumerism. Few pointed out the combination of factors that stood behind this upward mobility party. The business industry, through the Wal-Mart Syndrome, contributed by providing ever cheaper goods. The advertising industry, through its artificial ego imaging, contributed by encouraging a never-ending shopping spree. The financial industry, through its easy loans and loan scams, contributed by offering the procurement of oversized cars, larger-than-needed houses, and a host of non-necessities.

However, underneath all of these factors was a much more powerful motivation, the devoted consumerism engendered by the lie of the American Dream. The lie promotes the notion that the greater the acquisition of goods the greater the elevation of self-worth. This baseline appeal plugged directly into that which drives the living of every human being, namely, the desire to be viewed as worthy in the social order. If the consumerism of America contributed to the meltdown, then primal to that consumerism is the lie of the American Dream.

Further, this conversion of internal self-worth into an external social product is:

> ➢ the baseline for society's devotion to all things meaningless in the realization of true human fulfillment.
> ➢ the manufacturing of desire to possess that which is totally irrelevant to spiritual health or human well-being.
> ➢ the reduction of capitalism to a marketplace for the selling of superficial social charm.

To say the least, the cost of the lie of the American Dream is a demotion of human capacities from their noblest and most fulfilling to their most ignoble and most demeaning.

The Loser

In whatever way the conversion of internalized self-worth into an externalized social commodity is evaluated, democracy is the loser. When any citizen, for whatever reason, is viewed as an inferior, democracy loses. When any citizen is treated as a thing, democracy loses. When any status is viewed as superior to its holder, democracy loses. Inherently implied in the very notion of democracy is an equality of self-worth that is innate to being human. This inheritance is beyond all social status whatever the source of that status.

Social Harm

History reveals that the end result of converting human self-worth into an external procurable commodity is an evolution of social harm that grows by feeding upon itself. The ultimate expression of this social harm is a greed for more that replaces all other motivations as primal to existence. Such greed supplants nobility morality with ignobility morality. There is not an individual or a business in America that does not wrestle with the degree to which greed will dominate morality.

The only motivational alternative is the morality inherent in the spirit of democracy. This morality is a "do unto others as you would have them do unto you" scenario that is demanded of a view of mutual worth and is grounded in a covenant of mutual benefit. This morality is inherent in a fundamental realization of humanness, namely, that our most appealing social benefits and our physical survival depend on relationships of goodwill with each other that translate into the necessity of a government that fosters nobility in social relating. The ultimate political translation of this philosophy is democracy.

This is not a Christian influence. The philosophy of doing unto others as one would have done to self, is announced in all major societies throughout history. It is a basic human understanding, accumulated over history, as to how humans survive their darker selves and permit nobility to positively transform their living conditions. It is a behavior belief that derives from the human drama, irrespective of time or place. That is, it is rooted in universal human experience in social relating. It is the primal historical understanding of what maximizes human blessing for both the individual and the community.

Reduction to Vote

In a society that elevates the personal morality of individualism over the social morality of community and seeks to escape the guilt that greed imposes on this exploitation, the easiest absolution is to claim that the privilege and demand of democracy is nothing more than the vote. This divests democracy of the "do unto others as you would have them do unto you" morality of a social covenant and releases one to imbibe of whatever morality pacifies the demands of greed. Ironically, reducing democracy to mere vote enables one to expect to be treated by others with a morality of endowed worth while, at the same time, feeling no obligation to reciprocate. In effect, one can ignore the needs of the community and vote for personal benefit without feeling any pangs of conscience.

This posture is given definitive support by the spirit of excessive individualism that runs rampant through the American culture. This posture is why all those groups within the culture who have been deprived of democratic benefit have had to struggle and fight with great historical perseverance in order to attain to those benefits. Standout examples are the struggles of Blacks and women. Interestingly, while these benefits have been legally secured by law, the requirement of actually honoring such laws has been the recognition of a social relationship covenant inherent in the spirit and conscience of democracy and ultimately affirmed in the Constitution. That is, any law that justifies the morality of "do unto others as you would have them do unto you" is grounded in a view of democracy as social covenant.

A legal system designed merely to protect the right to vote is the weakest guarantee of voting rights. The history of the black population's struggle for democratic inclusion is a sufficient example. Social attitudes (community covenants) that excluded the black vote were all that was necessary to preclude this privilege for almost two hundred years. Only when the nation decided that the right of blacks to vote was a part of the democratic social covenant did that right become a social reality. In brief, the democratic right to vote for any citizen cannot be disconnected from the democratic spirit of equality and mutual worth inherent in social covenant. All critical human battles are relational in nature, whether or not their social expression is legal. The notion of one-person-one-vote is only a legal perspective that affirms a covenant of social equality. It is the social covenant that guarantees the vote and not vice-versa.

The Behavior

The lie of the American Dream, whatever form it takes, inspires behavior that elevates the individual over the community and self-aggrandizement over the national interest. While the spirit of democracy suggests that citizens view their neighbors as equals and envision concern for their welfare, the lie of the American Dream encourages a competitiveness of spirit and a propensity toward one-upping that would view neighbors as inferiors and permit one's own welfare to take precedent over that of others. Whatever favors a greater acquisition of external self-worth increments is smiled upon, even if such behavior summons the darkest of human attitude and action.

The lie of the American Dream is an ally of everything false and unprincipled that promises to enhance one's externalized worth. Throughout American history the lie of the American Dream has been used to justify the most demeaning and destructive ways of relating humans can devise. It is why the majority of Americans testify to the workplace as an environment that holds minimal promise of fair play or fulfilling relationships. In a national poll taken by a leading news network during 2008, 72 percent of those responding felt the workplace to be a totally negative experience in their living.

Escaping the Lie

From the inception of the nation, the lie of the American Dream has been and remains the paramount obstacle to the full realization of American democracy's potential. Wherever the spirit and work of democracy wanes in strength and succumbs to the tyrannies of excessive individualism, it is fed by this lie. If America is to escape the debilitating stranglehold of the American Dream's lie on its democratic possibilities, then the citizenry must engage the following:

> ➤ Recognize the lie of the American Dream for the retarding and destructive force it represents in the democratic process.
> ➤ Decidedly reject both the lie's validity and attainment practices.
> ➤ Proclaim the innate sense of worth of their neighbors that rises from being born of a common human womb.

> ➢ Distinguish between innate self-worth and the legitimate social gains earned by personal endeavor.
> ➢ Relate to one another through democratic egalitarianism irrespective of any perceived inequalities rooting in social status.
> ➢ Embrace both the material and spiritual blessings of an unfettered democracy.

A lie will always diminish but never enhance human worth. And a democracy built on a lie will never fulfill its promise. The lie of the American Dream is the most insidious and destructive force aligned against the democratic spirit, conscience, and process.

What is desperately needed is a third American Revolution. The first was its birth. The second was President Franklin D. Roosevelt's legitimization of government as democracy's processor and protector. The third would be the rejection of the lie of the American Dream and a corresponding endowment of every citizen with an innate worth as viewed through egalitarian eyes.

The Least Government Myth

As indicated in Part III, Chapter 6: The Necessity of the Vision, the notion that there can be a minimally involved government to process democracy in a maximally complicated world is an illusion. The reality is the need for a strong government that can exert influence over the democratic process in a protecting and enhancing manner. This reality extends to America's interaction with the global community. Everything in the modern world is simply too big and too complicated for least government to have any measure of effective positive influence. The advocates of least government neither understand the nature of today's world nor grasp the requirements of democracy within this world. They live in perceptions based on a national past that has no ability to inform the present with wisdom.

To underscore the historical truth that the American government exhibiting strength and acting in assertive and regulating ways has been the preservation of our democracy, consider the following:

> ➢ Since it is government that has acquired the land that makes up the nation's geography, without government our country's geography would only be about a quarter of its present size.
> ➢ Since it is government that provided incentive and land grants

for the building of the east-west connecting railroads, without government the rapid settlement of the West and the unity of the nation would have been radically delayed.

> Since it is government that acquired the rights and built the Panama Canal, without government ocean shipping might still move around the southern tip of South America.

> Since it is government that built the dams that provided cheap electrical power for the development of industry and cities, without government America would neither be modernized nor a global power.

> Since it is government that built the federal highway system, without government the nation's growth, commerce, and mobility would be severely hampered and its homogeneity severely retarded.

> Since it is government that established labor laws and fair practices of negotiation with management, without government citizens would still be subjected to the unscrupulous predatory practices of big business management.

> Since it is government that established a national Social Security system, along with Medicare and Medicaid, without government multitudes of citizens would be languishing in financial and medical disaster.

> Since it is government that created the Federal Reserve Board, without government the American economy would exhibit minimal stability.

> Since it is government that created the Federal Deposit Insurance Corporation, without government the citizenry would have no protection against bank fraud and failure.

> Since it is government that established the regulation of Wall Street, without government the nation's economy would be totally subject to the greed machinations of the financial industry.

> Since it is government that makes and enforces the laws guaranteeing citizenry civil rights, without government such rights would be at the mercy of prejudice and power-mongering.

> Since it is government that makes and enforces safety regulations for all areas of national life, without government there would be no adequate protection regarding food, drugs, air, water, transportation, hazardous waste, occupations, etc.

➤ Since it is government that provides for the nation's security, without government there would be no Homeland Security, Armed Forces, National Guard, Coast Guard, Marshals, Secret Service, FBI, CIA, ATF, Bureau of Prisons, Immigration and Naturalization Service, foreign embassies, Customs Service, etc.

➤ Since it is government that purchases and maintains national parks and public lands (presently almost 500 million acres) for citizen benefit, without government these acres would all be privately owned or commercially developed.

➤ Since it is government that protects the nation's economy on a global scale through trade regulations, without government the nation's businesses would suffer great disadvantage.

➤ Since it is government that provides insurance and relief from natural disasters (hurricanes, tornadoes, floods, fires, earthquakes, droughts, etc.), without government the citizenry would have little recourse for financial survival when facing such calamities.

➤ Since it is government that provides a national and uniform monetary system with bullion backing, without government economic chaos would reign.

➤ Since it is government that provides social programs in areas such as fair housing, subsidized housing, health, parenting, food, welfare, energy, and education, without government the disenfranchised would be more completely destitute.

➤ Since it is government that provides disease research and control, without government the citizenry could only rely on the economic motivations of the drug industry for relief.

➤ Since it is government that conducts a national census, without government there would be no way of processing democracy with numerical fairness.

➤ Since it is government that supports in an ongoing fashion and rescues when necessary the free-enterprise system, without government there would be no subsidies, bailout, loans, etc. for private business.

➤ Since it is government that prohibits racial, gender, and religious discrimination, without government there would be no equal opportunity programs or recourse from discriminatory practices.

> ➤ Since it is government that addresses physical and mental disability issues though laws and assistance, without government many citizens would be victims of more profound prejudices and behaviors toward such disabilities.

> ➤ Since it is government that promotes research and projects relative to natural science, aerospace, and oceanography, without government neither private citizens nor private enterprise would reap the benefits of these programs.

> ➤ Since it is government that sustains programs like the Job Corp and Peace Corp, without government neither American citizens nor other nations would be recipients of the benefits of these programs.

> ➤ Since it is government that provides national services for the aging, without government this segment of the citizenry would be deprived of much needed services.

> ➤ Since it is government that establishes the laws of the seas and outer space, without government there would be no laws, treaties, or enforcement of such endeavors.

> ➤ Since it is government that establishes international treaties among nations, without government there would be no such protections for the citizenry.

> ➤ Since it is government that provides monetary aid and support of state governments, without the federal government no such aid and support would exist, despite its necessity for the well-being of the citizenry.

> ➤ Since it is government that provides laws benefiting the total citizenry and prohibits conflicting state laws, without government the legal system of America would be a quagmire of inconsistencies and conflicts, reflecting the prejudices and protectionisms of individual states.

Although incomplete, this listing affirms in dramatic fashion that it is only a strong government that is capable of both upholding and preserving the democratic myth in a manner that ensures both its survival and its embodiment as a viable process for cultural living.

Spurious Rhetoric

When the citizenry recognizes this reality they will no longer allow themselves to be subjected to the spurious rhetoric of government as the enemy of democracy and will be ready to:

➤ Elect politicians whose primary goal is an efficient government that intends to function for the benefit of the entire nation.

➤ Demand the elimination of wasteful bureaucracies, earmark legislation, and campaign funding that holds politicians captive to special interests.

➤ Engage their citizenry responsibilities as a sacred privilege and duty.

When the citizenry assumes its rightful role as the power that guides the democratic process, then government will be of the people, for the people, and by the people. Until then, it will be of, for, and by those who have hijacked the government.

Refocusing democracy to the benefit of the citizenry will require not only recognizing the necessity of a strong government but also of the necessity of a strong citizenry exerting control over that government for its intended purpose.

The Messianic Myth

It has become not only a wise perception but a necessity for the American citizenry to actually make a clear separation of state and religion. Playing around the edges of such a separation by participating in irrelevant debates about whether or not the nation should observe the rituals and affirm the beliefs of the Judeo-Christian faith is insufficient to make this happen. Separation requires that the citizenry divest democratic function of the theology of Judeo-Christianity that stood at the altar of the nation's birth as a shadowed bridesmaid to democracy. That shadowed theology is embodied in the messianic myth.

The Premise

It is singularly enthralling to believe that there is a divine entity that rules the universe who has chosen you as his special arm of action in the affairs of humans. This is the foundational premise of the messianic myth. Here are the essential affirmations of this myth:

> ➢ The Judeo-Christian god rules the universe, and by extension, human affairs.
> ➢ This god has chosen American as his special representative on earth.
> ➢ Since America is made up of this god's chosen people, then whatever action it takes in the world is always right.
> ➢ Therefore, America is invincible as long as it is doing this god's will.
> ➢ Since the government of America is democratic, that is this god's chosen political myth.
> ➢ This god's mission for America is to see that democracy prevails in the world community.

The Chosen People

The messianic myth roots in the biblical notion that Israel is God's chosen people and persists through this notion's embodiment in institutionalized Christianity. It found abundant concrete expression in European history during the Middle Ages and realized a new incarnation following America's victory in World War II. It became an unrecognized failed social doctrine with the loss of the Vietnam conflict. And, ever since that conflict, it has sought to again insinuate itself as a valid doctrine back into American's behavior in world affairs. Its most recent incarnation is the George W. Bush administration's 2003 war to "liberate Iraq for democracy."

To accept the affirmations of the messianic myth is to affirm the Judeo-Christian myth as democracy's guide for national and international behavior. Such a validation endorses a merging of state and religious myths and trumps all notions about the distinction between the state and religion.

The Problem

The essential problem with this merger is that the religious component will inevitably rule over the secular component, as it has since the nation's inception. That is, God's myth will instruct the government's myth. The messianic perception will rise above the democratic perception. Or, they will simply be seen as synonymous, which is the same as religion triumphing over democracy. However, being ruled by God is not the same as being ruled by people. The people become subservient to God's rule, which is synonymous with God's will. And God's will is either announced by the tenets of the messianic myth or by those who claim to be the official interpreters of that will.

In Control

That the messianic myth is presently in control, howsoever subtle it may be, is evidenced by the fact that a politician who denies belief in the Judeo-Christian god risks rejection by the citizenry, even when a large portion of that citizenry may hold to a similar unbelief. It is evidenced in the expectation that the politician should invoke the name and blessing of this god during moments critical to the cultural drama's well-being. It is evidenced in the fact that almost all conflicts the nation enters are justified by a posturing as the world's democratic savior. It is evidenced by the fact that no wise politician is willing to tackle the problem of religious language that has insinuated itself into the artifacts of the culture, such as money and public oaths.

Whether yielding to these expectations is an act of hypocrisy or an act of sincerity is irrelevant to the necessity of a pubic affirmation of the messianic myth. They simply seem to be gestures that bring a sense of cozy social comfort to the American public during times of national need or stress. That is, whether the citizenry actually believes the messianic myth or not, it is habituated to its public affirmations in the same way that superstition becomes habituated to a reliance on magic. And public affirmations tend to dictate both national behavior and international perceptions. Such affirmations, then, facilitate perpetuation and instill new vitality.

Counterproductive

This nexus of assertions wraps a cloak of expectation around the democratic myth that encourages America to behave in ways that are counterproductive to democratic ideal, process, conscience, and spirit. It encourages a model of arrogance and behavior that runs roughshod over the self-determination rights of other nations in favor of facilitating the self-interests of politicians and the politically skewed interests of the nation. As long as the messianic myth holds sway in America's national and international life, the democratic model will be captive of Judeo-Christian religious baggage contradictory to democracy and America's behavior will continue to be open to ridicule by both its friends and enemies.

If there is a posture that awakens the interest of others in democracy and entices them to imbibe of its meaning and possible application, it is a humility that characterizes the principle of doing unto others as one would have others do unto one's self. It is the freedom to affirm equality produced by this humility that attracts to the democratic model. It is the acknowledgment of mutual worth and mutual benefit that this principle implies that stimulates envisioned potential. Far more than the announced tenets of democracy, it is the activated model of democracy that lures.

Democratic Antithesis

The messianic myth and its affirmations are the antithesis of democracy and the principle of do unto others. It usurps the democratic ideal. It warps democratic meaning. It prostitutes the notion of equality. It is a harbinger of weakness and death for democratic process.

Only when the American citizenry recognizes the messianic myth for the enemy of democracy that it is and strips every vestige of its affirmations from democratic ideal, will democracy stand alone as the model it needs to be for American behavior, both nationally and internationally. Only then shall democracy present itself in all of its potential for transforming the nation's behavior.

The Extreme Individualism Myth

The tendency is to define both individualism and communityism in a manner consistent with one's bias. This makes the bias easier to defend. To seek definition without bias is difficult. Here are the definitions used in these observations, however biased they may seem:

> ➤ Individualism is a focus on the individual as the ultimate human value.
> ➤ Communityism is a focus on a group of individuals as the ultimate human value.

Here are the actions and values for which these definitions stand:

> ➤ Individualism is solitary decision-making that favors the part.

> Communityism is companioned decision-making that favors the whole.
> Individualism values the one over the many.
> Communityism values the many over the one.
> Individualism is a view that the whole exists for the sake of the part.
> Communityism is a view that the part exists for the sake of the whole.

Without the individual, the community could not exist. Without the community, the individual could not exist. By nature, individualism and communityism, in concert and consort, represent the blended compromise that makes it possible for an individual to exist within the scope of the group without either of them losing its identity or meaning or purpose.

Both/And

This compromise rests in the lap of both/and. Both/and recognizes that human possibility partakes of both in some measure at any given moment of human existence. In brief, this compromise affirms the potential relationship choices that exist in each human being, that of being alone or being together.

The purpose of both/and is to underscore the benefits of reciprocity. The reason for the individual is to empower the community. The reason for the community is to empower the individual. Both empowerments are expressions of freedom based on the lure of benefit. For example, there is no platform to express the individual's voice except that of the community. And there is no need to have a platform except to address the community. Therefore, the use of the platform is an affirmation of the individual's dependency on the community for beneficial living.

The opposite is also true. The community provides a platform for the individual so that it can listen to itself speak. The provision of this platform affirms that the community needs to hear the individual's voice and is dependent on the individual for beneficial living.

Here are the principles that govern these observations:
> Apart, each defines the other; therefore, each must have the other to exist.

> Apart, each is unattainable in exclusivity because to so attain would be to negate the other.
> Together, both speak to a ground of choosing in opposite directions.
> Together, both speak to a wholeness that resides within human possibility.
> To move toward either polarity is to move away from the opposite without ever totally leaving it.
> It is not possible to totally forsake either polarity since both are connected by the distance between them, which is the relationship that defines them.
> It is only possible, therefore, for either individualism or communityism to be expressed through extremity and never through exclusivity.
> Together, individualism and communityism affirm the highest potential that can be derived from engaging either.
> When given equal weight, blended individualism and communityism become the highest social attainment of human possibility.

Benefits

The benefits that exist for the individual's full participation in the community are the collective benefits of civilization. These consist of the fruits of the group's combined thinking, energy, and focus. Art that feeds the soul of spiritual living and technology that elevates the quality of physical living are prime examples. Within these benefits resides that which is critical to all human fulfillment, namely, the possibility of relationships that grandly enhance one's personal well-being and sense of human worth. Thus, the individual could not attain to the possibilities inherent within human nature without some depth of participation in the life of community. Moreover, whatever the value of longevity in respect to the retention of benefits and the enhancement of values is a community benefit. The future belongs to the community as society's value carrier. As Alexis de Tocqueville suggested in his book *Democracy in America*:

> Among the laws that rule human societies there is one which
> seems to be more precise and clear than all the others. If men are

to remain civilized or to become so, the art of associating together must grow and improve in the same ratio in which the equality of conditions is increased.

The benefits that exist for the community's embrace of individualism within its midst are what the lone individual brings into the community from the experience of apartness. The visions, the inventions, and the creativity generated by the individual acting alone are processed in the community's civilized experience. These unique contributions constantly enrich the community's own understanding of the meaning of human existence and increase the depth of the community's own experience of itself. Moreover, as the individual acts as an individual within the context of community events, the outcome may be a heroism that inspires or a sacrifice that ennobles the community. Some of the most generative actions that vitalize the life of the community derive from individuals behaving beyond the normal expectations and constraints of the collective.

The principle is simple:

The greater the individual and the community contribute to each other the grander are the rewards for both.

Thus, to pit one against the other is the ultimate human folly. There is not a natural antagonism that exists between them. They were intended by human nature to be highly complementary.

False Pitting

However, there are those who seek this for the sake of a personal aggrandizement that is always less in quality than those rewards that come from the reciprocity of mutual commitment. Some of the more apparent false pittings have been:

 ➤ schemes of acquiring externalized social worth that cause individuals to demean one another's well-being and behave toward the community in a utilitarian manner
 ➤ nondemocratic forms of government that belittle both the individual and the community and use them for the benefit of exclusive groups of people
 ➤ views of reality that traffic on perverted notions of special entitlement that elevate individuals above their peers

➢ converting upper-class benefits into postures of superiority that establish social warfare

The downside of these pittings is that they entice citizens to invest in extremism. Extremism is a lifestyle that elevates the individual or the community over the other. Extremism courts perceptions of purity and perceptions of purity tear the paradox of both/and apart so that the polarities appear to stand alone as social choices. Extremism converts reality into black and white simplicities. It divests morality of tension. It invites activities of destruction based on a false face of polarity as the enemy. It fosters inequities of opportunity and contexts of unfairness.

Extremism

Extremism is not the same as a momentary elevation of either the individual or the community over the other for the sake of some correction or long-term benefit to both. There is always a constancy of correction going on within the relationship between the two. However, the criteria for correction are that of mutual benefit. It is when these criteria become that of exclusive benefit that the danger of extremism rears its head.

Those times in American history that communityism has found a real measure of extreme expression is generally during war or battles focusing on citizen civil rights. Examples of such extremism that benefited both the community and the individual are the Civil War, World War II, the civil rights movement, and the feminist movement. Examples that had negative consequences for both were when the government claimed the prerogative to violate citizenry constitutional rights during the McCarthy communist witch hunt of the 1950s and government attempts to suppress the freedom to protest during the Vietnam War. Expressions of community extremism appear to be sporadic but well defined and related to national and international issues that were interpreted as threats to unity or the democratic conscience. Whether such threats were valid or not is a moot issue in extremism's expression.

On the other hand, the extremism of individualism has simply been a constant throughout American history that has been pervasive of cultural life. That is, it has been a lifestyle of the population rather than an available choice. Because of individualism's insistent constancy and refusal to imbibe of the principle of reciprocity, its extreme expression has posed a primary threat to the both the spirit and conscience of democracy. It has become one of democracy's great enemies since democracy is fundamentally a community endeavor.

Self-Aggrandizement

The root of this opposition lies in the spirit of self-aggrandizement that extreme individualism generates in those who embody its spirit. It encourages demeaning behavior toward others, one-upsmanship, me-first-ness, destructive forms of competition, and the arrogance of superiority. Whatever the social benefits of democratic culture, extreme individualism seeks to usurp them for exclusive use. It epitomizes all the vulgarities and immoral behaviors of self-centeredness. In respect to the democratic process, it has been one of the ultimate corrupting factors of democracy because the extreme individualist votes for politicians, platforms, and programs that will abet its self-aggrandizement goals. Thus, it sucks the beneficial possibilities of democracy into a black hole of selfishness.

Excess

To be opposed to those expressions that exemplify excessive individualism is not, ipso facto, to be opposed to individualism. The very opposition to excess recognizes the validity of individualism as vital to the polarity of communityism. It favors the both/and benefits that are brought to democracy. The enemy is neither individualism nor communityism. The enemy is sustained excess. Sustained excess is to provide more than is either necessary or desired. The qualities of sustained excess are measured by weight and time. Excess in weight is unwarranted stress. Excess in time is an enduring focus. Excessiveness is an obvious and recognizable favoring of either the individual or the community over the other. It is a utilitarian employment that breaks the sustaining cycle of mutual support. It grants a greater worth to one above the other. It pushes toward an I-It relationship. It undermines synergistic enhancement.

Excessiveness is not the same as a momentary expression of either weight or time. As already suggested momentary excesses may be nothing more than natural measures taken to give needed correction for the sake of mutual benefit.

Unfortunately for democracy, American history is a testimony to the citizenry's investment in a sustained excessive individualism that feeds off of the spirit of self-aggrandizement. It has been a drama where the individual has constantly sought to subjugate the community to the whims of private benefit. It reeks of all the negative outcomes of the individual investing in the lie of the American Dream and all of the corruption of electing politicians who will abet private agenda. It has found a clear ally in the view that the individual should be at liberty to engage free enterprise with the same self-aggrandizing extremism that disregards any negative effect on community.

The irony of this excess is that the blessings of reciprocity that rise from the synergism of both/and are diminished. Thus, to whatever extent the individual elevates itself above community for personal benefit, in the long run, the possibilities of such benefit are decreased. Indeed, everything the individual does that weakens the reciprocal power of community correspondingly weakens the potential benefit of democracy because democracy is, above all else, a community event.

What America has euphemistically referred to as "rugged individualism," with some sense of pride about its expression as an act of courage and human superiority, is nothing less than an excess that demeans and demotes the spirit, the conscience, and the process of democracy. Only when the citizenry recognizes that such excess actually decreases the possible blessings of the synergism that flows from a mutually supportive and reciprocal both/and relationship between the individual and the community, will the full blessings of democracy become apparent. Until them, all expressions of excessive individualism decrease the maturing of the democratic experiment.

Recap

Here is a recap of some of the principles that govern the relationship between the individual and the community as symbolized by the part and the whole:

> ➢ Democracy is, above all else, a social covenant that intends the part and the whole to benefit from the vitality they create for each other.
> ➢ Since democracy is a form of government that intends to maximize the blessings of the total citizenry, it is not possible for

that government to succeed in this intention without expressing itself through a variety of socialisms.

➤ Since it is the community that creates and sustains those blessings that most benefit the life of the individual, the individual
owes its ultimate allegiance to the well-being of the community.

➤ To whatever extent either the individual or the community assumes a utilitarian posture toward the other, to that extent the
reciprocal benefits of democracy decrease for both.

➤ Since the ultimate blessings of democracy are dependent on
the mutual commitment of both/and, therefore all sustained
expressions of either/or will diminish these blessings.

➤ While excess at any temporary moment may bring corrective
benefit to both the individual and the community, sustained
excess can only have a debilitating impact on both.

American historian and critic Bernard DeVoto suggests in *The
Easy Chair (1941)*:

*The trouble with the sacred individual is that he has no
significance, except as he can acquire it from others, the social
whole.*

Yet these truths do not diminish the indispensable role the individual plays in the human drama of community. Nor can it ignore the
truth that there is no individual without this community drama.

Challenge

Whatever else might threaten the American democratic experiment, these five myths are critical enemies. As previously suggested,
all but the myth of the superior white male have existed in confused or
disguised form throughout American history. They sit at the cultural
table and draw vitality from their anonymity. In this anonymity, they
combine in force to create a foe much larger and more powerful than
any could pose alone.

It is the recognition of their true nature that causes the confusion
to disperse and the disguise to fall away and targets them as the enemies of democracy. When this recognition occurs, then the citizenry

can dispense with the threat they pose. When this dispensing occurs, democracy will open itself for a full maturing and the power of its model will become available to not only the American people but to the people of the world. Historian Arnold Toynbee states the issue this way:

> *Civilizations....come to birth and proceed to grow by successfully responding to successive challenges. They break down and go to pieces if and when a challenge confronts them which they fail to meet.*

There is a shorter version by Trammel Crow, American innovative property developer:

> *There's as much risk in doing nothing as doing something.*

The Gage of the Vision
(Patriotism and Myth)

I pledge allegiance to the flag of the United States of America, and to the republic for which it stands: one nation, under God, indivisible, with liberty and justice for all.
— The Pledge of Allegiance (Modified June 14, 1954)

You can't prove you are an American by waving the flag.
—Helen Gahagan Douglas

Patriotism is a lovely sense of collective responsibility. Nationalism is a silly cock crowing on its own dunghill.
—Richard Aldington

Patriotism

During the 2008 presidential election campaign, through media ads and campaign speeches, John McCain was posed as worthy of becoming president by virtue of being a superior patriot. The implied basis of this superiority was that McCain had endured and survived severe torture as a prisoner of war during the Vietnam conflict. One way this superior patriotism was endlessly pushed was by reminding the public that all McCain's decisions were based on the personal motto of "Country First." Without questioning McCain's patriotism, using this term during any political campaign or other public venue raises issues about the true meanings of the word.

For example, the implication of being a superior patriot raises the issue of whether or not there is a scale of strength to patriotism that can be measured by degrees. From this issue ensues endless questions.

Is one more patriotic if they serve in military uniform than others who wear overalls on the military production line? Is one more patriotic if they serve in Congress than others who serve in the various service industries of the nation? Is one more patriotic if they serve in a spy organization than one who digs ditches for the construction of the spy organization's headquarters? Is one more patriotic who dies defending the nation's flag than one who sews the flag that drapes the hero's casket? Is one more patriotic who is taken by the enemy as a prisoner of war than others who sacrifice the lives of their daughters and sons to the same war? Is one more patriotic who resists enemy interrogation techniques as a prisoner of war and dies as a result than one who succumbs to these same techniques and survives because of issuing a false confession?

Definition

A common definition of patriotism is devotion to one's country. The problem with this definition is that it is a perspective without depth. That is, it does not go beneath the symbol of country as a focus of patriotism's commitment and, thus, stops short of engaging that which creates the country's character and destiny. Country, as a symbol, stands for more than geography but still does not plug into a nation's attributes of being and its role in history. Being supportive of the symbols of the country is not necessarily the same as being supportive of the content that fills these symbols. It is that which creates the character and destiny of a country that is the legitimate focus of a patriot's allegiance.

When a nation fails to push past its symbols to get to their deeper meaning, then it is apt to substitute all manner of superficial focuses for its allegiance. These substitutes are invested with awry devotion. That the investment is awry does not obviate the power of the conviction applied to the substitute. It only announces that a depth has been missed that is a more profound focus for allegiance and, thus, a more insightful way of being in the world has also been missed. Since insight dispels ignorance, what has been missed is the opportunity to be guided by a greater wisdom and a deeper motivation.

American Patriotism

The deeper definition of patriotism invests in a country's mythic purpose. In America, this purpose is devotion to a special form of democracy that insists on the citizenry's right to directly participate in the nation's decision-making through elected representatives with the view of national well-being in mind. According to America's mythic documents, this national well-being is characterized by commitments to egalitarianism, civil rights, the facilitation of a liberating community, and attitudes and actions that intend reciprocal benefits.

Willingness

A question primal to patriotism is whether or not willingness is an essential element of devotion to this mythic purpose. For example, is military service an act of patriotism if the soldier is forced into participation? Most of the soldiers during World War II willingly entered military service. But that has not necessarily been the case since then because there has been no conflict that has equally compelled a commitment to volunteer. The Vietnam conflict was a low point of willing engagement. During this war people resisted induction into military service in every possible way. There was a minimal sense of the war as a patriotic endeavor by the majority of the troops. Indeed, surviving rather than winning was the primary goal of those forced into it by the draft. On the other hand, there were those, particularly career military types, who believed that America was doing the world a democratic service by being in Vietnam and who interpreted their own engagement as a patriotic duty. They self-declared as patriots by virtue of their willingness to serve.

Both those who saw the Vietnam war as having no patriotic relevance and those who saw it as having grand patriotic relevance died in the conflict. What qualified their respective deaths to be labeled patriotic, given the polar reasons for their participation? Is willingness of sacrifice more patriotic than forced sacrifice? Indeed, is the former patriotic and the latter not?

The Iraq War of 2003 was initiated by the George W. Bush administration. Congress relinquished its sole constitutional right to declare war by voting away its powers to the president. However, within this relinquishment there was no draft to compel soldiers into military service. Thus, the National Guard, ostensibly existing for homeland security, was used by the commander in chief to engage an international conflict. Some of this body of weekend warriors willingly went to serve in Iraq while others went because they were forced into participation.

388 Creating America's Story

Both those who went willingly and those who were forced to go were maimed and killed. What requirements, other than the act of being forced to do battle, are necessary ingredients for applying the label of patriot to these soldiers? Is being forced into battle by a single person, the president of the country, as patriotic as being forced into battle by an act of Congress?

One of the primary complaints of soldiers serving in the Iraq War during its early stages was a lack of adequate protection from physical harm, whether it was vehicles or gear. Who was responsible for this lack that eventuated in unwarranted maiming and death? Was it the vendors who created the equipment or the military leaders who ordered the equipment? Whoever made the decisions, did such justify labeling them as unpatriotic or even traitors despite the fact that they may have been wearing military uniforms? Does shoddy planning or shoddy products that create physical harm and death for combatants imply that whoever is responsible is a traitor? Using euphemisms such as "a mistake" or "an oversight" to refer to such irresponsible decisions does not obviate the implications of being a traitor. Again, the issue is whether willingness is a part of being a traitor. If so, then would not willingness also be a necessary concomitant to being a patriot?

Motivation

Perhaps the key to the deeper meaning of patriotism does not lie in a sacrifice made but in the motivation behind such a sacrifice. Any sacrifice can be forced upon a soldier or a citizen. Thus, are we back to willingness as a critical ingredient to the deeper meaning of patriotism? Must patriotism be a positively motivated activity?

Causal Myth

Another question has to do with the ground of motivation for such willingness. The answer to this question is the key to the deeper meaning of patriotism. This motivation plugs directly into the dynamic that actually shapes the character of a culture and gives direction to its destiny. To shape the character of the culture is to shape the motivational aspirations of the citizenry. To give direction to a culture's destiny is to give direction to citizenry attitudes and actions. This motivation, then, rises from that which is the wellspring of the culture's existence. It is the causal factor of this existence.

That around which a nation is organized and through which a culture is created and by which direction is given to its decision-making is the primal myth that fuels its being. In America, this myth is composed of two inseparable components. The first component is that of the processes of democracy. This is the notion of citizenry rule through both shaping input and actual vote. It is a sustained process of fair and open elections in which the general citizenry is guaranteed both a voice and a vote, and the outcome of which is majority rule.

The second component is the originally stated purpose and directions given•to the institution of this democracy. It is that which instructs the nature of the citizenry's input and vote. So, the total myth is not just the implementation and processes of the voting ideal of democracy. It is also the content of purpose and direction that imply those values which undergird why the democracy is to be implemented and processed. It is the desired ends of the democratic process.

In America, this second component is clearly stated in the Declaration of Independence, the Constitution, and the Bill of Rights. These documents declare the goals of the democratic process and vote. They state the intent of cultural structures and living. They announce the implied values that should motivate citizenry attitudes and action. This second component is the ground of the covenant that both defines the nature of the national community and the goals by which this community is to live out its existence. This covenant transcends all other motivations.

This covenant loathes any motivation that seeks to defy the spirit and conscience of democracy as defined by these documents. This covenant declares as illegitimate all political and economic views and actions that seek to instruct citizenry attitudes and actions that undermine the covenant's goals. This covenant decries all international behavior that does not accord with the implied values and principles that naturally rise from these documents.

The democracy of this covenant has two aspects. The first is an equality of vote. The second is an equality of social existence. Within this foundation of equality reside notions of liberty, justice, a stable union, national welfare, and civil rights. There is also the notion of self-determination that is wrapped in a transcending community that makes such freedom possible. Everything about this democracy is anchored in this transcendent community that is covenanted around both the meaning of democracy and the originating documents of the nation. Not inconsequential in this covenant is the notion of a nation's self-determination, its right to give direction to its own destiny. The meaning of patriotism is tied to the interrelatedness of all of these notions.

Thus patriotism, while involving willingness, is more than willingness. It involves a commitment to this complex of notions. The idea that patriotism is simply a positive response to a governmental call to join in arms or to express a certain attitude is, at the most, shallow. Indeed, it is misleading and false.

This understanding of the nature of patriotism makes the simplistic notion of democracy as freedom a paucity of perception. Dictators are free. Criminals are free. Terrorists are free. All of these people are free to behave in ways that accrue their labeling. Freedom must be modified by purpose and its responsibility and even then it can be a dark venture that owes nothing of nobility to the social order. So, while freedom is certainly a part of American patriotism the goals and the nature of that freedom are essential to any judgment about its social legitimacy.

National Purpose

Patriotism, then, cannot be adequately or truly defined outside of the combined purpose of the establishment of the nation as indicated in the aforementioned documents. Any attempt to define patriotism outside of the documents that describe the nature and meaning of this brand of democracy will inevitably be false and misleading. Therefore, patriotism is any attitude and action that derives from the intent and meaning of this democratic covenant. Fulfilling this covenant is not simply a single act but a life of devotion that leads to all single acts. As Adlai E. Stevenson, American politician, presidential candidate and ambassador to the United Nations, once observed:

> *I venture to suggest that patriotism is not a short and frenzied outburst of emotion but the tranquil and steady dedication of a lifetime.*

Any instinctive or rational motivation to act based on the following can be legitimately interpreted as patriotism:

> A sense of the rightness of attitude and action that affirms the purpose of the democratic covenant and its implied values.
> A willingness to sacrifice for the sake of this purpose and these values even though one might prefer avoiding such a necessity.

Traitor

Being a traitor is the opposite of being patriotic. It is to fail to support the democratic covenant. It is to be motivated to fulfill goals that benefit self above the fulfillment of this covenant and its sustaining community. It is a refusal to sacrifice for the sake of the covenant when the well-being of its members is at stake. It is to take deliberate action for personal profit when such action will be harmful to the covenant or to the members of the covenant.

Is one a traitor to the democratic myth if one is involved in a war that transgresses the basic spirit of the covenant? For example, if one is involved in a war that seeks to deny the right of political self-determination to another nation, is one a traitor rather than a patriot? And, again, is one a traitor if involved in a war that is seeking to impose, through force, a particular political myth on another nation from the outside? And what about military personnel who are required by law to engage conflicts that violate the intent and spirit of this social covenant? Can soldiers be patriots when they are engaged in an unpatriotic war? Does being forced to be a combatant in an illegitimate war obviate the requirements of patriotism? And what of the citizenry? Can non-combatants be patriots when they support a war that violates the letter and spirit of their nation's mythic covenant?

Moreover, what about those whose attitudes of greed and power-mongering translate into actions which are harmful to the majority of the citizenry? What about those who use the democratic process for a self-aggrandizement that is harmful to both the well-being of the nation and the citizenry of other countries? What about the denizens of Wall Street and the corporate executives largely responsible for the economic meltdown of America and much of the rest of the world in the first decade of the twenty-first century?

Could these denizens possibly be referred to as patriots? Indeed, given the obvious placement of private goals above the goals of the democratic covenant their actions imply, would it be more accurate to describe them as traitors? Why are they not in courts of law answering for their violations instead of being bailed out by the federal government by the tax dollars of the very people they have harmed so grievously? Can patriotism either exist or survive when it is warped and twisted so dramatically as to fit the expediencies of economic machination rather than the well-being of the nation?

What about executive and congressional leadership that condones or encourages behaviors which are anathema to the egalitarian premise of the nation's covenant? What about the deliberate torture of prisoners of war at Bagram Air Force Base in Afghanistan, at Abu Ghraib Prison in Iraq, and at Guantanamo Bay Naval Base in Cuba—all in violation of the accords of the Geneva Convention of which America is a signatory? Are not these kinds of covenant violations blatant acts of the traitor? If such are identified as war crimes by the Geneva Convention accords, should not all of those responsible be held accountable in courts of law? Can such a grievous violation of the nation's covenant be ignored because pursuing such might prove uncomfortable to the nation's political leadership? Is it right that those of the lowest rank are thrown to the wolves for such violations while those of the highest rank enjoy complete immunity? Duplicity of justice is not an act of patriotism. A true democratic patriotism will demand equal justice for all since its very essence is egalitarianism. If those at the top of the citizenry ladder are treated differently from those at the bottom of the citizenry ladder then democracy does not exist for anybody on the ladder. Such is only a dictatorship of the privileged.

Full Meaning

What is important to keep in mind in all of these questions and observations is the full meaning of the democratic covenant. Patriotism is not simply a defense of the right to vote or of the freedom to participate in profit-taking. It is a support of the goals of the democratic covenant as defined by the nation's grounding mythic documents.

Awareness

It is not possible to keep a covenant when one is not aware of either its meaning or of the vitalness of one's participation. It is a primary task of politicians and the educational system of the nation to reduce the level of ignorance on the part of the citizenry in respect to that which is absolutely basic to their cultural living. To say this in a positive manner: It is the obligation of both politicians and the educational system to keep the meaning of the democratic myth before the citizenry in such a manner that it is foremost in the nation's awareness. Uppermost, this means modeling patriotism, as opposed to simply mouthing its nuances or declaring that one is a patriot by virtue of self-ordination.

Assuming this obligation, it is obvious that both politicians and the educational system have grossly failed. A 2008 poll of high school graduates revealed that well over 40 percent could not name the three branches of American government that intends a system of checks and balances on power. If one cannot name the basic structure of the government designed to facilitate the nation's mythic covenant, is it likely that one will have any awareness of the true nature of the covenant itself?

The obvious factor in this lack of perception is that this mythic covenant is clearly spelled out in the nation's founding documents. Is this discrepancy an indictment of the entire American system of politics and education? Is it possible that politicians and educators are the source of this mythic ignorance on the part of the general public? What has happened that the myth so basic to the culture's existence has become submerged beneath layers of misunderstanding, ignorance, and superficiality? Has the notion of patriotism been so twisted to fit the needs of political expediency that the twisters actually believe the distortions they have invented?

Certainly politicians are to blame for skewing the meaning of American democracy in the world by behaving in ways that totally disregard the democratic covenant. Nationally, what the majority of politicians have modeled with eloquence is how to convert their role into a self-aggrandizing enterprise by submitting their services as congressional prostitutes to the highest financial bidders. Internationally, the government's support of dictators, its overt and covert actions in helping to overthrow legitimate democratic governments for the sake of economic motivations, and its general disregard for the right of other nations to self-determination, along with its attempts to cover these actions by cloaking them in democratic rhetoric has earned America the contempt of a significant part of the global community. While this rhetoric has fooled a large percentage of the American public, it has not fooled the people of other nations who look to America as the model of democracy.

It may be that educators will have to double their efforts to raise the consciousness of students about the nature of the democratic covenant in ways that cannot be so easily warped or ignored by politicians. It is possible that a significant measure of the hope of American democracy lies in the lap of the educational system. This means that educators must be determined to lower the level of ignorance and raise the level of knowledge about America's brand of democracy. No student should be allowed to graduate who does not know the simple structure of our government and the purpose of the democratic covenant as defined by the nation's founding documents.

A Peerless People

Because the citizens of a nation are raised within the structures and nuances of its culture, they are prone to view living within that nation, irrespective of its deficits, as the ultimate life condition. They are apt to view the people of that nation as incomparable in respect to character. Moreover, their personal identity, which is the root of their sense of self-worth, is deeply tied to who they are within their culture of birth. These factors, born of familiarity, easily convert into the notion of patriotism as devotion to a peerless people. Thus patriotism is understood as a devotion to the nation whatever its behavior might be. It is the same as the notion that blood is thicker than all other allegiances—that family comes before all other devotions.

This sense of the meaning of patriotism seems to be endemic to the human enterprise and its ultimate tendency is to focus on this birthed relationship. Indeed, such a view of patriotism is normally satisfied with this relationship perception and rarely ventures into mythic territory. It is summarized in the familiar phase, "My country, right or wrong." A part of the strength of this view of patriotism is that it takes on a tinge of elevating self-righteousness. That is, it seems to increase one's sense of self-worth by virtue of the posture of national superiority. However, this view also makes the holder susceptible to being conned into supporting any action the nation takes because whatever that action might be, it will be assumed as right.

The essential error in this way of defining patriotism is that it shifts the meaning of the word from its mythic base to its cultural context. And, possibly even more important, it voids the privilege of questioning the behavior of one's nation among nations.

False Patriotism

It is a false sense of patriotism that either refuses to question the nation's behavior or sees such questioning as unpatriotic. To refuse to measure national behavior against its rightful gage of covenant is to convert the nation into an idol. Idolatry is a devotion that denies full reality. It is the Don Quixote Syndrome: an adoration that acknowledges beauty without being able to see moles. Unquestioning loyalty is a narrow vision that can only make decisions of disaster. The true patriot will forever question the failure of one's country to live up to its covenant potential precisely because of a true adoration anchored in the nation's mythic reason for being.

Wrestling

It is obvious that during the early drama of the birth of America there was a keen awareness of both the political and social nature of the democracy that was being created. This awareness was grounded in strong debate and resolute purpose and was also grounded in an understanding of the potential cost of making their dream a reality. Thus it was carefully chosen and defined because the cost was both recognized and committed to with willingness. That cost was the probable death sentence of being a traitor to the British crown. In today's America, this clarity of cost and commitment is easily erased by the comforts of living. Moreover, the sense of community necessary to make America's brand of democracy work has been submerged beneath the excesses of individualism's self-centeredness. John Brockenbrough, in a letter to John Randolph concerning the Embargo Act of 1808, saw this at work in his own era when he observed:

> *Patriotism is a mighty precious thing when it costs nothing, but the mass of mankind consider it a foolish thing when it curtails their self-indulgence.*

Only when we wrestle anew with the meaning of patriotism in the manner of America's creators will we find its roots. To put it in the words of Adrienne Rich in her poem *An Atlas of the Difficult World*:

A patriot is one who wrestles for the soul of her country as she wrestles for her own soul.

Patriotism ought to be a combined rational and emotional response to that which is loved. Thus it is the character and behavior of the nation that is ultimately responsible for the level of patriotism its citizens express. As Edmund Burke suggested in his *Reflections on the Revolution in France* (1790):

To make us love our country,
Our country ought to be lovely.

Without a deeper form of patriotism that is anchored in its myth, most of the citizenry will only have some vague perception of a patriotism grounded in cultural relationships and stories about the glories of the past. May our nation rise above these shallow perceptions and find its ground in the potentials of its mythic ideals. May it find glory in that part of its past that was faithful to these ideals and seek to build its present and future stories upon this nobility.

The citizen who criticizes his country is paying it an implied tribute.

—J. William Fulbright

The modern patriotism, the true patriot, the only rational patriotism is loyalty to the nation all the time, loyalty to the government when it deserves it.

—Mark Twain

Who are the really disloyal? Those who inflame racial hatreds, who sow religious and class dissentions. Those who subvert the Constitution by violating the freedom of the ballot box. Those who make a mockery of majority rule by the use of the filibuster. Those who impair democracy by denying equal educational facilities. Those who frustrate justice by lynch law or by making a farce of jury trials. Those who deny freedom of speech and of the press and of assembly. Those who demand special favors against the interest of the commonwealth. Those who regard public office merely as a source of private gain. Those who would exalt the military over the civil. Those who for selfish and private purposes stir up national antagonisms and expose the world to the ruin of war.

—Henry Steele Commager

The Hope of the Vision
(Optimism and Pessimism)

Hope is the thing with feathers
That perches in the soul
And sings the tunes without the words
And never stops at all.
                                    —Emily Dickenson

When hope is hungry, everything feeds it.
                                    —Mignon McLaughlin

Substitution

There is a general recognition that something very basic is wrong with American democracy. And there are many who espouse a variety of reasons for this. One such proposed reason is that there is too much democracy. That is, there is a creeping populism that is undermining the republican structure of American democracy. While unwitting, there are a variety of means such as ballot propositions by which the general populace can encroach on the processes that ensure considered and wise decision-making by elected officials. The California election process is often cited as an example of this encroachment that constantly shrinks the decision-making focus of elected officials and reduces their power to determine the makeup of the state's budget. That is, a constant excess of ballot propositions significantly minimizes their reason for being, obviating the role of representative government.

While examples of such encroachments are held up, there is usually little blame assigned to politicians who have relinquished the trust of their office to the pressures of self-aggrandizement and corporate greed. In brief, it is easy to blame the citizenry for seeking to do the job of failed politicians instead of blaming the politicians who have failed. Moreover, once the citizenry tastes the power of filling the gap of such default, they will inevitably tend toward excess because it is a tool that is so readily available for use and feels supremely democratic.

There is little doubt that limitation needs to be imposed on the capacity of citizens to place on the ballot any issue of their momentary concern in willy-nilly fashion. This means of addressing citizenry concerns is not only costly and often tragic, it replaces considered debate with emotional heat and permits the heaviest monetary investors to determine the outcome. However, the primal issue to be addressed in correcting this substitution is the failure of politicians, rather than the frustration of the citizenry. And, in this respect, it is the citizenry which is ultimately responsible. This substitution of citizenry action for the failure of politicians is the citizenry's own failure for not electing trustworthy office holders. The way to confront the problem is to elect trustworthy politicians rather than constantly initiating ballot propositions that seek to deal with the issues which office holders should be addressing.

What Is Needed

So, while admitting that there is logic in the charge that there appears to be too much democracy in America, there is another way of coming at what is happening in the political arena. What is needed in America is not less democracy, but a more responsible democracy where both the elected and the electors assume a moral and principled obligation to fulfill the trust that the nation's covenant demands for success. If this were to happen, then there would be little concern about the need for more or less democracy. Here are some things that the elected could do that would enhance this possibility:

➤ Exhibit a mythic integrity: Know and engage the American covenant of democracy inherent in the nation's founding documents. Be a true patriot by allowing the myth to define attitudes and actions.

➤ Exhibit a wholeness integrity: Transcend provincialism and invest in what is best for the entire nation. Live the principle that what is best for the whole is inevitably what is best for the part.

➤ Exhibit an ownership integrity: Assume a posture of public service that motivates the creation of policy and law. Keep the noble purpose of being a trustworthy elected official in the forefront of all decision-making.

> Exhibit a congressional integrity: Refuse to compromise the intention of an elected Congress. Insist on a system of financing elections that denies the possibility of special interests converting government into a tool of self-aggrandizement and ban the unprincipled and wasteful action inherent in voting earmarks. Doing away with the economic reason why most political lobbies exist also will do away with most political lobbies.

Here are some things that the electorate could do that would enhance this possibility:

> Vote your conscience: However, be sure your conscience is grounded in the patriotism defined by the covenant of America's grounding documents. Be sure your conscience is democratic.

> Honor your community: Transcend the self-centeredness of an overstressed individualism, and decide in favor of that which is both the reason for democracy and its sustainer, namely community well-being. Remember that the ultimate community is the nation.

> Pay your way: Accept the fact that everything is a trade-off. Acknowledge that there can be no benefits without cost and, thus, no quality of national existence without a commensurate taxation that pays for and sustains these benefits.

> Demand your accountability: Insist that your elected representatives live up to the nation's democratic covenant. Know their voting record and the meaning of that record, and communicate your expectation of their aforementioned integrity. Be willing to vote them out of office as well as into office.

> Fulfill your responsibility: Vote in all elections and know the issues of each election. Assume the final responsibility of American citizenship.

Mythic Abuse

The myths that offer hope to our living are often severely abused.

However, to give up on mythic possibility because of such abuse is to abandon our grandest human gift—the ability to create. As long as we hold this gift in the forefront of living there is always hope because it empowers us to change the old and invent the new. This has always been the case in human history because this gift resides within us and can be beckoned at our will.

Consider the following examples:

➢ Government: The form of government that has dominated human history is totalitarianism. Yet the very birth of America was predicated on a sustained conviction that a workable democracy could actually happen.

➢ Religion: Institutionalized religions in the West have tended toward dehumanizing authoritarianisms characterized by rigid conformities and brutal suppressions. Yet there are religions that advocate freedom of belief, human respect, tolerance, and redemptive transformation.

➢ Worth: The notion that human worth is an external purchasable commodity has been endemic to most every culture in recorded human history. Yet the perception that every human is born worthy and should be treated accordingly continues to grow in the civilized world.

To give up on what we consider to be ennobling of the human enterprise is to capitulate to cynicism and despair. It is to bow the knee before those who live from the dark side of their nature. Those who have opened us to the fulfillment of our most noble longings have all bet their lives on hope and that hope has become the empowering edge of new creations. Before any myth becomes a created reality it is envisioned hope.

A Primal Message

A primal message of history seems to be that devoted human greed and the aspiration of self-aggrandizement continues to foster a slow decline of the human enterprise into ecological and relationship disaster. A message of equal strength seems to be that human nobility, or at least the desire to experience the mutual rewards of cooperative community, has stemmed this tide of ignobility to the extent that hope in the grander possibilities of human relating continues to empower the human enterprise. In brief, while hope in the survival of the human enterprise is severely threatened by the dark side of human nature, it is also strongly enhanced by the light side of human nature. This competition cannot be a stalemate. Stalemate always favors the opposition. Hope and its actions must triumph. As F. Scott Fitzgerald (*The Crack-Up*, 1936) once mused:

> *The test of a first-rate intelligence is the ability to hold two opposed ideas in the mind at the same time, and still retain the ability to function. One should, for example, be able to see that things are hopeless and yet be determined to make them otherwise.*

Typical of the glass as either half-empty or half-full being an interpretation of choice, one may choose whether the approach to present world circumstances should be viewed through the eyes of despair or hope. However, deciding about the content of the glass is minor in comparison to choosing despair or hope as a life motivation. It is a momentous choice, for the nature of the energy the choice releases in the world will shape both the chooser's life and the world in which the chooser lives.

➤ The choice of despair shapes life into an exercise in despair. The choice of hope shapes life into an exercise in hope.

➤ Despair molds life into an acquiescence to the forces that make up life's context. Hope molds life into a determination to creatively utilize life's context for benefit.

➤ Despair gives in to what appears to be a determining inevitability. Hope invests in altering the nature of the inevitable.

➤ Despair views one's self as a victim. Hope views one's self as a cocreator.

➤ Despair gives away one's power to external forces. Hope retains one's power as an internal force.

➤ Despair endows life with a negative aura. Hope endows life with a positive aura.

Thus the difference between choosing despair or hope is the same as choosing between death and life:

> It is the difference between drifting on the tide of destiny that others create or riding on the crest of a tide that one helps to create.
> It is the difference between giving up control or remaining in control.
> It is the difference between being changed or being a changer.

In essence, what one chooses creates the chooser. It defines character and shapes destiny. Each of us is a chooser and the choice is inherent in how we see life. As England's former prime minster Winston Churchill once observed:

A pessimist sees the difficulty in every opportunity, an optimist sees the opportunity in every difficulty.

Beyond the individual life of the chooser, the larger picture in which one participates as a purveyor of despair or hope is the future of American democracy as an experiment in the grander possibilities of human nature and community nobility. Whatever happens to either increase or decrease the application of the American democratic spirit and conscience as a mythic way of life will be consequential in human survival and quality of life. The world must have a compelling model of the payoff of our nation's brand of democracy. It must be inspired by the myth of democracy embodied in cultural form. Nothing else will empower the quality of relating among humans that can transcend the motivations of materialistic greed and the dark side of human nature. The potential outcome will alter the shape of human history and the fate of the planet.

The commitment to hope must prevail because it is this singular commitment that will translate itself into the attitudes and actions of the democratic myth. Or, as has been so vigorously proclaimed on the American political scene, the dream must not die and the hope cannot fail. If they do, then so does the growth of the human enterprise toward a redeeming nobility.

I saw the angel in the marble and carved until I set him free.
—Michelangelo

To defy Power, which seems omnipotent;
To love, and bear; to hope till hope creates
From its own wreck the thing it contemplates.
                              —Percy Bysshe Shelley

One measure of civilization, either of an age or of a single
individual, is what that age or person wishes to do. A man's hope
measures his civilization.
                              —Ezra Pound

A Tale of Larger Realities
(Continuous Confrontation)

My story is a tale of my mythic box within larger mythic boxes. My mythic box dwells within the larger mythic box of my region, which dwells within the larger mythic box of my culture, which dwells within the larger mythic box of my civilization. It has forever been and will forever remain that larger mythic boxes are the context of my living. Only the first human was exempt from this truth.

As I stand on the horizon of my moment in history and look backward over the eons of time, my box seems larger than those of my ancestors. But when those of the future stand on the horizon of their moment in history, they too will look backward at my box and pronounce theirs as larger. It has forever been and will forever remain that my largest box is the box of the moment. Even with the first human this was true.

I may decide that my box is too small to contain the gift of my life. I may trade my smaller box in for a larger one any time I choose. It has forever been and will forever remain that larger boxes are my option. Even the first human was presented this choice.

My humaness requires that I create a box large enough to explain the mystery of my existence. I cannot make meaning without this explaining box. But it has forever been and will forever remain that this mystery is larger than any box I can ever create. Yet even the first human was required to reduce mystery to an explaining box.

My life drama has been shaped by continuous confrontation with larger realities. These confrontations are the provocateurs of my evolution. It has forever been and will forever remain the essential fact of my existence. And the first human began this confrontation.

My story is a tale of larger realities.

Addenda

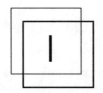

Principles that Govern Myth

Every individual and culture is governed by myth. Every myth has its upside and downside of character. This composite is its uniqueness. But however unique a myth may be it is governed by the same principles as all other myths. This governance is not inherent in myth, but in the human nature that creates and inhabits the myth. Following is an outline of some of the basic principles that govern myth in human experience.

General Principle

All myths are boxes that limit their devotee's view of reality and determine their devotee's destiny.

Personal Myth

(1) My myth creates my life story.

(2) My myth determines all meaning I make.

(3) My myth prescribes my relationship to myself, others, and the universe.

(4) All realities I create through my myth are perceptions of faith.

(5) The myth upon which I bet my life shapes my character and defines my sense of self-worth.

(6) I can change my life stories by changing my myth.

(7) An unquestioned myth shifts control of my life from me to my myth.

Cultural Myth

(1) All cultural stories are created through myth.

(2) All cultures maintain themselves through a system of mythic propagation.

(3) Cultures secure citizen support through systems of rewards and punishments and schemes of externalized social worth.

(4) Every culture will find a comfort level within the conservative/liberal continuum that defines both its character and drama.

(5) All deliberate cultural change comes through a raised consciousness provoked by an admission of complicity with evil.

(6) Cultural change is only made permanent when it is sustained by a corresponding change in the culture's social heart.

(7) The stories of all cultures are choreographed by the obsessions to find answers to the mysteries of the universe and human existence.

General Principle

All myths are continuously confronted with realities larger than themselves.

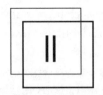

Why Cultures Fail and Succeed
(Factors of Weakness and Strength)

The characteristics of cultures are the characteristics of institutions that are the characteristics of individuals. Thus cultural weaknesses and their counterpart strengths are a complex expression of individual humaness. Cultural dynamics are human dynamics writ large.

Given time, all cultures will fail because of the cumulative effect of human weakness to starve and destroy social creations. This is the unquestioned judgment of history. The only issue is what factors of human weakness contribute to and hasten this process.

These factors of weakness are the polarities of cultural strengths. As the cumulative factors of strength contribute to a culture's longevity the cumulative factors of weakness contribute to a culture's demise.

Following are some of those factors that invite social starvation and destruction. One or more will be involved in a culture's decline toward failure.

> The loss of mythic reason for being. The failure to keep mythic purpose alive through the culture's propagating agencies.

> A fractured mythic focus that leads to loss of a cohesive social vision and a unified driving force. The failure to bond internal diversity.

> Uninspired, unskilled, and unimaginative guidance that leads to mythic lethargy and to addressing problems rather than possibilities. The failure to receive bold, artful, and visionary leadership that motivates mythic allegiance and inventively confronts critical decisions and crises of survival.

> The inability to fulfill the promise of its essential myth that leads to internal dissolution and rebellion. The failure of mythic realization and government capacity.

> The unwillingness to maintain historical relevance that leads

to obsolete coping mechanisms and misdirected internal support. The failure to adequately respond to accumulated knowledge and change.

➤ A major unaddressed discrepancy between mythic ideal and actual behavior that leads to diminished citizenry allegiance and discontent. The failure induced by apparent and sustained hypocrisy.

➤ The elevation of a part of culture over the whole of culture that leads to loss of synergistic power. The failure to recognize the mutual dependency of all the components that make up the social body.

➤ A squandering of resources on external goals that short-changes internal needs and leads to financial disaster, citizenry disillusionment, and discontent. The failure of internal social maintenance.

➤ A reluctance to accommodate to the larger world drama that leads to a vulnerability to cultural predators. The failure of an isolationism that shuns external political realities.

➤ A corruption of government that leads to citizenry cynicism and withdrawal of support. The failure of government to inspire trust.

➤ A capturing of the systems of maintenance by alternative myths that leads to mythic weakness, revision, or destruction. The failure to renew and vitalize mythic allegiance.

➤ A lack of images and events that sustain and enhance the citizenry's spirit and pride in its collective ego. The failure to adequately translate mythic identity from concept to symbol and celebration.

➤ The military conquest of the culture that ensures absorption into a competing myth. The failure to protect the culture with adequate posturing or force.

Cultures succeed because they not only avoid weaknesses but manifest their opposite strengths. These opposites are:

➤ a mythic devotion that transcends all other social considerations

➤ a strong mythic vision that enthralls and unites the citizenry

➤ a bold and visionary leadership capable of inspiring toward mythic fulfillment, of engaging necessary decisions, and of creatively meeting threats to mythic well-being

➢ a myth that is capable of cultural incarnation through governmental guidance

➢ the willingness to accommodate mythic expression to new perceptions of reality

➢ a continuous devotion to actualizing mythic ideal

➢ an acknowledgment that every major component of the cultural body is worthy and plays a vital role in its dynamic of power

➢ a dispensing of resources that cares for both internal and external mythic goals

➢ an understanding that the citizenry's trust in government is indispensable to the citizenry's support of government

➢ an alertness that assures the culture's maintenance systems are appropriately upholding mythic ideal

➢ a body of symbols and calendar of celebrations that gather the citizenry into common identity and mythic pride

➢ a processing of external relationships that concerns itself with mythic and territorial identity preservation

These same weaknesses and strengths translate into institutional failures and successes. Cultures are mirrors of their institutions as institutions are mirrors of their individuals.

A Vision of Personal Myth
(The Five Compelling Questions)

Simplicity and Complexity

Life is both simple and complex. These two concepts reside in each other. This is one of life's paradoxes. Correspondingly, answers to the compelling questions of existence can be stated in either a simple or complex manner. Neither way of stating is superior to the other. The degree of simplicity or complexity of statement is dependent on the level of our experience, the extent of our knowledge, and the purpose or group to which it is addressed or by which it is held. Following are four versions of my personal answers to the compelling questions of human existence followed by a synopsis.

Version I

Who Am I?

I am a human—a unique and worthy expression of the universe and my society. Because I create meaning, I make my own choices. While I may permit society to influence my choices, I am still responsible for their outcome.

How Do I Know What I Know?

I create meaning out of the mystery of creation. I do this by faith because I can't prove my meaning is true. This is how I know. I am my own authority.

Who or What Is In Charge?

The universe is in charge of itself. I just live in it. Everything that exists is made of the same stuff, including me. It all deserves respect. It's a living and communicating whole.

What Is My Purpose?

My purpose is to enjoy what it means to be human and to help others do the same. I do this by living up to my most noble capacities and treating others as I would like to be treated. By living this way, I feel worthy of the gift of life.

What Does My Death Mean?

When I die my body will be absorbed into the stuff of the universe and become something else. But my influence will live on in human history whether it's good or bad. Since I could die at any time, I will live as fully as possible.

Version II

Who Am I?

I am a human born on the earth, which is part of the larger universe. I am made of the same stuff as everything else in this universe. Everything that exists is my family. This family is holy.

As one of the humans on the earth, my life is shaped by my society and what I inherited at birth. But I am still free to make those choices that create the special person I am. I am responsible for how these choices affect both me and others.

I am a creation of both myself and the world in which I live.

How Do I Know What I Know?

Everything is a mystery—including me. I give meaning to this mystery and live by the meaning I make. I cannot prove that any of the meanings I make are true. I just have to believe they are. To be as sure as possible, I learn everything I can about the planet, the universe, and how other people have lived. I take what I learn and correct the meanings I make. I use all of my human gifts while I do this.

The bottom line is that nobody else can make up my mind. I create my own meanings. I am my own authority. But still, it's all a mystery.

Who or What Is In Charge?

I know I'm not in charge—except of my own life. The universe is just too big for humans to control and I don't know anything else that is bigger. So the universe must be in control of itself. And since everything in it, including me, is always changing, that's what it must be all about.

Everything in the universe is made of the same stuff. Maybe it's stardust! But whatever it is, if humans deserve to be treated as special, then everything else deserves to be treated the same way.

While humans and the things that make up the universe come and go, it remains. It just *is*. But while all these things exist, they kind of hold hands and talk to each other in a secret language—like humming or an *ooohhmm* that doesn't stop. This is their way of saying that they depend on each other.

What Is My Purpose?

My purpose is to enjoy life through the meanings I make—like friendship, love, caring for the environment, finding fulfillment, and learning new things. Being a responsible person is making meanings that allow other people to enjoy life like I do. This is the same as respecting others, being kind, and keeping my obligations. This means being humble because I know that my talents are a gift and other people make it possible for me to enjoy life. It also means I owe a lot to my planet and the people who live on it. Fulfilling this purpose is like a thumbs-up for the worth I was born with.

I am a special and growing person. To treat everyone and everything else as special is to enjoy my right and privilege of being a meaning-maker.

What Does My Death Mean?

When I die the same thing happens to my body as everything else that exists—it decays and becomes a part or what's on earth and in the universe. Like dust on the wind, I scatter in all directions.

My influence does the same thing—my friendships, my loves, my respects, my carings, my kindnesses, my good deeds, and all the bad stuff, too. Everything I've ever said or done just keeps on working in the world and the universe. So even after I die, my influence lives on.

Knowing that I could die any time and knowing my influence keeps going makes me live with passion and deliberateness so I can get all the joy in life I can and help others to do the same.

It's a mystery why I was born. And life is a mystery. When I die I will just go back into all this mystery. This means that mystery is sacred stuff because it's what living is all about.

Version III

Who Am I?

I was born on my planet within the vastness of the universe. My being partakes of both. And I am worthy because I exist.

I am made of the stardust of the universe—sharing a kinship with all else that exists. I am a member of its ecological family of mutual interdependence. Within this family, I have my peculiar identity and special place. So I am, at the same time, both myself and the stuff of the universe.

I am also shaped by the forces of my existence on the planet—my genes, my gender, and my geography within my moment of history. Yet I am free to take the givens of my birth and mold them according to my capacity for good or evil. Whatever this self-molding, I am responsible for its consequences to both myself and others.

I am, at once, the child of my universe and the child of my own creations. And my power is in meaning-making.

How Do I Know What I Know?

My universe, my planet, and myself are inexplicable mysteries. And the challenge of my living is to seek the meanings that reside within them. Yet because these mysteries are beyond my human grasp, I must live the meanings I give them through faith. I draw these meanings from creation, history, and my own personal experience. Everything that exists can become a revelation. And I access and shape them with my intuition, my reason, and my imagination.

I am my own final authority. Yet what I claim to know is always eventually swallowed by the mystery I seek to know.

Who or What Is In Charge?

The universe is in charge of itself. It is a continuous process of invention. And it delights in transformation. From one moment to the next, its face changes while remaining the same. Paradox is its revelation—being divided while whole, changing while changeless, visible while invisible, accessible while inaccessible, known while mysterious.

Every form of its being is its unique expression while sharing a common essence. Every form of its being has a unique purpose while sharing a common destiny. Being whole and holy within itself, all its forms are whole and holy. While the wholeness of its forms may cease through cosmic judgment, their holiness of essence continues forever.

The universe just *is*. And within this *isness* all is alive, all is related, all is communing.

What Is My Purpose?

My purpose is to reap the enjoyment of being the meaning-maker while upholding this enjoyment for other humans. This reaping and upholding requires the ultimate of my capacities for nobility. It requires seeking harmony and wholeness in all my relating. It requires acknowledging the sacredness of creation and maintaining hope for human destiny within this creation. It requires walking through life with the humility of being gifted by the past and the obligation of owing to the future. Such nobility is to leave my grateful and graceful imprint on the universe. Living this purpose continually reminds me that I was born worthy.

I am a creative and unfolding being. To achieve the noble potential of my being is to achieve the intended enjoyment of meaning-making.

What Does My Death Mean?

Cosmically, my death is the signal of physical transformation. My peculiar human form is spread throughout the universal womb to become the substance of its continual birthing. It is the end of my form while being the beginning and nurturing of other forms. I am scattered through creation as divine essence.

Socially, my death is the signal of continued influence. The released energies of my being invade the flow of human history and contribute to its quality and destiny. Even when my name is buried in history's archives, my spirit remains an imprint on humankind's journey through time.

Knowing that death is inevitable, I am compelled to live with cosmic and social awareness, imbibing its thrill with passion and engaging its challenge with deliberateness.

While the boundaries of my humaness define my moment in time, my death announces that my essence is reentering the mystery of the universe that birthed me. Thus my death will be as sacred as was my birth and life.

Version IV

Who Am I?

I am birthed of concentric wombs. I am a living equation: two-in-one, both-and.

I am a child of the cosmos. I am a mirrored form of the encompassing universe—a unique expression of both its substance and essence. I am, at the same time, a part of and apart from creation. Being a part of, I reflect creation's essence—sensing my kinship with all other existing forms. Being apart from, I exhibit the peculiarities of my embodied humanness—sensing my differences from all other existing forms. I am one of a myriad family. I am all of which *is* while being alone who I am.

I am a child of the planet. I am a mirrored form of the scope of my culture—a unique expression of evolution and historical circumstance. I am, at the same time, that which is given to me without choice and that which I willfully choose from option. In paradox, option opens me to freedom while binding me to ambivalence. Out of freedom I seize control of my existence. Compelled by my uniqueness, I create reality with this freedom and bet my life on the creation. I frame my creations around the realization of self-worth and live them with passionate devotion. In this freedom I become what I create. Out of ambivalence I mold choice into morality. Encouraged by my intrigue, I am prone to indulge both the nobility of good and the ignobility of evil. I am co-moral. In responsibility, both I and others harvest the effect of my choosing. In this choosing I give shape to destiny.

I am, at once, creation's own child and the child of my own creations. Power is companion to my uniqueness and the improbable is its measure. I am the meaning-maker.

How Do I Know What I Know?

I commence my knowing in the domain of mystery. As a seeker, I am drawn to those meanings that remain hidden in the shadow of infinity. I am forced to leap in faith from the answers I seek but cannot discern to the answers I must give to create meaning. I live within the tensions of this leap between doubt and certainty. At one end of my mind I am rebuked by the boundaries of my human limitations. At the other end I am encouraged by the frontiers of my human capacities.

I know through the eyes of both-and. Being conscious of my existence, I experience an awareness of inner knowing. Being conscious of existing others, I experience an awareness of outer knowing. Knowing comes to me as an alloy of this within and without consciousness. Outwardly, it comes through the accumulated wisdoms of history, social encounter, and the revelations of creation. Inwardly, it comes through the intuitive connections I make with infinite realities, my imagination, and the shaping craft of my analytical genius.

The final authority in my knowing is the selective creativity of my own mind and being. I know because I experience. And what I know ends where it begins—in mystery.

Who or What Is In Charge?

The universe is in charge. It is the ultimate value. The universe is its own final and absolute truth—the total, the whole, the divine, the holy. It exists as its own drama of being. With one hand it invents itself. With the other it alters the invention. The principle of its existence is changing changelessness. It vibrates with the unending beat of transformation. The government of its existence is an inner relating of its interdependent body of being. It pulsates with the patterns of paradox—harmony and discord, order and chaos, wholeness and division, visibility and invisibility, fusion and diffusion. It is a seamless fabric of reality, a dynamic self-awareness.

Every expression of its selfhood is its essence shaped into form. All its forms are geared to the uniqueness of a peculiar seasonality. Each is driven to fulfill its purpose within the whole. And the whole is a honeycomb of bonded destiny—the action of single parts rippling through its total frame of existence. The fate of individual forms is administered by a cosmic judgment that eventually consumes them into its own evolutional transformation. The universe is in charge of itself and all that is embraced in its body of being.

An essence pervades this *isness*, forging each part into a common dialogue. The universe hums with intimate communication. It is the word made form. It is the ultimate I-Thou relationship.

What Is My Purpose?

My purpose is to indulge joy by making those meanings that glorify life with nobility. Nobility is to enhance the quality of existence for all that is, to evolve by adapting to the unfolding truths of creation's design, to commit to that which bridges alienation into wholeness, to choose that which is life-giving over that which is death-dealing, to look through the depression of despair into the ebullience of hope, and to endow creation with the sacredness of acknowledged kinship. To glorify life with nobility is to relate as to holy. In fulfilling this purpose my sense of self-worth is sustained.

This purpose is realizable only in the active tense—recognizing that I am a journey of becoming from birth to death. The means of this becoming is a devotion to the worth of all that exists. The struggle of this becoming is constant choice between the polar possibilities of my nature. The reward of this becoming is the thrill of marking life with sanctity.

Inspired by communion with past luminaries and convicted by my own faith in meanings made, I conjure courage to face the vicissitudes of life. Enabled by capacities yet fully tested, I imprint creation's existence with nobility.

As I become I create myself into that which is not master but servant of the universe. This is my reason for being. This is my saving drama.

What Does My Death Mean?

Cosmically, my death is as my birth—a transition of energy into different form. It is the conclusion of my personal human season. It is a return to the body of the universe to be redistributed according to its principle of ecology, evolution, and transformation. It is to be reabsorbed into the being of the universe to be reinstated in the seasons of alternate forms. So my death is simultaneously an end of my peculiar form and a beginning of new modes of existence.

Socially, my death is a finalization of my personal contributions to the planet's ongoing life. It is my contribution to those accumulated fields of energy that alter human consciousness, my contribution to those memory pools that determine the genetic flow of human destiny, and my contribution to those harmonies or discords that imprint the ecology of the earth's future.

Both cosmically and socially, death is the placement of my peculiar and permanent seal on the environment of existence. It is to release my essence from the restraints of time to permeate creation.

Yet, while I live in time, the prospect of death provokes my passivity into passion. An awareness of the brevity of my human season awakens in me a sense of life as sacred. An acknowledgment of the capricious nature of death incites me to live with intentionality. An admission of the certainty of death beckons me to create meanings that infuse living with nobility.

As life wraps me in the boundaries of finite humanness, death discloses me into the body of infinite mystery. In between, I am graced with the power of becoming.

Synopsis

Who Am I?

I am a child of the universe.
I am a child of the planet.
I am a child of my culture.
I am a child of my own creation.
I am responsible for the consequences of my actions within all the
*   families of which I am a child.*
I am worthy of the gift of life.

How Do I Know What I Know?

I was born out of mystery into mystery.
I creatively shape this mystery into meaning.
I sustain this meaning by faith.
I bet my life on the knowing I create.
I can never fully know this mystery.
I am my own authority for knowing.

Who or What Is In Charge?

The universe is in charge.
The universe is a divided wholeness.
The universe is self-aware.
The universe invents and reinvents itself.
The universe is an interdependent body of communion.
The universe is made of the same stuff.
The universe is a holiness.
The universe just is.

What Is My Purpose?

My purpose is to enjoy life by glorifying it with nobility.
My purpose is to aspire to nobility through meaning-making.
My purpose is to live in wholeness as the universe lives in wholeness.
My purpose is to live with deliberateness through hope.
My purpose is to relate as to holy.
My purpose is to be a journey of becoming.
My purpose sustains my sense of self-worth.

What Does My Death Mean?

My death is a transformation of substance to essence to substance.
My death is a release of my influence to roam time.
My death is my seal of life on existence.
My death humbles my living by recognizing that my existence is a gift
  of universal grace.
My death spurs my passion for life by underscoring its brevity.
My death reabsorbs me into the universe's body of mystery.

The Journey
(A Metaphor of Control)

There is no going alone on a journey. Whether one explores strange lands or Main Street or one's own back yard, always invisible traveling companions are close by: the giants and pygmies of memory, of belief, pulling you this way and that, not letting you see the world life-size but insisting that you measure it by their own height and weight.

—Lillian Smith

The journey is my home.

—Murial Rukeyser

I was born between the clarion call of words and the passionate beckoning of hearts; between the ferocious clap of lighting and the delicate patter of raindrops; between the end of history and its beginning. In this between is my journey.

To save me from the fragilities of my humaness, others have sought to prescribe this journey. Some have said it is in my head; others that it is in my heart. Some have challenged me to walk on lightning tips and know power, others to nestle in raindrops and know peace. Some have insisted I must live at the end of history; others have insisted I must live at its beginning. Each prescription is a myth, contained in its own encircled reality.

But there is a stirring within me that rejects the prescriptions of others. There is a voice that cries for self-direction. Some say listen to this inner voice. Others say listen to the outer voices. I will listen to both. Yet I will trust the judgment of my own humaness. It is all that finally belongs to me.

But which way the journey? Words call and hearts beckon. Lightning attracts and raindrops whisper. The beginning and end of history implore. I am the chooser, and I will claim them all. I will know the fullness of both-and. I will not yield to the notion that I am too fragile to chart my own direction. If I relinquish this privilege, my life becomes only a parody of outer prescription.

I will create my own mythic map. I will gather my strength and strike the road with boldness. I will be my own journey.

No journey carries us far unless, as it extends into the world
around us, it goes an equal distance into the world within.
                                                —Lillian Smith

About the Author

Robert T. Latham grew up in a radically conservative religious tradition. As a result of enlightened educational experiences, his religious perspectives were transformed; due to military service during the Vietnam conflict, his cultural perspectives were also transformed. Out of these two transformations, along with his involvement in the 1960s civil rights movement, grew his insights into how mythology defines and shapes all human experience, whether personal, institutional, or cultural. This book is the product of these insights.

He is presently working as a consultant and writer.

His website is www.mythinglink.com.